Born in the UK and now based in Sydney, Australia, **ROBIN BOUSTEAD** (above, right) has been trekking in Nepal since he fell in love with the Himalaya in 1993. During countless trekking holidays he and a group of friends developed what was initially only an idea for the most challenging alpine trek in the world, the Great Himalaya Trail, from one end of the range to the other.

Since 1992 he has been researching new trekking routes in some of the most remote mountain regions of Nepal. He completed a full traverse over two seasons: the post monsoon of 2008 and pre-monsoon of 2009. This epic journey took a total of six months and on both treks he lost over twenty percent of his body weight.

Nepal Trekking and the Great Himalaya Trail
First edition: 2011

Publisher
Trailblazer Publications
The Old Manse, Tower Rd, Hindhead, Surrey, GU26 6SU, UK
Fax (+44) 01428-607571, info@trailblazer-guides.com
www.trailblazer-guides.com

British Library Cataloguing in Publication Data
A catalogue record for this book is available from the British Library

ISBN 978-1-905864-31-7

© **Robin Boustead** 2011
Text (except pp67-112) and photographs (unless otherwise credited)

© **Bryn Thomas** 2011
Kathmandu and Pokhara sections pp67-112

© **Himalaya Map House** 2011
All maps except Kathmandu and Pokhara maps (© Trailblazer)

Editor: Paul Wilson
Series editor: Bryn Thomas
Layout: Nick Hill
Typesetting and proof-reading: Nicky Slade
Colour Cartography: Himalaya Map House
B&W Cartography: Himalaya Map House & Nick Hill
Photographs: © Robin Boustead unless credited – RR: © Robert Rosenbaum,
YP: © Yann Piron, SB & TR: © Sandra Butler & Tim Reynolds
Index: Jane Thomas

Warning: mountain walking can be dangerous
Please read the notes on risks (p6), when to go (pp12-17), trekking grades (pp28-31),
safety (pp52-3, p57) and health (pp59-64). Every effort has been made by the author and
publisher to ensure that the information contained herein is as accurate and up to date as
possible. However, they are unable to accept responsibility for any inconvenience, loss or
injury sustained by anyone as a result of the advice and information given in this guide.

A request
The author and publisher have tried to ensure that this guide is as accurate and up to date as
possible. However, things change even on these well-worn routes. If you notice any changes or omissions that should be included in the next edition of this guide, please email or write
to us (address above). You can also contact us via the Trailblazer website at ☐ www.trail
blazer-guides.com. Those persons making a significant contribution will be rewarded with
a free copy of the next edition and an acknowledgement in the front of that edition.

Printed on chlorine-free paper by D'Print (☎ +65-6581 3832), Singapore

Nepal Trekking

AND THE
GREAT HIMALAYA TRAIL

A ROUTE & PLANNING GUIDE

ROBIN BOUSTEAD

TRAILBLAZER PUBLICATIONS

Acknowledgements

Of all the people who have helped, supported and assisted me over the last seven years on this project, I must firstly thank the three Sherpas who came every step of the way along the GHT: Pema Tsiring Sherpa, my Nepali guide; Lakpa Sherpa, my climbing Sherpa; and Karma Sherpa, the 'engineer'. To share the trail with them was an honour and a delight.

Over the last seven years there have been many Nepali crew who came on various research treks and I must apologise if I have missed anyone or misspelled a name. From the early days I must thank Lakpa Sherpa, Saroj Kanal, Pasang Sherpa, Dawa Sherpa, Lille, Krishna, Kumar, and Jamka Paneru, Takendra Tamang, and Ram Nepal. The last few years have seen a predominance of sherpas with me including Tendi Sherpa, Renji Sherpa, Pasang Sherpa, Tenzi Sherpa, Dawa Sherpa, Ang Dawa Sherpa, Tendi Sherpa, Ang Tendi Sherpa, and Tashi Sherpa. Three cooks have impressed with their ability to create meals from meagre supplies time and again: Chanda Magar and his brother Birbahadur Magar, and the irrepressible Hom Bahadur Magar, the 'pirate'.

Along the trail I have received help from countless individuals but four people really stand out for their amazing generosity: Pradeep and Mickie Giri from Kolti, Pasang Sherpa in Gokyo, and Lakpa Gurung in Jomsom.

Of our friends in Kathmandu, a very special thank you goes to Jamie McGuinness, who helped provide inspiration for the entire project, was a route advisor throughout and a key member of the editing team for this book. Others who have provided advice, support and enormous amounts of help and assistance to both myself and Judy while researching this book are Pema's wife, Dolma, who spent many days running between government offices; Puru Dhakal, our dear friend and advisor; Mads Mathiesen, for his advice on route options and trail information; Yam Bahadur Bam, Uttam Jung Thapa, for his help throughout the Far West regions; all the staff at Hotel Karma; Verena and the boys at Sam's Bar, Barga and Shangarsa Bista at Northfield Café. Udyog R Suwal, Rasik Shrestha, Dr DR Kafley, Era Shrestha, Santosh Maharjan, Pawan Shakya and everyone at Himalayan Map House; Irwin and Ben Grayling from BOA-Overland for collecting us at the end of the trip; Sam at Flight Connection for tickets and many valiant attempts to get us the stoves we needed, and Siddhartha Gautam for flying in such difficult weather conditions.

To our dear friends in Australia who never quite know when we will return or for how long, especially Geoff Chapman without whom this project would never have happened, Geoff Schwartz for his work on graphics, Julie Anderson, Almis Simans, Neal Gardner, Steve Vey-Cox, Annette Irwin and Susan Watson, who have always been on call in times of need.

A special thanks to companies who have helped me with gear and food: Earth Sea Sky, Outdoor Performance, Outdoor Agencies, Mont Australia, Sea to Summit and a huge debt of appreciation to Trek & Travel, Sydney, who have put up with my eclectic gear demands.

To Bryn Thomas at Trailblazer for taking on this project, Paul Wilson's amazing patience whilst editing many drafts, Nick Hill for putting the layout together and Nicky Slade for proofreading the text and Jane Thomas for the index.

My three long-haul trekking companions who had to put up with situations I am sure they had never expected! From 2008, the charming and down-to-earth Bob Rosenbaum, and from 2009, my dear trail buddies Tim Reynolds and Sandra Butler, who were stoic when times got really tough.

And finally, the most important person in my life, without whom this project would never have started or been completed, my dearest Judy. My deepest and sincerest thanks for her encouragement when things got tough, efforts with resupplies, help with the book, and being wonderful company on the trail and in life.

Front cover: The impressive kani gateway of Samdo village, Manaslu

CONTENTS

❑ **Warning**
All outdoor activities involve an element of risk, which could endanger you and those
with you. It is impossible for any guidebook to alert you to every possible danger or
hazard, or to anticipate the limitations of your party. The descriptions of trails, passes,
routes, geographical features in this guide are therefore not in any way a guarantee
that they will be safe for you or your party. When you follow the advice and/or route
information in this book you do so at your own risk and assume responsibility for your
own safety.

Ensuring that you are aware of all relevant factors and exercising good field-craft
combined with common sense is the best way to enjoy the mountains. If you feel
unsure about your skill level, experience or knowledge base then you should not
assume responsibility for yourself or a party.

The political situation in Nepal will change and could affect your plans. It is wise
to keep abreast of all developments and check government and relevant agency websites for your own safety. You assume the risk of your travels and the responsibility
for those with you. Be safe, be prepared, be informed.

Great Himalaya Trail Code

COMMUNITY

● **Respect cultures and traditions** – be a considerate guest, understand protocol, offer appropriate gifts when necessary, ask before taking a photo, do not show affection in public, and donations to gompas or shrines are appreciated.

● **Benefit local communities**, **commercially and socially** – share skills and experience, offer a fair pay for services, participate in activities. Do not encourage begging, publicly argue, drink excessively or fight.

● **Adopt new customs** – do not wear tight or revealing clothing, do not enter someone's home unless invited, avoid touching people of the opposite sex, do not use your left hand to eat or pass objects and try to learn as much Nepali as possible.

ENVIRONMENT

● **Tread softly** – stick to trails and recognised camping areas. Avoid creating new tracks, or damaging the environment in any way. Follow the adage: take only photos and leave only footprints.

● **Pack it in, pack it out** – avoid taking tins, glass, or plastic containers and bags unless you plan to carry them back to Kathmandu or Pokhara. Wash away from water sources, and always use local toilet facilities when available. Bury all organic waste at least 30cm below the ground and ideally 50m away from water sources.

● **Conserve natural resources** – what few resources there are belong by right to the locals. Always ask permission before using anything along the trail. It is illegal to disturb wildlife, to remove animals or plants, or to buy wildlife products.

SAFETY

● **Beware of altitude sickness** – use the buddy system to watch for symptoms of altitude sickness. Make sure everyone remains fully hydrated by drinking water throughout the day, everyday. Stay together along the trail, and communicate frequently with everyone.

● **Be safe** – carry an extensive first-aid kit and know how to use it. Have multiple plans for emergency evacuation and designate decision makers. Leave your itinerary details with someone responsible at home. Beware of yaks and other animals on narrow trails.

● **Be self-reliant** – don't assume you will receive help or assistance. Ensure your group has extensive field-craft and navigation skills. Research thoroughly: is your route appropriate for your party? Do you have the necessary skills, experience, resources and equipment?

INTRODUCTION

The Nepal Himalaya is amazing; a place where you can immerse yourself in authentic cultures and be inspired by the greatest mountain scenery on the planet. Since the early 1950s, trekkers have been exploring the countless valleys and peaks of the mid-hills, *pahar*, and high ranges, *himal*, throughout Nepal. Recent democratic elections and relative political stability have led to a surge in visitors and the mountains once again offer unhindered trails for anyone to explore.

The three main trekking regions, Everest, Annapurna and Langtang attract tens of thousands of trekkers every year. Facilities have never been better and easily rival those found in Europe or elsewhere: there are even country-style teahouses in the Everest and Annapurna should you want a touch of luxury. Trails are well maintained and safe, and locals will welcome you with a genuine friendliness that will make your heart melt.

The other two-thirds of Nepal's mountain terrain is normally considered 'off the beaten track' and counts visitors in mere hundreds. From the lush rhododendron forests of the east to the dense woodlands of the west there is wilderness, and remote communities that have remained relatively untouched. In these regions, a small trekking group can make a real difference to lives that often barely subsist.

Although the mountains are beyond compare, it is the people you meet along the trail that linger in your memory. You can't help but admire their indefatigable boldness and energy, their independence, strength and resilience when times are bad, and their fun, open-hearted, generous nature towards strangers who may never return. It's impossible to make a comparison, but surely the people of the high himal are the very best of mankind?

In 2002, the Nepali government reconciled all border disputes with its northern neighbour China. This de-militarised seven border areas and for the first time in over fifty years tourists were allowed to explore them. All of these areas offer unique trekking opportunities, with many resembling the now popular regions as they were thirty or more years ago. They also tend to be next to the major trekking routes so it's possible to design itineraries combining old and new routes thus making your holiday a more 'complete' Nepali experience.

For many years, one of the great trekking 'holy grails' has been a possible route through the remotest peaks of the entire Himalaya, which would join all the major trekking regions. The author is the first person to survey, plot and describe such a route: the Great Himalaya Trail (GHT). The Nepal section of the GHT would take about 160 days of continuous walking so for convenience it is broken into sections, all of which have easy access through the pahar. The introduction of new trekking routes through impoverished communities will encourage micro-tourism projects in places that are too remote for infrastructure development. By creating value in regions that previously had little to offer to tourism, it is hoped that the relevant governments will establish a network of National Parks and Conservation Areas as a trans-boundary corridor for animal migration, which would reduce illegal hunting and help save many endangered species. The snow-covered crown of Asia may then become one of its greatest assets.

The Great Himalaya Trail

The Great Himalaya Trail runs through regions and countries that have cultures dating back thousands of years, and for much of the time they have been trading with each other across the mountains. Salt, wood, grains, wool and livestock, gold and gems are just a few of the products that helped to establish a network of trails from Indochina to Afghanistan, including sections of the famous Silk Route.

It is easy to imagine local traders plying trails with their yak or donkey trains throughout the region. Over centuries, they explored remote valleys trying to find the easiest trails over the never ending 'Abode of Snow', the Himalaya. In the larger valleys small communities sprang up and developed their own unique languages and traditions. For over a thousand years the people of the Himalaya were cut off from the rest of the world as Ladakh, Nepal, Sikkim, Bhutan and Tibet all kept their borders closed from prying, colonial eyes.

Jesuit missionaries were the first Europeans to penetrate deep into the Himalaya in the early seventeenth century. The first was Father Antonio Andrade, in 1626, who crossed from India to western Tibet and then enjoyed the local Tibetans' open-minded hospitality which still exists today. However, it is William Moorcroft who is considered the father of modern Himalayan exploration. His first trip, in 1812, was in search of Tibetan goats; another followed this in 1819-25, when he disappeared without a trace. In his wake came a long succession of missionaries, botanists, geographers and traders who crisscrossed the mountain ranges from east to west and began mapping the himals. Exploration activity increased from the 1850s with the Great Game, a period when the British Raj, Russian Tsar and Chinese Qing empires all vied for ascendancy in the region.

The then new sport of mountain climbing arrived in the Himalaya in the 1880s with WW Graham, Sir Martin Conway and Freshfield who pushed deep into the unexplored valleys of Sikkim and the Karakorum. However, most of the

Himalayan Kingdoms still discouraged visitors, leaving many areas 'blanks on the map'. After the First World War, a number of expeditions were organised to reconnoitre and climb significant peaks. However, it was the mysterious disappearance of Mallory and Irvine on Mt Everest in 1924 that really ignited the world's imagination for Himalayan exploration, and was a precursor to the successful expedition led by Lord Hunt that placed Sir Edmund Hillary and Tenzing Norgay on the summit on the 29th May 1953.

It was the research expeditions to identify new peaks and climbing routes that began what we now call 'trekking'. In 1949, Bill Tilman visited the Helambu, Langtang, Kali Gandaki valley and Everest regions intent on walking rather than climbing any specific peak, and so became the first Himalayan trekker. In 1965, Colonel Jimmy Roberts introduced the world to organised trekking holidays and began a revolution in adventure holidays that made regions of the Himalaya accessible to anyone.

All of the activity to date was largely north to south across the Himalayan ranges, so when an east to west route along the entire range was suggested in the 1970s it was considered a radical idea. Yet the challenge had been set: who could be the first to traverse the entire range?

At the time, the eastern ranges through Bhutan and Tibet were closed so the first attempts could only start at Sikkim, then an autonomous region of India. The first expedition was in 1980 with Harish Kohli leading an Indian Army team; he was quickly followed by Peter Hillary (son of Sir Edmund), Graeme Dingle and SP Chamoli in 1981. These treks began at Kanchenjunga, on the border of Nepal and Sikkim and ended at the India-Pakistan border. A nine-month trek over 1981-82 saw Hugh Swift and Arlene Blum complete a traverse from Bhutan to Ladakh in India. This was to remain the longest attempt until 1990, when Sorrell Wilby and her husband Chris Ciantar made a traverse from Pakistan to Arunchal Pradesh (northern Assam in India).

All of these expeditions suffered from restrictions on where they could trek, which meant they frequently had to detour to the pahar, away from the Great Himalaya Range. Even Nepal, perhaps the most accessible of the countries, had strict 'no-go' areas along the border with Tibet. However, in 2002 things changed and Nepal has since opened every one of her himals to permit-based trekking. Along with new trekking areas in Tibet, Bhutan and India, the Great Himalaya Range is now open to trekkers for the first time in history.

How to choose a trek

Nepal has become one of the world's best trekking destinations with thousands of trails and endless mountain views. Choosing the right trek to suit your holiday has become a challenge in itself as the Nepal Himalaya offers a path for everyone, regardless of fitness level, experience or time available. This book is designed to help you first identify when to trek and what style of trek best suits your needs, and then which destination matches your expectations of the Himalaya.

In taking the time to carefully choose your trekking destination and style, there is a much greater chance of returning home having had a memorable experience. You never know, you may end up wanting to trek every region and immerse yourself entirely in the various cultures of the high Himalaya.

When deciding on a trek, you should consider the following:

● **Time of year** – First decide when you would like to visit Nepal, and then choose which regions suit you best. Or, if you have a clear idea of which region you would like to visit, what is the best time to trek?

● **Trek style** – Most trekking regions are only accessible to camping trips, but in the Annapurna, Everest or Langtang regions teahouse-style treks are an attractive alternative.

● **Trek duration** – The amount of time you can spend away from home is a major factor in deciding which trek to do; remember to leave yourself some buffer time before and after the trek in case of transport delays.

● **Trek grades** – Finally, consider the trekking grades for your chosen region(s) and try to match your expectations of 'life on the trail' with the grades; the summary table at the back of the book offers a short overview of the major options.

❏ **Important notes**
● Walking times, both of total trek duration and daily walking times are for the average trekker of good fitness.
● Total trek durations are for itineraries that begin and end in Kathmandu or Pokhara.
● Quoted altitudes have an average accuracy of + or – 15m; however, considering trail and demographic changes, it is wise to assume a general accuracy of + or – 50m.
● Place names are given in their most common current form but pronunciation may vary considerably.
● Directions are given as you look ahead, or in the direction of movement on the trail, rather than the 'true' direction (facing downstream) normally used when referencing rivers.
● Make sure you are not over committing yourself: your mental and physical health combined with environmental factors can affect your trekking speed on a daily basis.
● Daily walking times are *without* rest breaks.

PLANNING YOUR TREK

First decisions

WHEN TO TREK

Seasons

The most important factor in deciding when to trek in Nepal is the weather. Nepal has a monsoonal climate; heavy rains driven north from the Bay of Bengal engulf the country from June/July to September, and sometimes into October. This means that regions in the east, like Kanchenjunga and Makalu, receive heavier amounts of rain than in the west. The result is that the eastern ranges of Kanchenjunga and Makalu tend to have slightly shorter trekking seasons than the west of Nepal, which is drier. However, Far West Nepal tends to have longer, more severe winters due to its more northerly latitude.

The monsoon season from June to the end of September is not a popular time for trekking as the valleys that approach the mountains suffer from high rainfall, lots of leeches, transport delays and limited views. However, the Annapurna and Dhaulagiri massifs block the northerly push of the monsoon clouds and create a partial 'rain-shadow' along the border with Tibet. So Naar, Phu, Mustang and Dolpo only receive brief showers each day during their rainy season, which transforms their arid landscape into fields of wildflowers, and the local villagers get busy planting their one crop of the year.

After the monsoon has finished, stable, dry conditions predominate throughout the Himalaya for two or three weeks until a storm front of unpredictable intensity will affect most areas, usually in the third or fourth week of October. The weather then stabilises again, probably until late November when the chance of occasional showers coincide with the beginning of a colder weather pattern. The clear skies and cold nights of December and November are in turn replaced by winter storms in mid to late February. The beginning of March sees the sun regain intensity, and the weather becomes unstable for alternating periods of three to five days. By the end of March dry, warm weather is the norm but haze begins to build in the lower valleys. As temperatures rise through April the remaining rain clouds disperse to be replaced by hot, hazy conditions largely produced by dust blowing up from the plains of India, and local fires. May is the hottest month of the year, only cooled by occasional pre-monsoon storms, which gradually gain in intensity until the monsoon begins with vigour, usually in mid-June.

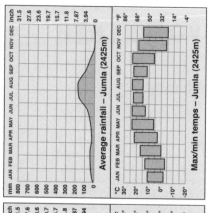

Average rainfall – Kathmandu (1336m)

Average rainfall – Pokhara (833m)

Average rainfall – Jumla (2425m)

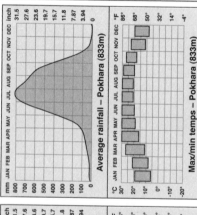

Max/min temps – Pokhara (833m)

Max/min temps – Jumla (2425m)

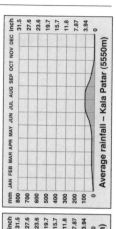

Average rainfall – Kala Patar (5550m)

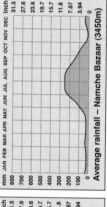

Max/min temps – Kathmandu (1336m)

Average rainfall – Namche Bazaar (3450m)

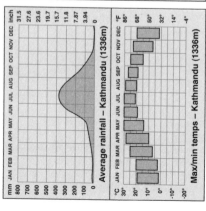

Average rainfall – Jomsom (2800m)

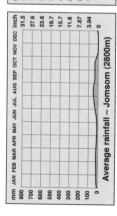

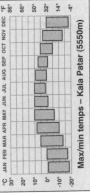

Max/min temps – Kala Patar (5550m)

Max/min temps – Namche Bazaar (3450m)

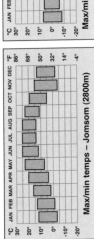

Max/min temps – Jomsom (2800m)

● **October to November** is a very popular trekking season as the entire country has long spells of fine weather with relatively clear air for photography. Occasional storms can dump large amounts of snow at higher altitudes, and the night time temperature frequently falls below freezing above 4000m (13,123ft).

● **December to January** boasts the clearest skies for photography and the coldest temperatures, frequently falling below -5°C above 4000m. Many of the locals who live above 4000m in warmer months begin to move down during December, so it is important to check that you'll be able to re-stock or find shelter prior to departure.

● **February to March** is warmer than January but occasional heavy rain and blizzards regularly sweep over the mountains, sometimes closing passes for weeks. With rain comes the first blooms and rhododendrons flower at lower elevations. Dust from India begins to obscure views towards the end of March and temperatures climb considerably in the lower valleys.

● **April to May** is renowned for the progressive blooming of rhododendron up to the tree line (some sheltered flowers will continue into June). In May temperatures start to get very hot at lower elevations and haze obscures views of distant mountains. However, this is a good time to spot migratory birds.

In the introduction to each trekking region there is a brief description of the ideal times to visit.

Festivals

The other major factor to consider when deciding when to visit Nepal is the festival calendar. There are more than 365 festival days in Nepal, so there is always something happening somewhere. Almost all festivals are related to phases of the moon and do not occur on specific dates.

It is a good idea to avoid travelling during some of the major festivals like Dasain or Tihar as transport systems tend to suffer from overcrowding and delays throughout Nepal. You should also be aware that some festivals traditionally require the slaughter of a goat and/or payment of a cash amount, and that visitors are expected to contribute. If you are unclear of what the impact of a festival could be on your plans ask local people and be prepared for your plans to change a little. Below is a summary of the most popular and for further information and specific dates for major festivals see 💻 www.visitnepal.com, 💻 www.nepalvista.com or 💻 www.qppstudio.net.

NEPALI FESTIVAL LOCATIONS THROUGH THE YEAR

	East Nepal	Central Nepal	West Nepal
January	Maghe Sankranti; Shree Panchami; Lhosar (Tibetan New Year)	Maghe Sankranti; Shree Panchami; Lhosar (Tibetan New Year)	Maghe Sankranti; Shree Panchami; Lhosar (Tibetan New Year)
February		Maha Shivaratri mainly in Kathmandu	
March	Holi	Holi	Holi; Gatunath**
April	Nepali New Year*	Nepali New Year*	Nepali New Year*
May	Buddha Jayanti; Mani Rimdu in Thame (Everest region)	Buddha Jayanti; Teeji in Mustang	Buddha Jayanti
June			
July	Gunla in Sherpa and Tibetan communities	Gunla in Sherpa and Tibetan communities;	Gunla in Sherpa and Tibetan communities
August	Gai Gatra	Bhairav Kumari Jatra in Dolkha, Gai Gatra; Tamu Dhee in Gurung villages	Gai Gatra
September	Krishna Janmastami; Teej	Krishna Janmastami; Teej	Gaura Parva; Teej
October	Mani Rimdu in Tengboche (Everest region); Dashain; Tihar; Bhai Tikka	Horse festival in Manang***; Dashain; Tihar; Bhai Tikka	Dashain; Tihar; Bhai Tikka
November	Dashain; Tihar; Bhai Tikka	Dashain; Tihar; Bhai Tikka	Dashain; Tihar; Bhai Tikka
December	Bibah Panchami	Bibah Panchami	Bibah Panchami

*Nepali New Year is celebrated nationwide usually on 14th April.
**Gatunath is a spring festival and held for three days in most Magar villages in west Nepal during March or April.
***Horse Riding festival, held for one day in Manang in the Annapurna region.

❑ Hinduism

Over 85% of Nepali people are Hindu, a religion that dates back to 1500BC. Hinduism has thousands of deities, but there are three main gods: Brahma the creator, Vishnu the preserver and Shiva the destroyer. Most Hindus are Vaishnavites (followers of Vishnu) or Shaivites (followers of Shiva).

Popular gods are also Ganesha (the elephant-headed god who is the remover of obstacles), Laxmi (goddess of wealth), Saraswati (Brahma's consort and goddess of wisdom), Hanuman (the monkey god who symbolises strength and protects against accidents), Kali or Durga (the blood drinking consort of Shiva and goddess of change and death), and Krishna (an avatar of Vishnu), the blue-skinned cowherd who had a way with milkmaids, and is usually depicted with his flute.

Hindus believe in reincarnation and that the circumstances of your rebirth are determined by your deeds in the present life. The caste system is an important part of Hindu culture in Nepal, but its influence is less noticeable in the major cities. The highest caste is Brahmin (usually priests or civil servants), followed by Chhetri (warriors and rulers), Vaisyas (traders and farmers) and Shudras (artisans). Below this are the Dalits (untouchables) who traditionally have performed menial tasks such as sweeping, butchering and tailoring.

Hindu festivals

● Maghe Sankranti worships the god Vishnu. It is held for one day in all Hindu communities during mid-January.

● Shree Panchami celebrates the birthday of Saraswati, the Goddess of Learning and is combined with Martyr's Day all over Nepal during late January to early February.

● Maha Shivaratri worships the god Shiva. The focus of celebrations is Pashupati Temple in Kathmandu where large crowds pack the temple for days. It is also celebrated at most Shiva shrines throughout Nepal during February.

● Holi, or Fagun Purnima, is a week-long festival culminating in a day of coloured water and paint fights. Held for one day in all Hindu communities during late February or early March.

● Bhairav Kumari Jatra worships the gods Bhairav and Kumari at Dolka and Bhairav Kund. Held for five days in early August.

● Gai Gatra (Cow Festival) allows any sort of joke, or prank, to be played on someone, but is traditionally an offering to Yamaraj, the god of death. Held for one day in all Hindu communities during August/September.

● Krishna Janmastami celebrates the birth of the god Vishnu. Held for one day in all Hindu communities that have a Vishnu shrine during August/September. This festival is also celebrated as Gaura Parva for two days in west Nepal at about the same time.

● Teej is a married women's festival to honour the god Shiva. Held at all Shiva and Parvati shrines across Nepal during September.

● Dashain, or Dasain, is the largest festival in the Nepali calendar and celebrates the goddess Durga. Held for 15 days in all Hindu communities during October/November.

● Tihar, Diwali or Deepawali, is the festival of lights and honours the goddess Laxmi (the Goddess of Wealth). It is held for five days and ends with Bhai Tikka (the brother/sister festival) in all Hindu communities during October or November.

● Bibah Panchami is to celebrate the marriage of the god Ram to Sita and is held for seven days all over Nepal during December.

❑ Tibetan Buddhism

Buddhism is the second most popular belief system in Nepal and is dominated by Tibetan monasteries, or *gompas*, of four major sects called Nyingmapa, Kagyupa, Sakyapa and Gelugpa. The Dalai Lama is the head of the Gelugpa sect, and their gompas normally boast a large statue of the sage Tsong Khapa who re-introduced Buddhism to Tibet in the 14th century. The Buddha was born in Lumbini in the Nepal *terai*, the plains along the southern Indian-Nepal border in 560BC as a prince, and renounced his worldly possessions to find the 'middle path' – the way to enlightenment is not through suffering or excess, but by realising that desires lock people into the cycle of suffering and rebirth.

Although Buddhism does not have gods as such, their gompas are decorated with figures depicting certain good or bad characteristics, such as hungry ghosts with tiny necks who were greedy people in a former life, or Buddhas with particular characteristics, or scary looking temple protectors to keep away evil spirits. Each sect has its own practices and traditions, and the Newar people have combined Hindu and Buddhist beliefs to form a complex religion called Newar Vajrayana Buddhism. The World Heritage Listed temples of Boudhanath and Swayambunath are the main Buddhist sites in the Kathmandu valley.

You will frequently hear Buddhists chanting throughout the day, and especially while walking clockwise around a place of worship. The most popular chant is *Om MaNi PadMe Hum*, a common translation being, 'Hail! The Jewel in the Lotus.'

Buddhist festivals

● Lhosar, Buddhist New Year, held for one day in all Buddhist communities the day after the new moon appears in late January or during February.
● Buddha Jayanti (Buddha's Birthday) is focused on Lumbini and all major Buddhist places of worship. Held for one day in all Buddhist communities on the full moon night in May/June.
● Teeji is a spring festival and ritual cleansing ceremony. Held for four days in Lo Monthang, Mustang during late April to mid-May.
● Tamu Dhee is a ritual cleansing festival to protect homes and fields owned by Gurung communities. Held for one day during August.
● Gunla is a month-long festival to celebrate the beginning of the monsoon and when Buddha led his disciples into a month-long teaching retreat. Held in most Buddhist communities during July/August.
● Mani Rimdu, held for 4 days in the Everest region. The festival at Tengboche is held during mid-October, and at Thame in May.

TREKKING STYLES

There are three main 'styles' of trekking, each of which has pros and cons, but your choice will depend on your destination, budget, time available and personal preferences. There is no better or worse style, in fact you might find yourself combining styles in some destinations to provide a broader experience.

Fully independent trekking or independent teahouse trekking

For many, the idea of finding one's own way and living off the land is what the mountains are all about. To be completely free to plan your day, to have all your gear on your back, and to interact one-on-one with locals is a liberating experience. Due to the nature of independent trekking it is normally a good idea to trek with a friend or in a small group of up to four for safety – larger groups tend to find it difficult to secure accommodation. Being an independent trekker doesn't mean to say that you cannot have a porter or a porter/guide. The introduction of the TIMS (Trekkers Information Management System) has made this option a little more complicated, but it is still possible to employ a local for almost any period of time, which can make tricky navigation and strenuous sections considerably easier.

Most independent trekkers prefer to trek the main routes of the Annapurna, Everest and Langtang regions as they offer a broad spectrum of teahouse accommodation to suit every budget, and a standardised menu. Trails in these areas are well marked and many of the local people speak enough of a range of languages that the individual can get by with basic Nepali. Even though you may walk on your own, or with a local porter, it is in fact very rare that you will find yourself without company, especially in the evenings when you sit in the teahouse communal dining room. The main trails are normally busy with local traffic so if you carry a guide and map it is unlikely that you'll take a serious wrong turn, although getting a little lost is almost inevitable.

Independent trekking is also the cheapest way to explore the mountains so it is popular with budget conscious travellers. Expect to pay anything from US$1.50-15.00 a night for a bed depending on room type, teahouse location, and season demand (in extreme cases teahouse owners have been known to auction beds!). Food per day will average from US$5-6 for Nepali fare, which is normally *dhal bhat* (rice, vegetable curry and lentil soup), to US$10-14 for three western meals. You should probably also budget for the occasional hot shower (US$1-2) and battery re-charge (roughly US$4 per hour). If you do employ a local porter or porter/guide, you will probably have to pay US$6-10 (plus meals) a day depending on the region and trail difficulty.

❑ **Bon**

The Bon religion was historically confined to Tibet and surrounding areas such as Dolpo, Sichuan, Yunnan, Bhutan and Assam, and is a combination of Buddhism with older animistic and shamanistic beliefs. Although many of its tenets melded with Buddhism, Bon is distinctly different in its day-to-day practices. There are very few Bon gompas remaining in Nepal, and most of them are in Upper Dolpo. People who follow Bon are called Bon Po.

The main differences between Bon and Buddhism are: Bon followers go around *chorten* (memorial or decorated cairn built on a pass, ridge or other significant spot) and monasteries counter-clockwise (keeping the object on their left side) whereas Buddhists keep the building on their right and go clockwise, the power symbol of Bon is a left facing swastika (Hindus use a right facing swastika), whereas Buddhists use the *dorje* (thunderbolt). The original Bon religion was based largely on magic, spirits and blood sacrifice to propitiate the gods, who lived in all natural things. Bon followers also chant throughout the day, the most common being, *Om Matri MuYe SaLe Dhu*, which means much the same as the Buddhist mantra: 'Hail! The Jewel in the Lotus.'

There are a few drawbacks to independent trekking: dealing with altitude and health problems on your own, logistical challenges, communication issues and safety concerns. None of these are insurmountable but they do need to be taken seriously both before and during your trek. Altitude and health problems are best monitored and dealt with as part of a 'buddy system' – that is, you and your trekking companion look after each other (for more details, see p61).

There are also some potential logistical issues in high season: the most common is that many teahouses are booked in advance by organised trekking groups and you may find getting a room, or even floor space to sleep on, difficult and/or expensive. It is therefore best to start trekking before or just after the main rush of tourists (see pp13-5). It's a good idea to be able to speak basic Nepali on the trail to find your way, order food and drinks, and get to know the locals, which is after all one of the main advantages to independent trekking.

If this is going to be your first visit to the Himalaya then the independent option probably isn't the best style to kick off your adventures, unless you really are the ultimate mountain goat and you stay on the main trails. Independent trekking in remote wilderness areas is far more suited to trekkers who have already learnt how their body deals with altitude, developed some knowledge of Nepali and the various customs of mountain communities, and have a good knowledge of Himalayan terrain and navigation.

Teahouse trekking with a guide

Recent years have seen a dramatic increase in both the number and quality of teahouses on the main trails. For example, Namche in the Everest Region now boasts 24-hour electricity, a laundrette, multiple Internet cafés, bakeries, and all the trappings of Thamel (the tourist district in Kathmandu) but at 3500m! It is no surprise therefore that teahouse trekking has become incredibly popular.

The convenience of the main trekking routes in Everest, Annapurna and Langtang is a major drawcard for tens of thousands of trekkers every year. The subsequent level of investment by local communities in these regions is extraordinary compared to the level of poverty elsewhere in the Himalaya. Large teahouses with comfortable communal dining rooms, private bedrooms (some with en-suite bathrooms) with mattresses and bedding, extensive menus or speciality restaurants and bakeries can make your trek a very comfortable experience. Commercial trekking companies from all over the world sell organised walking holidays using these teahouses and a local guide agency, and they're flexible enough to suit almost any fitness and experience level.

❑ **Top tip – bring a padlock**
There is always the risk of being robbed anywhere you care to travel in the world, and Nepal is no exception. Ironically, there is probably more chance of having something stolen by a fellow trekker than by a local, so always lock away your belongings when in shared accommodation and lock your bag to an immovable object at night or when unattended. You should also carry a spare lock to secure your bedroom door when staying in a teahouse.

Guides are normally hired through a trekking agency in Kathmandu or Pokhara, as professional registration is a necessary qualification to lead groups within National Parks. It is important to make sure your guide has been to, or preferably comes from, the area that you want to trek – it is surprising how many guides have only trekked a few trails. The role of a guide can encompass a great many activities. Apart from being the person who escorts you along the trail, they often explain flora, fauna, customs, culture and history. A guide may also manage any porters (should you only want to carry a small pack), ensure your accommodation is booked, transport is confirmed, and that the food is well prepared; in fact your guide will probably become your personal assistant, man-Friday, guardian, and best friend. For this reason most good guides are normally snapped up by the bigger agencies and accompany groups booked by overseas trekking companies.

There are no major drawbacks to this style of trekking, however there are a few issues that people regularly complain about. One is that teahouses that accept larger groups can be very noisy at night; for most it's tougher to sleep at altitude so anything that disrupts sleep is irritating. Another involves the decisions that your guide makes without consultation, like where to stay, or route options. Make sure you have a clear understanding of who makes which decisions. Small groups trekking with a guide may find it difficult to secure rooms or even meals in some teahouses that devote themselves to larger, more profitable parties. If you are a woman trekking alone with a guide then be aware that even simple acts can be misconstrued as a proposition (see *Trekking as a Single Female*, p50).

Booking a trek through an overseas operator means you don't get to have any choice of guide, but you do have the reassurance that they are probably going to be excellent and if not, you have recourse to complain. The size of group that you will be trekking with becomes important when you choose a 'packaged trek'. Some companies are still in the habit of sending over twenty trekkers into the hills with a single guide and a few porters, this is both irresponsible and a good way to have a bad holiday. A group size of twelve to fourteen is normally considered a 'manageable maximum' and you'll still get the opportunity to chat with your guide and spend time with any crew that they might hire.

One main advantage of hiring your own guide and teahouse trekking is that you can control your costs and stay within a budget that would be considerably less than booking with a big travel company. The logistical convenience of having someone with local knowledge handling routine details like where to stay, negotiating prices, and route directions is a great peace of mind. The safety and security of local knowledge should not be underestimated, nor should the ability to communicate to your heart's content through your guide's interpreting. Finally, the chance to build a friendship with someone is perhaps the most remembered feature of any trekking holiday. You might forget the name of the mountains you'll photograph, but you'll never forget your guide.

Trekking with a camping crew

The most flexible, comfortable, and hygienic way to explore the Himalaya is on a camping trek. To have unrestricted access to trails, viewpoints, and passes you need to be self-sufficient, with the support of a team of experienced staff. For many trekkers their first trip to Nepal will be teahouse based, but the lure of what lies beyond the main trails is so strong they return for a camping trek, often to the more remote areas.

Trekking in Nepal was initially exclusively camping based so there is a substantial experience pool that means even the first-time camper will be comfortable and well looked after. Each morning you will be woken with a mug of tea delivered by a smiling sherpa (as opposed to Sherpas, the famous ethnic group from the Everest Region), followed by a bowl of water to wash your face. Breakfast is preferably served al-fresco in the morning sun as your crew packs up the camp. At some point along the day's trail your cook will have prepared a lunch for you at a scenic spot before you complete your journey to the next campsite and an extensive dinner menu. Shower, toilet and dining tents with tables and chairs complete your campsite and comfort comes courtesy of a foam mattress and pillow (usually an optional extra). In fact, camping in Nepal is frequently more comfortable and less crowded than teahouses.

Nearly any remote or exploratory trek will be camping based as a group needs to have sherpas and crew available to help cross passes and break trail. The roles of various crew members are normally well-defined: the guide (or *sirdar*) is in charge; the sherpas look after clients on the trail, serve meals and make/break camp; the cook and kitchen staff prepare meals and wash dishes for the group, while the porters carry everything else. Normally, a guide discourages trekkers from becoming too friendly with the crew as companies are paranoid they might lose your future business to prospecting staff.

With the increasing popularity of teahouse trekking, companies that specialise in camping treks are becoming more competitive so it is important to check the details of your trek before you depart. The two most common ways companies cut costs are: firstly, increasing the amount of load the porters carry and not pro-

---

❑ **Crossing high passes**

A feature of many treks is a high altitude pass, for example the Cho La and Renjo La in the Solu-Khumbu (Everest Region), the Thorong La or Mesokanto La in the Annapurna. These passes are difficult and very challenging for the majority of walkers. Steep terrain combined with the effects of altitude mean that many people fail to cross what is an unavoidable part of their itinerary. If you plan to book a trek that incorporates one or more passes it is essential that you develop a high level of fitness and walking experience before you depart. You should also ensure that there is sufficient acclimatisation time in your itinerary to allow both you and your group to adjust to higher altitudes. It is wise to also add an extra day or two of flexibility into your itinerary to accommodate bad weather and illness that could delay your group while attempting to cross a pass.

viding them with necessary clothing and equipment (see the International Porter Protection Group, 🖳 www.ippg.net for how you should care for your porters and your obligations towards them); secondly, either the agency or the cook reduces the money dedicated to your food allowance. It is important that the group leader should keep an eye on the quantity and quality of food stocks.

The obvious drawbacks to camping-style treks are perceived inconvenience and potentially having to share a tent with someone you would rather not sleep next to. To solve both issues research is necessary. Camping really is more convenient than teahouses on the condition that you have a slightly flexible itinerary, so you can ensure washing and relaxing time for all, especially when the weather is good. Almost all camping groups offer single occupancy tents but you normally have to specify when you book, and you should always check the terms and conditions.

For many, these drawbacks are easily mitigated and, in fact, are over-whelmed by the advantages of camping-style treks. Being able to choose your own path and rest spots offers a level of itinerary customisation that not even teahouses in the most popular regions can compete with. The main benefit however, is being able to explore remoter regions away from the main trails and meet some of the inhabitants of the wild Himalaya. It is hard to believe that there are still many villagers who have never seen a tourist, and communities that greet you as an honoured guest and not an opportunity to make another buck. Away from the main routes is where you'll most likely see many of the species for which the Himalaya is famous: red panda, black bear, musk deer, snow leopard and a multitude of birds.

For many trekkers and trek leaders, camping-style treks are their favourite method of exploring Nepal; they often say that their experience feels more genuine. Camping brings you closer to nature, and the camaraderie built around a campfire often outlasts that of a teahouse trek.

For a list of trekking agencies in Nepal see pp246-9.

CHOOSING A TREKKING STYLE

The desire to make the most of what may be a once-in-a-lifetime trip to Nepal means that there is a temptation to choose itineraries that are too hard or long for your group's level of walking experience or fitness. Surprisingly, many trekkers choose teahouse treks with tough itineraries believing that by staying in a room they will recover faster from the day's walk. This doesn't actually make sense and the number of rescue helicopters taking overstressed or injured bodies back to Kathmandu grows each year. However, it is easy to understand that trekkers want to tackle a route that leaves them feeling they have achieved the most from their holiday. Perhaps the most important things you need to know before choosing a trek are:

● Fitness level – join a walking club or a gym to get a comparative assessment of your fitness level. How long does it take you to climb 500 metres? Test your stamina: can you walk for four or five hours a day? Try to find people who have done the trek before and ask them what it was like and how fit they were.

PLANNING YOUR TREK

❏ SUMMARY OF TREKKING STYLES

	Independent trekking without a guide	Teahouse trekking with a guide	Trekking with a camping crew
Ideal destination	Everest, Annapurna, Langtang	Everest, Annapurna, Langtang, Mustang	Anywhere in Nepal
Average number of days on the trail	A couple of weeks per trek	One to three weeks per trek	Two to four weeks per trek
Level of flexibility in your itinerary	Good, you dictate your own pace	Generally poor, but depends on group arrangements	Generally poor, but depends on group arrangements
Cost level	Low to Medium	Medium to High	Medium to High
Fitness/experience level	Need to be strong and fit to carry all your gear. Prior experience advisable	Training advisable but not with a heavy pack. Prior experience sometimes necessary	Training and experience advisable depending on trek
Amount of time to organise the trek in Kathmandu	Short – a few hours to one day	Medium – a couple of days	Long – at least three days

● Walking experience – how easily and confidently can you cross rough trails? Do you have a good sense of balance? Can you cope with slippery surfaces or exposed trails? Try to find some walks near to your home with steep up and down sections. Does the trek operator offer training walks or suggested programs?

● Have you been to altitude before? If not, then choosing an extreme altitude trek (over 5500m), or a trek that stays at high altitude for long periods may not be a good idea. Why some people and not others suffer from altitude sickness is still a mystery for medical science, so prior experience is still the best method of trying to predict how your body will cope up high.

● Find other people who have done the trek – use the Internet to search for blogs, or reports on the same or similar treks. Is their experience the sort of thing you are looking for? Are they the sort of people you expect to be trekking with?

Your choice of trek style should reflect your experience and expectations: is this your first time to Nepal? Do you want a cultural experience? Or to explore remote areas or climb a trekking peak? Do you have specific needs or require more flexibility than an organised tour will allow? Do you want to camp or use teahouses? And is it necessary to be an experienced camper/trekker/ mountaineer before booking?

The major trekking routes in Everest, Annapurna and Langtang are all well equipped with teahouse and camping grounds, but the convenience of not having to carry camping gear means that teahouses are the preferred option. In Manaslu, Makalu, Kanchenjunga, and Mustang there are some small teahouses that you might want to use but you will almost certainly need to camp at times. In the remoter regions of Humla, Dolpo, Ganesh Himal and the valleys that were once closed to foreigners, you will have to camp all of the time. It is almost impossible to find a bad campsite, unless you are intent on exploring the remotest and least accessible areas of Nepal; in those places any flat ground is hard to find. Whatever your choice of destination, a good crew (guide, sherpas, cook and kitchen, and porters) will become your surrogate family and maybe lifelong friends.

Each trekking region covered in this book will give you a summary of trail options and trekking styles. However, there are always exceptions and options, so for example, although the Everest region is an ideal teahouse style area there are some trails where camping is essential.

TREKKING THE GREAT HIMALAYA TRAIL (GHT)

The Great Himalaya Range stretches 2400km, forming a natural barrier between India and China, with Nepal covering the central third (865km) of the highest peaks. The Nepali section of the Great Himalaya Trail takes about 160 days to walk, which means multiple visits if you want to walk it all (tourist visas are only for 150 days each calendar year). The eastern third of the Nepali trail connects Kanchenjunga with Makalu and Everest regions, and then on into the Rowaling. A central section joins the Rolwaling to Langtang valley, then on through the Ganesh Himal before ending in Manaslu. The western section runs from the Annapurnas through Mustang, Dolpo, Mugu, Humla and ends on the banks of the Mahakali Nadi.

Although the GHT crosses many high passes, there are lower elevation sections in-between suitable for the novice trekker. Much of the trail requires full camping equipment, but as it passes through all of the major trekking routes, it is possible to rely on teahouses for the sections through the Everest, Langtang and Annapurna regions.

Logistical issues, fitness and weather all combine to make trekking long sections a major challenge for even the most experienced and well equipped trekkers. For some sections, campsites and trails are very hard to locate, requiring local guides to help you find your way. It is advisable to purchase large-scale topographic maps and relevant tourist maps to assist route finding; a GPS and a satellite phone are handy too. Groups should carry the minimum possible and rely on the least number of tents (ideally not more than ten), as most places to camp are very small. Villages will probably not be able to sell you much food, so expect to be self-sufficient.

There are many high passes that have to be crossed, some requiring ropes, so groups should have alpine climbing and rescue experience. Plans and contingencies for emergencies should be taken seriously; rescue from many areas along the trail could be very difficult.

However, the experience of exploring remote regions, meeting the challenges of route finding, crossing unnamed passes, and sharing in the life of communities who are always surprised and pleased to see you is simply amazing. There is no 'main trail' that can duplicate the joy and sense of achievement of the Great Himalaya Trail.

TREKS WITH A CAUSE

Many people who visit Nepal fall in love with both the country and her people. However, the level of poverty and tragic circumstances that some of the locals are suffering from often results in a desire to help. There are many 'pro-poor' or poverty alleviation programs throughout the country as well as community development schemes from providing and distributing emergency stretchers to installing toilets and water pipes.

The GHT is designed to help local communities by encouraging trekkers to visit areas 'off the beaten track' in the belief that any help is better than no help. Nearly all of the programs and initiatives currently operating in Nepal rely on donations and volunteer assistance, so if you want to get involved and make a positive difference there is always a cause to suit.

If you are providing support to someone attempting a long section of the GHT you might, in your spare time, want to offer your services to a local organisation. The notice board at the Kathmandu Guest House in Thamel is a good place to begin searching for an organisation that matches your interest. There are also some websites, 🖳 www.ngofederation.org, 🖳 www.ain.org.np and 🖳 www.nepalngo.org that list registered organisations.

A couple of popular organisations for volunteer work in the Kathmandu valley are Just One, 🖳 www.just-one.org that works with marginalised children and impoverished mothers, and Maiti Nepal, 🖳 maitinepal.org who help victims of human and sexual trafficking. You could also check with your embassy or consulate to see if they are sponsoring any projects you can help with. On a final note, you might like to check the prisons to see if there are any foreigners doing time. They always appreciate visitors, and gifts such as fresh fruit, bread, cigarettes and batteries. The food supplied in prisons is meagre and not good quality, so any supplement you can give is welcome. These people are not supported by their embassy and rely on the kindness of strangers to get by.

Community

The financial benefits to a community are obvious in the main trekking regions of Everest, Annapurna and Langtang. But when you visit the remoter regions of the GHT it becomes apparent that even US$10 can make a difference to some villages. By spreading tourist dollars the GHT helps to alleviate poverty and address the enormous wealth disparity in Nepal. For anyone wanting to make a difference for the better, the GHT offers many opportunities to support almost countless causes along the trail.

There are a number of International Non-Government Organisations (INGOs) that have long-term projects in Nepal. If you choose to help a local NGO you should carefully check its credentials.

Follow this link ⌨ www.ain.org.np/member_ingos.php to get a list of all INGOs registered in Nepal. A few examples of those that operate in areas of particular interest for mountain communities and projects are:

● Eco Himal: ⌨ www.ecohimal.org, is an Austrian initiative that specialises in grassroots projects to help create sustainable village living. They have created the Eco Himal lodges in the Rolwaling.

● ICIMOD: the International Centre for Integrated Mountain Development, ⌨ www.icimod.org aims to help people of the Himalaya understand the effects of globalisation and climate change on their delicate ecosystems, and develop economically sustainable practices.

● The Nepal Trust: ⌨ www.nepaltrust.org, is based in the UK and provides integrated rural development in the Far West areas of Nepal and is probably the most active organisation in the poorest regions of Humla and Mugu.

● SNV: ⌨ www.snvworld.org, a Dutch-funded organisation, which uses its expertise to advise and support local groups to promote sustainable development and improve access to basic services, such as health and education.

● ⌨ www.tenfriends.org is a group of people who work in the Sankhuwasabha (between Kanchenjunga and Makalu), who first started donating emergency stretchers to remote villages. They are now involved with orphanage and school programs, water filtration, sanitation and female empowerment projects in both East Nepal and Kathmandu.

● Australian Himalayan Foundation: ⌨ www.australianhimalayanfoundation. org.au run a number of projects in education, health & medical services and the environment, mainly in the lower Solu-Khumbu area. It aims to ensure, where possible, the long-term viability of schools, to provide health, education and medical services and to support environmental projects for remote communities.

● The Himalayan Trust: ⌨ www.himalayantrust.co.uk, founded by Sir Edmund Hillary is perhaps the most famous of the non-government organisations operating in Nepal. Its successes in the Sherpa region of the Solu-Khumbu have been outstanding and are considered to be a role model for best practice by many.

● IPPG: ⌨ www.ippg.net, the International Porter Protection Program, works to improve the conditions of mountain porters in the tourism industry world-wide and is active in Nepal. With representatives throughout the world, it is possible to assist this organisation both at home and overseas.

Environment

Many communities continue to hunt and log without any thought for the environment upon which they rely so heavily. By promoting sustainable tourism throughout the Himalaya it is hoped that remote communities will stop destroying pristine habitat and that the government will see the benefit in declaring more conservation and National Park areas. Eventually, this could link current reserves and create the first international trans-border animal corridor, truly a goal of Himalayan size!

● The World Wide Fund for Nature ▭ nepal.panda.org is active throughout the country and is always in need of support.

● The National Trust for Nature Conservation in Nepal ▭ www.ntnc.org.np is a local organisation that has projects in various districts, all of which require support and volunteers.

TREK DURATION

Trekking agents are often asked: 'What is a good length of time to go trekking?' and, 'There are treks from three days to treks that last months, is any one duration better than another?' The simple answer to both questions is no, any amount of time that matches your vacation plans is a good amount of time, but there are some issues you should consider before trying to squeeze as much as possible into your itinerary:

● **Trekking grades** Trekking grades give you a good idea of whether you should allow for a little extra time or speed things up along the trail. For example, the Everest Base Camp trek is normally operated as a 16 to 17 day itinerary, but could be done in 14 days by pre-acclimatised or very fit people, or 22 days should you want to explore around each village along the trail.

● **Festivals** If you are lucky enough to coincide your visit with a festival either in the Kathmandu valley or out in the hills then you should try and extend your itinerary to give yourself time to enjoy the event. You may also need to leave some spare time available in case of transport delays during some festival periods.

● **Weather buffer** The mountains always have unpredictable weather and only in exceptional circumstances will you have perfect weather every day. Flights to mountain airstrips are particularly susceptible to delays or cancellations, so it is wise to add an extra day or two to your trip just in case you can't make a connection.

TREKKING GRADES

Trek grades have always caused debate among guides and trekking companies alike, as what is simple for one person can be beyond comprehension to another. So instead of a single grade this book uses a multi-grading system. There are two major components, each split into three categories:

● **Trail conditions** – includes the type of terrain you will cover, navigation difficulty, level of skills required.
● **Trail difficulty** – includes the maximum altitude attained, how much ascent and descent, and the general level of fitness recommended.

Remember to consider both the grades and the total duration to gain an accurate idea of what the trek will be like. For example, a trek to Everest Base Camp with two different companies could take the same route, but one does it two days faster than the other. You would have to consider the various grades to decide if the faster itinerary suits you better, or whether you should give yourself more time to cope with the rigours of the trail.

Trail conditions

Type of terrain – whether you are in forested valleys or climbing high alpine passes the type of terrain you have to traverse is dependent on gradient and trail conditions. Major trekking routes sometimes have sections of moderate gradient but are normally on well-maintained trails of easy gradients. Remote, exploratory style treks, especially some sections of the GHT and the more difficult alpine passes normally incorporate steep climbs and very rough trails, called *shikari bato* by the locals.
● **Level 1**: **Easy** – trails generally with an incline of 25% or less (although there might be short steep sections) on loose dirt or stone paved trails in good condition.
● **Level 2**: **Moderate** – trails with an incline of up to 45% and some sections are on rough loose ground including scree and boulders.
● **Level 3**: **Hard** – trails where you may have to use your hands to ascend very steep sections of rock, snow or ice and/or shifting boulders or scree.

Navigation difficulty – trails in the main trekking areas are normally broad and easy to follow with switchbacks to make ascent and descent of steep sections easier. There are sometimes direction signs, and you can normally ask a local and get accurate information. In remote areas you will sometimes have to follow very narrow and ill-defined tracks, which can easily be confused with trails created by grazing livestock. Asking for directions is sometimes a bad idea in remote areas as only a few villagers will travel regularly and their concept of time and distance is vague at best.
● **Level 1**: **Easy to follow trails** – broad, well-maintained trails, sometimes with signs and/or reliable sources of local information.
● **Level 2**: **Some navigation skills** – route is sometimes hard to find, use of map and compass combined with judicious use of local information necessary. Employing a knowledgeable local guide is probably advisable.
● **Level 3**: **Challenging navigation** – trails are hard to find, no reliable local information, you will need a high degree of navigation skills in all weathers and conditions. Employing a knowledgeable local guide is a very good idea.

Skill level – for many treks the only 'skill' you need is to be a confident walker, that is, be able to balance easily, hop from rock to rock, and cope with slippery or treacherous ground. However, other skills are sometimes necessary, especially on harder treks where you might need to abseil, rock climb and cross glaciers.

● **Level 1: Confident walker** – you walk regularly and are familiar with assessing obstacles and hazards along a trail. You might require a helping hand now and then on slippery surfaces, but you feel confident being unassisted most of the time.

● **Level 2: Scrambling** – you rarely need a helping hand and can negotiate tricky steep or rough sections without having to sit down or be assisted. You can cope with loose, rocky ground, tracks only a foot-width wide and ascending or descending on all fours.

● **Level 3: Ropes needed** – you have experience with rock climbing, abseil and glacier crossing techniques. You should know how to tie knots, put on crampons and a harness, and self-arrest using an ice axe. Successful completion of a mountaineering course is advisable.

Trail difficulty

Highest point – for many trekkers the highest point of a trek is both a goal and a potential hazard. Altitude can affect you in many ways, some extremely serious, and for many people this may mean restricting themselves to an altitude limit, depending on prior trekking experience and fitness level.

● **Level 1: Low altitude** – for treks up to 4500m.
● **Level 2: Mid altitude** – for treks up to 5500m.
● **Level 3: High altitude** – for treks up to 6500m.

Amount of ascent/descent in a day – treks that go against the lie of the land, that is, across ridges and valleys, tend to be harder than those that following geographic features. The amount of ascent and descent (up and down) in a day can cause knee, ankle and hip problems as well as exhaust the body far more than following gentler gradients.

● **Level 1: Moderate** – the trail tends to follow natural geographic features like valleys and ridges, and if there is a significant ascent or descent of up to 500m there are plenty of places to stop and rest.

● **Level 2: Energetic** – the trail crosses ridges on a regular basis and/or has frequent sections of ascent or descent between 500 and 1000m, places to stop might be limited.

● **Level 3: Strenuous** – the trail frequently has major sections (over 1000m) of ascent or descent where it can be hard to find any place to stop.

Fitness level recommended – your fitness level does not help you avoid the effects of altitude, but it can have a direct bearing on how well your body copes with the continuous physical exercise of trekking. The fitter you are, the faster and more easily you will become 'trail fit' and the more likely that you will enjoy every day in the mountains. Ideally you should concentrate on cardiovascular fitness, build stamina and undertake a bit of strength training to add muscle mass.

● **Level 1**: **Basic fitness** – you should be able to walk, with rest breaks, for 5 to 6 hours on uneven walking tracks. If you are training on even, tarmac or paved surfaces you should be able to sustain a brisk walking pace (4 to 5km/hr) for the same time.

● **Level 2**: **Good fitness** – maintain a brisk walking pace (4 to 5km/hr) for three or four hours over rough ground, or jog on even tarmac or paved surfaces for an hour.

● **Level 3**: **Excellent fitness** – walk rapidly and/or jog for hours on uneven ground.

TRAIL CONDITIONS	LEVEL 1	LEVEL 2	LEVEL 3
Type of terrain	Easy, up to 25% incline	Moderate, up to 45% incline	Hard, very steep sections
Navigation difficulty	Easy to follow trails	Some navigation skills	Challenging navigation
Skill level	Confident walker	Scrambling	Ropes needed

TRAIL DIFFICULTY	LEVEL 1	LEVEL 2	LEVEL 3
Highest point	up to 4500m	up to 5500m	up to 6500m
Amount of ascent/ descent in a day	Moderate, up to 500m	Energetic, between 500 and 1000m	Strenuous, more than 1000m
Fitness level	Basic fitness	Good fitness	Excellent fitness

Trek summaries for the treks in this book follow overleaf, using this grading system.

TREK SUMMARY

Trek	Highlights	Best time	Accommodation
Kanchenjunga Base Camp; p117	Lush forests to the north face of the third highest mountain in the world	Apr–May/ Oct–Nov	Basic teahouse or camping
Kanchenjunga BC with Olangchun Gola extension; p122	Add the intriguing village of Olang for the complete east-Nepal experience	Apr–May/ Oct–Nov	Camping
Great Himalaya Trail from Jhinsang La to Hongon; p123	Visit six ethnic groups and some of the most remote territory in Nepal	Apr–May/ Oct–Nov	Camping
Makalu Base Camp; p126	The trail to the fifth highest mountain on the planet is high and wild.	Apr–May/ Oct–Nov	Camping
Makalu BC, Sherpani Col, West Col & Amphu Labsta; p130	Add the high passes and really get among the Himalayan peaks	Apr–May/ Oct–Nov	Camping
Great Himalaya Trail from Hongon to Chhukung; p132	Perhaps the toughest route along the Great Himalaya Range	Apr–May/ Oct–Nov	Camping
Everest Base Camp; p137	The classic must-do trek to the highest point on earth	Mar–May/ Oct–Jan	Teahouse or camping
Everest BC, Cho La and Renjo La; p137	Put the best of the best into one amazing trek	Mar–May/ Oct–Jan	Teahouse or camping
Great Himalaya Trail to Thame via passes; p142	It's short, convenient and really spectacular.	Mar–May/ Oct–Jan	Teahouse or camping
Last Resort to Laduk via Bigu Gompa; p144	A bit of wild combined with an authentic cultural trek	Mar–May/ Oct–Nov	Camping
Rolwaling and Tashi Labsta from Bharaibase; p144	Mountains, glaciers and valleys merge into a trekking extravaganza	Mar–May/ Oct–Nov	Camping
Great Himalaya Trail from Thame to Bharaibase; p151	A bit of everything that Nepal has to offer	Mar–May/ Oct–Nov	Camping

EAST NEPAL

Duration	Terrain	Navigation	Skill	High point	Asc/desc	Fitness
20 days	2	2	1	2	2	2
28 days	2	2	1	2	2	2
17 days	3	3	2	3	3	3
20 days	2	2	2	2	2	2
25 days	3	3	3	3	3	3
16 days	3	3	3	3	3	3
14 days	2	1	1	2	2	1
20 days	2	1	2	2	2	2
6 days	2	1	2	2	2	2
8 days	2	2	1	1	1	1
23 days	3	2	3	3	3	3
15 days	3	2	3	3	3	3

TREK SUMMARY

Trek	Highlights	Best time	Accommodation
Helambu to Gosainkund; p153	Pure Himalayan magic; great views, sacred lakes and amazing wild flowers	Mar–May/ Oct–Dec	Teahouse or camping
Langtang Valley; p157	Comfort, convenience and a quality Himalayan experience.	Mar–May/ Oct–Jan	Teahouse or camping
Great Himalaya Trail from Bharabise to Syabru Basi; p161	From the wilds of Bhairav Kund, Panch Pokhari and Tilman Pass to Langtang	Mar–May/ Oct–Nov	Camping
Tamang Heritage Trail; p166	An easy-going trek through the most vivacious ethnic communities in Nepal	Oct–May	Basic teahouse or camping
Manaslu Circuit; p172	An absolute gem of a trek, perhaps the best in Nepal	Mar–May/ Oct–Nov	Camping
Great Himalaya Trail from Syabru Besi to Dharapani; p180	Wonderful cultures and amazing mountain scenery	Mar–May/ Oct–Nov	Camping
Naar, Phu and the Thorong La; p185	Traditional Tibetan villages and the extraordinary Kang La	Mar–May/ Oct–Jan	Basic teahouse or camping
Annapurna Sanctuary & Poon Hill; p192	Fabulous mountain amphitheatre and all the comforts of some great teahouses	Mar–May/ Oct–Dec	Teahouse or camping
Great Himalaya Trail from Dharapani to Jomsom; p196	The Annapurna Circuit and the Thorong La are still somewhere special	Mar–May/ Oct–Nov	Teahouse or camping

CENTRAL NEPAL

Duration	Terrain	Navigation	Skill	High point	Asc/desc	Fitness
9 days	1	2	1	1	1	1
10 days	1	1	1	2	1	1
14 days	3	3	2	2	3	2
10 days	1	1	1	1	1	1
19 days	2	1	1	2	2	1
18 days	2	3	2	2	2	2
17 days	2	1	1	2	2	2
10 days	1	1	1	1	2	1
5 days	1	1	1	2	2	1

PLANNING YOUR TREK

TREK SUMMARY

Trek	Highlights	Best time	Accommodation
Mustang Circuit; p197	Like nowhere else does today collide so obviously with the Middle Ages.	Apr–Nov	Basic teahouse or camping
North of Lo Monthang; p205	Add the valleys and gompas along an ancient trade route to Tibet	Apr–Nov	Camping
Southeast of Lo Monthang; p206	The remote Damodar Kund and trails to Phu and Muktinath	Apr–Nov	Camping
Upper Dolpo Circuit; p210	Mysterious, spectacular, rarely visited and authentic cultures	Apr–Nov	Camping
Lower Dolpo Circuit; p217	Amazing variety in the Trans-Himalayan biodiversity area	Apr–Nov	Camping
Great Himalaya Trail from Jomsom to Ghamgadi; p217	Nine 5000m+ passes and authentic cultures make this beyond compare	Apr–Nov	Camping
Rara Lake; p227	Sublime beauty, old-growth forests and ancient history all in one trek	Mar–May/ Oct–Nov	Camping
Khaptad National Park; p232	The Gods choose to honeymoon away from the crowds...	Mar–May/ Oct–Nov	Camping
Great Himalaya Trail from Ghamgadi to the Mahakali; p235	What Nepal was like before trekking began	Mar–May/ Oct–Nov	Camping

WEST NEPAL

Duration	Terrain	Navigation	Skill	High point	Asc/desc	Fitness
12 days	1	1	1	1	1	1
14 days	1	1	1	1	1	1
17 days	2	2	2	2	1	2
20 days	2	2	1	2	2	1
12 days	1	1	1	2	2	1
19 days	3	3	2	2	3	3
13 days	1	1	1	1	1	1
9 days	1	1	1	1	1	1
11 days	2	3	1	1	2	2

PLANNING YOUR TREK

Before departure

Life in Nepal is more 'fluid' than what you might be used to, which makes working with the locals' concept of time and efficiency a particular source of frustration for many tourists. If you are planning and organising an independent trip then make sure you pack some patience and a smile – anger achieves only negative results. If you are on a packaged trip then let your tour leader do the worrying and just go with the flow. Whatever your plans once you have decided to visit Nepal the first thing to do is book your flight as most airlines run at full capacity in peak season.

VISAS AND PERMITS

Barely a year goes by without a change to the entry visa regulations to Nepal. You can check arrangements with one of the Nepali Embassies or Consular offices, but the most reliable source of information is currently the Nepal Department of Immigration website – 🖥 www.immi.gov.np

Many tourists organise a visa prior to arrival in Nepal, but it is straightforward to apply for a visa if arriving in Kathmandu at Tribhuvan International Airport (currently US$100 for 90 days). The visa available on arrival tends to be cheaper and lasts longer than applying for one from an embassy or consular office. To save time, complete the current visa application form (which can be downloaded from the website above) prior to arrival, and bring some passport photos. Other entry points are Kodari (on the Tibet border and normally only open for groups), and nine overland borders with India, for current details see the website above.

❏ **Getting weather reports**
It is a good idea for those walking long sections of the GHT to receive regular weather reports. This is most commonly done by phone. The following websites are a great resource for compiling a forecast, although you will often find they are a little contradictory.

🖥 www.monsoondata.org/wx/ezindia.n.html
🖥 www.imd.gov.in/section/satmet/dynamic/iso.htm
squall.sfsu.edu/scripts/nhemjetstream_model.html
🖥 www.wunderground.com/global/Region/A2/2xJetStream.html
🖥 www.stormsurfing.com/cgi/display_alt.cgi?a=nindi_250
🖥 weather.cnn.com/weather/forecast
🖥 news.bbc.co.uk/weather/forecast
🖥 www.weather.com/weather/today/Kathmandu+Nepal+NPXX0002
🖥 www.meteoexploration.com/mountain/forecastHimalayas.html
🖥 www.expeditionweather.info/index.php?page=200

Similarly, the trekking permit system undergoes almost constant change. Currently most trekking regions require: (1) a National Park or a Conservation Area Permit, (2) Trekkers Information Management System (TIMS) permit. You may also require a special area permit and/or a special trekking permit depending on the region. It is essential that you organise permits through a registered trekking company, and if this is all you do the company will charge you a processing fee. You should always carry a photocopy of your passport when trekking, and be prepared to register at police check posts whenever requested to do so.

A final formality is to register online or in Kathmandu with your embassy or consulate or register at the Himalayan Rescue Association. If there is no consulate, find out which, if any, country represents your country in Nepal. This can be determined from your Foreign Affairs Department, or corresponding office in your country.

The essential information needed by your embassy is your name, an emergency contact number, passport number and itinerary. It is also a good idea to provide the contact details of your hotel and trekking agency in Nepal should you need to be contacted. One major benefit of this process is to facilitate your rescue and repatriation should it be necessary.

MAPS AND WALKING GUIDES

During the 1990s, the INGO Finaid sponsored a new topographic survey of Nepal, which resulted in a broadsheet 1:25,000 (covering the terai and pahar) and 1:50,000 (covering the high mountains) series of maps of the entire country. They are sold on the Bhaktapur Road from a small shop called Maps of Nepal (near the Everest Hotel, New Baneswor) for the modest amount of NRs150 each. These maps are essential for many of the GHT sections and should be referred to as your primary reference, but never considered 100% accurate.

The Finaid maps are ideal for the remoter regions of Nepal, however for nearly every popular trekking route there are full colour maps available from the Map Centre shops in Nepal or from good trekking equipment shops in your home country. The tourist maps produced by Himalaya Map House are probably the most up to date and accurate on the market, for range details see 💻 www.himalayan-maphouse.com.np.

There is also a broad range of less expensive, and less accurate, maps available in Nepal. The best of these are produced by Kartographische Anstalt Freytag-Berndt und Artaria, Vienna, Austria (normally referred to as the Schneider maps after the original cartographer) but the place names on these maps often do not reflect local pronunciation and some of the routes have now changed.

The most detailed of the specialist pocket trekking guides currently available are from Trailblazer: *Trekking in the Everest Region* by Jamie McGuinness and *Trekking in the Annapurna Region* by Bryn Thomas. There are some older publications that review the major trekking routes, or the Annapurnas, Manaslu and Kanchenjunga in detail.

EQUIPMENT

Kathmandu has a broad range of outdoor equipment shops that sell gear for anything from light day walks to high altitude expeditions. Prices and quality vary enormously and it is wise to know what to look for in a product as shop staff will promise the world. In general, it is wise to equip yourself at home as you then have the opportunity to wear-in and become familiar with your kit. This may be something as simple as getting used to carrying things in certain pockets, to breaking-in your boots, to developing an exercise program around an increasing pack weight. Choosing footwear is normally the first equipment decision so take as much time as possible to discuss lacing and fitting options in a reputable outdoor gear shop.

Footwear

You are about to embark on a walking holiday, it makes sense to choose your footwear with care and ensure a *perfect fit*. It may take a considerable amount of time to shop around and find the boots that fit your foot so that there is no discomfort when you wear them. Your feet will swell and become more sensitive at altitude, your sense of balance may change and the terrain may provide unknown challenges, so a full boot that immobilises the ankle joint and has excellent grip is a must. It is relatively simple to adjust lacing for varying thicknesses of sock, so pack a few different types to suit terrain and climate. Thin, skin-hugging liner socks are always a good idea for longer treks as they reduce the need to launder thick socks (which are hard to dry), and help to keep the skin surface dry (thus reducing the chance of blistering).

You also need a pair of light shoes or sandals to wear when you finish trekking for the day. These will allow your feet to dry out and relax. Sandals can also be used for river crossings, and when showering.

Trekking poles

If you want to be walking in your dotage then use trekking poles now. The prolonged impact of steep downhill on ankles, hips and especially knees will have a noticeable effect on everyone in your group. The best and most reliable method for reducing shock on joints is to use trekking poles – that's a pair of collapsible poles, not a single stick. It is wise to purchase them well before your trek so that you have time for their use to become second nature.

Clothing

There are days that barely an hour goes by without having to make some adjustment to your clothing so most trekkers and mountaineers rely on a series of different clothing layers when on the trail. When you think about layers there are three distinct types of fabric:

● Next-to-skin fabrics are soft, easy to launder (that is, they dry quickly) and may be thermally insulating. Three, or even four, different fabrics are ideal; (1) **for warm to hot conditions** – a very light synthetic that can dry in minutes, is UV resistant, and has an antibacterial treatment, (2) **for cool to warm conditions** – a light long sleeved top with a pocket, that can be worn as sun protection or as a lightweight insulator on a cool evening, (3) **for cold to cool conditions** – a thermal fabric that can be worn all day or as a night shirt, (4) **for very cold conditions** – a very warm thermal shirt for high altitudes or very cold nights. It is also handy to have a loose-fitting, well-ventilated synthetic shirt for warmer or more humid days. Cotton is NOT advisable next to your skin in the mountains as it can increase the chances of hypothermia.

● Mid-layer fabrics include synthetic fleece garments for warmth, especially when you stop walking and need to protect against a sudden cooling, and soft-shells for warmth in wind and/or light rain. Soft-shell garments come in an enormous range of combinations; the most popular are lighter weight fabrics that can be worn while walking in a cold wind so that you don't have to put on your weatherproof shell. However, it is important to make sure that the garment provides some insulation, and is made from a fairly tough fabric, as you will be wearing it under your pack harness at some point.

● Shell fabrics are 100% waterproof and windproof, preferably breathable, and/or well ventilated. Whenever you venture into the Himalaya it is essential that you always carry a waterproof jacket and pants. Pit-zips or similar ventilation is a good way to prevent condensation from building up, especially in less breathable garments.

You should also pack a sun hat, warm hat, warm and weatherproof gloves, a light pair of liner style gloves, and a light scarf to wrap around your face on dusty sections of trail, especially when a train of yaks goes past.

Lightweight walking pants or trousers with detachable legs have become popular with some trekkers. For cultural reasons this might not be a good idea in some areas, see *Dos and Don'ts: How not to Cause Offence*, pp54-7.

Packs

The range and methods of using packs is almost limitless, whether you are carrying all of your own equipment, or just a small daypack. The majority of trekkers use a 40 litre (or thereabouts) pack for all the items they are likely to need throughout the day and a kit bag (carried by a porter or pack animal) to stow the remainder of their equipment. Packs should have a number of generic features, like at least one lid pocket for bits and pieces, external stash pockets and compression straps, and someway of keeping wet and dry gear separate. However, the most important feature of a pack is that it should fit properly (and that you know how to adjust it).

The back panel length of a pack should match your own back length, try on different models and check in a mirror to see if the lengths match. You should understand the principle and placement of balance straps and how to adjust a harness to fit. It is inevitable that your pack will need readjusting at some point on the trail and knowing how to do this is as important as knowing how to lace your boots.

The kit bags that you are given to stow spare equipment are normally not waterproof so to protect valuables, your sleeping bag and spare clothing against water damage use roll-top, durable, waterproof stuff sacks.

Sleeping gear

You are going to spend roughly one third of your holiday in your sleeping bag so it is worth making sure you're comfy inside it. The European Union has introduced a sleeping bag insulation rating system, which is a good method of comparing and choosing a bag. Most treks in Nepal require a bag that can keep you warm at -10°C but that you can also sleep in when it's 15° or 20°C at night.

PACKS – FITTING AND PACKING

Begin by adjusting the harness system with no weight in the pack, then once you think the pack is as comfortable as possible put roughly your average carry weight inside the pack and try it on again. Try to distribute the weight inside the pack as you would for a trip – the idea is to make the load distribution as realistic as possible. Walk around for 10 or 20 minutes to feel how the harness performs as you move – this is the only accurate way of appraising a harness system. To adjust the harness:

1 Loosen the pack's shoulder straps, top stabiliser straps and hip belt.

2 Lift the pack using the haul loop (never lift or move the pack with the pack harness) and slide your arms through the shoulder straps.

3 Bend over so that the pack sits on your spine allowing you to adjust the straps without the pack sliding down your back.

4 First do up the hip belt making sure that it straddles your pelvis (iliac crest) and then tighten the straps. Note that the two ends of the hip belt should not be touching, nor pushing into your stomach.

5 Cinch the shoulder straps so that they fit snugly (no gaps should be visible) over your collar bone – check that the top stabilisers connect with the pack about 3cm above your shoulder. The shoulder straps should not compress your spine, nor restrict your arm movement – they are there to take about 20% of the load, the hip belt takes the rest.

6 Adjust shoulder and hip stabiliser straps for comfort. The pack should not swing or bounce as you walk – it should remain stable over your natural centre of gravity. Make sure that the shoulder straps do not extend beneath your armpits – they will chafe if they do. Use the sternum strap to prevent the shoulder straps from slipping sideways and make sure that you do not hit your head on the pack when you look up.

7 Now check for comfort by moving around. Walk up and down stairs, crouch down, hop from spot to spot, and move your arms about – make sure that the harness is not causing any irritation or overly restricting movement.

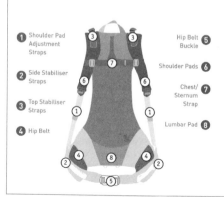

1. Shoulder Pad Adjustment Straps
2. Side Stabiliser Straps
3. Top Stabiliser Straps
4. Hip Belt
5. Hip Belt Buckle
6. Shoulder Pads
7. Chest/ Sternum Strap
8. Lumbar Pad

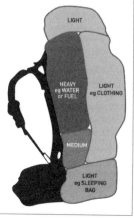

A full side zip, and preferably a foot zip, adds a little weight but it makes your bag more versatile across a broad range of temperatures. It is also a good idea to use a sleeping bag liner to prevent body oil or sweat from making your sleeping bag smelly. Silk liners are a popular choice as they are lighter, easier to launder and slightly warmer than those made from cotton.

A good quality insulation mat is also recommended for teahouse and camping trekkers alike. In most teahouses you are provided with a foam mattress, which can have a well-worn pit in the middle, which an insulating mat will negate. Camping treks sometimes provide sleeping mats but it is normally a good idea to take your own mat as well, unless you are certain that you will be comfortable and well insulated from the ground.

Tents and shelters
Nearly all camping treks will provide tents for the trip. However, if you want to take your own for an independent trek choose one that: (1) can withstand extreme winds – such tents are normally rated as 'alpine', '4 season' or 'extreme', (2) has enough room for people and gear as sometimes it is unsafe to leave your kit in a vestibule, (3) is well ventilated – most treks start in the hot and humid lower valleys before climbing into alpine regions. Bring a footprint or light tarp for use on wet ground, and carry an extensive field repair kit, as even glue can be hard to find in the hills.

Cooking gear
If you are planning to do a teahouse trek to high altitudes and/or out of season (when the chance of snow fall is higher) then a small gas stove is a good safety measure. Some people find it very difficult to sustain body heat at altitude and the ability to prepare a hot drink quickly can prevent frost nip or frost bite. Gas fuel is widely available in Kathmandu.

Camping groups tend to prefer locally made heavy kerosene stoves, as they are robust and easy to maintain. For expedition-style treks then the MSR Whisperlite International and MSR XGK Ex models both burn low-grade kerosene (good quality fuel is rare in Nepal) and are fairly easy to field-maintain. It is essential that you carry a field repair and maintenance kit for your stove as it will clog and require cleaning on a regular, almost daily, basis.

Miscellaneous
A first aid kit is essential – see p44. Perhaps the most useful item is a head torch: for reading in bed, finding gear in the bottom of bags and to be hands free in the toilet. An essential piece of equipment is a water bottle or bladder, which should ideally have the capacity to carry a minimum of two litres. You also need to pack biodegradable soap, a travel towel, and general toiletries in a waterproof bag.

Instead of cotton hankies, which can become quite unpleasant, it is a good idea to use lightweight kitchen cloths (for example Chux, Super Wipes, Jay Cloths), as these are easy to clean, dry incredibly fast and weigh very little.

Technology in the shape of a GPS or wrist-computer can be invaluable as a backup to a map and compass (declination in most of Nepal is a marginal 2 or 3°) but carry enough batteries so the device will continue to work in cold conditions.

PLANNING YOUR TREK

First Aid kit

Name	Uses	Dosage	Remarks
Betadine liquid iodine	Water sterilisation, throat gargling	8 drops/litre, leave for 30mins, or 2 drops/20ml for gargling	For external use when cleaning cuts and grazes; water treatment, gargling
Antiseptic cream/Savlon	Burns, grazes	Apply directly on affected area	External use only
Aspirin	Aches, pains, flu, headache, fever	1-2 tablets up to four times a day	May cause indigestion, stomach bleeding
Paracetomol	Aches, pains, flu, headache	1-2 tablets up to four times a day	Best painkiller at high altitude
Ibuprofen	Pain with inflammation	400mg, 3 times daily with food	May cause indigestion, stomach bleeding
Norfloxacillin (Norflex)	Chest, skin, urinary infections	500mg, 12 hourly for 5-10 days	Avoid in quinolone sensitive patients
Ciprofloxacillin (Cipro)	Diarrhoea (except giardia, amoebic dysentery)	500mg, 12 hourly for 2-3 days	First choice for non-specific diarrhoea. Give on empty stomach. Avoid alcohol
Erythromycin (Erythrocin)	Alternative for penicillin/sulpha allergics	250mg, 6 hourly for 5-10 days	Avoid alcohol
Tinidazole (Tinibar), Metronidazole (Flagyl)	Specific for giardia and amoebic dysentery	2g in a single dose daily for 3 days	May give metallic taste. Avoid alcohol
Maxolon, Stemetil	Nausea/vomiting	Maximum of one every 8 hours	Avoid at altitude. Avoid alcohol
Immodium, Lomotil	To slow bad diarrhoea	1 tablet, 3 times daily	Do not use if blood present. Will not cure you.
Acetozolamide (Diamox)	Altitude sickness	Half tablet morning and night	May produce tingling in extremities. Use with caution – better to descend. Avoid in sulfa sensitive patients
Antihistamine	Allergies, bites	Usually 1 per day – check packet	Avoid at altitude. Avoid alcohol
Tyotocin eardrops	Earache, ear infection	3-4 drops, 3-4 times daily	Antiseptic, anti-inflammatory, pain-killing eardrops

Other items for First Aid kit

thermometer	**surgical gloves** (disposable)	**ear plugs** to help keep wind out
roll of sticking plaster	**scissors**	
Bandaids	**tweezers**	**Vaseline** (use inside nostrils to stop drying out)
Steri-strips	**antibacterial hand gel**	
elastic bandages	**rehydration salts**	**anti-itch cream**
triangular bandages	**eye infection drops**	**SPF 30 sun lotion** or **zinc cream**
crêpe bandages	**eye drops**/saline solution	
roll of cotton wool	**antacids**	**SPF 30 lip balm**
safety pins	**Tiger Balm/Vicks**	**sweets** or **gum** to keep mouth and throat lubricated
gauze squares	**Lemsip** (generally not available in Kathmandu)	
thin panty liners – to keep pressure on wounds		**moisturiser**
	cough medicine (very good herbal one in Kathmandu; avoid preparations containing alcohol)	**cotton buds** (Kathmandu ones not very good)
alcohol swabs		
butterfly closures		**waterproof storage bags**
Dettol (small bottle)		
blister pads	**Wet wipes** (Wet Ones)	

Waterproof stuff sacks of different colours make identifying items very easy. Clothing items are easy to find in heavy-duty transparent compression bags, Eagle Creek make some good ones. A spare bag for a clean set of clothing to be left in Kathmandu should be lockable, and take another lock for your on-trail kit bag. Small ziplock bags (sandwich size) are handy for toilet roll, bottles of liquid, and to protect your money and documents.

Think about what might break down on the trail and how you might carry out repairs. A sewing kit is handy, as well as a strong glue for boots, a polyurethane glue or sticky patches for when repairs need to be flexible, a repair kit for your sleeping mat, enough spare batteries (those available in Kathmandu are frequently adulterated), a pen knife or multi-tool of some description, and a length of 3 or 4mm cord as a washing line, spare laces, etc.

If you write a diary it is worth carrying some spare pens, and a few photos of your family and friends will help to build new friendships wherever your path takes you.

POWER AND RECHARGING ON THE TRAIL

Recharging electrical devices while in the hills can be problematic. Many villages have at least one building with a solar panel connected to a 12v battery to provide low wattage lighting. These set-ups often look very rudimentary with bare wire connections, but they can be a useful source of power in an emergency. It is now commonplace to pay a rate per hour for charging from a local battery (roughly US$4 per hour). Alternatively, purchase one of the many compact and lightweight solar panel and in-built battery chargers.

Many satellite phones require higher ampage outputs than regular mobile phones and they may require additional connectors. This is also true of different generation iPods and other mp3 players for which you may need to purchase special adaptors. Solar charging times are often more than eight hours so you might need to consider two chargers for longer trips or during cloudy months (eg before and during monsoon). Thorough testing of your charger with your device is highly recommended prior to embarking on your trek.

❑ **TYPICAL GEAR LIST FOR SOMEONE JOINING A TREKKING GROUP**

Clothing

1 pair of trekking boots, well broken in, with spare laces
1 pair of sandals or camp shoes and a bag to store them in
4 pairs of liner socks
2 pairs of warm weather walking socks (at least 50% wool)
2 pairs of cool weather walking socks (at least 40% wool)
1 pair of warm weather walking socks (at least 30% wool)
2 warm weather T shirts (lightweight synthetic)
2 long sleeve shirts with pocket (lightweight synthetic)
1 long sleeve thermal shirt and 1 pair of long johns
1 long sleeve heavy weight thermal shirt, long johns are only necessary for high altitude or if you especially feel the cold
2 lightweight walking shirt with pockets (ideal for travelling to and from the trek)
2 lightweight walking pants, detachable legs are not essential
1 fleece pullover or lightweight jacket
1 warm fleece or soft shell jacket and pants
1 waterproof jacket and pants
1 sun hat
1 warm hat
1 pair of warm, weatherproof gloves
1 pair of lightweight liner gloves
1 trekking scarf

General equipment

1 pack of about 40 litres
1 kit bag or suitcase to leave in Kathmandu with a clean set of clothes
1 kit bag to take on the trek (check with your agent if this is provided)
1 pair of trekking poles
1 sleeping bag rated to at least -10°C for treks over 5000m
1 sleeping bag liner sheet, preferably silk
1 inflatable sleeping mat (optional)
1 pillow (optional)
1 head torch with spare batteries
1 selection of waterproof bags to organise your gear
1 bag of toiletries
1 first aid kit
1 repair kit
1 note book, pens and reading materials
1 camera, spare batteries and memory cards

Speciality gear

1 pair of gaiters if going above the snowline
1 pair of crampons to suit trekking boots
1 ice axe, 1 harness, 2 locking karabiners and descending device

Nepal and you

Yes, the mountains are spectacular but it will probably be the people who draw you back to Nepal time and again. Building relationships with your crew and those around you will not only enhance your holiday, it may well change your perspective on your own life. Nepali people live life 'immediately', they have been accused of wearing their hearts on their sleeve and lacking foresight, but they are disarmingly openhearted and hospitable. For them, the opportunity to make a friend today is more important than what might or might not happen tomorrow.

CHOOSING A GUIDE AND CREW

Trekking with a guide and a crew is a wonderful opportunity to develop a better understanding of Nepal. The days or weeks that you'll spend on the trail together will provide many opportunities to delve into the lives and perspectives of those around you. So if you have the opportunity to select your own guide it is worth spending a little time in making the right choice. Once you've found your ideal guide they will take responsibility for the choice of crew, but you can have input as well.

If you are on a fully organised trek and the guide is already chosen for you there are issues and ideas that you should be aware of, so please take the time to read this section.

Finding a guide can be difficult in peak season, but if you arrive before the rush of groups in mid-October or April you should be able to find a good candidate in a couple of days. A good start is to ask returning trekkers, or some local trekking agencies if they know any guides with knowledge of a specific area or issue and the 'grapevine' will do the rest.

Guides sometimes present their trekking or climbing history in a scrapbook or simple résumé, and it is important to ask for, and then check, references from the outset. Perhaps choose a modest local teashop as place to meet for a snack or lunch as a 'get-to-know-you' session. Try to only ask open questions as most Nepalese will almost certainly answer 'yes' rather than lose face. It is surprising how many 'guides' will assert knowledge of places they have heard about second or third hand. So your first question could be, 'What is it like in … ?' If they have been there before, how many times, how long ago, and have they been the senior member or guide of the group each time? Perhaps your guide's home village is in or near the region you wish to trek, if so can you take the time to visit their home? Such opportunities are a great way to really get to know what life is like in rural Nepal.

Your guide's general experience is also important. A long history of leading groups to different regions proves a deep level of competence. Having taken 'a few groups teahouse trekking in the Everest region' should not inspire confidence. There are a few formal technical mountaineering and climbing courses run by the Nepal Mountaineering Association in Manang, which are world class in standard, and qualifications from here are evidence of genuine skill and ability. However, you should be cautious of the Trekking Agency Guide Identity Card for which very little training or few qualifications are necessary.

Rates of pay for guides vary depending on experience, level of responsibility, trek difficulties and demands. You may not get to negotiate with many guides, as they will insist on using a particular agency to organise your trip. This has become common since the introduction of TIMS (Trekkers Information Management System) and porter insurance. KEEP (Kathmandu Environmental Education Project), IPPG (International Porter Protection group) and the Nepali government all have recommended minimum wages and conditions for guides and crew. By trekking with a crew you are undertaking to look after the welfare of your staff, so also ask your trekking company, IPPG and KEEP about your responsibilities towards your crew. You should also develop a clear idea of which jobs and responsibilities belong to you, and those your guide will handle.

Some guides can speak multiple languages and dialects from Nepal (there are more than eighteen ethnic groups each with a distinct language), which can make bargaining and trail finding much easier. You should also test the first aid knowledge of your guide; many have only a very basic idea. After you have asked all your questions and developed a good idea of how well you get along together, you can discuss plans for the trek.

Perhaps the most common problem trekkers suffer from is the Nepali propensity to answer questions with a 'yes'. As well as using open questions, also make sure the person is qualified to answer your questions. It's amazing how often you hear trekkers asking how long it takes to walk somewhere and being answered by a local who doesn't own a watch and has a completely different concept of time.

Before you and/or your agency start buying food, booking tickets and employing staff you also need to get the rules of the trek agreed with your guide and/or trekking agency. Some common issues you should be completely clear about:

● How do you organise a rescue? Is the trekking agency going to organise a helicopter if needed? You might need to obtain details of a rescue organisation before you depart. Leave a copy of everyone's insurance details with the agency.

● Who decides on rest days? Is your itinerary rigid or could you take an extra day here or there to rest and explore a place?

❏ **Top tip – grade your language**
When researching treks or contacting trekking companies by email remember to use open questions, itemise questions and try to use simple language so that the meaning cannot be misinterpreted.

● If there is an injury who treats the patient? The crew are considered your responsibility as well as that of the guide and agency.
● Are there any special dietary needs for the group?
● Is anyone in the group on medication? Are there any other pre-existing medical conditions that the guide or agency should know about?
● If equipment is damaged or lost who pays for the repair or replacement?
● Will you be happy if the crew drink alcohol or smoke in camp? If you have a little party or celebration, who is paying for the drinks?

Once you have a clear understanding about the roles of the agency, guide and your own responsibilities it is time to select a cook, sherpa assistants if necessary, kitchen crew and porters. Normally your agency and guide handle all the recruiting and planning, but you can be involved should you have particular needs.

Cooks vary greatly in skill: from almost as bad as the extremely comical Pong described in WE Bowman's *The Ascent of Rum Doodle*, to five-star hotel-trained cooks who produce seven- to eight-course gourmet meals. Your guide should be able to find a cook who can cater for your tastes, and if you have special dietary requirements, don't be afraid to ask for a sample meal to check their skills.

The Sherpa people of the Solu-Khumbu (the Everest Region) have developed a reputation for enormous energy and skill at assisting climbers to Himalayan summits. In recognition of this senior role within a group, 'sherpa' has come to mean someone who helps clients along the trail, scouts ahead to find the safest route, and prepares and dismantles camp on a daily basis. Many groups employ at least one or two sherpas on teahouse treks to go ahead and book rooms for the night, be a helping hand on tricky sections of trail, and they may serve your meals to help out the teahouse owners.

Your cook will normally select the kitchen crew, who tend to be staff they have worked with in the past. The kitchen crew may also lend a hand when pitching tents or dismantling camp if necessary. Porters carry the heaviest loads, normally 25 to 30kg, but sometimes they might elect to carry a double load up to 60kg for short periods. You should not encourage double loads. Regional Maoist groups often check porter loads and you will have trouble continuing your trek if the loads are considerably over 30kg and/or your staff are too young. As the majority of staff on any trek or expedition are porters it is important to take a little time in their selection.

Although the Nepalese are very socially and religiously tolerant, different castes may chose to prepare and eat meals separately, so ideally, you shouldn't have just one or two porters from a low caste as this may make meal times hard work for them. There are a number of theories about the selection of Hindu versus Buddhist staff but none are reliable. The bottom line is, you can always get a bad apple in a group but the chances are small. A very general (and therefore wrong) rule is that the only discernible difference between Nepalese of different ethnic groups is that the main Hindu castes tend to have a better sense of rhythm when singing and dancing.

Encouraging your crew to have a small party after a day on the trail is an excellent idea for a number of reasons:

● Sharing a communal bowl of *chang* (a locally made beer throughout Nepal) is the best way to break the ice and get to know your crew. By making the effort to share some social time you'll find your crew willing to share stories and relax.

● Nepalese love a party and it will help to bond the crew together, and you will notice that the whole crew will start to work as a team.

● Some low impact dancing will help to flush lactic acid from tired muscles, thus make the walking easier tomorrow.

❑ **Trekking as a single female**

There are many specialist trekking agencies in Nepal, including some who target the female-only trekking group market by providing only female staff. They have some highly skilled guides, cooks and sherpas, and can organise anything from a light trek to climbing Mt Everest.

If you plan to trek on your own with a male guide and/or porter you should choose your staff carefully. Make sure you interview them, preferably with a friend or someone from your hotel present, and get some contact details from them. Check their ID and leave details with your hotel when you go trekking. Generally speaking, an older, more experienced guide will be better in these situations than a younger one, who may just believe everything he has seen on MTV.

Always make sure you put your money and any valuables you take in the bag you are carrying yourself every day.

Local customs throughout Nepal deem it improper for you and your staff to share a room in a teahouse, and even innocent offers to help room allocations can be mis-construed or cause offence. It is a good idea to make it clear to your guide before you hire him that you will not tolerate any advances, and that he will be fired if he tries to become intimate.

One major problem for female trekkers is hygiene. As it is not always possible to get a shower, so wet wipes are always a handy thing to have in your pack. Thin panty liners help keep your knickers fresh and may keep thrush at bay. You may not be able to wash your undies every day, and even if you do you'll need to hang them like flags off the back of your daypack to get them dry. Although a local would never display their underwear like this it is accepted as 'one of those things tourists do'.

Another problem that really irritates many female tourists who come to Nepal is their 'invisibility'. The shopkeepers see you, the beggars see you, but nobody seems to hear you. Traditionally in Nepal, women (especially Hindu and Muslim women) do not usually travel alone, nor do they speak out in public. You may have a conversation with your guide about where you will walk to, or where you would like to stay, only to find that you have been completely ignored. It's all part of the Nepali culture. It's not unusual for your guide to believe that he has a much better idea of where to stay or walk than you do, and he is just trying to make sure you have a good day. The more experienced your guide is at dealing with Westerners, especially women, the less likely this will happen. Standing by the side of the trail and shouting at him won't make any difference, it's best just to sit down with him and tell him that you are disap-pointed that he overruled you and next time if he disagrees with your choice he should say so. That way nobody loses face and you can all still be friends.

Judy Smith

SHOPPING, TIPS AND MONEY

Money issues like tipping, bargaining and the payment process are perhaps the most common complaints tourists have when visiting Nepal. This need not be so when you understand a few simple principles.

Firstly, you are the visitor and are therefore perceived to be wealthier than the vast majority of Nepalese you will meet. Traditionally, a wealthy person travels in Nepal with an entourage of family, servants and assistants, so the expectation exists that you will do the same. This expectation is reinforced when you see all the support that comes with a trekking group. The simple fact that you are travelling in Nepal, and it is very difficult for a Nepali to travel in your country, probably exacerbates the perceived wealth divide. It is perhaps no surprise, therefore, that the government charges a higher price for entry to places of interest for tourists than for locals (the average annual income in Nepal is only around US$1400 per capita, 2003 est.). You will also begin most negotiations with a seemingly outrageous amount being quoted by the vendor, which is just a 'water-test' and all part of the process.

Haggling and bargaining

Bargaining can be a harrowing or fun experience depending on your expectations. The entire process is as much about the vendor and purchaser getting to know each other as it is about actually buying something. A major complicating factor in making a purchase is ethnicity. Some ethnic groups do not negotiate at all; they just offer a fixed price, whereas others expect to haggle. The best way to find out what to do is to be relaxed, start haggling, and if the vendor won't move on the price, make up your mind if you are happy to pay that price or move on. A few ideas to make 'haggling' more enjoyable:

● Start haggling over something you do not want to buy to help build your confidence and rapport with the vendor and then progress on to your desired object but do not show much enthusiasm, as this will push the price up. It is best to only start haggling if you genuinely have an interest to purchase something from the vendor.

● Your first counter offer should be less than half the first price quoted by the vendor. The vendor will undoubtedly act offended, but this is all part of the process. If the vendor insists that you make the first offer, then say half of what you are prepared to pay and then work up to what you think is a fair price.

● Have the actual amount of money you are prepared to pay ready in your pocket. If the negotiation has hit stalemate then showing that you have the money ready can sometimes swing the deal. Also, when it comes to paying most transactions happen very quickly with the transfer of goods ending the conversation.

● Always keep smiling, keep the conversation friendly and not too serious, and never, ever get angry.

Tipping

For many tourists the tipping process either in Kathmandu or at the end of a trek leaves them confused and sometimes feeling offended. However, tipping is a

> ❏ **Top tip – price check**
> When you are out in the hills you should always confirm prices before accepting a
> service or product. Some teahouses may even charge you for sitting in a dining room,
> especially if you do not order something from their menu. Check if there is a room
> surcharge if you choose to eat elsewhere.

traditional part of Nepali life and a vital component of a local's income. Tipping
is therefore expected and you could seriously offend if you do not tip. The big
question is: *how much*?

Tipping in restaurants is normally 10%, but this is now optional in tourist
restaurants, which, as per union demands, add an automatic service charge.
Your bill must specify if the service charge has been included. Nearly all local
restaurants, that is those out of the main tourist areas, will not add this sur-
charge, so pay a tip as you see fit.

Tipping your staff at the end of a trek is more complicated; a general rule is
US$1 per day for a porter or kitchen crew, US$1.25 for sherpa helpers, US$1.50
for your cook and US$2 for your guide. However, these amounts depend on the
duration and difficulty of your trek, how well the crew as a whole has performed and individual performance. It is reasonable to increase or slightly
reduce tips for each crew member, and to tell them why, when you give them
out on the last night of your trek. You should put tips in individually named
envelopes. Your crew won't open the envelope immediately as it is considered
rude to do so; they'll just put the envelope in their pocket and say 'thank you'.

It is therefore important that you have sufficient cash for your general
expenses and tips before you start the trek. You'll need to take a mix of Rupee
note denominations (make sure the notes are in good condition) with you for the
trek. It is almost impossible to get additional cash in the mountains. Trekkers in
a camping group are less likely to buy soft or alcoholic drinks and snacks along
the trail, whereas teahouse trekkers have such luxuries within temptation's
grasp everyday. Prices vary dramatically; in the first days of a trek a bottle of
soft drink may cost US$1-2, but in the highest teahouses it may be US$5-6.
Beer, chocolate and luxury snacks are more expensive.

YOUR SECURITY

Since the Maoist 'People's War' there has been a breakdown in law and order
in some areas of Nepal; combined with an increase in the availability of weap-
ons, this has led to a general increase in crime across the country. However,
serious crimes very rarely involve tourists, who are much more likely to suffer
from opportunistic theft. It is also more likely that the thief will be a fellow tourist rather than a local. Most Nepalese are still very respectful of other people's
possessions and are often protective of your belongings. Some ethnic groups,
most notably nomadic Tibetans, have been known to take items which they think
have been discarded. So when you leave a solar charger or some laundry in a

sunny spot make sure it is watched. Any bags left unattended, including those on bus roofs and checked onto domestic flights, should be locked shut. Keep spare money on your person in a money belt or buried deep inside your pack, your kit bag is not as safe as the bag you always carry with you.

The role of women in Nepali society is changing in good and bad ways; strip bars and pornography accompany greater emancipation. The Nepali government is trying to cope with an underground sex industry that now flourishes throughout the country. It is unfortunate but perhaps no surprise therefore that women sometimes suffer from sexual harassment from young males, especially in urban centres or if a woman's attire seems suggestive.

INSURANCE

Most travel insurance policies will cover you while you are trekking and will include emergency medical evacuation costs. However, you should read the policy carefully and check for any exclusions. For example, using a rope (even as a handline) or itineraries that go higher than a stipulated maximum altitude during your trek could void your policy.

It is also vital that you establish some contacts in Kathmandu that could help you should an accident occur, see *Rescue* p63 for more details.

COMMUNICATIONS

Nepal's **phone** system has expanded rapidly, and the cheap cost of calls is hugely enabling for local and visitor alike. The downside is almost perpetually overloaded circuits. It can take multiple tries to get through between different service providers and line interference is common. International calls are still comparatively expensive and it may take many re-dials to finally make a connection. **Mobile phones** are now very popular throughout the country, as the landline system is notoriously unreliable. Inexpensive and good quality Internet phone services are also cropping up and a subsidised satellite network is spreading throughout mountain areas. If you want to set your phone to roaming it is wise to first check call charges, and that your provider offers roaming in Nepal. You may find it easier to buy a SIM card in Nepal (available at the airport on arrival through Ncell or Nepal Telecom); you will require photo ID and they generally cost about US$12 (with $8 worth of calls).

Recharge scratch cards are widely available and come in many denominations, the largest being Rs500 for which there is a Rs10 charge. You will find that calls home are pretty reasonable, and calling local numbers and even other mobiles in Nepal is inexpensive, but the service can sometimes be erratic. There is no voicemail in Nepal. Texting is popular as is 'give me a missed call' when

---

❏ **Top tip**
Never carry something around town or on the trail that you can't afford to lose.

❏ **Top tip**
The best time to call is in the early morning: the mobile network is less congested.

arranging to meet people. When you try to call and can't get through there are a variety of messages you will receive – they range from the phone is unavailable, the caller is busy to the number called doesn't exist. Persist, as the other person may just be on the phone. Expect to be cut off at some point in most calls.

Thuraya satellite phones can receive SMS directly from the Thuraya website for no charge, see 🖳 sms.thuraya.com and there is a local operator who sells phones and accessories, see 🖳 www.constellation.com.np.

There is also a new phone on the market in Nepal from Isat PhonePro, which is available for $US700. For more information see 🖳 www.isatphoneproreview. com.au.

When a Nepali answers a call they do not say their name, which can cause a great deal of confusion. Likewise, they do not normally say 'goodbye', they just hang up. Years of bad phone connections mean that most locals talk very loudly or even shout down the line and expect the line to cut out at the most inopportune moment.

Internet access is readily available in nearly all urban centres, and during the climbing season there is even a satellite Internet café at Everest Base Camp!

Snail mail operates from the GPO (Sun-Fri 10am-4pm), a 25-minute walk south of Thamel on the corner of Kanti Path and Prithvi Path. When sending a letter or small package don't put it in a post-box but ask them to frank it or the stamps may be removed and resold. Sending mail is easier done through the various bookshops in Thamel, which are usually more reliable than the hotels.

For **parcels**, in addition to the GPO you have the choice of international couriers with reliability at a price, and cargo agents who specialise in bigger consignments. The cargo companies will often accept much smaller airfreight shipments for the same price per kilo, usually around US$5, for common North American and European destinations.

DOS AND DON'TS: HOW NOT TO CAUSE OFFENCE

Almost anyone who visits Nepal returns with a story of another tourist's inappropriate behaviour or dress. To commit the occasional faux pas is inevitable when exploring foreign shores and Nepali people will often make light of your indiscretion. However, taking advantage of traditional hospitality without understanding the implications, overt ostentation, disrespecting ceremonies or customs, and dressing inappropriately are all considerable insults and should be avoided at all costs. If you are unsure how to behave then follow the lead of a Nepali, and if necessary ask questions. Everyone will understand that you are trying to do the right thing and you'll be given all the support to participate in local lives to the fullest. This list of Dos and Don'ts is by no means exhaustive, so please apply liberal amounts of common sense to your day.

Community
Respect cultures and traditions:

● **Consideration** – Be a considerate guest at all times. Nepali culture is rich and diverse and can sometimes confuse a visitor but if you are friendly, approachable and consider those around you before yourself, you will always earn the respect of local people.

● **Photos** – Ask before taking a photo, as many people prefer not to be photographed for personal, cultural or superstitious reasons.

● **Gift giving** – The complex patina of Nepali society sometimes calls for gift giving or making a donation; this may be to a monastery or shrine, at a wedding, or at a cultural program. Whenever you are faced with the need to give a gift you should seek the advice of a Nepali to work out what is appropriate. The method of or the formality associated with giving a gift is often as important as the gift itself so make sure you are aware of any protocols.

● **Affection** – Do not show affection in public.

● **Bathing** – Showing your genitalia when bathing is offensive. Use a sarong, screen or shower tent and when visiting a hot spring try to behave modestly.

Benefit local communities, commercially and socially

● **Share skills and experience**, offer a fair rate of pay for services, participate in activities whenever invited.

● **Do not publicly argue, drink excessively or fight**. Demonstrations of anger are considered an embarrassing loss of face on your behalf.

● **Begging** – Of all the negative impacts tourists have had in Nepal, the encouragement of begging along the trail is probably the most problematic. Handing out candy (referred to as sweets, *mitai* or bonbons) to children who never clean their teeth is thoughtless and irresponsible. Giving money to small children in return for picked flowers is destructive and illegal in all National Parks. If your conscience struggles with the wealth divide then provide skills through training and education, or donate to one of the major charities in Kathmandu or Pokhara. But do not just give away items along the trail and so perpetuate a habit that ultimately only reduces self-esteem and can cause long-term problems. If you aren't convinced of the negative effects of pandering to cute children then trek away from the main trails and experience the genuine, openhearted joy that children show tourists without the expectation of a 'reward'.

Adopt new customs:

● **Clothing** – Do not wear tight or revealing clothing, especially if you are a woman. There is a firm dress code followed by Nepalese and is only not observed by the very poor or for special reasons.

It is considered offensive to expose your knees, shoulders and chest at all times and especially in any place of worship. This means that detachable leg pants are not very useful in Nepal, and cropped tops of any description should be avoided. Men can wear long shorts but should avoid exposing their chests.

It is also considered offensive to highlight genitalia, so avoid wearing stretch or very tight clothing around the chest or groin area.

● **Entering homes** – It is critical that you wait to be invited into a home. The caste system prescribes a rigid hierarchy of which rooms you may or may not be allowed to enter, respect the wishes of the homeowner. The cooking-fire area is often sacred so always check if you can dispose of burnable rubbish before consigning it to the flames.

● **Greetings** – Nepalese greet eat other with the traditional, 'Namaste!' Sometimes they will shake hands, especially if they are involved in the tourism sector or have retired from the Royal Gurkha Rifles, but in general you should avoid touching people, especially of the opposite gender. A namaste, or thanks, or taking a little time to play or practice English is always preferable to a short or quick reply. It will both build respect and relieve any stress you may feel from curious locals.

● **Eating** – Do not use your left hand to eat or pass objects. Traditionally Nepalese eat only with the right hand, the left being considered unclean. Therefore pass foodstuffs to another person with your right hand and use your left as little as possible. You should also avoid touching the lip of a vessel to your mouth, just pour the drink into your mouth.

● **Offering payment and/or gifts** It is respectful to use both hands, or with your right hand while touching your left hand to your right elbow.

● **Language** Learn some basic Nepali phrases and use them as often as possible.

Environment

● **Tread softly** – Stick to trails and recognised camping areas. Avoid creating new tracks, or damaging the environment in any way. Follow the adage: take only photos, leave only footprints.

● **Pack it in**, **pack it out** – Avoid taking tins, glass, or plastic containers and bags unless you plan to carry them back to Kathmandu or Pokhara.

● **Conserve water quality** – Wash away from water sources, and always use local toilet facilities when available. Bury all organic waste at least 30cm below the ground and 50m away from water sources.

❏ How long does it take to degrade?	
Cotton rags	1-5 months
Paper	2-5 months
Orange peel	6 months
Wool socks	1 to 5 years
Plastic bags	10 to 20 years
Leather shoes	25 to 40 years
Nylon fabric	30 to 40 years
Aluminium cans	80 to 100 years
Plastic bottles	Forever
© WorldWise, Inc.	

● **Conserve natural resources**
What few resources there are belong by right to the locals. Always ask permission before using anything along the trail. It is illegal to disturb wildlife, remove animals or plants, or buy wildlife products.

Safety

● **Beware of altitude sickness** – Use the buddy system to watch for symptoms of altitude sickness. Make sure everyone remains fully hydrated by drinking water throughout the day, everyday. Stay together along the trail, and communicate frequently with everyone.

● **Be safe** – Carry an extensive first-aid kit and know how to use it. Have multiple plans for emergency evacuation and designated decision makers. Leave your itinerary details with someone responsible at home.

● **Be self-reliant** – Don't assume you will receive help or assistance. Ensure your group has extensive field-craft and navigation skills. Research thoroughly, is your route appropriate for your party? Do you have the necessary skills, experience, resources and equipment?

● **Remain hydrated** – Drinking between two and four litres of water per day will help prevent altitude sickness and improve your body's recovery time.

● **Don't rush** – There are no prizes for coming first on the trail and rushing will probably over-stress your body and may increase your chances of suffering from altitude sickness. Frequent stops to drink water and rest often become photo opportunities and a chance to chat with locals.

● **Trekking poles** – That more people aren't impaled by absent-minded trekkers swinging their poles is amazing. Be aware of the pole tips, especially when crossing bridges or negotiating narrow or steep trails.

● **Beware of yaks** – Many porterage animals you meet along the trail are yaks or hybrids of yaks and cattle, and all of them can be dangerous. Every season at least one tourist will die because they got too close to the large horns or were knocked from a bridge. If you see any pack animals (even donkeys cause accidents) coming along the trail you should scramble up the hillside of the trail and wait until they pass.

● **iPod use** – Rather than listening to the noise of life along the trail some people prefer to plug in to an iPod. Doing so puts you at greater risk from animals and rock fall.

● **Common courtesy** – The trail is often busy, especially at steep or difficult sections. A common courtesy is to give way to people walking up-hill, or to those who are obviously struggling or carrying a very large load.

GREETINGS AND BLESSINGS

Religious practitioners of all faiths are normally happy to show you around and answer questions, but there is a strict etiquette to follow when in their company.

They will greet you with both hands together in front of their chests and with a light bow of their head. You should respond in the same way. Shaking hands is not required unless the other party extends a hand. If you do shake hands, your sleeves should always be unrolled to show respect.

If you are a guest, you should begin by handing over a *khadag* (aka *khata*), or ceremonial scarf. Use two hands with the palms towards the sky and take the khadag between your thumb and the palm of your hand. This is a traditional greeting in order to pay respect to your host, who may, as a sign of respect, hand back the khadag, hanging it over your head onto your shoulders. Receiving a khadag from a *lama* is considered a form of blessing. Your khadag should be folded three times width-wise and presented with the opening towards the receiver; to not do so will be considered offensive.

When receiving a blessing from the lama or presenting a khadag, monks and nuns are generally asked to go first, in order of seniority. In Buddhist cultures, monks go before nuns. You approach the lama holding out a khadag; he may then touch your head with his hands as a blessing, and then either he or his assistant may give you a red blessing cord with a small knot on it. The cord should be treated with respect and not dropped. Buddhists tie the cords around their necks or place them in their shrines. You should knot the thread around your right wrist or your throat, depending on the size. You may also receive a blessed parcel or small picture amulet, which can be suspended from the thread, like a pendant. You should not remove this (unless for washing) as you will also remove the blessings it bestows. It is always polite to offer money to the temple when you receive a blessing – NRs100 or more is reasonable.

If a Hindu holy man, or *sadhu* approaches you on the street with a little tray of coloured powder or flowers and you accept a blessing, it is appropriate to give Rs5-10 – this is his way of living. However, if you take a blessing from a sadhu, especially in tourist areas and places of interest, expect to pay a few hundred rupees at least.

TEMPLE ETIQUETTE

Many temples are closed for periods throughout the year and you should check if the 'key-holder' is nearby otherwise you might have a pointless walk. Personal contact is frowned upon, so you should avoid touching monks or nuns at all times. You should ask if it is necessary to remove your footwear when entering any religious building. Both men and women should have their chests and shoulders covered at all times, whereas your head should be uncovered.

Remain quiet and avoid speaking loudly. Also turn off your phone. Many Buddhists make prostrations when they enter a temple. If you do not wish to do the same, either bow your head slightly with the palms of your hands together at the chest or simply stand quietly until others have finished.

If you enter a monastery or shrine you may be led to the main statue where you can pay respect to the Buddha or deity by laying down a khadag in front of the Buddha in the same way, as you would present it to a lama – folded correctly and with your palms facing towards the sky. Lighting a candle is another way of paying respect; this should be done facing towards the central Buddha or deity statue. Do not touch Buddha statues, or any of the ritual objects around the temple.

When teachers, monks and nuns enter and leave the main shrine room, visitors should stand to show respect. Otherwise, it is good manners to bow down low when walking directly in front of people, in particular monks, who may be sitting against the walls of the temple.

Sit with your feet folded cross-legged or folded under yourself. If you feel the need to stretch your legs while in a temple, do so in such a way so as not to point your feet directly at the teacher or altar.

If you wish to take pictures, verify beforehand that it is acceptable to do so, and find out when a good time would be so as not to disturb any ceremonies.

Always ask before you enter Hindu temples, as many do not allow non-Hindus inside. Please respect their wishes and do not go in if the people outside ask you not to. You will need to remove your shoes and any leather objects you are carrying (wallets, belts etc). If you are allowed inside, do not touch any of the objects and always ask before taking photos.

Health and wellbeing

Trekking is good for you! The daily exercise, consumption of significant volumes of water and controlled exposure to sunlight all combine to make many feel healthier than they ever have before. However, there are occasions when this is not the case, and being aware of your and your groups' health is critical to safe trekking.

This chapter is not an exhaustive review of health, first aid and rescue issues; it is merely a guide to help you understand what information and experience you need to have to trek safely. It is essential that somebody in your party has up-to-date first aid knowledge, that everyone has a clear idea of general health problems and their prevention, and that your party and guide understand what to do in an emergency situation.

An excellent resource for anyone trekking into mountainous regions is *Pocket First Aid and Wilderness Medicine*: Drs Jim Duff and Peter Gormly (Cicerone Press). Every group should carry at least one copy.

GENERAL HEALTH ISSUES

All trekking companies and medical staff recommend a regular exercise program of increasing difficulty some months prior to embarking on your trek. If you arrive in Nepal in an unfit state you will find trekking tough on your body and mind.

Regular aerobic exercise for a couple of hours at a time is the least you should be able to achieve. It is also wise to take at least one long walk a week, for up to five or six hours (of walking time), so that your body is not unfamiliar with sustained exercise. The fitter you are before you arrive the faster your body will adapt to the rigours of walking all day on sometimes rough and difficult trails. It is often hard for people to imagine that you can spend *days* walking up just one hill and that a climb of 100m or 200m is considered *flat* by most Nepalese. Aerobic fitness will also make acclimatisation easier for you as your body will begin to adapt to, rather than just coping with, reduced levels of oxygen.

You must visit your doctor at home and check your immunisations and any general health requirements or issues. It is also a good idea to get some recommendations about specific medications for your trip and research potential health issues. Whenever you prepare a field first aid kit there is one major consideration: only pack what you know how to use. Any items or medications that you are not familiar with will at best be a waste of time, at worst, they could cause a serious problem. You should also include enough supplies to cover your crew as well as group members.

When you are trekking you will come across health posts in some villages, if you have additional medical supplies these could be a good place to leave them. You should avoid giving out medications to locals unless absolutely necessary and you know exactly what you are doing. It is far better for everyone that you encourage them to visit their health centre as quickly as possible. Sometimes, you may be asked to give medicines to people along the trail or in villages; this is because many Nepalese believe foreign medicines are stronger and more effective than those available locally. If this should happen, ask your guide to explain that your medicines are the same as those prescribed by their local health practitioner. Local people frequently use traditional remedies to cure general ailments, but as you may react to them, so it is wise to avoid them.

Although malaria is rare in Nepal, mosquitoes and numerous other insects and nasties that bite, including bed bugs, fleas, small spiders, leeches (in the wetter months), horse flies and ticks are common. Packing both an insect repellent (with DEET) and a bite-balm is a good idea, especially for remoter trips.

If you wear contact lenses you will probably find the chance of an eye infection higher than at home, especially on dusty trails. Pack sufficient amounts of sterilising/disinfecting solutions and do not exceed recommended wearing times. Use boiled water that has cooled for cleansing, and remove contacts at the first sign of irritation. The disposable extended-wear lenses tend to perform better than those you change or clean daily.

The supply of plastic bottles of water in the mountains is causing a major environmental problem, and boiling water frequently puts a strain on meagre fuel supplies. Taking a water filtration or purification treatment means that you can be sure your water is good to drink. Ultra-violet light (for example Steri-pen) and chemical treatments tend to be easier to use and lighter to carry than pump systems.

FOOD AND DIARRHOEA

It's rare that some form of stomach malady doesn't affect the trekker at some point, and you should be prepared with a range of medications, see p159 in *Pocket First Aid and Wilderness Medicine* for specific details. Many travellers to Nepal pick up a stomach bug in Kathmandu and continue to suffer while trekking. It is important that you eat and drink correctly-prepared food from the moment you arrive in Nepal and maintain high levels of personal hygiene throughout your trip. However, there are a few general precautions that will make the chances of sudden dashes to the toilet less likely.

● Only eat food that has been freshly prepared, which is normally dhal bhat. Many teahouses are guilty of preparing food hours or days in advance, which will certainly cause a stomach upset at least. If you doubt the level of hygiene then visit the kitchen and check for yourself before ordering.
● Avoid excessively oily food.
● Keep to regular eating times.
● Increase the amount of vegetables in your diet, even to the extent of avoiding meat altogether when in the mountains.
● Drink plenty of treated water.
● Only consume raw vegetables and fruit if properly treated.
● Be very careful of all roadside restaurants, even if they are busy serving fresh food, as hygiene in these places is frequently very poor.

ALTITUDE SICKNESS

The effects of altitude are many and various, and still largely a mystery to modern medicine. One year someone may suffer from altitude sickness, but not the next, even if they are doing exactly the same trek at the same time of year. For this reason the effects of altitude have become the most common dinner conversation in teahouses and dining tents alike. For a comprehensive review of HAPE, HACE, AMS and related issues see p138 in *Pocket First Aid and Wilderness Medicine*. If someone is beginning to feel unwell then the first assumption is always altitude sickness until proven otherwise.

A healthy level of observation should exist between all group members and each trekker should have a 'health buddy', normally a tent or roommate, with whom you will form a 'watch me, watch you' relationship. Sometimes the effects of altitude are subtle, eg a slight slurring of speech, or loss of coordination, that only regular examination will notice. It is essential that all group members take altitude seriously and maintain a vigilant approach and openly discuss how they feel; self-medication without telling anyone is extremely dangerous. When ascending, most people suffer from some symptoms of altitude sickness, but cautious acclimatisation and continuous vigilance will help to limit the effects you will feel.

LOOKING AFTER FEET AND JOINTS

Carry a blister treatment kit and examine your feet regularly for any signs of irritation or nail problems, see p128 in *Pocket First Aid and Wilderness Medicine* for blister treatment information. When you have finished trekking for the day it is a good idea to remove your boots and socks and let your feet 'breathe'. Some people like a footbath but these are best saved for times when your feet can completely dry out. Trim your toenails regularly and clean out any dead skin from around the nails. If you develop any aches or pains in your feet you should first check that your boots are laced correctly, your sock or boot lining hasn't creased or folded differently, or that your laces are not too tight. If pains persist it is wise to rest and seek medical attention.

Legs and joints can frequently feel painful with deep muscle aches lasting for days. Pack a little massage oil and apply it to affected areas gently. If a joint is twisted or sprained then first apply something cool: along the main trails this is frequently a chilled bottle of soft drink. Then compress and elevate the joint, make sure the patient is comfortable and relaxed and then give pain relief and/ or anti-inflammatory medication, see p111 in *Pocket First Aid and Wilderness Medicine* for more information.

HYPOTHERMIA AND HEAT STROKE

Two very common conditions suffered along the trail are hypothermia (aka exposure) and heat stroke, and even mild forms (including dehydration) can significantly reduce your walking performance. See *Pocket First Aid and Wilderness Medicine* (pp148-158) for a comprehensive review of symptoms, diagnosis and treatments.

Hypothermia occurs when your body loses heat faster than it can generate it, and is most common in cool to cold conditions during or after periods of high exertion. Typical combinations of factors that cause hypothermia are physical exhaustion, wet or insufficient clothing, cold and/or wet weather conditions, failure to eat enough food, dehydration and high altitude. Ultimately it can result in death. The patient needs to be warmed immediately, ideally with a hot drink, high-energy food, and hot water bottle next to the skin. They should also be insulated from the weather using a sleeping bag, and/or a blanket/mat wrapped around them.

Heat exhaustion, and the more severe heat stroke, is common at lower altitudes, especially at the beginning of the trek. It occurs when your body's ability to regulate temperature fails, normally in hot and/or humid conditions, especially when you have arrived from a very different climate. Symptoms include dizziness, vagueness, rapid heart rate, and possibly nausea, vomiting and headache. It is best avoided through the regular intake of substantial quantities (up to eight litres a day) of water, salt, resting at the hottest periods of the day and the application of moist scarves to the head and neck. Rest and avoiding vigorous exercise for a few days is the best method of recuperation.

FIRST AID   [see also pp44-5]

A comprehensive first aid kit suitable to cater for the needs of your party is essential. It should be kept available throughout the day and not packed away in a porter's load that will not be seen again until camp. There are two components to most first aid kits: medications and dressings. A simple list and explanation is given on pp44-5 but see *Pocket First Aid and Wilderness Medicine* (pp213-235 in that book) for a comprehensive guide, and remember to keep your first-aid skills updated through regular training. It is also a good idea to have a small subsidiary first aid kit with the person responsible for your crew during the day.

❏ **Top tip – more uses for tampons and condoms**
Take a few tampons for (1) packing or dressing deep cuts, (2) a fast way to help light a fire. It's also a good idea to pack some condoms, as they are useful for making hand and foot dressings waterproof.

RESCUE AND EMERGENCY

None of the rural health posts throughout Nepal can provide the sort of emergency care that tourists take for granted back home. If an emergency occurs you must evacuate the patient either by land, or at times of a life-threatening emergency, by rescue helicopter, see pp94-5 for more information. Some tourists are wealthy enough to pay for non-medical evacuations and if you choose this option you must explain that it is a not life-threatening situation.

Telecommunication options (see *Communications* p53) in Nepal are expanding year by year and it is rare that you will be more than a few days away from a telephone. Better still, carry your own satellite phone system to contact the emergency services. However, phone numbers frequently change in Nepal and it is essential that you confirm emergency contact details before you start your trek. It is wise to have a clear idea of the costs of a rescue before you start your trek and you may also need to organise a method of payment in Kathmandu and obtain permission from the relevant insurance company prior to rescue. When you make an emergency call you must relay the following to your trekking company and the pilot of the helicopter:

● Degree of urgency. **Most Immediate** means death within 24 hours. **As Soon As Possible** is used in all other cases.

● The patient's present location or, if the patient is going to be moved, where to and how quickly. You should provide a latitude, longitude and altitude if possible, alternatively a map reference with publisher's name and title, and give as many local details as possible.

● Name, age, sex, nationality, passport number, visa and permit details, trekking agency name and contact details, and any other relevant contact details (family, embassy, etc).

● Medical information, including sickness or injury details, and any special requirements for the rescue, eg is supplementary oxygen or neck brace required?

● Is a doctor present or does one need to come in the helicopter to administer treatment prior to and during the flight?

● The names, ages, nationalities and sex of all persons who need to be evacuated.

● The name and organisation of the person who is going to pay, and the method of payment. Most helicopter charter companies will only fly once a payment guarantee has been provided in writing or paid in cash in Kathmandu.

A rescue may take a number of days to organise, especially if the weather is bad. Wait until 10am or 11am each day before moving the patient to give the helicopter a chance of arriving when the weather is normally clearest. In each cleared landing area mark your position with a large emergency orange X – you may need to light a large smoky fire if it's hard to spot your location from above. Try to make a windsock and a signal mirror, which should be used with great care. If you are signalling to a helicopter stand, at the end of the landing site with your back to the wind and wear brightly coloured clothing. As the helicopter prepares to land remove the X marker.

Do not signal a helicopter if you cannot direct it to the victim or you are not directly involved in a rescue. Do not approach the helicopter until indicated to do so, and only approach from the front.

If the worst should happen and a porter or trekker dies you will probably have to charter a helicopter to transport the body; domestic airlines will refuse transport. It is best to organise a cremation and have it witnessed by at least one senior local, perhaps a village chairman, policeman or teacher; they should not be associated with anyone in your group. Record all personal possessions and details if known and have at least one witness sign to the effects. There are many logistical issues facing the transport of bodies to Kathmandu and then out of Nepal, if you need to do this, contact your embassy.

Colour section

● **C1 (Opposite)** Perhaps the best viewpoint for Everest (8848m) is from the Renjo La (5306m, see p141) to the west of Gokyo.

● **C2** Kanchenjunga region – **Top left**: Descent from the Lumbha Sambha La (5159m, see p124) towards the remote village of Thudam. Makalu is in the distance. **Bottom left**: Mani wall at Olangchung Gola. (Photo © RR). **Right**: Lhomi man in Chyamtang.

● **C3** Makalu region – **Top**: One of the five Panch Pokhari Lakes in the Honku Basin. (Photo © RR). **Bottom**: Rai children.

● **C4** Everest region – **Top left**: Thame Gompa (see p142) where trekkers can receive a blessing before attempting the Tashi Labsta pass (see p149). **Right**: Drolambu Glacier on the west side of the Tashi Labsta (Photo © YP). **Bottom left**: Typical Sherpa kitchen. (Photo © RR).

● **C5** Dolpo – **Top**: Standing on the top of the Nyingma Gyanzen La (5563m, see p236), in the centre of the Great Himalaya Range, is like being on the spine of the planet. **Bottom left**: Many rivers in the remote regions of the Far West have no permanent bridges. **Bottom right**: A woman in Bhijer prepares wool for weaving.

● **C6 Top left**: Langtang region – Looking down into the Chilime valley. **Top right**: Trekker on the Manaslu trail with Shringi Himal (7187m) ahead. **Bottom left**: Suspension bridge on the Manaslu trail. (Photo © SB & TR). **Bottom right**: Phoksundo Lake (see p212), one of the most impressive in the entire range, was made famous by the movie, *Himalaya*.

● **C7** Mustang – Teeji Festival (see p203) in Lo Monthang. **Top**: Lama musicians. **Bottom left**: Novice monks enjoying a snack. **Bottom right**: Purification dance.

● **C8** Dolpo – The nunnery of Ribum Gompa (see p220) and Regu Chorten above Dho Tarap.

● **C9** Winnowing buckwheat in Bhijer, Dolpo.

C2

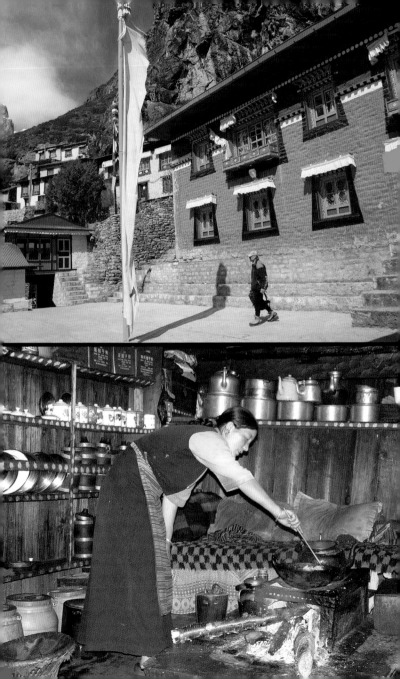

C4

KATHMANDU

The Kathmandu Valley is enigmatic and unique; the colour, chaos and complexity of life in Nepal's capital will fill your days with wonder and amazement. For almost two millennia, people from across the Himalaya, and now the world, have been drawn to this broad and fertile Valley and its three cities of Kathmandu, Patan and Bhaktapur. Some say that if you belong nowhere else on earth, then this is your home.

HISTORY

Origins

According to legend, the Kathmandu Valley was once a lake upon which a beautiful lotus grew surrounded by light. The Buddhist deity Manjushri (Buddha of Transcendent Wisdom) drained the lake by cutting a gorge at Chobar so he could examine this lotus. The flower settled on a hill now called Swayambhunath and the retreating waters left rich soil in the Valley that was ideal for grazing cattle and buffalo.

The founder of the first dynasty here was a sage known as Ne and in ancient chronicles the area became known as Ne-pāla, literally 'the land protected by Ne'.

By the second half of the first millennium BC the invading Kiratas, who are distantly related to the Limbu (p118) and Rai (p128) people, had occupied a number of sites in the region. They were succeeded by the Lichhavi in the 9th century AD. The settlements were centred around religious sites known as piths or power places, usually on the tops of hills. The Lichhavis worshipped the sun and the moon, which are two symbols that appear on Nepal's uniquely shaped flag, and they are responsible for many of the oldest religious sites in the Valley, although none of their architecture remains.

A transitional period, also called the 'dark period' of the Valley's history, began with the disintegration of the Lichhavi empire towards the end of the 9th century. A series of shadowy kings ruled a Valley that was rarely at peace, but the period is notable for the founding of Kathmandu city at some point between AD980 and 998. The towns of Patan and Bhaktapur were already established by then. The name Kathmandu is believed to be a corruption of Kasthamandap ('square house of wood'), the 1000-year-old *dharamsala* (rest-house) that still stands in Durbar Square.

Everything changed in 1200AD when Ari Malla founded a dynasty that was to last until 1769. However, the early years of a peaceful unified Malla empire soon ended with the creation of the three separate city-kingdoms of Kathmandu, Patan and Bhaktapur. The cities had their own courts, which frequently engaged in intrigue, quarrelled and went to war against one another. Competition between the Valley's kings helped to create some of the region's most notable buildings and art. Throughout this period the Valley grew wealthy on trade with Tibet and India, which led to ever-grander and more flamboyant festivals and events. The success of the three cities meant that the Valley became synonymous with Nepal as a whole, and this largely excluded the surrounding kingdoms to the east and west.

Times present

While the Malla kings squabbled, the nearby kingdom of Gorkha grew stronger to become the dominant power in central Nepal. In 1769, Pritvi Narayan Shah conquered the Valley and so began a dynasty that unified dozens of regional principalities into what has become modern Nepal. However, the rule of the Shahs was often challenged. One night in 1846 almost the entire court was massacred thus making Jung Bahadur Rana de facto ruler of Nepal. For almost 100 years the Rana family kept Nepal isolated from the rest of the world, yet they travelled widely. They introduced garish Western-influenced building styles incorporated into enormous palaces throughout Kathmandu. The tight control held by the Ranas didn't extend much beyond the edge of the Valley beyond which the concept of a unified Nepal meant little. Ethnic groups throughout the country identified themselves with clan, caste and district far more than a national identity.

In 1951, the Shahs returned to power with the support of India, who also encouraged the new King Tribhuvan and his son, Mahendra, to adopt democracy. A system of local government through village committees known as Panchyat was established across the country in 1959. Although this system continues to

---

❏ The Newar

Newars are the indigenous inhabitants of the Kathmandu Valley, and claim an ancestry dating back to the 6th century BC. They are a cultural entity rather than an ethnic group, and have Mongoloid and Mediterranean features. They speak Nepali and Newari. Newars traditionally travelled for trade or business, and many now live west of Kathmandu in Pokhara, Butwal and Silgadhi. Newar houses are usually several storeys high, with a veranda, and large framed doors and windows. Many of the beautiful old buildings in Kathmandu highlight the complexity and beauty of their woodcarving. Newars may be either Hindu or Buddhist, and sometimes both, so they celebrate most festivals and feast days. There are 1600 sub-castes in Newar culture, as every profession forms its own caste.

Newars, particularly the Hindus, still prefer arranged marriages. Every family is a member of a *guthi* or club, which come together for religious services (such as weddings and cremations), social events (picnics and the like) and public services (maintaining temples, rest houses and bridges). This means that Newar communities are close knit and can be difficult to understand.

Newar woodcarvings and stone masonry are famed throughout the Himalaya, including India and Tibet, and have influenced many of the most popular works of Asian art.

work well in India the rampant corruption and self-interest in Nepal undermined its effectiveness. A series of riots and civil unrest throughout the country led to democracy in 1991, where the Nepali Congress (symbol: the tree, a neo-conservative, pro-business party akin to the UK Conservatives or US Republicans) won, putting the United Marxist Leninists (UML, symbol: the sun, a strongly socialist party akin to the UK Labour or US Democrats) and the royalist RPP into opposition. However, corruption continued unabated as governments regularly fell and what seemed like a procession of the same old faces moved in and out of power.

When in 1994 the UML split sending the charismatic Baburam Bhattarai and his Communist Party of Nepal 'underground' no-one predicted the extent of suffering Nepal was going to endure. The subsequent 'People's War' between the Maoists and the Nepal army and police services killed 15,000 people and many more died or suffered indirectly through the conflict. Accusations of war crimes will continue for many years to come.

Two of the most tangible changes in Nepal during what is euphemistically called, 'the troubles', were a gradual creation of national identity so that impoverished and marginalised groups realised they had a voice and a right to be heard, and perhaps more importantly, the monarchy was removed as head of state making Nepal a Federal Democratic Republic. At the same time many Nepalese left their country to work overseas, a practice that continues today. The funds sent home keep the economy afloat and it's hoped that exposure to stable governments elsewhere is, in some way, positively influencing expectations and practices back in Nepal.

As the country lurches forward in fits and starts and attempts to write a new constitution it is hard to see other short term gains from what seems to be an extension of a traumatic, feudal history. Everyone hopes that peace will continue, that law and order will prevail and that corruption and self-interest are replaced by good governance, altruism and a system of government that benefits every Nepali.

Modern Kathmandu

Kathmandu today is plagued with the problems that beset all rapidly expanding cities in the developing world: overcrowding, severe pollution and traffic congestion to name but a few. Many parts of Kathmandu have degenerated into an urban sprawl of unsightly concrete block buildings. The district of Thamel, that today looks no different from tourist ghettos in the other Asian capitals on the backpackers' route, was largely fields 40 years ago. The population of the Kathmandu Valley stands at around 1.8 million, with a very high growth rate of almost 5%. None of these problems seems to tarnish the allure of the city as far as the tourist is concerned. Until the recent decline in tourism, brought on by the ten-year Maoist insurgency and global terrorism concerns, Kathmandu drew more than a quarter of a million tourists each year and can still boast more than 150,000 per annum, most of whom, you'll no doubt be glad to know, venture no further than the capital. Tourist numbers grew in 2008-9 following the end of the Maoist insurgency and, if political stability is achieved, look set to rise further.

ARRIVAL AND DEPARTURE

By air

● **Arrival** Tribhuvan International Airport is a 20-minute drive from the centre of Kathmandu. The domestic terminal is next door.

After completing **visa formalities** (see p38) head down to the baggage claim and then pass through **customs** where you may be required to put all your luggage through an X-ray machine. If you've brought film with you don't let it go through this.

Reaching the main hall, pick up a free city map at the **tourist office** here and a copy of *Nepal Traveler* magazine. There's also a **post office, communications agency** (for telephone calls), **bank** and **hotel reservations** counter.

Outside, screens and barricades attempt to keep an enthusiastic mob of hotel touts and taxi drivers at bay. If you stop to negotiate a fare expect to be quickly surrounded. Anyone other than your driver who pushes your trolley, even a few metres, will expect a tip. However, some hotels (and even some of the budget places) offer free transport from the airport. Taxis to the city centre and Thamel should cost Rs300 if you get your own, or Rs400 with the pre-paid taxi desk just outside to the left of the arrivals entrance. If you're really counting the pennies you can reach the bus stop for the crowded local bus (Rs10) by walking to the end of the airport drive and turning left.

● **Departure** At the bank in the international terminal you can convert into hard currency (usually US$) only up to 15% of the rupees for which you have encashment certificates. Alternatively you can dispose of surplus rupees at the shop in the corner of the departure hall, that sells gift packs of tea and Coronation Khukri rum in exotic khukri knife shaped bottles.

By road

Some of the tourist buses will take you all the way to Thamel. Most go no further than the new bus station about 3km north of the city. Buses from the Everest region still use the old bus station by the clock tower in the town centre. Frequent shuttle buses link the two, passing by the northern end of Thamel. Sajha buses usually stop at the GPO, which is closer to Thamel.

ORIENTATION

Greater Kathmandu, which includes Patan as well as Kathmandu itself, lies at about 1400m/4593ft. The Bagmati River runs between these two cities. The airport is 6km to the east, near the Hindu temple complex of Pashupatinath, with the Buddhist stupa at Baudha 2km north of Pashupatinath. The other major Buddhist shrine, Swayambhunath, is visible on a hill in west Kathmandu. The third city in the Valley, Bhaktapur, is 14km to the east.

Within Kathmandu, most hotels and guesthouses are to be found in Thamel, north of Durbar Square, the historic centre of the city. Freak Street, the hippie centre in the '60s and '70s, which still offers some cheap accommodation, is just off Durbar Square. Some of the top hotels and the international airline offices are along Durbar Marg, which runs south from the modern royal palace.

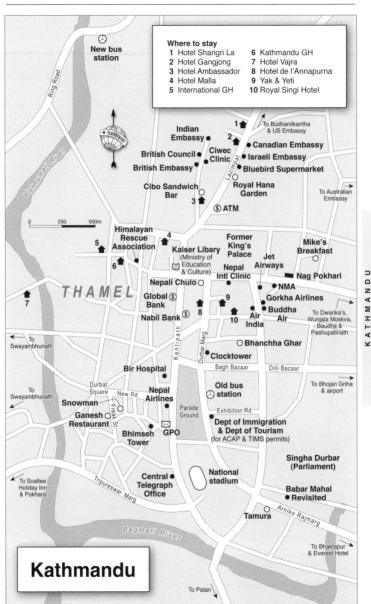

Where to stay
1 Hotel Shangri La
2 Hotel Gangjong
3 Hotel Ambassador
4 Hotel Malla
5 International GH
6 Kathmandu GH
7 Hotel Vajra
8 Hotel de l'Annapurna
9 Yak & Yeti
10 Royal Singi Hotel

New bus station

Ring Road

Vishnumati River

Indian Embassy
To Budhanilkantha & US Embassy
Canadian Embassy
British Council
Ciwec Clinic
Israeli Embassy
British Embassy
Bluebird Supermarket
Lazimpat

Cibo Sandwich Bar
Royal Hana Garden
To Australian Embassy

ⓈATM

0 250 500m

Himalayan Rescue Association
Former King's Palace
Mike's Breakfast
Kaiser Libary (Ministry of Education & Culture)
Jet Airways
Nepal Intl Clinic
Nag Pokhari

THAMEL
Nepali Chulo
NMA
Global Ⓢ Bank
Gorkha Airlines
Nabil Bank Ⓢ
Buddha Air
Air India
To Dwarika's, Wunjala Moskva, Baudha & Pashupatinath

To Swayambhunath
Bhanchha Ghar
Kantipath
Clocktower
Durbar Marg
Bag Bazaar
Dilli Bazaar
To Bhojan Griha & airport

To Swayambhunath
Bir Hospital
Durbar Square
Nepal Airlines
Old bus station
New Rd
Freak St
Snowman
Parade Ground
Exhibition Rd
Ganesh Restaurant
Bhimseh Tower
GPO
Dept of Immigration & Dept of Tourism (for ACAP & TIMS permits)

To Soaltee Holiday Inn & Pokhara
Central Telegraph Office
National stadium
Singha Durbar (Parliament)
Babar Mahal Revisited
Tripureswar Marg
Tamura
Arniko Rajmarg

Bagmati River
To Bhaktapur & Everest Hotel

Kathmandu

To Patan

KATHMANDU

WHERE TO STAY

Hotel areas

● **Thamel** Most travellers find Thamel the most convenient area to stay in, although it's largely a tourist ghetto. Everything you could want is available here, with over 100 guest houses and hotels, good restaurants, souvenir shops, book shops, communication centres and travel agencies.

● **Freak St** In the halcyon days of the '60s and '70s when Kathmandu was a major stopover on the hippie trail, Freak St, just off Durbar Square, was the place to hang out. Although the hash dens are now all closed it still retains a quaint charm. A banner proclaims 'Welcome to Freak Street – free entry to all tourists', a sly dig at the Durbar Square entrance fees. Its 15 or so hotels and restaurants are all in the rock bottom to cheap bracket.

● **Other areas** Away from the intense tourist scene are other small hotels scattered throughout Kathmandu. In Patan, there are two budget hotels off Durbar Square and also a few good upmarket hotels. Baudha and Swayambhunath have some simple hotels favoured by Buddhists and travellers.

Prices

Intense competition means you can find bargain accommodation in all price brackets. Although it is still possible to get a small room for as little as US$1.50, budget accommodation with a common bathroom is more usually around the US$3 a night mark. Basic rooms with an attached bathroom are around US$3-6, and for a nicer room expect to pay around US$10. Three-star hotel rooms off peak can be had for somewhere between US$15 and US$25. A travel agent or trekking company can usually get better rates for the four- and five-star hotels than are available through their websites. Accommodation prices can vary enormously between off-season and peak season, and there is plenty of choice.

Prices given in this section are for the high season (Oct-Nov/Mar-Apr) for single/double rooms, with **common (c)** or **attached (a)** bathrooms as indicated. In low season, however, many hotels cut their prices or offer significant discounts – sometimes 50% or more for stays of more than one night.

Many hotel owners quote their prices in **US dollars**; you pay in rupees, though. Given the changing rate of inflation in the country, this is a sensible idea so US dollars are also used in this section. The dollar/pound exchange rate hovers around US$1.50 = £1.

Budget guest houses (less than US$5/£3.50)

In **Thamel** there are around 50 places to choose from in this price bracket, and in some you'll even get an attached bathroom for this price. A few hotels have triple or quad bed rooms. Check that the hot water works and try to get a room that faces away from the roads – Kathmandu is plagued by noisy dogs and honk-

❏ An increasing number of even the smallest of Kathmandu's hotels have **websites**. www.hotelnepal.com is a good place to start.

ing taxis. The cheapest hotels tend to be in Narsingh Camp (behind Pumpernickel Bakery), in Chhetrapati on the southern end of Thamel and the noisy stretch on the right between Tom and Jerry, and Sam's Bar. A few Thamel hotels offer dormitory accommodation for around $1 a bed. These include the basic *Hotel Happy Home* [105] and *Hotel Jjang* [25]. These may be the cheapest options, but they're not the best value: for just a few rupees more you can have your own room.

Recommended budget hotels include the wonderful *Hotel Potala* [84], run by a Tibetan family, with satellite TV lounge and a roof terrace, which is swamped by gap-year students who take over the place for much of the year.

Nearby, there is a knot of cheap guest houses across the street, including *King's Land* [83] and *Thamel* [82]. These currently have the cheapest rooms in a very central location. Alternatively, try some of the cheap guest houses in the north of Thamel: *Holyland Guest House* [43], *Delight Guest House* [39], *Hotel Easy* [20] and *Hotel Cosmic* [15] all have rooms for around $5.

For a bit of peace and quiet away from Thamel, check out the collection of six guest houses just to the north which each have their own garden area. Though the quality of all six suggests that they should belong in a higher price bracket, at least two – *Tibet Peace Guest House* [5] and *Nirvana Peace Home* [4] – are prepared, after a little negotiation, to offer discounts though not to rock-bottom rates, presumably because many tourists don't want to stay a ten-minute walk away from central Thamel.

The following budget guest houses are **keyed to the map on p75**:

4 Nirvana Peace Home (438 3053; nirvanapeacehome.com) $3/4 (c), $4-8/6-12 (a)

5 Tibet Peace GH (438 1026; tibetpeace.com) dbl $5 (c), $5-20 (a)

15 Hotel Cosmic (470 0415; hotelcosmic.com) dbl $4-6 (c)

19 Hotel Lily (470 1264; kajbabu26@ hotmail.com) $6-7/10-12 (a)

20 Hotel Easy (470 1462; hoteleasy@yahoo.com) $3/5 (c)

25 Jjang (470 1536; nepal-jjang.com) drm $1.30, sgl/dbl $3.50 (c)

26 Hotel Namche Nepal (441 7067; hotelnamchenepal.com) $3/4 (c), $4/5 (a)

27 Laughing Buddha Home (442 5056) $4/7 (a)

34 Souvenir GH (441 0277; souvenirguest house.com) $1.50/3(c), $4/4-5(a)

39 Delight GH (441 6951) dbl $3-5 (c)

42 Namaskar GH (442 1060) $4/5 (a)

43 Holyland GH (443 3161; lodgenepal.com) sgl $4 (c), $5-10 (a), $4-5/4-9 (a)

46 New Dhaulagiri GH (470 0761; nwdhaulagiri@ yahoo.com) $4/5 (c), $6/8 (a)

47 Yeti Guest Home (470 1789; yetiguesthome.com) $4/5(c), $6/8(a)

48 Mustang GH (470 0053; mothersland.com) $2/3(c), $3-4/4(a)

49 Hotel Seoul (470 0668) $3/4 (a)

60 Third Pole GH (470 1736) $3/5 (c), $10/18 (a)

61 Hotel Royal Grand (470 0945) $3/4 (c), $5/6(a)

63 Classic Down Town GH (217 4349; b2magar@hotmail.com) $3/4(a)

65 Red Planet (470 0879; redplanet_ thamel@hotmail.com) $6-10/9-15 (a)

67 Deutsch Home (470 0989; allnepaltour@gmail.com) $5/8(a)

69 Thamel White Lotus GH (442 9386) $3/5-8 (a)

70 Tourist Home (441 8305) $2/4 (c)

71 Wonderland – Trekker's Inn (441 8197) $4/6 (c), $10/16 (a)

78 Potala Tourist Home (441 0303) $3/4 (c), $7/10 (a)

79 Student GH (425 1551/1448) $4/6.50 (a)

80 Marco Polo (425 1914) $3/3(c), $6-8/5-10 (a)

82 Thamel GH (470 0747) $2/3 (c), $4/5-8 (a)

83 King's Land GH (470 0129) $2/3 (c), $3/3.50 (a)
84 Hotel Potala (470 0159) $2/3.50 (c),
87 Hotel World Wide (425 8420) $3/3 (c), $4/4 (a)
88 Hotel Global (425 8320) $1.50/2 (c), $2/3-3.50 (a)
89 Hotel Golden Star (421 2519) $3/5 (c)
90 Hotel Puskar (426 2956) $3 (c), $4/5-7 (a)
91 Mount View (421 2818) $3/5 (a)
97 Siesta House (421 2818) $7/10 (c), $10/20 (a)
100 Universal GH (425 9382) $3/4 (c), $3-5/6-8 (a)
103 Gorkha GH (426 6602) $1.50/3-4 (c), dbl $4-6 (a)
104 Cherry GH (425 0675) $2/2-3(c), $3/3-4(a)
105 Happy Home (424 2076 & 691 0479; happyhomeguesthouse.com) $5/7 (c), $10/15 (a)

112 Hotel Earth Mount Holiday (425 3555) dbl $4-15 (a)
113 Kathmandu City GH (426 0624) $3/4 (c), $4/5 (a)
116 Lucky GH (429 8250) dbl $3-4 (a)
120 Hotel Kathmandu Holiday Inn (423 3892) $4-9/5-10(a)
121 Om Tara GH (425 9634; bhim15@hotmail.com) $5/8 (c), dbl $10-15 (a)
122 Hotel Green Lotus Inn (425 8996) $3/5-9
123 Yak Lodge (425 9318; yakreslodge@ yahoo.com) dbl $3 (c), $4 (a)
124 Hotel Heera (425 9671) dbl $4 (c), $3/5 (a)
144 Shangri-La GH (425 0188; shangrila thamel.com) sgl $5 (c), dbl $10 (a)
145 Hotel White Lotus (424 9842) $3/6-8 (a)

Freak Street, near Durbar Square, is one of the few places in the world where it is still possible to find a room, admittedly small, for just over one US dollar a night. A slightly larger budget widens the choice considerably. The majority of hotels are on the main street but looking down alleys nearby yields more.

Cheap hotels in Thamel (US$6-15/£4-10)

Most Thamel hotels offer a range of rooms, the majority falling in this price bracket. The hotel should provide clean sheets, blankets and a desk while the better ones will also supply towels and toilet paper and perhaps be carpeted. Little features to check are: is there a vent or window in the bathroom, a clothes line and a rooftop garden? Features aside, when choosing a hotel, go by the reception staff – are they friendly and helpful or lackadaisical? Most people new to Kathmandu begin looking at hotels in the heart of Thamel. However, there are plenty of hotels in every direction, none of which is more than a few minutes' walk from the centre.

Holy Lodge [51] (☎ 470 0265) is recommended. *Hotel Karma* [44] (☎ 442 5476) also enjoys a burgeoning reputation and the patronage of many expats. If you're travelling with children, the small *Sun Rise Cottage* [109] (☎ 425 6850) is a good choice. It has large clean rooms with hardwood floors and shares a garden with Tibet Guest House.

At the top end of this price range is the wonderful *Pilgrim's Guest House* [28] (☎ 444 0565 ☐ www.pilgrimsguesthouse.com), set in its own peaceful and sunny grounds at the northern end of Thamel.

❑ The **Kathmandu area code** is 01. If phoning from outside Nepal dial ☎ +977-1 for more information see ☐ www.ntc.net.np/utilities/areacode.php

The ***Kathmandu Guest House*** [59 – see p76] is actually a three-star hotel but they have a few rooms with shared bathroom from US$2-10/4-14.

The following cheap hotels are **keyed to the map on p75**:

1 Kathmandu Garden GH (438 1239; hotel-in-nepal.com) $3-5/8-15 (a)

2 Family Peace GH (438 1138; peace_family@hotmail.com)

3 Hotel Paknajol

6 Kathmandu Peace GH (438 0369; peaceguesthouse.com) $8-12/12-16 (a) dbl $5-7 (c)

7 The Yellow House (438 1186; theyellow house2007@gmail.com) $6/8 (a)

9 Hotel Impala (470 1549; hotelimpala.com.np) $5/8-16 (a)

12 Lucky Star (470 1569; hotelluckystar.com) $15/20-35 (a)

13 Sweet Dream GH (470 1880; sweet dreamthamel@yahoo.com) dbl $5-15 (a)

17 Hotel Florid (470 1055) $10/10-15 (a)

18 Hotel Visit Nepal (470 1384) $8-12/10-18 (a)

22 Hotel Eco 2000 (470 0213; eco_hotel@ hotmail.com) $15-25/20-30 (a)

23 Hotel Shree Tibet (470 0902; sritibet@wlink.com.np) $10/15-60 (a)

28 Pilgrims GH (444 0565; pilgrimsguest house.com) $10/15 (c), $20/25-68 (a)

29 Hotel Kathmandu View (441 7212) $12/18-30 (a)

30 Hotel Encounter Nepal (444 0534) $6/15

31 Dolphin GH (442 5422; dolphinguest house.com) $6/8 (c), $10/12 (a)

33 Villa Everest (441 1593) $7 (c), $16/30 (a)

35 Hotel Shakti (441 0121) $20/30 (c), $25-30/40-50 (a)

37 Hotel Bright Star (442 0165) $5/7 (c), $7/10 (a)

38 Annapurna GH (441 7461; annapurna guesthouse.com) $8/10 (a)

44 Hotel Karma (442 5476; hotelkarma.com) $12-22/18-32 (a)

51 Holy Lodge (470 0265; holylodge1983 @live.com) $4/5(c), $9-12(a)

52 Hotel Down Town (470 0471; hotel-downtown-nepal.com) $5/7 (c), $8/8-20 (a)

55 Millennium Inn (426 2013; millennium@mail.com.np) $6/6-10 (c), $6-15/8-20 (a)

56 Kantipur Hotel (426 6518) $10/14-18 (a)

57 Hotel 7 Corner (470 0405; hotel7corner.com) $6/8-10 (a)

58 Prince GH (470 0456; princeguest house@hotmail.com) $6-8/10-12 (a)

59 Kathmandu Guest House (470 0800; ktmgh.com) $2-10/4-14 (c), $14-100/18-120 (a)

62 Hotel Garuda (470 0766; garuda@mos.com.np) $10-35/15-40 (a)

64 Acme GH (470 0236; acmeguesthouse.com) $5-20/8-25 (a)

66 Hotel Nana (470 1960) $10/15-25 (a)

73 Hotel Hana (442 4683; hotelhana.com.np) $6/8 (c), $10/12 (a)

76 Red Planet GH (441 3881; htlredplanet@wlink.com.np) $8/10 (c), $10/12 (a)

81 Newa GH (441 5781; newagh.com) $6-12/8-14 (a)

85 Legend Highlander (425 9086) $8/12 (a)

92 Hotel Silver Home (426 2986; hotelsilverhome.com) $5-8/6-10 (a)

93 Hotel Discovery Inn (422 9889; hotel_ discoveryinn@yahoo.com) $5-15 (a)

95 Hotel Adventure Nepal (442 4147) $13/17 (c), $40 (a)

96 New Pokhara Prince (424 9579; omshantiok@yahoo.com) $8/12 (a)

98 Thorong Peak GH (425 3458; thorongpeak.com) $12-24/18-30 (a)

102 Hotel Prime (426 0855; hotelprime.com.np) $5/7 (a)

106 Hotel Pyramid (424 6949; trip-nepal.com) $6 (c), $20/25 (a)

107 Hotel Horizon (422 0904; hotelhorizon.com) $4 (c), $25 (a)

109 Sun Rise Cottage (425 6850; src@mos.com.np) $7/10 (c), $15/25 (a)

110 Tibet GH (426 0383; tibetguesthouse.com) $16-65/20-75 (a)

115 Langshisa GH (425 5453) $9/12-18 (a)

117 Khangsar GH (426 0788; khangsar@wlink.com.np) $8/12 (a)

119 Potala GH (422 0467; potalaguest house.com) $13-17/20-48 (a)

125 Hotel Jagat (425 0732; jagathotel.com.np) $7/15 (a)

(*Continued on p76*)

Hotels in Thamel – keyed to map opposite

1 Kathmandu Garden GH
2 Family Peace GH
3 Hotel Paknajol
4 Nirvana Peace Home
5 Tibet Peace Guest House
6 Kathmandu Peace GH
7 The Yellow House
8 Hotel Manang
9 Hotel Impala
10 Hotel Tenki
11 Hotel Marshyangdi
12 Lucky Star
13 Sweet Dream GH
14 Hotel Nature
15 Hotel Cosmic
16 Hotel Courtyard
17 Hotel Florid
18 Hotel Visit Nepal
19 Hotel Lily
20 Hotel Easy
21 Hotel Buddha
22 Hotel Eco 2000
23 Hotel Shree Tibet
24 Hotel Vaishali
25 Jjang
26 Hotel Namche Nepal
27 Laughing Buddha Home
28 Pilgrim's Guest House
29 Hotel Kathmandu View
30 Hotel Encounter Nepal
31 Dolphin Guest House
32 Malla Hotel
33 Villa Everest
34 Souvenir Guest House
35 Hotel Shakti
36 Hotel Norbu Linka
37 Hotel Bright Star
38 Annapurna GH
39 Delight GH
40 Hotel Thamel
41 Samsara Hotel
42 Namaskar Guest House
43 Holyland Guest House
44 Hotel Karma
45 Hotel Tashi Dhargey
46 New Dhaulagiri GH
47 Yeti Guest Home
48 Mustang Guest House
49 Hotel Seoul

50 Hotel Mandap
51 Holy Lodge
52 Hotel Down Town
53 Hotel Tradition
54 International GH
55 Millennium Inn
56 Kantipur Hotel
57 Hotel 7 Corner
58 Prince Guest House
59 Kathmandu Guest House
60 Third Pole Guest House
61 Hotel Royal Grand
62 Hotel Garuda
63 Classic Down Town GH
64 Acme Guest House
65 Red Planet
66 Hotel Nana
67 Deutsch Home
68 Hotel Centre Point
69 Thamel White Lotus GH
70 Tourist Home
71 Wonderland – Trekkers Inn
72 Hotel Hana
73 Hotel Hana (annexe)
74 Hotel Blue Horizon
75 Hotel Magnificent View
76 Red Planet GH
77 Tibet Holiday Inn
78 Potala Tourist Home
79 Student Guest House
80 Marco Polo
81 Newa Guest House
82 Thamel GH
83 King's Land GH
84 Hotel Potala
85 Legend Highlander
86 Hotel Excelsior
87 Hotel World Wide
88 Hotel Global
89 Hotel Golden Star
90 Hotel Puskar
91 Mount View
92 Hotel Silver Home
93 Hotel Discovery Inn
94 Hotel The Great Wall
95 Hotel Adventure Nepal
96 New Pokhara Prince
97 Siesta House

98 Thorong Peak GH
99 Kathmandu Peace GH
100 Universal Guest House
101 Hotel Pisang
102 Hotel Prime
103 Gorkha Guest House
104 Cherry Guest House
105 Happy Home
106 Hotel Pyramid
107 Hotel Horizon
108 Nirvana Garden
109 Sun Rise Cottage
110 Tibet Guest House
111 Hotel Yanki
112 Hotel Earth Mount Holiday
113 Kathmandu City Guest House
114 Hotel Harati
115 Langsisha GH
116 Lucky GH
117 Khangsar Guest House
118 Hotel Tayoma
119 Potala Guest House
120 Hotel Kathmandu Holiday Inn
121 Om Tara Guest House
122 Hotel Green Lotus Inn
123 Yak Lodge
124 Hotel Heera
125 Hotel Jagat
126 Hotel Elite
127 Hotel New Gajur
128 Mt Annapurna GH
129 Si Hai Hotel
130 Hotel Diplomat
131 Lhasa Guest House
132 Tibet Himalayan GH
133 Hotel Planet
134 Hotel Utse
135 Hotel Blue Diamond
136 Hotel Norling
137 Namtso Rest House
138 Namaste GH
139 Hotel Suhung
140 Fuji Hotel
141 Hotel Holy Himalaya
142 Mustang Holiday Inn
143 Imperial Guest House
144 Shangri-La GH
145 Hotel White Lotus

KATHMANDU

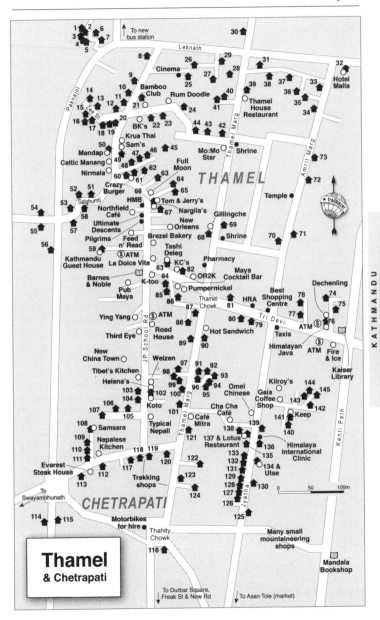

Thamel
& Chetrapati

126 **Hotel Elite** (422 7916; hotelelite@
   hotmail.com) $5/8-25 (a)
127 **Hotel New Gajur** (422 6623;
   taishan88zst@yahoo.com.np) $15/18 (a)
128 **Mt Annapurna GH** (422 5462; raj_
   kumarb@hotmail.com) $6-10/8-15 (a)
129 **Si Hai Hotel** (423 8109) $10/12-25 (a)
130 **Hotel Diplomat** (426 7798; hotel
   diplomat.com.np) $14-25/$20-35 (a)
131 **Lhasa GH** (422 6147) sgl $5 (c),
   $12/18 (a)
132 **Tibet Himalayan GH** (422 5319;
   tibethimalayan.com) $5/6 (c) $7/8 (a)
133 **Hotel Planet** (422 0258;
   hotelplanet.com.np) $8-12/$12-20 (a)
134 **Hotel Utse** (425 7614;
   hotelutse.com.np) $15-24/21-30(a)

135 **Hotel Blue Diamond** (422 6907; hotel
   bluediamond.com.np) $11-13/14-16 (a)
136 **Hotel Norling** (424 0734;
   hotelnorling.com) $15/$20-30 (a)
137 **Namtso Rest House** (425 1238;
   namtso4h@wlink.com.np) $10/20 (a)
138 **Namaste GH** (423 3734) $5/8 (a)
139 **Hotel Suhung** (422 6577) dbl $8 (c),
   $10/15 (a)
140 **Fuji Hotel** (425 0435; fujiguest
   house.com) $6/10 (c), $10-35/15-45 (a)
142 **Mustang Holiday Inn** (424 9041;
   mustangholiday.com) $15-30/20-40 (a)
143 **Imperial GH** (424 9339; imperial_
   guesthouse@yahoo.com) $12/15 (a)

Moderately-priced hotels

There are numerous reasonable hotels in the US$15-30/£10-20 price range, most of them with a restaurant attached. All rooms have attached bathrooms with hot water, and in the more expensive rooms a TV and perhaps an air-conditioner and heater. Some hotels have a few deluxe rooms in this price range too. Once again, a little bargaining with these hotels can go a long way if they're not full.

The best known of the hotels in Kathmandu must be the long-running *Kathmandu Guest House* [59] (☎ 470 0632, 🖳 www.ktmgh.com), a Thamel landmark. Popular with groups, it's bursting in the high season. It's a three-star hotel; rooms with bathroom attached range from US$14-100/18-120.

Nirvana Garden [108] (☎ 425 6200, 🖳 www.nirvanagarden.com) has a large tranquil garden. *Hotel Courtyard* [16] (☎ 470 0476, 🖳 www.hotelcourt-yard.com) was recently refurbished to a high standard. In Kaldhara, a five-minute walk away from the bustle of central Thamel, is the *International Guesthouse* [54] (☎ 425 2299, 🖳 www.intguesthouse.com) which offers discounts for online bookings.

The following moderately-priced hotels are **keyed to the map on p75**:

10 **Hotel Tenki** (470 1483) $25-40/35-50 (a)
14 **Hotel Nature** (470 0822;
   hotelnature.com) $28/33 (a)
16 **Hotel Courtyard** (470 0476; hotelcourt
   yard.com) $55-115 (a)
21 **Hotel Buddha** (470 0366) sgl $6 (c),
   $15/18-30 (a)
36 **Hotel Norbu Linka** (441 0630; hotel
   norbulinka.com) $45-85/50-100
40 **Hotel Thamel** (442 3968;
   hotelthamel.com) $30-45/40-55 (a)
45 **Hotel Tashi Dhargey** (470 0030;
   hoteltashidhargey.com) $20-35/25-40 (a)
50 **Hotel Mandap** (470 0321;
   hotelmandap.com) $30/40-50 (a)

53 **Hotel Tradition** (470 0217;
   hoteltradition.com) $30-55/$40-65
54 **International GH** (425 2299;
   intguesthouse.com) $10-18/19-22 (c),
   $24-32/30-36 (a)
59 **Kathmandu Guest House** (see above)
   $2-10/4-14 (c), $14-100/18-120 (a)
68 **Hotel Centre Point** (444 4399;
   hotelchangcheng.com) $55/65-85 (a)
72 **Hotel Hana** (442 4683;
   hotelhana.com.np) $15/20 (a)
74 **Hotel Blue Horizon** (442 1971;
   hotelbluehorizon.com) $12-15/15-20 (c),
   $25-50/30-60 (a)

75 Hotel Magnificent View (443 7455)
  $10/14 (c) $25-50/35-60 (a)
77 Tibet Holiday Inn (442 3530;
  viewnepal.com/tibet) $16-26/22-34 (a)
86 Hotel Excelsior (425 7748) $18-40/
  $25-50 (a)
94 Hotel The Great Wall (425 3543; hotel
  greatwallnepal.com) dbl $15-30 (a)
101 Hotel Pisang (425 2540; hotel@pisang
  .wlink.com.np) $25-50/30-60 (a)

108 Nirvana Garden (425 6200; nirvana
  garden.com) $40-80/$50-75 (a)
118 Hotel Tayoma (423 1920; tayoma
  hotel.com) $15-52/30-62 (a)
111 Hotel Yanki (425 6851) $14-18/16-20
  (c), $25-35/30-40 (a)
141 Hotel Holy Himalaya (426 3172;
  holyhimalaya.com) $24-49/$34-99 (a)

Three-star standard hotels

Close to each other in north Thamel are the *Hotel Marshyangdi* [11] (☎ 470 0105, 🖳 www.hotelmarshyangdi.com) with rooms from US$80/90 and *Hotel Manang* [8] (☎ 470 0993, 🖳 www.hotelmanang.com), with rooms from US$55/65, both popular with trekking groups. Nearby, with a large garden area is the modern and completely non-smoking *Samsara Hotel* [41] (☎ 441 7711, 🖳 www.samsararesort.com) which has rooms for $60-70/70-80 (a). Also good is *Hotel Harati* [114] (☎ 425 7907, 🖳 www.hotelharati.com.np) with spacious rooms for US$30-50/35-70.

Around the three-star standard are two well-managed traditionally built hotels. *Hotel Vajra* [see map on p69] (☎ 427 1545, 🖳 www.hotelvajra.com) was conceived and paid for by a Texas billionaire, and built by Newar craftsmen, with wall-paintings by Tibetan and Tamang artists. Rooms are from US$33-85/38-90 with attached bathroom and there are cheaper rooms for under US$14/16 with shared bathrooms. It is located near Swayambhunath.

The traditionally decorated *Summit Hotel* (☎ 552 1810, 🖳 www.summit-nepal.com) in Patan is popular with expeditions wanting a peacefully-located hotel. Prices range from €45/55 to €70/80 and they have a budget annex aimed at groups where twin rooms with shared bathroom are €15/20. Both hotels have a pleasant atmosphere, attractive gardens, restaurants and appropriate amenities.

In the Lazimpat district north of Thamel (see map p69) there are a couple of smart hotels popular with diplomats and dignitaries. The fully vegetarian *Hotel Gangjong* (☎ 443 9888, 🖳 www.gangjong.com) has rooms priced at $70-80/80-90 or there's the cheaper *Ambassador Hotel* (☎ 441 0432, 🖳 www.nepalshotel.com) where rooms are just $25-35/35-45. Another worth trying is the *Royal Singi Hotel* (☎ 442 4190, 🖳 www.hotelroyalsingi.com). Rooms here are $90/100-200.

Four- and five-star hotels

Until its unfortunate demise in 1970, the top place to stay was the Royal Hotel. Its success was largely due to its proprietor, the legendary White Russian émigré, Boris Lissanevitch. It was the country's first Western hotel, opened in 1954 in a wing of the palace that is now the Bahadur Bhavan. Virtually everything for it had to be imported from Europe, shipped to India and then carried in by porters. Staying here you'd be guaranteed to meet interesting people and many of the mountaineering expeditions made it their Kathmandu base.

Most of the city's top hotels are now much like expensive hotels anywhere in the world. The *Hotel Yak & Yeti* (☎ 424 8999, 🖥 www.yakandyeti.com) has rooms from US$185 to US$625. Centrally located, it has everything you'd expect from a five-star hotel, although the modern wings don't exactly blend with the old Rana palace which forms part of it. The Yak & Yeti Bar with its excellent Chimney Restaurant was moved here from the Royal Hotel when it closed. Rich Nepalis, however, consider the *Soaltee Holiday Inn Crowne Plaza* (☎ 427 3999, 🖥 www.ichotelsgroup.com) as the best of the big hotels, although it's not so well located, being in the west of the city, in Kalimati. Rooms range from US$80/140 to US$800. It's said to have the best casino on the subcontinent.

Back on Durbar Marg is *Hotel de l'Annapurna* (☎ 422 1711, 🖥 www.annapurna-hotel.com) with rather ordinary rooms from US$140-450/150-450, a large pool and casino. Similarly priced but inconveniently located is the *Everest Hotel* (☎ 478 0100, 🖥 www.theeveresthotel.com) on the road to the airport.

Hotel Malla [32] (☎ 441 8385, 🖥 www.hotelmalla.com), just north of Thamel, is pleasant with rooms from US$130/156. It has a fitness centre and swimming pool. The best value in this group is the *Hotel Shangri-La* (☎ 441 2999, 🖥 www.hotelshangrila.com), in Lazimpat, with rooms from US$180 and a peaceful garden. Both the *Hotel Radisson* (☎ 441 1818, 🖥 www.radisson.com/kathmandune) and a 400-room branch of the *Hyatt* chain (☎ 449 1234, 🖥 www.kathmandu.regency.hyatt.com), near Baudha, have opened in the last few years, both with rooms from around $175 per night; discounts are available.

Hotel Vaishali [24] (☎ 441 3968, 🖥 www.hotelvaishali.com), with pool, was Kathmandu's first four-star hotel. Rooms are around $90/110 but you should be able to negotiate discounts of 50% or so.

Probably the best hotel in Kathmandu is *Hotel Dwarika's* (☎ 447 3725, 🖥 www.dwarikas.com), which has opted out of a star classification. If Kathmandu is a living museum, this is the ultimate place to experience it. The red-brick buildings are decorated, inside and out, with ornate panels lovingly restored from old Kathmandu houses. Every room (US$175-220/180-230) is an individual work of art, and the restaurant's offerings are similarly exotic. The Friday evening poolside buffet is yet another reason to stay.

Note that all star-class hotels add a 13-15.5% government tax to the bill.

WHERE TO EAT

Kathmandu's restaurants have long been renowned amongst travellers throughout South Asia for their ability to serve passable approximations of Western dishes. Until recently, however, you'd probably have been more appreciative of Kathmandu's apple-pie and enchilada cuisine after a trek rather than on arrival direct from the West. Standards have risen quite considerably over the last few years with restaurants competing for more authentic dishes, some even importing chefs from abroad.

The cost of meals in restaurants doesn't vary as greatly as hotel prices. Most main courses cost less than US$2.50/£1.70 in the smaller places but in the best restaurants expect to pay US$5-10/£3.50-6.70.

The better restaurants charge 13% VAT; sometimes this is included in the menu price but in upmarket restaurants it is usually added to the bill. Some restaurants also add a 10% service charge to the menu prices.

Be especially careful about what you eat before you set out on your trek; you're more likely to pick up a stomach bug in a Kathmandu restaurant than in the hills. A test on the quality of the tap water in Thamel showed it to contain more than ten times the WHO-recommended safe maximum level of faecal matter. The better restaurants are serious about hygiene but don't believe all restaurants that tell you their salads are washed in iodine. Similarly, filtered water is not reliably clean; stick to bottled or hot drinks. Unless otherwise indicated the restaurants described are in Thamel (see map, p75).

Breakfast

Most hotels and guesthouses offer breakfast and snacks either as room service or in their own snack bars. Most of the Thamel restaurants have set breakfasts that can be good value, but for a leisurely breakfast or brunch in the sun there are a few places worthy of special mention. The *Pumpernickel Bakery* does a roaring trade in cinnamon rolls, bagels and other pastries and cakes. There's a pleasant garden behind it and the noticeboard here is a good place to track down trekking partners. *Brezel Bakery*'s rooftop offers competition, particularly as service is speedy. The best bread is at *Weizen*, where the wholewheat and sourdough are always good.

Most places offer yoghurt with fruit and muesli but the two best are *New Orleans* with great curd and *Northfield Café* with better fruit; both places have decent coffee, a great variety of food, tasteful music and the morning papers. Decent bacon can be found at Northfield Café, New Orleans and at Helena's. It may be flights of stairs to *Helena's* rooftop, but the view makes it worth it. Another place with a sunny terrace is *Mandap*, which is good all round.

If you don't mind being indoors, *K-too* has hearty breakfasts while *Himalayan Java* specialises in coffee, their cold blended banana mocha is hard to beat. The *Gaia Coffee Shop*, near the KEEP office, is a great place for a peaceful breakfast. There is still no Starbucks in Nepal; indeed none of the major food-beverage chains has made it here.

Out of Thamel the place to go for a relaxing start to the day is *Mike's Breakfast*. You breakfast on authentic American (hash browns, pancakes and syrup, fresh coffee with free refills etc) and Mexican fare in a garden, serenaded by items from the ex-Peace-Corps owner's classical CD collection. Lunch and dinner are also good.

Lunch and dinner

● **Western** The cheapest restaurants in Kathmandu serving 'Western' fare are in and around Freak St. The *Ganesh Restaurant* is still one of the best places to eat here. Their crêpes with garlic cheese are recommended. The long-running *Snowman* has been renovated, leaving it a little sterile compared with its hippie past but the desserts remain astounding value. The crème caramel is still the best in Kathmandu. The most recent addition to Freak Street's restaurants is *Jasmine*

Restaurant, small, intimate and excellent value with chicken and fish dishes for Rs160 and nothing over Rs190.

Back in Thamel, restaurant prices can be much higher but there are still places where you'll get a cheap meal that's reasonably filling and clean. At the long-running *Tashi Deleg* everything is around Rs100, including the delicious momos and thukpa and steaks which are Rs115. *Nargila's* is good value too, although steaks are more expensive at Rs285, it is popular with Israelis for its Middle Eastern fare: a plate of falafel with pita, tahini and salad is Rs145.

There are more bakeries than you'd imagine, all of which offer quick snacks such as spinach cheese quiche and chicken-stuffed rolls, and desserts including delicious strawberry tarts in season. Prices range from Rs20 to Rs75, and a few of the bakeries have seating. A word of warning about most bakeries in Thamel – croissant- and bagel-shaped things are a cruel, fluffy joke. The baked goods on display in the Yak & Yeti's lounge are more authentic, and good value. The *E-Z Bakery* next to Northfield has particularly fresh, fragrant bread.

The long-running *Hot Sandwich* and other similarly-named '24-hour' sandwich bars will sell you a cheese-cream sandwich for Rs60-100. Real sandwich connoisseurs will be disappointed – the fillings never go beyond cheese, ham, cream cheese, salami and tuna. But you can combine these any way, with mayonnaise, mustard and veggies. For upmarket sandwiches in chic surroundings try the *Cibo Sandwich Bar*. Situated near the British Embassy just off Lazimpat, it's popular with ex-pats. Steak sandwiches are Rs240 and the goat's cheese pita with walnut flakes and spinach is Rs325. They also serve pasta main dishes.

Helena's is popular; main dishes are Rs150-300, everything is good but nothing really stands out. Almost opposite, in the Ganesh Man Singh building (3rd floor) is *Delices de France*, which does a to-die-for all you can eat Saturday brunch platter for Rs750. *Weizen* has fresh, good food, and a similarly-priced menu. At *K-too!*, the beer and steak house, there's a range of steaks from Rs345-955 they also have a full-flavoured onion, anchovy and spinach quiche for Rs225 and to go with the large cable TV behind the bar is the best range of bar snacks in Thamel.

For a refreshingly different menu and good music *New Orleans* is recommended. Try their Jambalaya with veg for Rs270 or for a lighter meal spinach rice and steamed vegetables. It's a successful blend of a restaurant and bar; a White Russian made with blended ice cream (Rs190) will even do as a dessert.

❏ Babar Mahal Revisited

This place has to be seen to be believed! The crumbling stables of a Rana palace near the parliament building have been converted into a chic shopping centre that wouldn't look out of place in California. There are some distinctly exclusive boutiques and some excellent restaurants. *Chez Caroline* is one of Kathmandu's best, with authentic French cuisine, wine and good patisserie. Not to be missed for a celebratory dinner is *Baithak* (☎ 426 7346). In the grand long gallery, past Ranas stare down from their portraits as you feast on 'delicacies from the Rana court'. Main dishes are Rs500 and the set dinner, the Maharaja's Feast (Rs1200) is recommended.

A fancy dinner with gleaming silver, china, linen, and good service can be had at *Café Mitra*. The tossed salad, Zen mackerel and cheese soufflés are excellent, as is the pannacotta. This two-floor resto-bar has lounge seating, a private dining room, art on the walls, and the best toilet in Thamel. However, some find the prices a little high (Rs200-500 for appetisers and soups, Rs380-950 for main courses) and the portions a little small. Perhaps the best buffet-feast in the Valley is on a Friday evening at *Dwarika's*. It's a bit expensive at Rs999 but a post-trek appetite will mean you'll get your monies worth! Bookings are essential as it's very popular with local expats, call 4479488 for more info.

Many places have steak on the menu, usually (but not always) buffalo steak. It's often served as a 'sizzler' and arrives in front of you on a heated cast-iron plate doing just that. The enduring *Everest Steak House*'s speciality is a wide range of real beef fillet steaks (Rs280-475). *KC's Restaurant & Bambooze Bar* is as much a Thamel institution as the Kathmandu Guest House. The food's good but prices are distinctly upmarket. A sizzling steak from the people who introduced the 'sizzler' to Kathmandu now costs Rs340. Another Kathmandu institution recommended for its food is the *Rum Doodle*. It is one of the very few places that offer mashed potato. Try chicken with almond sauce and mashed potatoes (Rs380) or a steak (from Rs400).

Probably the best restaurant in Thamel is *Kilroy's* (☎ 425 0441). On the eastern edge of Thamel, you can dine indoors or outside. The Irish chef, seen posing in photos on his menu with distinguished customers like Sir Edmund Hilary and Princess Anne, oversees the creation of such delicacies as 'seared breast of chicken stuffed with nak's cheese, served with mushroom sauce', Irish stew, and beef and Guinness hotpot (Rs425). For a starter, chargrilled market vegetables (Rs205) is interesting. Their Royal Dal Bhaat (Rs400, veg Rs360) is indeed royal – when Nepal still had a royal family the king and queen ate here. The lemon tarts are superb and perhaps one is not enough. Lunchtime sandwiches are good value.

Samsara at the Nirvana Garden Hotel is a good, quiet multi-cuisine restaurant with lovely garden seating, a big menu, consistently safe and tasty food but occasionally slow service. The high rooftop of the *Tibet Guest House* is a great place to eat and drink respectably, particularly on a clear afternoon.

McDonald's hasn't arrived. However, there are plenty of places that serve a substantial burger, salad and chips, including *Northfield*, *K-too!*, *New Orleans*, and *Helena's*. BK's does chips (French fries) to take away while *Crazy Burger* has modelled itself on a Western fast food chain, and has food of the quality you might expect from such a place.

In the five-star hotels there are some excellent Western-style restaurants. Probably the best is the *Rox* at the Hyatt where a huge slab of salmon cooked to perfection is Rs1200. The *Yak & Yeti* often has specialty functions that are heavily advertised, and *Dwarika's* does a great Friday-night buffet barbecue with live music. Lazimpat has a wide range of good if more upmarket restaurants catering to the large expat community around there. For Finnish-style food try *Cross Kitchen* next to the Shangri-La.

● **Nepali, Newari & Thakali** There are many cheap local Nepali places out of Thamel that serve daal bhat or momos, usually for less than Rs50. *Mo:Mo Star*, to the north of Thamel near Namaskar Guest House, is cheap, cheerful and rough-and-ready. Also in Thamel the *Nepalese Kitchen* has a range of superior daal bhat specials (Rs155-185) The *Typical Nepali Restaurant* does the same in a typical building. Just outside Thamel, *Dechenling*, has a large and secluded beer garden away from the chaos of the nearby streets. The food is predominately Nepali but they have Tibetan, Chinese, Indian and Bhutanese under their culinary umbrella. Mains are Rs150-380.

   Lowland has perhaps the largest traditional Nepali menu in central Thamel. Nepali khasi (boneless mutton) is Rs165. A great accompaniment is tomato achaar, a traditional boiled tomato sauce, which is rarely found on menus. They also have a popular range of fish dishes and the grilled trout is superb and good value, too, at Rs195. *Northfield*'s fancy daal bhat is also recommended.

   One interesting option to try typical Newari food local-style is *Newa Bhanchha* in the same lane as New Orleans. The best dishes are bandel tareko (wild boar) for Rs325, kaju tareko (fried cashewnuts) for Rs225 and aloo sandeko (spicy boiled potatoes) for Rs125.

● **Tibetan restaurants** are amongst the cheapest places to eat in Thamel. Below the Kings Land Guest House, *Tashi Deleg* is popular and also does Western food that's good value. The best-known Tibetan place here is *Utse*, at the hotel of the same name. The pingtsey soup (meat soup with wontons) is excellent, as are their momos (vegetable, mutton, buffalo or pork). Given a couple of hours' notice, they will prepare a complete Tibetan banquet (Rs1500 for four people and Rs2220 for six). *Tibet's Kitchen* in the Sherpa Guest House has an open-plan kitchen and the food is similarly clean and fresh. *Gillingche* is an authentic Tibetan eatery with all the usual favourites for Rs50-85.

● **Indian** Serving reasonable Indian has made *The Third Eye* popular but *Mandap*'s quality is more consistent. Delicious yogurt chicken is Rs350. Palak paneer (spinach cheese) is Rs200. *Northfield Café* was the first place in Thamel to have an open clay oven, while *Lowland* does a good Indian thali with nan, rice, and four different dishes in a size to suit one hungry person

   Surprisingly, *Feed n' Read* is the only decent place in Thamel that serves southern Indian Masala dosas which, for Rs195, make a great lunch. Their momos are original too. Dosas can also be had at *Green Ice*, *Angan* at the edge of Durbar Square, and sometimes at *Satkar Pure Veg* next to Thorong Peak Guest House.

   The top Indian restaurant is the Hotel de l'Annapurna's *Ghar-e-kabab* (☎ 422 1711). It specialises in the rich cuisine of North India, main dishes are around Rs450 and there's live music in the evenings. You may need to book.

● **Mexican** *Walter's Bodega* is popular, with its chimichangas (meat-filled tortilla with green rice) at Rs220 and 10 different tequila cocktails (Rs180). *Northfield Café* and *Mike's Breakfast* are the only places for a tostada. They are also among the most hygienic Thamel area restaurants. Northfield's attached

Jesse James Bar serves free corn chips and salsa with drinks. Finally, ***Bamboo Club*** specialises in Mexican fare but also serves European and Nepali dishes.

● **Italian** Many restaurants serve pizza and pasta but one place stands way above the rest. ***Fire & Ice Pizzeria & Ice Cream Parlour*** has to be experienced to be believed. Run by an Italian woman who's imported her own computer-controlled Moretti Forni pizza oven, some of the best pizzas on the subcontinent are now turned out here – to the sound of Pavarotti. Prices range from Rs270 to Rs380 and there's wine by the glass for Rs250. Queues can be long, though. *Northfield Café* turns out the next best pizzas.

For authentic pasta try ***La Dolce Vita***, which has great food (especially salads, pesto and deserts) and sometimes lacklustre service. The pasta at *Café Mitra* is excellent but choice is limited. The ***Cha Cha Café***, hidden down a small alley, is tiny with room for just a few bar stools. Pasta mains are Rs160-240.

● **Chinese** Most restaurants have spring rolls and chowmein on their menus although what appears on your plate is usually unmemorable. The ***Friendship Restaurant*** on Durbar Marg is the best of a new breed of Chinese-run restaurants, which import their own cooks. The soups (Rs220-260) are delicious and good for two. This and the restaurant at *Hotel Centre Point* are popular with Chinese expats. The ***New China Town Restaurant*** is good, sometimes excellent and the ***Lotus Restaurant*** is good value with curries for Rs 110-195. The nearby ***Omei Chinese*** was under renovation at the time of research and may change its name once it reopens.

● **Thai** *Ying Yang*, opposite the Third Eye, is one of Thamel's best restaurants. Their Pad Thai for Rs395 is the most consistent and best, and with the curries

KATHMANDU

❑ **Stylish traditional dining**

There are now some very upmarket traditional restaurants in Kathmandu. *Bhanchha Ghar* (see map p69) was one of the first restaurants in Kathmandu to serve a 9-13 course banquet with lots of complimentary raksi, floor seating, and traditional singing and dancing. Located in an old Rana building in Bagh Bazaar, Bhanchha Ghar (meaning Kitchen House) offers wild boar or dried deer meat to accompany drinks, and the dinner menu is similarly exotic (Rs1200).

Others include *Bhojan Griha* in Kamaladi and *Nepali Chulo* on Lazimpat behind the Hotel Gangjong, which occupies an extensive Rana palace that's worth exploring if you want a private dining room. Similar in spirit, though classier – and without live entertainment – are *Baithak* in Babar Mahal Revisited (see p80) and the spectacular *Krishnarpan* at Dwarika's Hotel, where the service and décor are entertainment enough.

At the slightly bizarre end of the scale is *Wunjala Moskva* in Naxal. At this Russian-Newari eatery, you sit in a garden courtyard eating blinis and momos, watching Nepali dancing and knocking back vodka!

Thamel House in Thamel is a well-maintained 100-year-old Newari building. As at the other places, you can order á la carte (main courses start at Rs100 here) or go for the set meal (Rs550 for vegetarian, Rs650 for non).

you have a choice of heat. They also have a range of Western cuisine, including decent pastas. For a cheaper but authentic alternative there is *Krua Thai* where a Red Chicken Curry is Rs325.

● **Israeli** Catering to the large number of Israeli visitors that the country is attracting, there are two Israeli restaurants in the heart of Thamel. *Nargila* is a cavernous first-floor establishment that unfortunately suffers at the moment from a lack of clientele, and as a result a lack of atmosphere, though the food (felafel, hummus etc) is fine. *Yamini Restaurant*, however, 50m further north, is probably that little bit better, with authentic and good value hummus with chapattis, Israeli salad and felafels. They put on special meals for Jewish festivals.

● **Japanese** Many serve authentic portions at almost authentic prices. *Koto*, towards Chetrapati, is the most conveniently located and has salmon sushi. Warm towels greet you and the dishes are works of art.

At *Royal Hana Garden*, on Lazimpat, the California rolls are great after you've had a shiatsu session upstairs or soaked in the hot tub.

For consistently delicious Japanese food in Kathmandu, you need to find the little hillock in Thapathali on which Hotel Kido stands. Its restaurant, *Tamura*, a well-kept secret, serves wonderful fresh food.

● **Korean** Like Japanese restaurants, there are more and more Korean places popping up. *Picnic* may not serve bibimbap in a stone bowl, but its beef bulgogi (Rs200-300) and egg rolls (Rs60) are unbeatable. It also wins hands down for hygiene, value for money, and good service.

● **Vegetarian** All restaurants have some dishes for vegetarians who are sick of daal bhat. *Nirmala* is simply the best value restaurant in Thamel, soups are Rs48, quiche mushroom spinach is Rs105 and a small pot of herbal tea is Rs30. The meals are consistent, delicious, and wholesome. The Israeli restaurant, *OR2K*, is clean and comfortable and specialises in imaginative veggie dishes. Couscous with soup is Rs190.

On Freak St, *Ganesh Restaurant* continues to provide excellent service.

● **Juices** *Just Juice and Shakes* down the alley heading to Hotel Red Planet is a favourite. Their secret is using frozen fruit instead of ice for incredibly thick shakes; a coffee banana shake is Rs70 and their cappuccino (Rs60) is one of the best in Thamel if you like it strong.

NIGHTLIFE

● **Bars** *Rum Doodle Restaurant & 40,000 ¹/₂ft Bar* is a Kathmandu institution, with yeti prints on its walls inscribed by the members of many mountaineering expeditions. As well as a wide range of drinks (hot buttered rum, Rs160) the food here is good although a little expensive. *Tom & Jerry's* is large, noisy, and popular. There's a couple of pool tables and satellite TV. *Maya Cocktail Bar* has a wide, usually well-made, selection of cocktails and a three-hour-long two-for-one happy hour. *Sam's Bar* is a small, friendly local where the bartender is charming and the service good, while **Full Moon** is a hip place for lounge music and the suspiciously smoky ambience that goes with it. **Celtic Manang** is Kathmandu's answer to the ubiquitous faux-Irish bar.

● **Clubs** *Scores*, *Fire* and *Spin* pump till late (when there isn't a noise crackdown) and the crowd is increasingly Nepali.

● **Live music** It's a long weekend of music in Thamel with a band playing somewhere almost every night, just listen for the noise as you walk around. Friday nights are popular with the Nepali working crowd. The best music is at **New Orleans** and **Full Moon**, while the cover bands that play at places like **Lhasa** and **G's Terrace** ensure that you will never want to hear *Hotel California* again.

The **Hyatt** on a Friday night attracts the wealthy Nepali crowd; beers are Rs275. **Dwarika's** gets a nice crowd and usually has a good female vocalist. A few times a year the **Yak & Yeti** has month-long jazz guitar gigs or one-off a cappella performances by the Yale Whiffenpoofs. Hotel de l'Annapurna's **Juneli Bar** often has live music with a decent flautist.

● **Other entertainment** Look out for posters advertising **Chris Beall's slide shows** covering the main trekking regions. He's a professional photographer and lecturer and the slide shows, held in the early evenings, usually at the Kathmandu Guest House but sometimes in other hotels, offer good unbiased advice for trekkers about to head into the hills and are well worth the ticket price.

The **French Cultural Centre** and **Russian Cultural Centre** occasionally sponsor a play, jazz night or films and details are advertised. Kathmandu is home to two top-notch film festivals, **Film South Asia** in alternate Septembers, and **Kathmandu International Mountain Film Festival** in alternate Decembers.

The top hotels all operate **casinos**. If you recently flew into Nepal you're entitled to Rs100-worth of free coupons if you show your air ticket.

See *The Himalayan Times* or *The Nepali Times* for current events.

SERVICES

Banks

Larger hotels can change money at reception and around every corner in Thamel are authorised money changers.

There are numerous **automatic cash dispensers** (ATMs) in central Kathmandu. In Thamel the most convenient machines are in the courtyard of the Kathmandu Guest House and next to its main gate, in front of the reception of Garuda Hotel, and adjacent to the Roadhouse Café. There is also one next to La Dolce Vita and another on the right-hand side on the road down from Fire and Ice. These last two are tiny brightly-lit cubicles. There have been no reports of theft or muggings around ATMs but you should use your judgment at night. There is a withdrawal limit of Rs10,000 per transaction set by the machines but some will allow up to five withdrawals a day if your card limit permits.

You can withdraw unlimited amounts in person from banks, either in rupees or travellers' cheques but not in foreign currency. The most convenient bank foreign exchange counter is the Himalayan Bank in the same building as Fire & Ice. The Global Bank and Nabil on Kantipath are convenient too, and the Nepal Investment Bank on Durbar Marg works 365 days a year, though only from 9am to 12 noon on weekends and public holidays.

Bookshops and libraries

Kathmandu has some of the best bookshops on the subcontinent, including many small second-hand shops where you can trade in your novel for another. There's even a **Barnes & Noble**, and although it's not connected with the American chain, it still offers the biggest selection of new and secondhand books in Thamel. Most international news, computer and fashion magazines are regularly available. One of the best is the jam-packed **United Bookshop**, which is slightly cheaper than the others and has a good selection of new and used titles; it's at street level, slightly off the main drag in the new building almost opposite the Himalayan International Clinic.

The **Kaiser Library**, Kaiser Sumshere Rana's private collection, is worth visiting as much for the building as for the 30,000 plus musty volumes. This Rana palace just west of the modern royal palace is now the Ministry of Education & Culture. There's also an old garden with six pavilions in the same compound. This is now being renovated and turned into an upmarket shopping, café and bar area – the Garden of Dreams.

The **British Council Library** by the British Embassy is open to all and has the main UK newspapers and plenty of magazines.

Health clubs, swimming pools and gyms

Most five star hotels have pools you can visit even if you aren't staying there, but with prices averaging between Rs500-600 a day they soon become expensive for multiple visits. The **Hotel Malla** has a good pool and gym, which has season passes (April to October) for Rs12,000 for the pool and Rs20,000 for pool and gym. The **American Club** opposite the Palace Museum has a wonderful pool, gym and café but you need to know a member to get in, although most expats and long-term residents are members so ask around. Guest entry is Rs250, or a current member can support your application for a Friend and Family short-term membership (3 or 4 months) it's around Rs3000 per month. This allows you free access to the pool, gym and café.

The British embassy operates the **Sterling Club**, which is a restaurant open for lunch every day, Sunday Roast on the last Sunday of every month, and has yoga classes, bingo nights, plays and other entertainments. It costs Rs1500 to join – get forms at the embassy gate and find two members to vouch for you. As usual, just ask around.

There are a few public pools in Kathmandu but they aren't recommended for solo women. Their standards of cleanliness may not be what you are used to, either. The pool at the **Mahendra Police Club** is the most reliable and safe to use. There are many local gyms, more information is at 🖳 www.hotelnepal.com/kathmandu/health_club.php

Left luggage

All hotels and guest houses are happy to store excess luggage for you free of charge while you go off on your trek, although they expect you to stay with them on your return.

Medical clinics

CIWEC (☎ 4424111, 🖳 www.ciwec-clinic.com, open Mon-Fri 9am-5pm for consultations, 24hr for emergencies) is an exceptionally competent clinic. It's opposite the British Council, which is next to the British Embassy in Lainchaur. Consultations cost US$55 ($70 after hours and at weekends) or equivalent in any currency. Credit cards are accepted.

Nepal International Clinic (☎ 443 5357, 🖳 www.nepalinternationalclinic. com; open Sunday to Friday 9am-5pm, appointments only on Saturday) is also excellent. Consultations cost US$45 or equivalent (US$50 on Saturday). It's opposite the Royal Palace, slightly east of Durbar Marg.

There are a couple more convenient and slightly cheaper clinics in Thamel. Try **Himalayan Traveller's Clinic** on the edge of Chhetrapati (☎ 426 3170, after hours ☎ 437 2857) or **Himalaya International Clinic** (☎ 422 5455, open 9.00-17.00 every day) virtually next to Hotel Norling in Jyatha.

For dental problems the best option is **Healthy Smile** (☎ 442 0800) on Lazimpat, opposite Ambassador Hotel. The dentists are competent and experienced, and have been trained overseas.

Markets and supermarkets

Apart from the numerous street-side vegetable sellers around town, there is a new **Organic Farmers Market** in the garden of 1905 Restaurant on Kantipath from 9am each Saturday morning. With an excellent selection of veggies, honey, cakes, bread and cheeses (from French, Italian and Australian local initiatives) this is an inexpensive way to buy quality and fresh produce.

A chain of Western-style supermarkets, **Bhat Bhateni**, has an incredible array of everything from fresh and dehydrated foods to homewares and clothing. Two large multi-storey shops are in Baluwatar and on the ring road in Maharajgunj. If you use a taxi to get there ask them to wait while you shop. Alternatively, walk or ride as they even offer free home delivery. **Best Shopping Centre** near Marco Polo Guest House has lots of imported goodies. **Bluebird Supermarket** in Lazimpat has an even wider stock. There are two small supermarkets in the heart of Thamel, at the junction just down from the Kathmandu Guest House.

> ❏ **Embassies**
> * Australia (☎ 437 1678), Bansbari
> * China (☎ 441 1740), Baluwatar
> * France (☎ 441 2332), Lazimpat
> * Germany (☎ 441 2786), Gyaneshor
> * India (☎ 441 0900), Lainchaur
> * Israel (☎ 441 1811), Bishramalaya House, Lazimpat
> * New Zealand (Honorary Consul ☎ 441 2436), Dilli Bazaar
> * Russia (☎ 441 2155), Baluwatar
> * Thailand (☎ 437 1410), Bansbari
> * UK (☎ 441 0583), Lainchaur
> * USA (☎ 441 1179), Pani Pokhari

KATHMANDU

GETTING AROUND

If you want to **cycle** and brave the traffic and pollution problems, which get worse each year, there are lots of rental stands around Thamel. No deposit is required; you sign the book and pay the first day's rental. Be sure you check the tyres, brakes, lock and bell before you cycle off. Lock the bike whenever you leave it as you'll be held responsible for its replacement if it gets stolen. A mountain bike for a day costs Rs100-200. If you're renting for more than one day (a good idea as you can keep the bike overnight at your guest house) you can usually negotiate a lower rate.

A number of places in Thamel, particularly around Thahity Chowk, now rent out **motorbikes**, mostly 100-250cc Japanese bikes made under licence in India. They cost around Rs450 (for 100cc) to Rs650 (for larger bikes) per day, plus Rs30 for a helmet; a cash deposit is sometimes required, usually they simply want to know where you're staying. You're supposed to have either an international driving licence or a Nepali one.

There are lots of **taxis** around Kathmandu but it's difficult to get drivers to use their meters, especially if you pick one up in a tourist district like Thamel or Durbar Marg. There are also auto-rickshaws, metered and costing about a third less than taxis.

Kathmandu's **cycle-rickshaw** wallahs understand just how your delicate Western conscience ticks, so hard bargaining is required if you're going to pay anything like local prices.

There are extensive **bus** routes around the city and out to the airport but this is a very slow and crowded transportation option.

WHAT TO SEE

You could easily spend a month in the Kathmandu Valley, such is the rich concentration of sights here. Several companies operate bus tours (ask in the larger hotels and travel agencies) but renting a bicycle and wandering round independently is rather more rewarding. Getting lost is all part of the fun.

The first seven places mentioned here have been declared World Heritage Sites, making the Kathmandu Valley one of the most significant cultural heritage sites in Asia.

Durbar Square

First stop on the Kathmandu sightseeing trail is Durbar Square, also known as Hanuman Dhoka, named after the Hindu monkey god and patron saint of the Mallas. This complex of ornately-carved temples and monuments includes the old royal palace (closed Tuesday; entry is Rs300), the Kumari Bahal (the home of the Kumari, the 'living goddess', a young girl chosen as the incarnation of the Hindu goddess, Durga), the Kastha Mandap (the wooden pavilion from which the city's name is said to have been derived), the tall Taleju temple, built in the 16th century and Kathmandu's protective god, the Black Bhairab, whose statue is of unknown origin and antiquity. The best time to be here is early in the morning when people are going about their daily pujas.

The authorities charge foreigners an entrance fee of Rs300 to get into the square. While this has raised a number of complaints from travellers, nobody should begrudge paying it – the entire square has, after all, been declared a World Heritage Site by UNESCO and a vast amount of funds are required to restore and maintain the square's many buildings. It's a good idea, having paid the fee, to go straight to the offices lining the southern end of Durbar Square (to the west of the entrance to Freak Street, behind the souvenir market) to convert your entry ticket into a Visitor Pass. You will need one passport photo and your passport. The authorities will then provide you with a pass that will be valid for the duration of your stay in Nepal, and which will allow you to visit Durbar Square as many times as you like for up to a week without further payment.

Baudha (Bodhnath)

This Buddhist stupa is one of the largest in the world. Seven km from the city centre (about Rs300 in a taxi from Thamel), it's a major place of pilgrimage, especially for Tibetans. There's a large Tibetan community here and several monasteries. There's now an entrance fee of Rs150 for foreigners.

From dawn to dusk the faithful make their circumambulations (always in a clockwise direction) under the fluttering prayer-flags and the all-seeing eyes of the giant white stupa. It's a fascinating place to visit, especially at the time of a new or a full moon when there are special festivities. Legend tells of a woman who wanted to build a stupa and asked the king for as much land as the hide of a buffalo could cover. The king agreed and she cut the hide into tiny strips, laying them in a giant square. The king gave her the land, but at the time there was a bad drought. The woman laid sheets of cloth on the ground to collect morning dew to make cement, so Baudha is known as the stupa of a million dewdrops.

❑ KEEP and HRA
The Kathmandu Environmental Education Project (KEEP) raises environmental awareness among trekkers and the trekking industry. Well worth visiting, they have an information centre (☎ 421 6755, 🖥 www.keepnepal.org, Sun-Fri 10am-5pm) offering unbiased trekking info, a coffee shop and library. They also sell iodine, potable aqua and steri pens for water purification. Their notice board is a good place to look for trekking companions. You'll find them down a side street not far from Kilroy's restaurant (see Thamel map p75).

The Himalayan Rescue Association (HRA, ☎ 444 5505, 🖥 www.himalayanrescue.org) was founded in 1973 with the primary aim of saving lives in the mountains by alerting trekkers to the dangers of altitude sickness. It's largely due to their unfailing efforts (passed into guidebooks) that the death toll from altitude sickness is now very low. They have an information centre in Kathmandu upstairs near Best Supermarket where they have an altitude awareness talk at 3pm each day during the main trekking seasons. They also have forms here so you can register with your embassy. Unless you're trekking with an organised group, you're advised to do this since your embassy's assistance is necessary if a helicopter rescue is required for you. In addition to the Kathmandu information centre the HRA has two medical posts, one at Manang and the other in the Khumbu at Pheriche. They operate only during the peak trekking seasons, however, from early October to early December, and March to April.

Nourishment of a basic nature is available at the *Oasis Restaurant* and several other places near the stupa. There are also a couple of *bars* serving momos and *tongba* (a drink made from fermented millet) just around the corner from the Oasis. Look for a curtain across a door; there are no signboards. Order a plate of sukuti (dried meat) to accompany your tongba and momos. It's all very cheap but not terribly hygienic – probably best enjoyed when you come back from your trek.

Swayambhunath

Offering the best view of Kathmandu and the first place of pilgrimage in the Valley is the Buddhist stupa at Swayambhu. A popular 40-minute walk west from Thamel; Rs200 by taxi. This is the best place to watch the sun set on a clear evening. There's now an entrance fee of Rs250 for foreigners.

Mythical creatures guard the entrance steps, while the all-seeing eyes of supreme Buddhahood gaze out over the valley and up to the snowy peaks along the border with Tibet. Statues from the 7th and 8th centuries have been found around the stupa but it is thought to date from a much earlier period. It's also known as the 'Monkey Temple' on account of the troupes of macaques here. Don't feed them as they can get vicious when your supplies of biscuits run out.

Pashupatinath

Hindu pilgrims come from all over the subcontinent to this Nepalese Varanasi. It's a very extensive complex of temples beside the Bagmati River, six km from the city centre. A taxi from Thamel will set you back around Rs400, or you can walk here from Baudha; leaving Baudha, turn left and cross to the small dirt track squeezed between the buildings on the opposite side of the road (look for the sign saying 'Peace snooker'). It's a twenty-minute walk from there (take a right at the fork in the path halfway along). There is now an entrance fee of Rs500.

Pashupatinath is the oldest Hindu site in the Kathmandu valley and derives its fame from the metre-long linga, carved with four faces of Shiva which is kept in the main temple (closed to non-Hindus). The first rites at Pashupati are lost in the haze of time, but it was well established by the time the Lichhavis arrived in the 1st century. The whole complex is dedicated to Shiva and is a focus for sadhus, wandering ascetics, some of whom may have walked here from as far away as south India. As at Varanasi, people perform their early morning ablutions from the ghats here. It's also the most auspicious spot to be cremated in the country. The funeral pyres by the river have become something of a tourist sight, attracting coachloads of scantily-clad foreigners who behave with astounding insensitivity, lenses zooming in on the burning bodies.

Patan

Also known as Lalitpur (meaning City of Beauty), Patan is the oldest of the three main city-states in the Kathmandu Valley but now just a suburb of the capital (Rs400 by taxi from Thamel). Patan's **Durbar Square**, probably the best collection of late Malla architecture in the country, is rather less touristy than Kathmandu's Durbar Square and, what's more, the officials here seem even less enthusiastic about collecting the Rs300 entrance fee than they do in Kathmandu's square. If there's only one museum you visit in Nepal it should be **Patan**

Museum, in the palace compound of Keshav Narayan Chowk on Durbar Square. The museum gives an idiot's guide to the Hindu and Buddhist faiths using statues, icons and sculptures from the tenth century onwards. Marvellous stuff. It's open daily except Tuesday; entry is Rs250 for foreigners.

It's also worth visiting Kumbeshwar Square. Water in the pond here is said to flow directly from the holy lake of Gosainkund in Langtang. At the north-east corner of the square is **Kumbeshwar Technical School**. Visitors are welcome at this school and orphanage set up to help the lowest castes in the area. Tibetan rugs and sweaters of considerably higher quality than those on sale in Thamel can be purchased here.

Bhaktapur

The third city, Bhaktapur, is a mediaeval gem, visited only fleetingly (if at all) by tourists. Fourteen km east of Kathmandu, it's an almost entirely Newar city that is strongly independent of Kathmandu. Some of the people who live here can't even speak Nepali. Much more than in Kathmandu or Patan, an atmosphere of timelessness pervades this place. Bhaktapur's main attraction is its **Durbar Square**, with its Palace of Fifty-Five Windows, but here, as in the rest of the city, many buildings have been damaged by earthquakes. Much of the reconstruction work has been done by the Bhaktapur Development Project, a German-sponsored urban renewal programme. To help support further restoration programs there is a Rs750 entrance fee, which is expensive but you can really see the benefit throughout Bhaktapur.

It's an hour-long cycle-ride to Bhaktapur from Kathmandu or you can take the electric trolley-bus from Tripureshwar which will drop you across the river, a 15-minute walk from Bhaktapur's Durbar Square. A taxi will cost around Rs800.

Changunarayan

Changunarayan Temple, roughly 10kms northeast of Kathmandu, rarely sees a tourist and has the earliest historical inscription with a date so far found in Nepal. It is believed that the first construction was in the 4th century and is dedicated to the Hindu god Vishnu. Entrance is Rs100; a taxi from Kathmandu costs Rs1200.

Thimi

This small Newar town is famous for its pottery and the streets and squares are lined with recently-thrown pots drying in the sun. Ten km from Kathmandu, Thimi makes a pleasant cycle-excursion and can be combined with Pashupatinath and/or Baudha.

Nagarkot

The most popular mountain-viewing spot near Kathmandu is Nagarkot, 32km from the city on the road that passes Bhaktapur. Since the view, which includes Everest and four of the other ten highest peaks in the world, is best in the early morning, most people spend the night here. There are, however, tours that leave Kathmandu before dawn to catch the sunrise. You can also get here by taxi (Rs1800), bus from Bhaktapur (two hours), on foot or by mountain-bike.

❏ STAYING ON IN KATHMANDU – LONG STAY TIPS AND IDEAS

If your partner or friend is walking the GHT, they may need someone in Kathmandu to look after logistics such as: crew changeovers, weather reports, trekking permits, food resupply, government departments, plane tickets, and just to be a voice at the end of the phone. You won't be doing all the touristy things, but you won't really be an expat either.

Getting organised

First, make sure that your hotel has **enough space** in your room to store all the stuff you will need to 'keep handy' – spare tents, stoves, clothes – all sorts of things have littered my room over the years. I find a blue plastic barrel handy as I can lock things in it, and use it as a side table as well. If you are buying food to restock, this is the place to keep it. If you can get a room with a balcony, you will be able to air things like down jackets, sleeping bags, boots and tents. Next best option is the rooftop garden of your hotel. Always try to make sure that you stay in a hotel with an outside place inside! Never leave your belongings out overnight.

Negotiate a **'long term' room rate** with your hotel. Most places are happy to offer discounts to long termers, and you will find that they are usually willing to do extra little things for you. If you go away for just a few days on a resupply visit, keep your room – it's worth the few dollars you pay while not in it to have everything in the same place when you get back. Just like home – well, it is home for now.

Thamel is the main tourist area and everything is in walking distance, which is a handy feature in a transport strike, but many people prefer the quieter areas like Lazimpat. You should always make sure the room has **good ventilation**, decent **locks** on the doors, and bars and **mosquito mesh** on the windows. Try to avoid ground floor rooms (monsoon floods or little squeaky visitors are no fun) and if the hotel has a generator try to stay as far away from it as possible. An airy sunny room is your best option, and if you are staying a while you may be able to negotiate a rearrangement or replacement of furniture to suit your needs. Make sure you have **wireless and/or cable TV** (even cheap hotels have it these days) and check to see if it is backed up by inverters or battery power when the power cuts begin after the monsoon (ask your hotel for the current schedule). Some of the wireless can be fairly unstable, especially if you are trying to video Skype someone. If you are taking the laptop for an outing, remember to take the power lead and adapter/powerboard as many places have outlets at every table. And a word of warning, most Nepali computer owners don't use anti virus protection. Don't let them use their USB stick in your computer, tell them to email whatever it is to you. Make sure your antivirus etc is up to date before you leave home.

Many hotels have solar heated hot water, which is fine until there is no sun for a day or two. During the colder months it's a good idea to purchase an **electric kettle** and a thermos, and borrow a bucket from the hotel. Have the kettle filled and ready to go so that when the power comes on (often at 3am) the water boils and then store it in the thermos till you need it later that morning.

Buy yourself a local **4-point powerboard** so that you can recharge everything at once. Most local boards have universal holes so that any sort of power plug will fit. That way your computer, phone, camera, iPod and whatever else will always be charged. Just get into the habit of plugging everything in every time you're in the room.

If you would prefer an **apartment**, there are many places available, it is just a matter of finding them. Check the local English newspapers, or the magazine ECS (though places listed there can be rather expensive), and ask the staff whenever you are somewhere for food or drinks. Almost everyone knows someone that has a room or apartment to rent. You should expect to pay around Rs 15-20,000 a month for a small furnished place. On top of this there will be utilities such as water, electricity (even though you hardly ever get any) gas bottles for cooking, and the 'didi' (house help) who will come to clean and cook for you. Then you have the cost of buying food to cook (this will keep you busy for quite some time as you generally can't store food for long due to the lack of electricity for the fridge). If you want to buy anything like a new mattress, sheets etc go to Bag Bazaar and haggle. It may be worth taking a local with you. Expect to pay about Rs 25,000 for a good 'big size' mattress. Beware of the sprung coir mattresses as they get hard and lumpy quite quickly. The best linen is by Bombay Dyeing, and the Korean acrylic blankets with ghastly floral patterns (unless you get the one with the horse on it) are surprisingly warm.

Once you're settled in
Many 'long-termers' hang out in Sam's Bar, Celtic Manang, New Orleans or Tom and Jerry's (all in Thamel) or Upstairs Jazz Bar (Lazimpat.) in the evenings and they are a **wealth of useful information** as well as good company. If you tell people what you are doing and what help you think you need, they are usually happy to offer whatever advice they can. Never leave your room without a small **notebook** and pen as you won't remember everything. Always make sure you have a head torch in your bag or pocket, too. Get yourself some **business cards** – they don't need to be flash but you should make sure they have your local phone number on them.

You will want to be in close discussions with the **trekking agent** who has organised your friend's trip, to make sure that all arrangements are going fine, and that they don't need more permits (the government often introduces new permits part way through a season), tickets, tents or whatever. Depending on the level of service you have requested and paid for, you may need to take a greater role in the forward planning. You will definitely need to have access to US dollars cash for the unexpected things that pop up – extra staff and charter flights are the big dollar items that you need to have money set aside for.

Make sure you know when any major **festivals** are coming – Dashain is the main one, usually in October, when the country effectively shuts down for about 10 days. This is a Hindu festival, so you should still be able to get some Sherpa staff, but don't try to set out anywhere in the days just before the festival as all the buses and planes are booked solid. There are plenty of one day festivals that you can see in Kathmandu – just check the festival calendar and the local papers, or ask around.

If you stay in Thamel or nearby, most of what you will need to access is within walking distance. Taxis are plentiful but the prices can vary wildly. They are all supposed to have meters, but many are 'broken', and plenty that aren't have been doctored to spin around so fast it is a wonder they don't take off. Always agree on a fare before you jump in. Ask the hotel what a fair price is before you head off. Try not to use the taxis that just cruise around Thamel clogging up the roads – there are a few taxis ranks close by – there are a few taxis ranks close by – TriDevi Marg outside the Mountain Hardwear shop – and you get a choice then if you don't like the first quoted price.

At some point you will need to go to the **Immigration Office**, which is inconveniently located in Maitighar – it is a taxi ride from just about anywhere in Kathmandu where you might be staying. Get the driver to wait while you extend your visa and pay the staff the Rs500 'express fee' to get your visa in 10 minutes – it is actually cheaper than two taxi rides there and frees you up from having to return later that day.

Judy Smith

MOVING ON

By air

There are about a dozen domestic carriers, all with expert pilots who cope with tricky navigation, rough runways, and the vagaries of mountain weather every day of the week. However, do not expect flying in Nepal to be like a city hop back home; the entire process from booking in, to reclaiming your luggage will appear chaotic and at times quite thrilling!

Since the deregulation of the domestic airline industry in Nepal there has been a dramatic increase in operators. One of the best known is **Yeti Airlines** (☎ 446 5888, 💻 www.yetiairlines.com), who are developing into a major competitor to the notoriously unreliable **Nepal Airlines** (☎ 424 4055, 💻 www.royal nepal-airlines.com). **Cosmic Air** (☎ 421 5771, 💻 www.cosmicair.com) has international services to Delhi, Kolkatta, Varanasi and Dhaka. **Buddha Air** (☎ 552 1015, 💻 www.buddhaair.com) flies five times daily to Pokhara with speedy new Beech 1900D aircraft and to Paro in Bhutan. **Gorkha Airlines** (☎ 443 5121, 💻 www.gorkhaairlines.com) operate two daily flights to Pokhara as do **Sita Air** (☎ 449 0103, 💻 www.sitaair.com.np).

If you are going to need many flights, or you're helping with the logistics of a long trek then get to know a good travel agent. One that takes your calls at all sorts of hours, and can arrange charter flights (plane or choppers) at short notice. If there is an accident where someone needs air evac, you or your trekking agency will need to be able to deposit about $US7000 as a surety before the helicopter will leave. The going rate for helicopters in March 2010 was around $US2500 an hour.

From Pokhara, airlines with connections to Jomsom include Cosmic, Gorkha, Agni and Nepal Airlines. Nepal Airlines flights to Humde/Manang from Pokhara. Most airlines have reliable flights to the terai cities of Nepalgunj and Biratnagar but services to mountain airstrips like Simikot and Juphal are irregular so check before booking. Prices for tickets do not vary a great deal from one airline to another, however, reliability does. It is also worth being aware that security luggage checks can occasionally result in opportunistic theft.

❏ **Taking the high road...**
If you thought flying in Nepal is a risky business then don't look at the road accident statistics! For many tourists a road trip by bus or car can be a harrowing experience, but here are a few simple guidelines to help make your trip more comfortable:
● If you suffer from vertigo don't take a window seat.
● Travel in daylight hours whenever possible, night buses are scary.
● Pack a light lunch for yourself.
● Be very careful of valuables and ensure any luggage on the roof is safe and packed in a waterproof bag.
● Try to sit in the middle of the wheelbase (not right at the front or back)
● Take some earplugs.
● Don't sit on the roof.
● Avoid 'local' buses for trips longer than a few hours, take a tourist service instead.

Departure tax applies to domestic flights (Rs169 per person per flight), is paid in local currency only and before you check in (turn right upon entering the terminal). There is a strict 15kg luggage allowance on most domestic flights.

Flights are frequently cancelled, delayed and rescheduled due to bad weather, which can be frustrating. It always pays to be patient when flying.

By bus

● **Pokhara** The easiest way to get to Pokhara is on one of the **tourist buses** that run from Thamel, leaving in the early morning. Tickets can be bought at most travel agents for Rs160 upwards. Top of the range are the air-con buses operated by Greenline Tours (tel 257544, on the corner of Kantipath and the main road into Thamel). They have daily buses at 08.00 to Pokhara ($18, seven hours) and Chitwan (five hours). Breakfast is included.

More interesting since they're also used by Nepalis are the **buses** which run from near the GPO. Tickets can be bought up to two days before departure from the green kiosk at the corner of the first alleyway across the road (to the south) from the GPO. Minibuses to Pokhara (Rs315) leave every half an hour, beginning at 8am, with the last at 2pm. There are also two big buses (Rs250) daily, at 7.30am and 9am.

Buses from the new bus station north of Thamel are considerably more crowded. There are ordinary buses to Pokhara (Rs310, 10 hours) from 06.30 to 09.00 and de luxe ('Swiss') buses (Rs400, 7 hours) at 07.00. Tickets can be bought from window No 20. The original 'Swiss Bus' was operated by an aid project funded by the Swiss but it no longer runs. The appellation is now indiscriminately applied by Nepalis to any 'luxury' bus service. The cheaper mail-service Sajha buses now run from here, too, leaving at 07.30 and arriving at 14.30. The Sajha night bus is not recommended.

● **Other destinations in Nepal and India** From the new bus station there are buses to most towns in Nepal, many departing early in the morning. Avoid the night buses, not only because they don't exactly make for a restful night but also because you'll miss some spectacular views. For the Everest region, buses use the old bus station in the centre of town.

If you're going on to India watch out for 'through' tickets. Since everyone has to change into an Indian bus at the border, there's actually no such thing. Travel agents give you a bus ticket to the border and a voucher to exchange with an Indian bus company with whom they've got an arrangement. Since things don't always run as smoothly as they might it's safer, cheaper and just as easy to buy the tickets as you go along. It also gives you a choice of buses and the option to stop off where you want.

The best crossing point into India is via Sunauli for Gorakhpur, Varanasi or Delhi. From the main bus station for Sunauli ordinary buses (nine hours) leave 06.00-09.00 and there are also night buses. For Patna and Calcutta it's better to go via Birgunj/Raxaul (11 hours). Buses leave from the main bus station. For Darjeeling you'll have to make the gruelling trip to Karkabhitta (12-14 hours) on overnight buses leaving between 15.00 and 16.30.

KATHMANDU

3

POKHARA

In all my travels in the Himalaya I saw no scenery so enchanting as that which enraptured me at Pokhara.   **Ekai Kawaguchi** *Three Years in Tibet*

Pokhara's superb mountain scenery has been enrapturing foreign visitors since Ekai Kawaguchi, the town's first foreign visitor, came this way in 1899. Modern travellers are no less impressed; there can be few other towns that are so close to such high mountains. Pokhara (pronounced 'POKE-rah') lies at 850m/2789ft yet peaks of over 8000m/26,267ft rise above it in a breathtaking panorama.

Two hundred kilometres (125 miles) west of Kathmandu, Pokhara is the starting and ending point for most of the treks in the Annapurna region. It's also the perfect place to rest weary limbs after a trek and the town's relaxed atmosphere causes many travellers to stay rather longer than they'd originally planned. Along the eastern shore of Phewa Tal (Lake) a waterside version of Thamel offers accommodation to suit every budget.

The joy of Pokhara is that there really is very little to do here except laze around by the lake and over-indulge in those culinary delights you may have been pining for while away on your trek.

HISTORY

Origins

Probably at the same time that the Kathmandu Valley was a lake (about 200,000 years ago) the Pokhara Valley was also under water. Now just a few lakes (tals) remain: Phewa Tal in Pokhara, and Begnas Tal and Rupa Tal 10km to the east are the largest.

Very little is known about the early history of this area but Pokhara's location between the mountain passes and the plains has made it a focal point for peoples from both sides of the Himalaya for centuries. The area was controlled by numerous small kingdoms, usually situated on hilltops around the valley, populated by people who had migrated from Tibet. They were the ancestors of the Gurung who now live in Pokhara and the surrounding hills.

In the 14th century, Moghul persecution of Hindus in India forced refugee communities north into Nepal and some settled in the Pokhara area. Rajput princes from Rajasthan brought their entire courts and armies with them to carve out their own principalities. These Indo-Aryans developed the agriculture of the Pokhara Valley and whilst the high caste Brahmins and Chhetries remained in their mountain strongholds, the lower castes were sent to work the land below.

Shah Rulers of Kaskikot

In the 17th century, Pokhara was being ruled as part of Kaskikot, one of the most powerful of the Chaubise kingdoms in Central Nepal. These Chaubise kings were cousins of the Shah kings of Gorkha (Nepal's last royal family). Kulmandan Shah is the best known of Kaskikot's kings and also the first of the Shahs to rule a Nepalese Kingdom. He is credited with establishing a winter capital in Pokhara and he encouraged trade along the Kali Gandaki Valley through Mustang to Tibet. Mule trains brought salt and wool down from Tibet to exchange for grain from Pokhara.

By the late 18th century the Chaubise kingdoms were no longer closely united. Prithvi Narayan Shah, the king of Gorkha who had conquered the Kathmandu Valley, turned his attention west to these kingdoms, sweeping through with his powerful army to conquer Kaskikot in 1785. In the period of peace and stability that followed Pokhara quickly grew to become the major trading town in the region.

The Ranas

Although the Rana prime ministers who ruled Nepal from 1846 to 1950 could claim ancestral connections to the Kaskikot area, only Jung Bahadur, the first of the Ranas, showed any particular interest in the region, declaring himself Maharaja of Kaski and Lamjung. None of the Ranas ever visited the Pokhara area.

Under the Ranas, Pokhara became the capital of Kaski and Lamjung districts. That there are few old buildings to see in Pokhara today is the result of a devastating earthquake in 1934, and in 1948 of a fire offering being made by a priest in the Bindyabasini temple that got out of control and reduced much of the town to ashes.

Pokhara since 1950

Until the middle of the 20th century, the only way to reach Pokhara from Kathmandu was on foot, a six- or seven-day journey. In 1951 the airfield was built but it was not until 1973 that the road linking Pokhara with the capital was finished.

By the turn of the century another major communications project, the Pokhara–Baglung–Beni highway, was complete, and by 2008 a dirt road had been constructed from Beni all the way to Jomsom. While some argue that the road has improved communications to the valley's remote communities there is no doubt that it has had a damaging effect on the Kali Gandaki valley as a trekking destination, as is evident from the sudden drop in trekker numbers and the boarded up lodges and teahouses. In 2010, however, ACAP completed a new trail on the eastern side of the Kali Gandaki, well away from the road.

Improved communications brought people from the surrounding villages to swell the town's population from just 5400 in 1961 to over 200,000 in 2008. The Chinese invasion of Tibet in 1951 brought 15,000 exiles to Nepal, many to Pokhara. Dervla Murphy spent some time working with Tibetan refugees in the 1960s and *The Waiting Land: A Spell in Nepal* provides an interesting description both of her experiences and of a Pokhara before apple pie and chocolate cake were being served on the shores of Phewa Tal. Numerous international aid agencies now have their regional headquarters in Pokhara.

Pokhara is the main recruiting area in Nepal for troops for the Gurkha regiments in the British and Indian armies. Together with tourism, army wages and pensions form the mainstay of the local economy. While the Gurkha contingent in the British army decreased, however, tourism throughout the nineties boomed in Pokhara and moved upmarket, too, with the opening of a number of five-star hotels. The beginning of the 21st century, however, brought nothing but bad tidings for Pokhara. The ten-year Maoist insurgency led to a decline in tourists visiting Nepal which caused financial ruin for more than just one hotel. The end of the Maoist struggles in 2007 and the slow road to political stability saw an upturn in fortunes for the tourist industry; foreign visitors have noticed the change in Nepal's prospects and have begun to return to the mountains.

ORIENTATION

The lake is the main focus for travellers. It's on the western edge of town and there are two main accommodation areas here, Lakeside (Baidam) and Damside (Pardi). Lakeside is one long strip of hotels, guest houses, restaurants and shops with more places to stay up the paths among the trees. Damside is the smaller district beside Pardi Dam, to the south of the lake.

The airport and bus station are also in the southern half of the town, a long walk or a short taxi ride from the lake.

In the centre of Pokhara is the modern town; the old bazaar is to the north. Pokhara is a surprisingly spread-out town, sprawling for several kilometres down an incline that is unnoticeable until you try to ride your gearless Indian Hero from the lake to the bazaar.

WHERE TO STAY

Hotel areas

There are now over 250 hotels in Pokhara so you shouldn't have any difficulty finding a place to stay. Most are simple guest houses with just a few rooms, many run by ex-Gurkhas.

Although there is also some accommodation near the bus station and in the centre of Pokhara, everyone heads for the lake. **Lakeside** has the greatest choice of places to stay and almost all the restaurants and shops. **Damside** is quieter and it has better views of the mountains; many of the guest houses here also have dining rooms so you don't have to go to Lakeside to eat. There are some good guest houses here, and as Lakeside continues to develop into Thamel-by-the-Sea, peaceful Damside becomes a more attractive alternative.

Prices

The prices given here are for single/double/triple rooms, with common (c) or attached (a) bathrooms, at the height of the season. You usually pay extra for a bathtub, or a room with mountain view. Intense competition means you can find bargain accommodation in all price brackets. For the cheaper places you may get

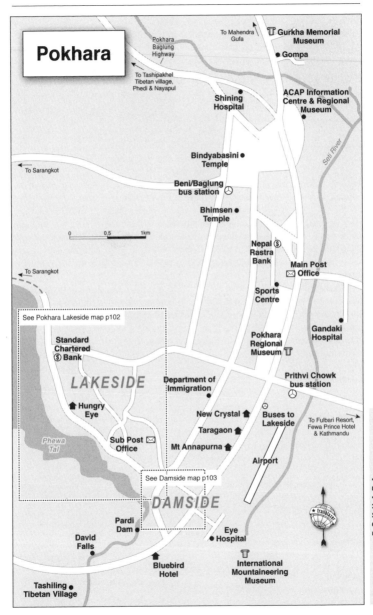

Pokhara

To Mahendra Gufa

Gurkha Memorial Museum

Gompa

Pokhara Baglung Highway

To Tashipakhel Tibetan village, Phedi & Nayapul

ACAP Information Centre & Regional Museum

Shining Hospital

Seti River

To Sarangkot

Bindyabasini Temple

Beni/Baglung bus station

Bhimsen Temple

To Sarangkot

Nepal Rastra Bank

Main Post Office

Sports Centre

Gandaki Hospital

0   0.5   1km

See Pokhara Lakeside map p102

Standard Chartered $ Bank

Pokhara Regional Museum

LAKESIDE

Department of Immigration

Prithvi Chowk bus station

Hungry Eye

New Crystal

Buses to Lakeside

To Fulbari Resort, Fewa Prince Hotel & Kathmandu

Taragaon

Phewa Tal

Sub Post Office

Mt Annapurna

Airport

See Damside map p103

DAMSIDE

Pardi Dam

Eye Hospital

David Falls

Bluebird Hotel

International Mountaineering Museum

Tashiling Tibetan Village

★ trailblazer

POKHARA

20-40% off but for mid-range hotels you should be able to get a discount of up to 70%, depending on how many people are chasing rooms at the time. There is 12-15.5% VAT payable on accommodation: make sure you ascertain whether this is included in the price agreed upon.

Budget guest houses and cheap hotels (less than $5/£3.50)

● **Lakeside** Many of the cheaper places lie at the northern end of Lakeside, including a few that actually stand on the western side of the road overlooking the lake, such as *Hotel Hollyhock* [7], *Phil's Inn* [8] and, behind the ACAP office, the *Amrit Guest House* [58]. While the accommodation is uniformly basic, these are the only places where you're likely to find a room with an uninterrupted view of Phewa Tal – something that few other hotels (except for the luxury Fish Tail Lodge, see p108) can boast. There are also some inexpensive options hidden behind the shopfronts on the other side of the road nearer the centre, such as *Sweet Dream* [113], *Holy Mount Guest House* [76] and *Alka* [103]; while certainly cheap, these lack the two main charms of Pokhara hotels, namely great views of the mountains and the lake. Also along this main drag and in the thick of things behind the giant Email One internet café is the surprisingly pleasant *Hotel Monal* [80], under German-Nepali management, which is good value, being a former mid-standard hotel that has had to drop its prices permanently to compete.

Probably the most popular of the budget guest houses is the *Holy Lodge* [157], partly because of the value of the accommodation (beginning at a ridiculously cheap Rs80 for a room in the older building) and partly for the laid-back, convivial atmosphere, for which the ever-smiling manager must take credit. Another enduring favourite with budget travellers, for which again the affability of the manager plays a large part in its success, is *Lubbly Jubbly* [85]; relatively charmless on the outside, it's nevertheless set in a peaceful yet central location, the rooms are fine and it's always busy.

Other popular options include: *Hotel Little Tibetan* [55], by some distance the most charming on this street; the popular *Hotel Yokohama* [22], which looks smart enough to belong in a higher price bracket, but which is fairly priced at $10-15 for attached singles/doubles; the *Summit* [195], set back from the lake and with a warm welcome; and the family-run *Eco Traveller's Lodge* [170], one of the first hotels on Lakeside, and one that still enjoys a reputation for friendliness and efficiency.

Finally, one that is rarely busy, but probably should be, is the *New Annapurna Guest House* [196], a pleasant, intimate little spot set back from the lake at the far southern end of the lake, where the owner grows and brews his own coffee, served with milk from his cow. The rooms are unexceptional but adequate.

● **Damside** The most competently-run places here seem to be those owned and operated by ex-Gurkhas. Rather different in character is the *New Sherpa Guest House* [236]. It's run by a friendly, helpful manager and there's also a cheap restaurant here.

❑ The Pokhara area code is 061. If phoning from outside Nepal dial ☎ +977-61

Mid-range hotels – lower (US$5-20/£3.50-13.50)

Several of the hotels which used to offer rooms for just a few dollars a night spruced them up and dramatically increased their prices. With the drop-off in tourist numbers, however, and particularly outside high season, you can get equally dramatic discounts if you bargain.

● **Lakeside** Despite some serious overcrowding, there are still some places where you can avoid the crowds on Lakeside. One 'remote' Lakeside hotel that's well worth recommending is *Green View Lodge* [44], which appears to be located in the middle of wasteground but, that aside, is a rather bright and spotless place. Also fairly isolated, the *Full Moon* [38] is unusual for Lakeside in that it's built on the only hill in the area, overlooking the district and the lake. With fountains and statues of deities decorating the garden it's a lovely place, though the steps up to it are a killer.

Keeping with the isolated theme, the manager of the aptly-named *New Solitary Lodge* [41], a hotel right on the eastern edge of Lakeside, is justifiably proud of the rooms and the tranquillity of his hotel, though some may find it a little too far from the lake to be ideal. The award for most lonely accommodation, however, must go to the rather incongruous *Hotel Saino* [190], which resembles an Italian villa transplanted to a quiet backstreet in Lakeside Pokhara. All the rooms have attached bathroom; if there are no tour groups staying this place is usually deserted, resulting in a lack of atmosphere but bargain rates.

Another way to avoid the crowds is to go for a hotel with a big garden, of which there are plenty to choose from. Most can be found by heading down one of the lanes off the main drag heading directly away from the lake, such as the friendly *Boardwalk Guest House* [125] and its slightly cheaper neighbour *Hotel ABC* [127], the former with a TV and en-suite bathtub in every room, the latter, run, seemingly single-handedly, by an affable man whose pride and joy is his lovely, well-kept garden. Also with large and well-kept grounds: the popular *Noble Inn* [119], the excellent German-run *Hotel Temple Villa* [68], which has some exquisitely furnished rooms; and its neighbour the *Octagon* [69], a bizarre place with individually furnished rooms housed within an octagonal building.

Another peaceful retreat is the long-running *Gurkha Lodge* [189] which, though its grounds are not particularly large, makes up for it by having perhaps the prettiest garden in Lakeside. There are five doubles at US$5-10 each in the bungalows here. *Nanohana Lodge* [194] lacks large grounds, but has some lovely balconies and very smart rooms; again, this is very good value at US$6-15.

Two places under the same Scottish-Nepali management that are proving deservedly popular are the *Hotel Nirvana* [150] and *Sacred Valley Inn* [142]. The former is an efficiently-run, smart little place with a variety of lovely, spotlessly clean rooms, some with mountain views. The latter is a little cheaper, a

(continued on p107)

POKHARA

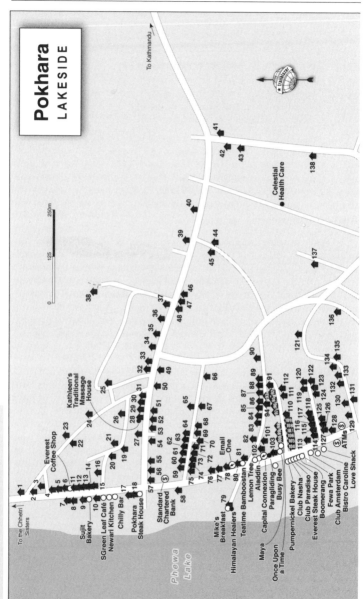

Pokhara
LAKESIDE

To Kathmandu

Celestial
Health Care

250m

125

0

Kathleen's
Traditional
Massage
House

Everest
Coffee Shop

Sujit
Bakery

SGreen Leaf Café
Newari Kitchen

Chilly Bar

Pokhara
Steak House

Standard
Chartered
Bank

Phewa
Lake

To the Chhetri
Sisters

Mike's
Breakfast

Himalayan Healers

Teatime Bamboostan

Maya

Capital Connexion

Once Upon
a Time

Lemon Tree
Aladdin

Paragliding

Busy Bee

Emall
One

Pumpernickel Bakery

Club Nasha

Club Paradiso

Everest Steak House

Boomerang

Fewa Park

Club Amsterdam

Bistro Caroline

Love Shack

ATMs

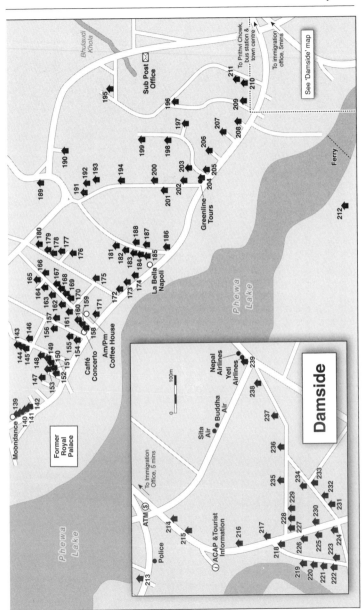

POKHARA

POKHARA

ACCOMMODATION IN POKHARA
Keyed to map on pp102-3

Lakeside
1 Hotel Supriya (462862) $7 (a)
2 Hotel Tropicana (462118) $7-10 (a)
3 Apex GH (462496) $4/5 (a)
4 Hotel Mandap (462088) $10-15/15-20 (a)
5 Be Happy GH (462454) $5-8 (a)
6 Laxmi GH (464928) $5/6 (a)
7 Hotel Hollyhock (461462) $5-7 (a)
8 Phil's Inn (462009) $5/8 (a)
9 Ganga GH (464784) $3/5 (a)
10 Hotel Peace Plaza (461505, www.hotel peaceplaza.com) $2.50 (c), $5 (a)
11 Machhupuchre GH (621751, www.guest house-nepal.20m.com/index.htm) $4/5 (a) & Pokhara Village Resort (462427) dbl $15 (a)
12 Hotel Crown (464821) $6-10/6-10 (a)
13 Pushkar GH (525053) $2-3 (c), $3-4 (a)
14 Hotel Plaza Annapurna (462606) $7/10 (a)
15 Hotel Blue Heaven (463647, www.hotel blueheaven.com) $14-18/18-22 (a)
16 Hotel Mandala (464690) $2 dorm, $3 (c), $4-5 (a)
17 Buddhi Home (463028) $5 (a)
18 New Elite's GH (462807) $3/5 (a)
19 Hotel Tiiicho (462021) $4-6 (a)
20 Hotel Peace Nepal (627008) $3/5 (a)
21 Gurung Village (984 602 5646) $5 (a)
22 Hotel Yokohama (462692) $10-15 (a)

23 Hotel Tibet Home (463101) $12 (a)
24 Hotel Brunei (463858) $4-7 (a)
25 Holy Shiva (463023,www.glocalnepal.com/ holyshiva) $5-13 (a)
26 Hotel Silent Peak (462857) dbl $10 (a)
27 New Winds Hotel (462643, www.thenew winds.com) $5-10 (a)
28 Hotel Hong Kong (463202) $12-20/15-30 (a)
29 Hotel Cordial (525723) $2-8 (c) $10-20 (a)
30 Hotel Shikhar (462033) $15-25/18-30 (a)
31 Hotel Nepal (527222) $3-4/4-5.50 (a)
32 Millennium GH (463544) $5 (a)
33 Hotel Buddha (462995) $5-15 (c/a)
34 Hotel Alpine (525161) $2.50 (c), $3.50 (a)
35 Bonny GH (463006) $3-20 (a)
36 Hotel My Home (461482) $3-15 (a)
37 International (463432) $3-5/3.50-6 (a)
38 Hotel Full Moon (462511) $4 (c) $20 (a)
39 Hotel Mount Everest (461846) $3-4.50 (a)
40 Welcome GH (521864) $2 (c), $2.50 (a)
41 New Solitary Lodge (461804, www.new solitarylodge.com) $6/8 (c), $12-15/15-20 (a)
42 Hotel Global (463117) $2 (c), $3-6/2 (a)
43 Garden GH (462596) $1.50/4 (c), $2/5 (a)
44 Green View Lodge (462408) $6-10 (a)
45 Hotel Rockland (461953) $20-30 (a)
46 Hotel Surya (461642) $5 (a)
47 Silent Park (980 414 7403) $4-6 (a)
48 Hotel Planet (980 418 4077) $2.50-3 (a)
49 Hotel Sindoor (462754) $3 (c), $6/12 (a)
50 Mountain Villa (521954) $4-5.50/5-9 (a)
51 Hotel Motherland (461712) $4/15 (a)

52 Hotel Diamond (462871) $4-30 (a)
53 Hotel Singapore (603260) $3.50-7 (a)
54 Fairmount Hotel (463252, www.travel-nepal. com/hotel/fairmount/) $18-30/25-40 (a)
55 Little Tibetan GH (531898) $3-4/4-5.50 (a)
56 Hotel Unicorn (532030) $2/3 (a)
57 Hotel Marigold (525065) $10-15/15-30 (a)
58 Amrit GH (464240, www.amritnepal.com) $2/3 (c), $5/6 (a)
59 Trans Himalaya (463131) $5 (a)
60 Hotel Monila (462014) $6 (a)
61 Hotel Baidam (525991) $5-7 (a)
62 Hotel Celesty Inn (984 602 0486) $5/8 (a)
63 Tranquility Lodge (463030, www.baidam.com) $5/7 (a)
64 Nature's Grace Lodge (527220, www.hidden kingdom.co.uk) $4 (c), $8 (a)
65 Silver Oaks Inn (462147, www.hotelpokhara.com) $10-20 (a)
66 The Mountain House (464613) $10 (a)
67 Beautiful View Inn (984 606 6714) $5-8 (a)
68 Temple Villa (521203) $3.50/8 (c), $10 (a)
69 Hotel Octagon (526978) $5-8 (c), $7-9 (a)
70 Hotel Green Peace (463884) $8/10 (a)
71 Sanctuary Lodge (523407) $5 (a)
72 Butterfly Lodge (461892, www.butterfly-lodge.org) $4-6 (c), $6-8 (a)
73 Hotel Khukuri (464614, www.landmark pokhara.com) $10 (a)
74 Elia GH (462129) $3/6 (c), $5/7 (a)
75 Hotel Gorkhali Dhee (463385) $12-15/ 20-35 (a)

76 Holy Mount GH (531123) $2-3(c)/$3-5(a)
77 Hotel Vimal's (462306) $4/5-8 (a)
78 Simrik GH (461497) $6/6-10 (a)
79 Hotel Fewa (463151, www.hotelfewa.com) $20/25-55 (a)
80 Hotel Monal (461459) $5/10-12 (a)
81 Yeti GH (521423) $8/10-13 (a)
82 Hotel New Family (980 412 2428) $3/4-7 (a)
83 Hotel City Annapurna (462913) $4/4-5 (a)
84 Future Way GH (984 602 0218) $4-5/6-7 (a)
85 Lubbly Jubbly GH (463810) $3 (c), $5/7 (a)
86 Fuji Sagamartha GH (463678) $3/5 (a)
87 Hotel Stupa (462608) $18-20/25-30 (a)
88 Hotel Lake Palace (462027, www.hotel-lakepalace.com) $16-20 (a)
89 Hotel River Park (462756) $6-7/8-9 (a)
90 Atlas GH (461971) $3/4.50 (a)
91 Teacher Krishna Lodge (461709) $3/4-5 (a)
92 Hotel Virgin Peak (984 604 6671) $4/5 (a)
93 Hotel Dulcify (461692) $3-8 (a)
94 Hotel Tenzing Hilary (984 602 9847) $5-7 (a)
95 Pokhara Peace Home (464960) $6-7 (a)
96 Nepali Cottage GH (461637) $4-5/5-7 (a)
97 Century GH (524461) $4/5-8 (a)
98 Pushpa GH (464332) $3-6/4-8 (a)
99 Hotel Avocado (463617) $5/6-8 (a)
100 Him-Trekkers Lodge (462817) $16/20 (a)
101 Peace Horizon GH (980 415 83307) $2/3 (a)
102 Mountain Top (461779, www.mttop.com.np) $6-7/9 (a)
103 Alka GH (463357) $2/3 (c), $4/5 (a)
104 Om Sweet Home (461523) $3/5 (a)

POKHARA

105 Hotel Lake Diamond (462064) $4/7 (a)
106 Vardan Resort (985 602 0241) $15/16-20 (a)
107 Hotel The Star Light (463705) $8-10 (a)
108 Mountain GH (462720) $8-15 (a)
109 Hotel Travel Inn (462631) $5-45 (a)
110 Hotel Serenity (463098) $3/5-8 (a), $3/3.50-20 (a)
111 Unique Mountain GH (532720) $4-8 (a)
112 Hotel Deep Oasis (463769) $6/7-10 (a)
113 Sweet Dream (980 413 2040) $3/3 (a)
114 Hotel Meera (462031, www.hotelmeera.com.np) $40-58/50-80 (a)
115 Hotel Tulsi Pokhara (462895, www.hotel tulsipokhara.com) $50-72/60-104 (a)
116 Mayur (464285) $4-6 (a)
117 Mera Peak GH (463318) $7 (a)
118 Hotel Greenland (461591) $1.50/2 (c), $3-8 (a)
119 Noble Inn (464926, www.nobleinn.com) $12-17/14-24 (a)
120 Hotel Fishtail Villa (462451) $10-20 (a)
121 Harvest Moon GH (462647) $2.50 (c)
122 Iceland GH (463082) $6-8 (c), $12-20 (a)
123 Hotel Mount Fuji (463274) $3 (c), $5 (a)
124 Candle Inn (463128) $10-25 (a)
125 Boardwalk GH (46492 7) $15-20/25-30 (a)
126 White Lotus GH (984 605 6804) $3 (c), $10 (a)
127 Hotel ABC (461934, www.hotelabc.com.np) $16/22 (a)
128 Hotel Snowland (462384, www.hotel snowland.com) $15-55/20-65 (a)

129 Fuji GH (462230) $5/7.50 (a)
130 Hotel Sakura (462555) $5-10 (c), $20-30 (a)
131 Hotel Barahi (460617, www.barahi.com) $42-75/53-94 (a)
132 Holy Heaven (461281, www.go2kathman du.com/holy-heaven) $24-42/31-42 (a)
133 Hotel Four Seasons (465777) $20-30 (a)
134 Green Tara Hotel (462698) $5/10 (a)
135 Hotel Panorama (463763, www.hotel panorama.com.np) $10-15/15-20 (a)
136 Lonely GH (462566, www.coara.or.jp/ ~nagata/Lonely/LGH1.htm) $5-6 (a)
137 Goodwill GH (527166) $4-5 (a)
138 Garden Rest House (461862) $3/4 (a)
139 Landmark Hotel (462908, www.land markpokhara.com) $35-55/45-75 (a)
140 Hotel Nasa (984 603 2143) $3/4 (c), $8/12 (a)
141 Traveller's GH (462131) $8/12 (a)
142 Sacred Valley Inn (461792, www.sacred valleyinn.com) $8-20 (a)
143 Hotel Himalayan Star (463846) $6 (c), $8 (a)
144 Pokhara Palace Hotel (464485, www.pokharapalacehotel.com) $12 (a)
145 Lodge The Placid Valley (465193) $5-10 (a)
146 Fire on the Mountain (465431) $5-8 (c), $7-15 (a)
147 Hotel Angel (464713) $6-10/10-20 (a)
148 Hotel Him Shikhar (446671) $5 (c), $8 (a)
149 Giri GH (464955) $3-5 (a)
150 Hotel Nirvana (463332) $4 (c), $6-20 (a)

P O K H A R A

ACCOMMODATION IN POKHARA
Keyed to map on pp102-3

Lakeside (cont'd)
151 Karma GH (984 604 9867) $2/2.50 (c), $2.50/3 (a)
152 Green Tara Hotel (462698) $7 (a)
153 New United Hotel (464824) $4-8/5-12 (a)
154 New Friendly Home (461677) $3/5 (c), $6/10 (a)
155 Hotel View Point (464648 www.hview point.com) $8 (a)
156 Hotel Eden (463838) $4-8 (a)
157 Holy Lodge (463422, www.hollylodge. com.np) $1/2 (c), $3/6 (a)
158 Hotel Glacier (463722, www.glacier nepal.com) $15-40/20-50 (a)
159 Broadway Inn (465796) $10-15/15-20 (a)
160 Pacific GH (462008) $5-7/8-10 (a)
161 Gauri Shankar (462422) $3-6/5-8 (a)
162 Gautama GH (463898) $1/1.50 (c), $2/3.50 (a)
163 Peace Eye GH (980 419 7125) $3/4 (a)
164 Rustika GH (465138) $3.50-4/$7 (a)
165 Shanti GH (463645) $2/3 (c), $3-6 (a)
166 Hotel Horizon (462893) $7-8/10 (a)
167 Karki GH (985 602 7312, www.karki guesthouse.com) $3/4 (c), $6-10 (a)
168 Royal GH (463443) $1.50-6.50/2-8 (a)
169 Penguin GH (527399) $1/1.50 (c), $2/4-5 (a)
170 Eco Traveller's Lodge (462421) $3-6 (c), $8-15 (a)

171 Trek-O-Tel (464996, www.nepalshotel. com/trekotel.html) $40/50 (a)
172 Lake View Resort (461477, www.pokhara hotels.com) $15-40/22-50 (a)
173 Moonlight Resort (465704) $20-30/30-40 (a)
174 Hotel Lakeside (465073) $17-27/22-37 (a)
175 Hotel Grand Holiday (984 505 0480, www.hotelgrandholiday.com) $12-15 (a)
176 Hotel Pleasant Home (464514) $5-7/7-10 (a)
177 Blue Heaven GH (463351) $2.50-4/ $5.50-6 (a)
178 Hotel Pokhara View (462592, www.ktmgh. com/pokhara/) $12-25/15-30 (a)
179 Pokhara Mount Resort (463465) $8/10 (a)
180 Pun Hill GH (462799) $3/6 (c), $6/12 (a)
181 Kiwi GH (463652) $6/10-20 (a)
182 Stay Well GH (463471) $5-18 (a)
183 Kumari Lodge (464384) $3/4 (c), $6/10 (a)
184 Pokhara GH (465228) $4-30 (a)
185 Dharma Inn (465232) $15-25/25-35 (a)
186 Nightingale Lodge (462638) $8-10/10-13 (a)
187 Hotel Bedrock (465524) $10-15 (a)
188 Hotel Yeti (462768, www.hotelyeti. com.np) $3/5-10 (a)
189 Gurkha Lodge (462798) $5-10 (a)
190 Hotel Saino (522868) $9/12 (a)
191 Hotel Miracle (463116) $3-5/4-8 (a)
192 Hotel Marco Polo (463154) $2-4/2-4 (a)
193 Mum's Garden Resort (463468, www.geocities.com/soho/exhibit/ 3246/mums.html) $25/30 (a)

194 Nanohana Lodge (464478, www.geo cities.com/nanohanalodge) $6-15 (a)
195 Summit GH (461421) $3/4-7 (a)
196 New Annapurna GH (465011) $1/2 (c), $3-7 (a)
197 New Pokhara Lodge (462493, www.pokharalodge.com) $10-17/15-23 (a)
198 Hotel Mount Kailash (980 651 9312) $3-15 (c/a)
199 Hotel Orient (464912, www.geocities .com/hotelorient/index.html) $5/6-8 (a)
200 Hotel Swiss Home (985 602 8607) $3-4 (a)
201 Hotel Raraa (465930) $5-8/7-10 (a)
202 Hotel Lovely Mount (463530, www.love lytravels.com.np) $30/50 (a)
203 Base Camp Resort (465949) $72/75 (a)
204 Hotel Green Park (463473) $4/5 (c), $8/10 (a)
205 Baba Lodge (462997) $20-25 (a)
206 Nepal GH (465271) $4-10/8-15 (a)
207 Snow Hill Lodge (465685) $18-25/25-35 (a)
208 Trekkers' Lodge (462854) $5-15/$15-25 (a)
209 Ever Green GH (463503) $1/2 (c), $2-4/ $3-5 (a)
210 Paramount GH (980 661 8363) $2/3 (a)
211 Hotel Mountain View (465281) $3-4 (a)
212 Fish Tail Lodge (465071, www.fishtail-lodge.com)

Damside
213 Kantipur (460286, www.hotelkantipur.com) $55-80/65-90 (a)
214 Hotel Nature Land (462577) $25/35 (a)
215 Hotel Holiday Pokhara (464763) $15/25 (a)
216 Hotel Lake City (534807, www.sanghimala.nl) $15 (a)
217 Fewa GH (463215) $3-20 (a)
218 Hotel KC (985 602 0477, www.hotelkc.com.np) $15/$20 (a)
219 Hotel Jharna (465925) $15/22 (a)
220 Hotel Monalisa (463863) $20-40/30-50 (a)
221 Hotel Cosmos (462464) $3-4 (a)

222 New Ashok Palace (520374) $4/5 (a)
223 Hotel Pokhara Prince (532632) $20 (c), $25 (a)
224 Hotel Gurkha Haven (464527) $12/20 (a)
225 Hotel Garden (463681, www.hotelgardennepal.com) $10-30 (a)
226 Hotel Peaceful (520861) $2/3(c),$6-8/8-10 (a)
227 The Central Inn (485283) $20/30
228 Hotel Nascent (464719) $1 (c),$2.50 (a)
229 Lumbini Resort (463541) $15-20/20-30 (a)
230 Hotel Mount Heaven (462860) $5/7 (c), $10-20 (a)

231 Purna GH (460986) $3/4 (c), $6-8/12-15 (a)
232 Hotel Green View (521844) $2-8/3-12 (a)
233 Hotel Aashika (462446) $4 (c), $5 (a)
234 Hotel Sports (464751) $3/4 (c)
235 Dragon Hotel (460391) $40/50 (a)
236 New Sherpa (984 173 5399) $5/7 (c)
237 Tibet Resort (460853, www.hotelkc.com.np) $23/34 (a)
238 Hotel Indra (460614) $1.50/2 (c), $2/2.50 (a)
239 Pokhara Holiday Inn (465094, www.pokharaholidayinn.com) $30-40/40-60 (a)

little more laidback and a little better value too, with a decent sunny roof terrace and eager-to-please staff. It's possibly the best value in Lakeside. The highly-recommended and extremely friendly *Hotel Tibet Home* [23], at the northern end of Lakeside is one of many places owned by a former soldier in the British Army Gurkhas. The hotel boasts rooms with tub, TV, phone and mountain views (US$12).

If you're a woman travelling on your own, the *Chhetri Sisters' Guest House* (☎ 524066) is recommended. Run by Lucky, Dicky and Nicky, the guesthouse is in the north of Lakeside, along the road that runs parallel to the lake. Double rooms with breakfast cost US$15 (shared bathroom) and $20 en suite ($12/15 for single occupancy). They also run a trekking agency for women.

● **Damside** The *Hotel Gurkha Haven* [224] is, as one would expect, efficiently run by a Gurkha. There are superb views from the rooftop. One of the newest guesthouses here is *Hotel Lake City* [216] which offers a warm welcome and a quiet garden away from the road.

The *Hotel KC* [218] is a business-class hotel on a busy corner near the lake: rooms are $15/$20. The staff are friendly and there are good views of the lake and mountains from its rooms with balconies.

Mid-range – upper (US$20-50/£13.50-33)
Owned by Mike of Mike's Breakfast fame, *Hotel Fewa* [79] is in an enviable location: it's the only hotel in the centre right down by the water. There are rooms with attached bathroom for $20/25-55, and 'for your peace of mind – no TV or telephone in room'.

The centrally-located *Landmark Hotel* [139] is a pleasant place to stay; rooms are $35-55/45-75 but there can be

POKHARA

attractive discounts. There's good food in the restaurant. *Baba Lodge* [205] is similar, with rooms at US$20/25, while the *Trek-O-Tel* [171], with its neatly manicured front lawn, lies just a few minutes west; singles/doubles cost US$40/50. Also surrounded by large grounds, the *Hotel Barahi* [131] is one of the only hotels in Lakeside with its own swimming pool. Nearer the lake, and well run by a Gurkha owner, is *Hotel Meera* [114] with a range of rooms some with attached bathrooms with bathtubs, perfect for a long soak after your trek.

In Damside, *Hotel Kantipur* [213] with its grey stone buildings is a deceptively large place away from the road, behind its own highly-recommended restaurant. The *Tibet Resort* [237] is a pleasant enough spot. Rooms in the *Dragon Hotel* [235] cost US$40/50 with bathtubs in the attached bathrooms. The restaurant here has been recommended.

Expensive (US$50/£33 and above)

The 'official' prices for rooms at the top places are given here but if there are few tourists some amazing discounts may be possible. The *Base Camp Resort* [203] charges US$72/75 and used to be regarded as the best in Lakeside, though it's now been rather upstaged by the smart *Mum's Garden Resort* [193], one of the more charming places in Lakeside, tucked away in secluded splendour at the end of a small dirt track. Constructed out of hand-cut stone, all rooms have a terrace with mountain views, a bathtub and telephone and go for $25/30, single/double occupancy. A third option on Lakeside is the old favourite, the *Fish Tail Lodge* [212], whose main attraction is its superb location on the southern side of the lake; it's worth visiting just for the wonderful view of the mountain panorama reflected in the water. All rooms have attached bathrooms and cost US$140-160/150-170. It's set in well-kept gardens and reached by raft across a narrow stretch of the lake. Contact the Hotel de l'Annapurna in Kathmandu (see p78) for bookings.

The *Hotel Fewa Prince* (☎ 524881), on the road to Kathmandu, was built in collaboration with a Japanese company. Rooms are US$90/110.

On the eastern edge of Damside, the *Bluebird Hotel* (☎ 525480) is a large marble-floored affair popular with Japanese tour groups. The comfortable rooms here are US$130/150. Use of the swimming pool for non-residents is Rs250.

Even more impressive is the nearby *Shangri-La Village Pokhara* (☎ 462222, 🖳 www.hotelshangrila.com). There are rooms with tremendous mountain views for US$180 and a garden which will get more attractive as it matures. The pool is not heated so somewhat chilly in the main trekking season.

Pokhara's top hotel is the *Fulbari Resort* (☎ 432451), attractively situated on the edge of a gorge about 5km from the centre of Pokhara. The opulent rooms cost US$165 up to US$600 for the top suite. There's a golf course, an excellent restaurant and Pokhara's best pool (Rs650 for non-residents, including lunch).

WHERE TO EAT

Calorie after delicious calorie line the main street of Lakeside, from the cake shops laden with waist-expanding chocolate croissants, to the larger establishments offering ever more scrumptious ways of putting the wobble back in your walk after weeks on the trail. It's difficult to give specific recommendations for restaurants: things change so fast. Some of the old favourites are listed below.

Breakfast

One place that's often recommended for its breakfasts is *Mike's Breakfast* at the Hotel Fewa. If you want something simple like a roll and coffee there are several bakeries, including *Sujit Bakery*, along the main road in Lakeside. They are not quite up to the standards of Thamel bakeries, yet, though there is a branch of Kathmandu's *Pumpernickel Bakery* in Pokhara.

Some of the best bowls of muesli and curd with fruit is served by the numerous small **fresh fruit stalls**. There's a particularly good, un-named one by the Hotel Fuji. The tiny *AM/PM Coffee House* is also good and they do half-decent coffee. For real filter coffee head to *Moondance* where you can also get pancakes with honey for around Rs100. Other relaxing places for a coffee and croissant are *Everest Coffee Shop* and *Green Leaf Café*, both at the northern end of town.

For a post-trek celebratory breakfast binge try one of the top hotels since they often have all-you-can-eat breakfasts.

Lunch and supper

● **Western/Have-a-go-at-anything** 'Tourist-friendly' restaurants now proliferate on Lakeside's main street. Characterised by thatched roofs and Western music, a new addition to one restaurant's menu is quickly emulated by the other restaurants here, thus most menus now look decidedly similar. That said, the food is usually of a fairly high standard, the attempts at copying different national cuisines continue to achieve higher levels of authenticity – and the beer's always cold. Most places have DVD screenings to entice customers in.

One restaurant that is consistently recommended is *Once Upon A Time*. A number of other places on this main central drag, such as the *Moondance* and *Lemon Tree*, have similar fare. The latter also does the most exquisite banana smoothies in Pokhara. Further north, the long-established *Tea-time Bamboostan* is still going strong, and if one of the ultra-hip waiters deigns to serve you, the food isn't bad at all. They now have live bands here some evenings.

Many restaurants have gardens stretching down to the lake. Very pleasant in the early evening as the egrets swoop by, it is also possible to get some decent nosh, provided the mosquitoes don't devour you completely first. *Fewa Park* and *Boomerang* are both good. The best, however, is *Bistro Caroline*, a French restaurant with a lovely little back garden that serves some scrumptious starters.

Love Shack is British-owned which is reflected in the menu: beef hotpot and fish and chips are two staples. They also do some typical Nepali dishes. *Aladdin* is a new place with plenty of Western choice on the menu. The *Chilly Bar* opened in 2008 and has lovely exclusive balconies that look out to the lake. The menu covers a range of world cuisines including Mexican, which is presumably what the restaurant's name is trying to hint at as there was nothing wrong with their thermostat when I was there.

The popular *Everest Steak House* is a branch of the Kathmandu restaurant, and serving the same menu: everything from the Rs250 breakfast cowboy special

POKHARA

to the Rs1700 chateaubriand. There is a cheaper steak house, the **Pokhara Steak House**, further up the road where the food is very good and the staff friendly.

In South Lakeside, **Baba's Restaurant** has been popular for many years. Main dishes include chicken cordon bleu and spinach mushroom lasagne.

As you might expect, the top hotels have good restaurants. There's a buffet lunch at the **Shangri-La Village** for Rs650.

● **Italian** The best Italian food is served at **Caffè Concerto**, in south Lakeside. There are pizzas, fresh pasta, gnocchi and even tiramisu. **La Bella Napoli** offers similar and does excellent juicy steaks.

● **Nepali/Tibetan** There are several small Nepali/Tibetan places offering daal bhat or momos at give-away prices. More upmarket, the **Little Tibetan Tea Garden** serves momos and many other Tibetan dishes. The **Lhasa Tibetan Restaurant** is also recommended and you can try gyakok here (four hours' notice required). Opposite Boomerang is **Rice Bowl Tibetan**.

● **Chinese** **Lan Hua**, in the south of Lakeside, is an authentic place with delicacies such as 'phoenix craws' and 'double cook gizzard' on the menu. A large selection of Chinese food can be found at many of the places here. Usually these are just variations on fried rice, but are nevertheless tasty and filling. The best Chinese on Lakeside, now, and indeed in Pokhara, is the central **Great Wall**, with a great waterfront location and rooftop view.

● **Japanese** Judging from the queues of Japanese backpackers in it, the **Ajino Silk Road**, near the Hungry Eye, is good. The **Koto Restaurant** nearby is comparable quality, while the most authentic Japanese cuisine is served up by **Tabemonaya**, at the south-eastern end of Lakeside by the Anma Shiatsu centre.

● **Indian** Most of the restaurants make fair attempts at Mughal and Tandoori dishes. The **Hungry Eye**, in central Lakeside, is recommended.

● **Vegetarian** All restaurants have some vegetarian dishes.

SERVICES

Banks

Standard Chartered Bank (open Sunday to Thursday 09.45-16.15, Friday 09.45-13.15, closed on Saturday and Sunday) has a branch on Lakeside. They will do cash advances on Visa or MasterCard. Their ATM tries to operate 24hrs, or you can walk a couple of hundred metres south to the grounds of the Hotel Snowland, which also has one. The nearest ATM to Damside is in Shahid Chowk.

There are exchange counters dotted all the way along the main drag; they all seem to offer exactly the same rates, too, though in the early morning there are some differences between them, depending on whether they have managed to hear the new rates yet. As a result, this may be the best time to change money with them. None of the moneychangers charges commission. Double check your money here as shortchanging always seems to work in their favour.

The main branch of Nepal Rastra Bank is in the centre of Pokhara.

Left luggage

As in Kathmandu, most hotels and guest houses will store excess baggage free of charge, as long as you promise to spend at least one night more there on your return. Keep all valuables with you, though.

Medical clinics

There are a number of clinics/pharmacies in Lakeside that do stool tests and also the **Western Regional/Gandaki Hospital** (☎ 520066), near the main post office. If you're hospitalised in Pokhara you may need a friend to bring you food and help look after you as nursing is minimal. Unless, that is, you are staying at **Celestial Health Care** (☎ 463271). Situated on the edge of Lakeside, this is a plush clinic with beds for 40 people, with each room furnished with TV and bathtub. A one-off $30 consultation fee covers all medicines and any further consultations. Call outs with medication cost $60, while overnight stays should be covered by your travel insurer.

For specialist eye treatment, the **Himalaya Eye Hospital** (☎ 520352) regularly treats foreigners for a nominal fee. Staffed by one Dutch and two Nepali opthalmologists it's to the south of the airport.

Annapurna entry permits

The ACAP desk is in the **tourist information office** in Damside. It's open daily from 10.00-17.00; permits for entry into the Annapurna Conservation Area cost Rs2000, which is half the price of the same permit bought at one of the offices on the trails (which may or may not still be selling them by the time you read this). Next to the ACAP desk is the TIMS (trekkers information management system) desk. You need to get a TIMS card from here, which is free, before you set off on your trek. For both the ACAP entry permit and the TIMS card you will need to show your passport and bring along two passport photos for each. It's not yet possible to get visas for the north Mustang area here; you need to get these from the immigration office.

Visa extensions

The **Department of Immigration** has a branch in Pokhara (☎ 521167) five minutes north of Damside. Opening times are from Sunday to Thursday from 10.30 to 13.00 for visa extensions, or Fridays 10.00 to 12.00.

GETTING AROUND

Some **taxis** have meters but most are meterless and you pay as much as the driver thinks you will stand. Between the airport or bus station and Lakeside you probably won't get away with paying less than Rs80.

Local **buses** are based at the Prithwi Chowk Bus Station in the centre of town. Buses run from here to Lakeside (Rs10), to the airport, and to Besi Bus Park (for buses to Nayapul for Birethanti etc).

The best way to get around Pokhara is by **bike**. There are lots of places to rent them from and prices are around Rs50 per day for the cheapest, to around Rs100 for a mountain bike. In Lakeside you can rent **motorbikes**.

WHAT TO SEE & DO

Apart from the impressive **mountain panorama** (best viewed at dawn) there really are very few 'sights' in Pokhara so you needn't feel guilty if you spend your time lazing around by the lake. Hiring a **boat** to paddle yourself around the lake or out to the small temple on the island helps pass the time until the next meal. You can **swim** in the lake (best from a boat in the middle – but wear a swimsuit) and the water can be surprisingly warm.

The **ACAP Information Centre** is interesting, with displays about the work currently being done as part of the Annapurna Conservation Area Project. To the south of the airport the huge **International Mountaineering Museum**, housed inside what appears to be an enormous hangar, is a project managed by the Nepal Mountaineering Association. Open 10.00-17.00 daily except Saturday.

The **Gurkha Memorial Museum** (Rs150, open 08.00-16.30 daily) is at the northern end of Pokhara near the Seti Gorge (see Pokhara map p99). It's more for those with a serious interest in the subject.

The **Pokhara Regional Museum** (Jan-Oct, Tue-Sun, 10.00-17.00, Mon 10.00-15.00; Nov-Dec, Wed-Mon, 10.00-16.00, closed Tue) has a small dusty archaeological and ethnographic display.

Other activities include, paragliding, ultra-light flights, river rafting, kayaking and parahawking (paragliding with a trained bird of prey that will find the best thermals).

❏ Brahmin & Chhetri people

Brahmins are the highest 'rank' in the Hindu caste system, and with the Chhetris (who formed the ruling Rana class) still form the majority of wealthy and influential society in Kathmandu. They speak Nepali and are spread throughout the country, especially in the pahar and terai. Of the Chhetri castes, the Thakuris have the highest social, political and ritual status, so many of the influential Khas, Gurung, Bhotia and Magar people who have converted to Hinduism have aspired to become Thakuris.

In most parts of Nepal Brahmin and Chhetri homes are painted with red ochre, or whitewashed and traditionally repainted during the *dasain* festival. The inside is usually whitewashed and the mud and cow dung floors are swept daily. Around the outside of their homes is a line formed from where rainwater falls from the roof. This is the external boundary for low caste people approaching a home, the next boundary is the veranda and reception room (in larger houses) where you, and people of a similar caste may be invited to rest and have a cup of tea. Same caste marriages organised by the family still predominate, although love and inter-caste marriages do occasionally occur.

Brahmins (who originally came to Nepal from India) form the priestly caste, and as such are often conservative in their outlook. Brahmin and Chhetri boys are given a 'sacred thread' when young, and every year this is replaced. This thread is worn diagonally across the body under clothing, and never removed.

Almost everyone you meet in Nepal who is in any position of responsibility will be Brahmin or Chhetri. This has made many of the lower castes feel marginalised, and in some way led to the Maoists success in the 2008 elections, with the promise of social change.

ROUTE GUIDE

4

Main trekking areas

KANCHENJUNGA   [pp116-124]

Kanchenjunga is the most easterly of the Nepal himals and forms a natural border with the Indian state of Sikkim. Incredibly lush temperate rainforest surrounds the third highest mountain on earth, with its many sentinel peaks providing dozens of remote glaciated valleys to explore. In Nepal, the southwest face, south ridge and west ridge of Kanchenjunga form a massive horseshoe-shaped valley system around Yalung, and are rarely visited. The main trekking route heads to the mountain's north face and Base Camp at Pangpema. The isolated communities of Olangchun Gola and Yangma are adventurous side trip destinations that can be used as bases to visit some of most far-flung corners of Nepal. There are many ethnic groups in the region, including Limbu, Rai, Sherpa and Lhomi as well as Tibetan nomads who cross the border to trade.

MAKALU   [pp125-134]

Sandwiched between Kanchenjunga and the Solu-Khumbu (Everest Region) this is perhaps the most stunning and challenging of the commercial trekking areas. The standard route to the base camp of the fifth highest mountain in the world, Mt Makalu, is reached after an arduous trek over the Kongma Danda to the incomparable Barun Khola valley. The Makalu-Barun National Park and Buffer Zone is also home to Rai, Lhomi and Sherpa people, but many think its really big attractions are the high, dangerous passes to the Everest region: Sherpani Col (6180m), West Col (6190m) and Amphu Labsta (5845m).

EVEREST REGION   [pp135-142]

The Everest Region, known locally as the Solu-Khumbu, is currently Nepal's premier trekking location. Tens of thousands of tourists visit each year, mainly in the post-monsoon months of October and November; come out of season and the well-maintained trails are almost empty. This is a region where you can stop at any point for stunning mountain scenery that will rival anywhere and, of course, there's Everest, the world's highest peak at 8848m. Add the famous hospitality of the Sherpa people, comfy teahouses and plenty of culture and history and you can see why some trekkers keep coming back.

ROLWALING [pp143-151]

The Rolwaling lies beyond the western boundary of the Everest region and the mighty Tashi Labsta pass (5760m). Perhaps one of the least visited areas in Nepal, the mountains and valleys of this region offer unbridled opportunities for the remote trekker and mountaineer. Bordered by the Arniko Highway (the Kathmandu to Tibet road) to the west, the Rolwaling also includes some excellent medium altitude trails over the Tinsang La and through Bigu Gompa. Tamang, Gurung and Sherpa people offer a genuine welcome to any visitor. Consider adding a bungee jump at the Last Resort to your itinerary.

HELAMBU AND LANGTANG [pp152-164]

Helambu and Langtang, to the north of Kathmandu, are perhaps the most convenient of all the trekking areas; it is even possible to begin your trek from your hotel door in Thamel. Any visitor to Nepal in April should see the rhododendron forests that cover the northern slopes of Helambu, which are only rivalled by those in the Kanchenjunga region. The Bhotia people here are just as friendly as the Sherpa elsewhere, and the intermingling with Brahmin, Chhetri and Newar people is a reminder of Nepal's harmonious ethnic diversity. It is almost unbelievable that so few trekkers continue past Kyangjin Gompa to visit the Langshisa Glacier, or cross the Tilman Pass, where the mountains are just amazing.

GANESH HIMAL AND MANASLU [pp165-182]

The Ganesh Himal and Manaslu lie in the geographical centre of Nepal and are perhaps the country's best kept trekking secrets. Many would argue that the Manaslu Circuit is the best general trek the country has to offer, and for those wanting to immerse themselves in some wild, but not high-altitude, trekking then the Ganesh Himal is the place. Gurung, Tamang, Magar, Larke and Siar people blend to create perhaps the most ethnically interesting series of valleys throughout the Himalaya. Add some majestic peaks, including Manaslu, the eighth highest mountain on earth, and these regions should be high on anyone's list.

ANNAPURNAS [pp183-196]

For many years the Annapurnas were the most trekked region of the entire Himalaya, only now overshadowed by the Solu-Khumbu region. Despite some recent road construction work this is still one of the most beautiful and convenient areas of Nepal to explore. When you add the variety of landscapes that you'll find in Naar, Phu and Tilicho it is easy to see that the region still has lots to offer.

MUSTANG AND DOLPO [pp197-222]

Mustang and Dolpo both lie in the 'rain-shadow' of the Annapurna and Dhaulagiri massifs, and are unique when compared to the rest of Nepal. Both regions are repositories of unchanged Tibetan culture, dating back at least 1200 years. Lush lower valleys lead up to an arid alpine desert and some of the highest permanent settlements on earth. Nomads herd yaks over windswept passes, and tales of sorcery and magicians are woven into everyday life.

FAR WEST   [pp223-243]

The least developed of the trekking regions of Nepal are in the Far West of the country: Humla, Rara, Khaptad and the Api and Saipal Himals. The local Khas and Chhetri people have rarely seen trekkers, so be prepared for a heartfelt welcome wherever you go. Logistics are a challenge throughout the region but the extra effort of organising a trek here is the price you pay for authenticity.

GHT NEPAL ROUTE SUMMARY

There is no one prescribed Great Himalaya Trail route, it is more a collection of trail options that you can use to develop your own GHT. This guide describes the most extreme and challenging route along the Nepal Himalaya ranges, but should you choose to avoid some sections, that won't reduce the validity of your GHT experience.

Section 1: Eastern Nepal – Kanchenjunga to Thame

From the Jhinsang La on the north side of Kanchenjunga the trail heads down past Kanchenjunga Base Camp to Ghunsa, then westwards over the Nango La to Olangchun Gola. Head northwest up and over the Lumbha Sambha, down through Thudam and along the Arun Nadi to Hongon. Climb back to the Tibetan border towards Popti Bhanjyang, but head west before the pass and then through the Saldim Khola and over to the Barun Khola. Then past Makalu Base Camp and over the Sherpani Col, West Col and Amphu Labsta to the Solu-Khumbu, where you cross the Cho La and the Renjo La to Thame.

Section 2: Central Nepal – Thame to Jomsom

Climb the Tashi Labsta and descend through the Rolwaling. Take the most northerly exit route towards Kodari, cross the Bhote Koshi and trek up to Bhairav Kund. To the northwest is a low mountainous region that must be crossed before crossing the Tilman East Pass into the Langtang valley. Descend to Syabru Besi, continue to Gatlang then cross the Ganesh Himal foothills to the Manaslu Circuit. Continue around to Dharapani then around the Annapurna Circuit to Kagbeni.

Section 3: Western Nepal – Jomsom to Mahakali Nadi

From Kagbeni head northwest into Dolpo via Chharka Bhot and then pick one of two routes; either westwards to Dho Tarap and Ringmo and then north to Pho, or alternatively, head northwest from Chharka Bhot to Shimengaon and then west to Pho. Then take one of the two routes to the Mugu Karnali Nadi valley and descend to Gamgadhi. From here there are two route options: the shorter is to Simikot and then to the Yari valley where the Tibet border effectively stops your trek; the other crosses from Gamgadhi to Rara Lake National Park, and then across minor passes to the south of Saipal and Api Himals and on to the Indian border on the Mahakali Nadi. The second route offers trail continuity, whereas the first takes you through the Great Himalaya Range.

Kanchenjunga region

Lush rhododendron forests, dramatic mountain vistas, communities that abound in folklore and the third highest peak in the world, Mt Kanchenjunga, all combine to make this a paradise for trekking off the beaten path. Located in far-eastern Nepal, on the border with Sikkim, the Kanchenjunga Conservation Area (KCA) was one of the first areas of the Himalaya to be explored in the nineteenth century and yet it remains largely unvisited by tourists outside of October.

The Nepal side of the Kanchenjunga massif is split into two sections: the remote valleys that lie beneath the horseshoe-shaped southwest face and ridges,

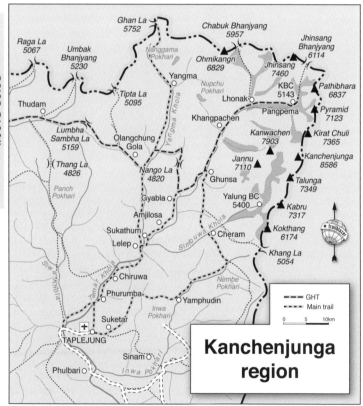

ROUTE GUIDE

around Yalung, and the north face where the Base Camp for mountaineering groups is sited. Dozens of peaks form a maze of ridges that isolate communities from the lower valleys. Treks to this region are a little longer than those to the most popular areas, but spending a little extra time here will prove more than worthwhile as you get to explore one of the wilder corners of the Himalaya.

Most trekkers arrive at Taplejung (Suketar airstrip), which attracts a lively combination of Sherpa, Limbu, Rai and Gurung people, especially for the Saturday market. You then drop to the Tamor Khola, through dense jungle and picturesque villages, before reaching some magnificent rhododendron forests on the way to Kanchenjunga Base Camp at Pangpema. A challenging side trip is up to the Jhinsang La, the starting point of the Great Himalaya Trail in Nepal. The GHT follows a route down through Ghunsa and heads west to Olangchun Gola, which also makes for a great side trip. From Olangchun Gola the GHT crosses the untamed wilderness of the Lumbha Sambha, home to snow leopard, blue sheep and, for the believer, the Yeti! Then you descend to what is perhaps the most isolated community in Nepal, Thudam, before reaching the welcoming and charming Lhomi people of the Arun Nadi valley.

The KCA is the first region in Nepal to be managed by local communities and has so far proved very successful along the main trail, but is yet to be fully effective in remoter valleys. Trekking is still in its infancy in much of the KCA so tread lightly and encourage sustainable practices wherever you can.

KANCHENJUNGA BASE CAMP

The return trek to Kanchenjunga Base Camp takes about 20 days and can be combined with a number of trails to explore some magnificent wilderness areas. If you want to visit the southern valleys of Kanchenjunga, then begin your trek by first heading to Yalung and then joining the main trail at Ghunsa.

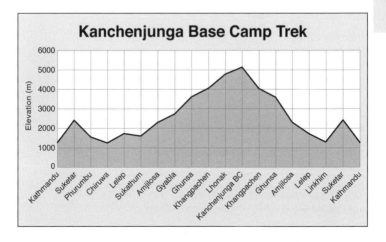

ROUTE GUIDE

KANCHENJUNGA BASE CAMP TREK

See the third highest mountain in the world up close, trek on glaciers, challenge yourself on high mountain passes, enjoy spectacular forests of rhododendron and the openhearted hospitality of Sherpa, Limbu, Rai and Lhomi communities.

Duration: from 20 days

Highest Point: 5143m

Best Season: Apr-May/Oct-Nov

Accommodation: camping or very basic teahouses.

Another great option is over the Nango La from Ghunsa to the intriguing communities of Olangchun Gola and Yangma, which can both be used to explore some really remote mountains.

There are two main seasons for visiting Kanchenjunga, April-May and October-November, which offer very different trekking experiences.

Being isolated from the other main ranges in far-east Nepal, Kanchenjunga is renowned for making its own weather and suffering from heavy monsoonal rains. After the monsoon has finished the mountains are free of lingering cloud and the views in late October and November are probably at their best.

By mid-December snow closes the higher trails, which will not open again until mid to late March at the earliest. The pre-monsoon period is famous for stunning forests of rhododendron that begin at Suketar and continue throughout the trek, and are perhaps the most extensive throughout the Himalaya.

Getting to and from the Kanchenjunga region can be time consuming. In the main trekking seasons a scheduled flight operates between Biratnagar and Suketar a few times a week.

For the remainder of the year, you either have to catch a bus to Taplejung or Phidim, or charter a helicopter to Suketar.

❑ **The Limbu**
Limbuwan (the Limbu homeland) extends east from the Arun Nadi to the Indian border at Sikkim, and includes Taplejung and Ilam. Most of their villages are between 750 and 1200 metres in altitude.

Like the Rai, their houses are in the middle of their fields and are generally single storey stone buildings with thatched roofs. Richer folk will use slate for their roof, and the house will be larger than average with a wooden balcony running around the first floor.

They cultivate maize, rice, wheat and millet, which they use for food and for *rakshi* and *tongba* (locally made alcohol). Limbus have arranged marriages, but more often prefer capture/abduction or elopement. Abduction marriages are where a girl is 'taken' from a public place and kept in the boy's home for three days. If the girl agrees, the wedding will be arranged; if not she is free to return to her parents. This is certainly a less expensive alternative to big arranged marriages.

Limbu marriage customs and religions are similar to Rai, who can be described as ethnic cousins.

DAY 1: KATHMANDU – TAPLEJUNG/ SUKETAR 2HRS

There are no scheduled direct flights to Suketar (2420m) from Kathmandu, you either have to fly via Biratnagar (causing an overnight delay), charter your own flight, or use a combination of flight and bus to the large Limbu settlement of Taplejung (1820m). Bad weather can delay flights so it is wise to organise a second option, just in case.

If you arrive late in the day at Suketar there are some simple teahouses next to the airport, alternatively it is an easy downhill walk for 2 hours to Taplejung.

DAY 2: SUKETAR/TAPLEJUNG – PHURUMBU 4HRS

Suketar sits within a web of trails that can easily confuse, so make sure you walk with your guide or ask locals for directions at trail junctions.

From the airstrip follow a grass-covered trail northwards for 20 to 30 minutes which brings you to a major trail junction where you turn right. Ask for Bhotegaon if you are confused. The trail slowly descends providing views of the Tamor Khola valley below to your left.

This is a very fertile region with three crops being produced per year; depending on the season and altitude it might be rice, millet, corn, potatoes, cauliflowers or green vegetables that surround you. Slowly curving northwards the trail moves on to a spur that suddenly steepens at Gadidanda (1890m, 2½ hours).

The 350m descent is on a muddy trail that is slippery when wet, so take care. There is a good camping site in the school at Phurumbu (1542m, 1 hour) to the left of the trail just before the end of the steep section.

DAY 3: PHURUMBU – CHIRUWA 6HRS

The trail dips and climbs slightly as you pass a stream, and then again after Baishakhe (1520m, sometimes also called Moyam, 1 hour). Now the descent towards the Tamor Khola continues, first to Linkhim (1300m), then Tawa (1120m, 1 hour) before finally reaching the valley floor before Nagadin (1050m, 4 hours).

The villages you pass through are part of a historically important region in Nepal; this is where the Kirati warriors came from who first tried to unite the many kingdoms of the Himalaya into a single sovereign state.

The trail climbs slightly as you approach Chiruwa (1270m, 40 minutes), a compact settlement of teahouses, shops and school, all squeezed between the river and steep hillside. The campsite is 10 minutes further on and off the main trail.

DAY 4: CHIRUWA – SUKATHUM 5½HRS

After the heat of the previous afternoon it's a relief to start walking in the cool morning air from Chiruwa. The main trail remains on the river's south bank and if you get an early start you won't need to walk in the sun until just before the National Park check post at Taplechok (1380m, 1¾ hours).

It is necessary to stop and complete formalities with the National Park staff, perhaps over a cup of tea, and confirm if there are any landslides ahead, which might mean taking an alternative trail. From there, the west bank (left) trail first winds through cardamom fields and then in to dense forest before gradually climbing away from the Tamor Khola to Lelep (1750m, 3 hours) which has a small teahouse. A trail descends rapidly from Lelep to a suspension bridge across the Tamor Khola to Sukathum (1576m, 40 minutes) and a large campsite.

The east bank (right) trail follows the river before climbing a little after Tamewa (1420m, 2 hours), then down to the Simbuwa Khola at Hellok (1550m, 1 hour) where there is a small teahouse. A trail winds around to the Ghunsa Khola valley and across a suspension bridge to Sukathum (1576m, 30 minutes) and the campsite.

DAY 5: SUKATHUM – AMJILOSA 6HRS

This is the toughest and most dramatic day of the trek so far. Cross the suspension bridge at the Sukathum campsite and follow a trail through dense forest until the valley narrows in to a deep gorge (2 hours).

Waterfalls cascade down both sides of the valley, and the sound of the river will

ROUTE GUIDE

make conversation difficult. It is essential you concentrate on the trail.

Locals have built a stone walkway beneath a cliff face along the river's waterline, which makes for some great pictures but care is needed at all times. After negotiating this section, there is another hour of dense forest trail before you come to a bridge at the base of a steep climb. Switchbacks ascend 350m (2 hours) before the gradient eases, about 1 hour before Amjilosa (2308m).

DAY 6: AMJILOSA – GYABLA (KYAPRA)   5HRS

The trail leaving Amjilosa wastes no time in climbing a minor ridge to a sharp turn to the north (30 minutes). The forest is dense and dark as you again descend towards the Ghunsa Khola at Thyanyani (2405m, 1 hour) and the first of a few slippery log bridges across a stream. There are a few small stone shelters here which are normally only used by herders in monsoon.

For the first time in a number of days the trail doesn't seem to continually climb up and down, as the valley widens slightly and feels less claustrophobic.

After the third bridge (2 hours) the trail climbs another steep track for roughly 300m (2 hours), the last section beside a stream can be slippery so care is needed.

You crest the climb and find yourself on the outskirts of the picturesque village of Gyabla (2730m).

For those with time and energy there is a pleasant walk up behind the village with views of the Birdhungga Danda.

DAY 7: GYABLA (KYAPRA) – GHUNSA   4½HRS

After the previous week this day marks a change in the flora and fauna along the trail. At first, the trail seems much like that of the previous afternoon; a broader valley bottom permits views of the river and hillsides, which continue for 1½ hours. Then the trail climbs for 200m (1 hour) and suddenly you notice rhododendron, camellias, and azaleas rather than bamboo and cardamom beside the trail.

The village of Phale (Phere, 3140m) is spread over a large area. The first houses are

the winter village for Ghunsa, before the village proper (30 minutes). This is a Tibetan refugee settlement where it's possible to buy handicrafts and homemade rugs from some of the locals, ask around when you arrive and potential sellers will soon find you.

From Phale a pretty trail winds through dwarf conifer and pine forest before arriving at Ghunsa (3595m, 1½ hours) in a very broad section of valley. Waterfalls fall from the steep cliffs above this Sherpa village that feels like the edge of nowhere on a cloudy day.

DAY 8: GHUNSA   ALL DAY

As you have now passed the 3000m mark, it is wise to take a rest day at Ghunsa. You can relax and explore the village.

Sherpa hospitality is legendary, and the local school is proud to show off its computer (you can charge iPods here for a donation).

Alternatively, explore the Yamtari Khola which boasts a fantastic view of Jannu (7711m) from the south – continue up the left hand side of the river until you reach some herders' huts, then climb to your left for a viewpoint.

This valley is also the route to the disused and dangerous Lapsang La (5161m), as well as Selele La (4290m) and Sinion La (4440m) both of which offer interesting route variations to/from Yalung if you have camping gear.

DAY 9: GHUNSA – KHANGPACHEN (KHAMBACHEN)   5½HRS

Pine, deodar and rhododendron forest, grassy glades dotted with wild flowers, and increasingly spectacular mountain scenery combine into what is perhaps the most impressive section of trail along the entire trek.

It will take about 1½ hours to reach the bridge across the main river before Rampuk Kharka (3720m), which is often blocked with sticks to prevent yaks from wandering. The trail now climbs almost 400m past, then through, a large landslide (beware of rockfall) beside the terminal moraine of the Kanchenjunga Glacier to 4100m (2½ hours).

A brief traverse of the hillside might offer a glimpse of Jannu before descending to the yak farming settlement of Khangpachen (Khambachen, 4050m, 1½ hours).

DAY 10: KHANGPACHEN (KHAMBACHEN) ALL DAY

A day to acclimatise is normally taken at Khangpachen, where there are two great day walks to help you adjust to the 700m altitude gain tomorrow.

One route is to explore the valley directly behind Khangpachen, and walk up to the base of Tha Nagphu (5980m), a massive snow and rock dome that you can see from the village.

Alternatively, for those feeling fit, cross the river and climb the left-hand side of the Kumbhakarna Glacier lateral moraine to the popular pilgrimage site beneath the massive vertical north face of Jannu – there is a large boulder and plenty of prayer flags to mark a viewpoint.

DAY 11: KHANGPACHEN (KHAMBACHEN) – LHONAK 5HRS

The trail away from Khangpachen is surprisingly easy as you gradually climb scrubby lateral moraine for 1 hour. Then comes perhaps the hardest and most dangerous section of the entire trek, a climb up a long section of landslide, mostly across large boulders, which takes about 2½ hours.

It is wise to keep moving, however slowly, across this section and complete the climb as early as possible as the risk of rock fall increases throughout the day.

Once across the stream from the waterfall section the trail climbs steeply (beware of rockfall) for a short section to the top of an ancient lateral moraine at 4670m (a popular lunch stop), where the gradient eases as you cross some scrub and grass covered moraine. On the far side is the Lhonak Khola, which you follow to a seasonal bridge and a few stone shelters at Lhonak (4780m, 2 hours).

DAY 12: LHONAK ALL DAY

The large sandy bed of the Lhonak Khola offers an inviting walk for an acclimatisation trip. It is important that you are prepared for, and understand the hazards of river crossings if you want to fully explore this valley.

It is possible to explore a rough track along the western edge of the Lhonak glacier to the confluence of the Chabuk and Chijima glaciers at 5080m, 5 hours return.

Alternatively, you can enjoy the views of Gimmigela, Wedge Peak, Nepal Peak and Tent Peak (Tharpu Chuli) that line and head the valley to the east. Try to spot the rock pinnacle on the far side of the glacier, just at the point it turns southwest.

DAY 13: LHONAK – KANCHENJUNGA BASE CAMP 4HRS

The trail from Lhonak climbs gently along the massive lateral moraine of the

ROUTE GUIDE

❏ **Olangchun people – the Holung**

One of the most important trade routes from Nepal to Tibet passes along the upper Tamur Valley, with its centre at Olangchun Gola (known locally as Holung). A local legend tells of a wolf that showed a passing trader the trail to Tibet, thus the village name Olang (wolf), chun' (trader) and Gola (place or village). The people here are closely related to the Thudam and Topke Gola communities. Exports to Tibet include cloth, cotton thread, grain, *gur* (brown sugar), matches, cigarettes and other items from India. These are exchanged for Tibetan salt, wool and carpets.

Holung people travel extensively for trade, as far as Lhasa, Delhi and even Mumbai, and they are therefore relatively well informed about the outside world compared to many of the mountain neighbours. Their houses are built of stone to the floor level and then completed with wood. The ground floor is for storage and the living quarters are above. The village houses are built in a row along a paved street. They practise Buddhism and have a beautiful but old gompa in the village, which desperately needs some repairs.

Kanchenjunga glacier for the first 2 hours. It's hard not to stop and admire the views of the peaks and the glacier below.

A short steep section of loose rock and landslide formed by a side river will take 40 minutes to 1 hour to cross. The trail then climbs more gently for another hour before you reach the few stone huts of Kanchenjunga Base Camp (5143m).

Expedition groups will probably not have a permanent camp here, however, as an advanced base camp across the glacier has become a preferred spot.

DAYS 14-21
Return to Suketar along same route, then fly to Kathmandu.

ROUTES FROM KANCHENJUNGA BASE CAMP

If you have experienced crew, or can employ a local guide, it is worth the effort to continue along a small, dangerous trail that climbs around the massive curve in the glacier to the north. This route is very rarely trekked and after 3 hours will require you to traverse and then walk across a glacier; beyond here you will need ropes and associated climbing equipment.

After two days you reach the Jhinsang La and the border with Sikkim and Tibet. Expect to take another two days to return, see the **GHT – Kanchenjunga** below. Be paranoid about the weather, this is not a place to get caught out.

The small river that creates the landslide and loose rock about 1 hour below Kanchenjunga Base Camp flows from a glacier complex on Mera Peak. To either side of the river are two minor rocky summits of close to 6000m, which do not require permits to climb and are fantastic viewpoints.

OTHER MAJOR TRAILS IN THE KANCHENJUNGA REGION

From Ghunsa, there is a trail to Olangchun Gola via the Nango La, which takes a total of three days to complete, see *GHT – Kanchenjunga* below for details. The trail from Olangchun Gola back to Lelep / Sekatum takes two days; there is a convenient riverside camp at Jongin, after 3½ hours of walking on the first day.

It is possible to trek to a remote 5700m Tibetan border pass via Yangma without any additional permits. Camping is the only option, but if you have the time this is one of the most remote corners of the entire Himalaya. Allow three to four days from Ghunsa to Yangma, then four days minimum (without an

---

❏ **The people of Thudam**
West of Olangchun Gola is a series of valleys where the people of Thudam, which is a place name rather than an ethnic group, live. These people have no land of their own, so they rent a little farming land east of the Arun Nadi from the Lhomi people. Individual families own pulping mills where they make juniper wood incense, which is very popular in Tibet. The mills are very basic: a wooden shaft a metre or so long is turned by a waterwheel. The rough block of sandstone, which is attached to the ground, is scraped with the small juniper log – the resulting pulp is dried in the sun and then sold. They also keep yaks, which are mainly used as pack animals.

acclimatisation stop) to reach the border and return to Yangma, and a further two tough days to Olangchun Gola, where it would be wise to rest for a day or two.

An alternative route from Suketar to Ghunsa via Yamphudin, Cheram (Tseram), Yalung Base Camp is a great trail to create a circular trek. It requires camping gear and takes 10 to 14 days depending on your route.

GHT – KANCHENJUNGA

The Great Himalaya Trail starts from the Jhinsang La, a two-day walk from Kanchenjunga Base Camp. The approach to the pass is along the left hand side of the Jhinsang Glacier; it is wise to employ a local guide from Ghunsa as the route changes frequently. Crossing the pass into Sikkim is not permitted.

From the pass follow the main trail to Ghunsa (see the reverse *Kanchenjunga Base Camp*, days 9-13, pp120) and then to Olangchun Gola as follows:

From Ghunsa, descend the main trail beside the Ghunsa Khola for 1½ hours to a trail junction, just before the Yangma Samba Khola (before Phale) that descends from the Nango La valley to your right. Ascend a small trail, first through scrubby pine forest and then grassy hillside for 3¼ hours to a series of *kharka* (summer grazing pasture), which offer some rough tent platforms.

The following morning get an early start for the Nango La (4776m, 1¼ hours), as cloud often obscures the view. Once over the pass descend to a bowl-shaped valley, where a *dharamsala* (emergency shelter) has been built recently. Livestock have made the ground around the dharamsala very muddy so only stay here if you have no other choice.

Descend to the west on the northern (right) bank of a stream, which rapidly grows in size, and then through dense woodland before entering the Yangma Khola valley. The trail swings north, up the valley, for about 1 hour before descending to the Yangma Khola bridge (3430m, 5 hours from the pass).

Walk downstream on the western (right) bank of the Yangma Khola and then turn west (right) into the Tamor Khola valley (2800m, 2½ hours). Do not cross the bridge over the river: you must stay on the northern (right) bank following a broad trail to Olangchun Gola (3191m, 1½ hours).

From Olangchun Gola head northwest for 3½ hours along the Tamor Khola, which brings you to a river confluence and bridge, which you cross to head up the Dingsamba Khola. There is a campsite at the confluence of the two rivers (3712m).

A small trail through dense rhododendron forest climbs to a large, flat valley used by herders (1½ hours). At the end of the valley a trail climbs up and over a black rock band into another, smaller valley (4453m, 2½ hours), where you should camp.

A stream cascades down a rocky slope on your left; climb the broken trail on the northwest side of the stream. You then reach a plateau (1½ hours) with a lake and views of the Lumbha Sambha.

Climb the ridge on your right (northern side of the small plateau), heading for the northernmost of three obvious saddles. There is a small trail to follow but

❏ The Lhomi

Lhomi live in the upper Arun Nadi valley in eastern Nepal in Sankhuwasabha district, one of the most remote regions along the northern border of Nepal. Their 'main' villages are Hatiya, Hongon (Hangaun) and Gomba (which has one of only two gompas for the region), which cling to the steep slopes above the Arun Nadi gorge. They are often isolated from each other, and they mainly trade to the south as far as the terai.

Lhomi marriages are always by choice. They grow enough maize, millet, barley wheat and potatoes for their own needs, and the villagers keep cattle and *dzum* (yak crossbreeds) for ploughing, and sheep for wool and meat. They have only recently learned how to milk their cows. The dzum are often sold to Olangchun Gola people. Their houses are erected on piles, with bamboo walls and wild straw thatch. Although not well off economically, they are friendly, hospitable and cheerful. They are not ardent Buddhists, as they will kill animals for meat and follow Shamanism.

snow often obscures your route. You should crest the saddle (5136m, 1 hour, Finaid: Topkegola, sheet: 2787 07, ref: 658 697) after another hour.

Do not descend into the Palun Khola valley below. There is a small trail that traverses beneath a peak marked 5422m on the map to another saddle and the Lumbha Sambha La proper (5159m, 30 minutes, Finaid: Topkegola, sheet: 2787 07, ref: 642 688), with views of Kanchenjunga and Jannu to the east and Makalu to the west.

An easy-to-follow trail descends to the northwest into a large valley and the source of the Lapsi Khola. This valley has many campsites and after another day you should reach the strongly Tibetan-influenced community of Thudam (3556m, 4 hours).

The trail gradually becomes overgrown and harder to follow as you descend the Medokchheje Khola. Just before a large wood-cutting camp the trail climbs (3020m, 1½ hours, Finaid: Tiptala Bhanjyan, sheet: 2787 03, ref: 512 707) and splits again after 30 minutes of climbing, take the west (left) fork.

A sometimes scrambly trail winds around ridges and climbs to a minor pass (3369m, 2 hours) before descending into dense forest beyond where you can camp in a small sloping *kharka* (1½ hours). The trail continues in much the same vein to another kharka (2 hours) dominated by a large rock.

The trail goes to the right of the rock and climbs steeply to another minor pass (2820m, 1 hour) before a long descent to a bridge over the Arun Nadi below (1850m, 2 hours).

You are bound to receive a warm welcome from the Lhomi people in Chyamtang (2187m, 1 hour), where you can also now enjoy the luxury of a main trail.

It is an easy day to Hongon (2323m, 5½ hours) where you will need to stock up on food and fuel before embarking on the next section to the Makalu region.

Makalu region

The Makalu region is known for being wild and high, and has some of the most dramatic mountain scenery in the Himalaya. Sometimes described as the Yosemite of Nepal, but with glaciers on top of the mountains, this region offers unbridled wilderness to explore. Sandwiched between Kanchenjunga and the Solu-Khumbu (Everest) regions, the massive Makalu-Barun National Park and Buffer Zone rarely sees more than a few hundred trekkers each season.

Dozens of peaks surround the Honku Khola and Basin in the west of the National Park, including the popular Mera Peak and the infamous Amphu Labsta

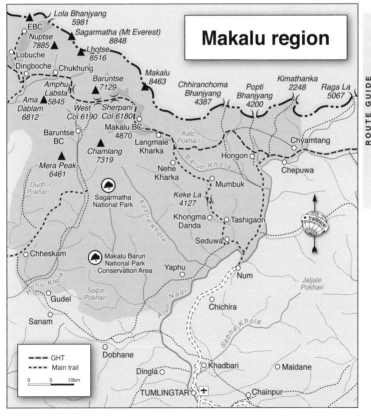

pass. To the north, Mt Makalu (8485m) straddles the border with Tibet and is reached via the Barun Khola, which flows east to join the Arun Nadi in Lhomi country. An outgoing mix of Sherpa and Rai communities populate the valleys in the southern Buffer Zone, but no one lives in the centre of the Park, which is home to many endangered species including snow leopard and red panda.

Most trekkers begin their adventure from Tumlingtar, a sprawling Rai settlement, and follow a long ridge-top dirt road to Num (via Khadbari), before crossing the Arun Nadi. The next few days are tough as you climb up and over the Khongma Danda, but the views and cloud forest adorned with orchids are ample reward. You then descend to join the Great Himalaya Trail through the sparsely populated Barun Khola valley to Makalu Base Camp. If you are coming from Kanchenjunga along the GHT then you'll get to explore some wild and remote trails that run parallel with the Tibetan border. Once at the Barun Glacier, above Makalu Base Camp, you can cross some of the toughest and highest mountaineering passes in the Himalaya: the Sherpani Col (6180m), the West Col (6190m) and the Amphu Labsta (5845m) to the Everest region.

A recent burst of teahouse-building activity means the trail to Makalu Base Camp has a ready-made stop for each day/night of the trek. Facilities and food are basic, and a little on the expensive side for Nepal, but it does now mean you can avoid carrying tents and cooking equipment during the main trekking seasons.

Makalu-Barun is the largest of Nepal's National Park and Buffer Zones. Local herders are permitted to graze animals and are encouraged to take an active role in conservation projects.

MAKALU BASE CAMP

The return trek to Makalu Base Camp takes about 15 days if you take a jeep to Num from Tumlingtar and return via the same route. However, you could create a long mountaineering route across the high passes to the Everest region, either via the Amphu Labsta or by descending the Honku Khola. Both of these routes take you to Lukla where you can either fly to Kathmandu or take the trail to Jiri (see *Other major trails in the Solu-Khumbu*, p142). If you are returning to Tumlingtar from Makalu, consider taking the rougher riverside trail along the Arun Nadi instead of retracing your steps from Seduwa.

Like most mountain regions in Nepal, the best time to visit is during the main trekking seasons of April-May or October-November. Throughout winter (December to March) and monsoon (June to mid-October) the

MAKALU BASE CAMP TREK

A genuine Himalayan wilderness experience, with towering cliffs and hanging glaciers. Stand at the foot of the massive bulk of Makalu, while old growth rhododendron and pine forests surround picturesque and welcoming Rai and Sherpa villages.

Duration: from 15 days

Highest Point: 4825m

Best Season: Apr-May/Oct-Nov

Accommodation: camping or simple teahouses

ROUTE GUIDE

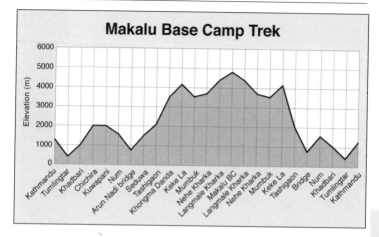

Makalu Base Camp Trek

Arun Nadi and Barun Khola valley systems funnel wet weather towards Makalu, dumping large amounts of snow on the both the Khongma Danda and Shipton's Pass, closing them. During the pre-monsoon spring season the extensive rhododendron and orchid forests that cover the Kongma Danda bloom in a multitude of colours and provide a welcome distraction from the tough climb. The clear air of the post-monsoon period makes for some excellent mountain photography and is probably the best time of year to cross the high passes to see Mt Everest.

There are several scheduled flights a day between Tumlingtar and Kathmandu, and Tumlingtar and Biratnagar, as well as bus services. If you cross to the Everest region then make sure you have purchased your flight tickets out of Lukla, as there can be long waiting lists in October.

DAY 1: KATHMANDU – TUMLINGTAR – NUM   ALL DAY

It is a good idea to get the earliest possible flight to Tumlingtar's grass airstrip (410m) and take the first available jeep to Num, but should you need to camp there is a good grassy site near the airport as well as some simple teahouses. The return jeep journey from Num to Tumlingtar will mean you'll have to overnight near the airstrip, so it is prudent to book teahouse accommodation or camping space when you first arrive.

For those wanting to walk to Num, either because they have the time or the road is closed, the trek takes three days. From Tumlingtar ascend a long ridge running north from the edge of the sprawling

town around the airstrip to the Newari and Rai village of Khadbari (1040m, 3 hours walking from the airport), it's an exposed trail so take plenty of water and sun cream. Khadbari is the administrative centre for the enormous Makalu-Barun National Park and Conservation Area and you will need to register at the park office. Try and coincide your visit with a market day on Wednesdays and Saturdays. There is a campsite next to the large school in the middle of the town.

The following day continue along the ridge through picturesque villages to Mane Bhanjyang (1100m, 1 hour), where you can see the trail climbing a small hillside basin to a minor pass at Bhotebas (1740m, 3½ hours). On a clear day there are good views of Makalu from a point about 10 minutes beyond the pass and from spots along trail for the next few hours. The next village, Gogane (1720m, 20 minutes) offers an excellent campsite if you are running a little late. Follow the road through moss-covered forest along the ridge to Chichira (1980m, 1 hour) and a large camping area; there are also some simple teahouses here.

It's a good idea to get an early start on the final day to Num to get clear views of Makalu before the jeeps drive by and kick up dust. The village of Kuwapani (2010m, 1 hour) sits hunched on a narrow section of ridge at a major trail junction. Take the right hand trail that traverses beneath a triangular hill and passes through Satbaini (Sakurate, 1920m, 20 minutes).

After another 1 hour you come to a minor pass, the Dauj La (Dhara Deurali, 2100m) before descending, gradually at first, and then through a steep section of forest with many trails. It is important to stick together through this forested section, as some trails lead down to the Arun Nadi valley and it is easy to take the wrong path. From the pass it is 2 hours and 30 minutes to the large village of Num (1560m), which has a grassy campsite and some teahouses.

DAY 2: NUM – SEDUWA   4½HRS

If you look across the valley to the north-west, you will see the day's destination, the village of Seduwa. The main trail from Num continues along the ridge before curving back on itself to lose height. However, there is also a direct route down some rough steps, which begins near the campsite.

In 1½ hours you should reach the Arun Nadi (760m) and its suspension bridge. The dense, moist forest of the east bank contrasts to the open deciduous forest on the west bank before giving way to cultivation.

It will take about 3 hours to climb to Seduwa (1500m), a large trading village with views of countless mid-hills receding into the distance. You will need to register again with the National Park office.

DAY 3: SEDUWA – TASHIGAON
4HRS

Today is the last day of walking though villages as you draw closer to the Khongma Danda, the large and imposing forested ridge at the end of the valley. An easy trail to Murmidanda (1560m, 1 hour) brings you to a school where the children will almost certainly break class to ask you questions.

The climb to Narbugaon (2000m, 1½ hours) eases to become a straightforward trail that traverses hillside through cultivated fields. As Tashigaon (2100m, 1 hour) is the last village on the trail, your guide will spend some time re-stocking food and fuel supplies. It is important that you also research trail conditions for the coming

---

❏ The Rai

Rai settlements are along the Dudh Koshi and Arun Nadi, usually between 1000 and 2000 metres in altitude. They live in single storey stone houses with thatched or slate roofs. Their villages are generally spread out, like Sherpas', with each house in the family field. Some Rai houses are built up on wooden piles, with a notched ladder to get you up to the first floor. Animals live under the veranda, and the walls and roof are made from bamboo. They use wet and dry fields to grow rice, maize, wheat, millet and vegetables and fruit such as beans, potatoes, bananas and guava.

Men and women smoke cigarettes of locally grown tobacco. Rais have arranged marriages, but more commonly capture/abduct or elope. Their religion is quite complex having been influenced by Tibetan Buddhism and Hinduism, and incorporates many local mountain deities. Within the home, the cooking fire is sacred and visitors should never throw anything into the flames. They frequently build stone *chautara* (resting platforms) and wooden benches shaded by a pipal tree, which provide shade and rest for travellers (yes, even trekkers!) as a memorial for their dead. Along with the Limbu, they often join one of the Gurkha regiments.

days, check if there is any snow or hazards on the trail, and that locals are using the route. You will be told that there are no supplies up the Barun Khola valley; this is not true during the main trekking seasons, as all basic supplies are available, although expensive, all the way to Makalu Base Camp.

DAY 4: TASHIGAON – KHONGMA DANDA   7HRS
The trail climbs, often steeply, through some of the most impressive cloud-forest in Nepal. It is important that you climb slowly, rest frequently, and perhaps take some time to admire the clusters of orchids hanging above. Make sure you have enough water and snacks to last the day, as there is no convenient lunch spot with running water.

Unshisa (3110m, 5 hours) is the first potential campsite and there is a small teashop open in the main trekking season.

You now climb on to the Khongma Danda and your campsite (3500m, 2 hours) will offer morning views of Makalu, with Peak 6 and Peak 7 in the foreground. When you reach camp you should check the entire group, including your porters, for symptoms of altitude sickness.

DAY 5: KHONGMA DANDA ALL DAY
Acclimatisation day. It is important that you begin the day by checking again for any signs of altitude sickness. Some of your group may have had a restless night, make sure they remain hydrated and rest. There is not much to do other than explore the surrounding forest and enjoy the views, so relax and unwind, soak your feet and consume as much water as possible.

DAY 6: KHONGMA DANDA – MUMBUK   7½HRS
Today is the toughest day on the trek so far and you must be on the lookout for altitude-sickness symptoms in the party. The day begins by continuing along the ridge past the prayer-flag-covered Kauma La (3603m, 1½ hours) with views of Makalu, Chamlang, Baruntse, and if the weather to the east is clear, Kanchenjunga and Jannu.

The trail now climbs to the left of the main ridge up to the Tutu La (Shipton's

Pass, 4125m, 2½ hours) before descending for 200m to a large lake called Kalo Pokhari, which can offer sublime reflections of Peaks 6 and 7 and Chamlang in calm, clear conditions.

A short climb up to Keke La (4170m, 1 hour) gives views of the Chamlang range and Tibet to the north, the Barun Khola flows almost 1000m below.

A two and a half hour descent is steep and rocky all the way to the stone huts and campsite of Mumbuk (3540m).

DAY 7: MUMBUK – NEHE KHARKA   4½HRS
The trail descends to the Barun Khola before turning left and traversing steep hillside, which is often affected by landslides.

Note: In 2009, this trail had become so dangerous that locals were discussing building a bridge to the far bank of the Barun Khola. Seek local advice for developments.

You should take care when crossing any loose ground, as well as watching for rockfall from above.

Then about 4½ hours of alternate loose landslide and stable trails brings you to Nehe Kharka (3700m) and a good campsite in a meadow surrounded by pine trees.

During the monsoon, normally for the August full moon, there is a fertility festival here as a tradition tells that a famous Buddhist sage, Guru Rimpoche, stayed in a cave high above.

DAY 8: NEHE KHARKA – LANGMALE KHARKA   5HRS
More loose sections of trail, with an occasional well-formed path, continue beside the Barun Khola before crossing on a log bridge to a wide grassy field called Yangri Kharka (Yangla Kharka, 3557m, 2 hours). There are a number of teahouses here, along with basic supplies and a very large campsite.

The next section of trail is perhaps one of the most spectacular in the entire Himalaya as you wind through rhododendron, fir and pine forest. Yosemite-like cliffs form an enormous U-shaped valley crested with glaciers, and a series of snowy peaks including Pyramid Peak, Peak 4,

ROUTE GUIDE

Peak 6, Chamlang and Peak 5 all show themselves. In one monstrous rock face a massive cave contains a waterfall in free-fall. *Lumdar* (strings of prayer flags) are suspended from poles to mark a pilgrimage site popular during the July/August full moon, when it is said that the waters here can cure many illnesses.

For 3 hours you'll keep stopping and absorbing the evolving panorama, before arriving in Langmale Kharka (4410m), which has a couple of teahouses and camp-sites well apart.

DAY 9: LANGMALE KHARKA – MAKALU BASE CAMP   4HRS

The avenue of mountains that line your route become ever more spectacular as Peak 3 and the snout of the West Barun Glacier appear. From Langmale Kharka the trail enters an ancient lateral moraine through which the infant Barun Khola flows. A large glacial lake fills the valley to your left and

an easy-to-follow trail leads to Shersong (4630m, 2½ hours), a large grassy area used by yak herders in the monsoon months.

Turn right and follow an obvious trail that climbs more moraine, and, once on top, maintain your height; do not descend into the valley to your left. A number of small trails (formed by yak herds) stay about 100m above the valley floor before finally descending to a small bridge and the stone huts of Makalu Base Camp (4870m, 2 hours).

Expeditions have left all sorts of sup-plies here over the years and it is possible to buy anything from kerosene to apple jam and dehydrated meals.

To the north, the massive bulk of Makalu rises almost two miles (3500m) to a pyramid summit; this is truly one of the most spectacular mountain viewpoints in Nepal.

DAYS 10-15

Return to Tumlingtar along same route, then fly to Kathmandu.

ROUTES FROM MAKALU BASE CAMP

Makalu Base Camp has now become a staging post for expeditions rather than a full-blown base camp. Most expeditions now climb to a valley on the north-east side of Makalu to an advanced base at 5780m. To get there, follow the trail up and past Hillary Base Camp before descending to and crossing the Barun Glacier on a loose trail (3 hours). A few small tracks run through the lateral moraine on the far north side of the glacier, beware of rockfall in this area. You eventually reach a small waterfall and the trail turns in to the Makalu La valley (2 hours). Some small stone shelters have been built by porters at 5500m, advanced base camp lies further up this valley on the left hand side (2 hours).

Sherpani Col, West Col and Amphu Labsta

Those with mountaineering experience and equipment may choose to cross three passes over 6000m (Sherpani Col, West Col and Amphu Labsta) into the Solu-Khumbu (Everest Region). If you want to attempt the high passes you should have a guide or climbing sherpa who knows the route well. Identifying the route and avoiding crevasses can be very difficult, especially if snow covers the trail.

From Makalu Base Camp follow the well-defined trail to Hillary Base Camp and then continue along a smaller trail on the south side of the Barun Glacier valley. Do not descend to the *ablation valley* (created by snow and/or ice melt from a glacier) beside the glacier until forced to do so, and camp at a small area known as the Swiss Base Camp (3 hours, Finaid: Mount Makalu, sheet: 2787 01, ref: 049 825). Just beyond the campsite the trail becomes hard to follow as it climbs towards a steep boulder-filled stream (Finaid: Mount Makalu, sheet: 2787 01, ref: 043 829) that flows from a valley opposite Makalu. Identifying this valley can be difficult, especially in cloudy weather. Climb to boulders to the north (right) of the watercourse for about 300m. The gradient then eases and ahead you will then see a small trail ascending the northern side of a rocky valley. There is a small flat area (1½ hours) before the trail climbs further. After another hour you reach the Sherpani Col Base Camp (5688m), at the snout of a glacier. There are two routes that climb either side of the glacier snout, so you will need to do some reconnaissance to decide on the appropriate route. The first is to the south (left) of the snout and climbs mixed rock and ice, before veering onto the glacier. Beware of rockfall and crevasses on this route. The second option is to climb the rocky slope and gully to the north (right) of the glacier snout.

Once the gradient levels, step across onto the glacier and head towards the base of a rock face on the southern (left) hand side of the glacier, where it begins to rise towards the Col. Do not get too close to the rock face as there is constant danger from rockfall. Traverse across the base of the rock face to a point beneath some prayer flags, which are easily spotted on the rocky ridge above. Climb towards the prayer flags from rocks beside the glacier; this will require a hand-line (20m) for the first, loose scrambling section, and possibly another fixed rope for an easy 20m rock climb to the top of the Sherpani Col (6180m, 3-4 hours from Base Camp, Finaid: Mount Makalu, sheet: 2787 01, ref: 007 819).

You will need to abseil (35m) down to the West Barun Glacier, which you reach after crossing a snow-bridge over a *bergschrund* (a deep crevasse between a glacier and mountainside). **Beware of rockfall** while descending to the glacier. Cross the glacier (2-3 hours – **beware of crevasses**) to Baruntse Advanced Base Camp and the only spot on the glacier with some shelter from constant wind. Most groups elect to camp here and prepare the abseil over the West Col for early the following morning. To reach the West Col (6190m, Finaid: Sagarmatha, sheet: 2786 04, ref: 993 805) cross another bergschrund and climb a loose rocky route at the far southern end of the distinct rock wall that forms the pass. From the summit there is a 200m abseil into the Honku Basin and some potential campsites (3 hours) if you are going to head to the Amphu Labsta, or Baruntse Base Camp (4 hours) if you are exiting via the Honku Khola route. The full traverse normally takes about 11 hours, as time is lost preparing the abseils and fixing a rope up to the Sherpani and West cols.

The route to, and over, the Amphu Labsta (5845m, Finaid: Sagarmatha, sheet: 2786 04, ref: 929 832) to Chukhung (4730m, 15 hours from West Col base) is now popular with groups that have climbed Mera Peak. However, this is still probably the most dangerous pass in Nepal and care needs to be taken on both the ascent and descent. Most groups that attempt the pass camp beside one of the Panch Pokhari lakes and get an early start. A series of cairns are reached after about 1 hour after which you have to choose one of two routes to the pass: the more popular is up a series of ice cliffs, while the other climbs an exposed and steep rocky and snow-covered section direct to the pass. Full climbing equipment is required for either route and it is wise to fix any ropes in the afternoon prior to crossing. The descent is a bottleneck as there is a short abseil to a ledge, which then leads down steep rocky ground to the Amphu Labsta Glacier and the trail to Chukhung.

GHT – MAKALU

The route through the Makalu region is probably the most difficult section of the Great Himalaya Trail as it follows some rough trails only rarely used by locals when they search for medicinal plants, has many river crossings (especially post-monsoon), and three of the highest and most technical passes in the Himalaya. Only small (roughly 12 trekkers with crew), experienced groups who have climbing skills and equipment should attempt this route.

This section of the GHT begins with some particularly remote and small trails with occasionally confusing junctions, so you would be foolish not to employ a local guide from Chyamtang or Hongon at least for the Barun Khola valley. This trail can be very hard to follow in the Dhunge Khola and Saldim Khola valleys, even with Finaid maps and GPS. You should take a 50m rope for river crossings.

If you want to climb the high passes you should have a guide or climbing sherpa who knows the way very well. Identifying the route can be very difficult especially if snow covers the trail and alpine climbing guides are required for glacial travel.

From Hongon, climb a well-used trail that goes straight up to a ridgeline behind the village. There are some tall prayer flags beneath the ridge that mark a burial site. Avoid going there or taking photos of the site as it will only offend the locals and your crew will believe that any disrespect will bring bad luck. There are many small trails towards the top of the ridge, most of which are created by grazing animals, so it might take a little time to find the *chorten* that marks a minor pass (2710m, 1½ hours Finaid: Kimathanka, sheet: 2787 02, ref: 354 726).

Just after the pass the trail forks: you must go right; do not descend to your left. The trail traverses a hillside, crosses a stream and then climbs a small ridge before meeting the Tojo Khola. You need to stay on the east bank of this river and follow a trail made by woodcutters through rhododendron forest covered in moss. The Bakim Kharka (3020m, 2 hours, Finaid: Kimathanka, sheet: 2787 02, ref: 338 749) is a good campsite, and after another hour there is a smaller campsite at Khazakhani Kharka (3480m). The trail becomes steep and rocky but offers great views south of the Arun Nadi valley. Climb for nearly 500m (2½ hours), as you near the top of the plateau (3950m) there are some scrambling sections. A series of chortens mark the end of the climb and the edge of Molun Pokhari, a picturesque lake.

Note: there is a direct route to the Popti Bhanjyang plateau and thence Molun Pokhari from Chyamtang (see *GHT – Kanchenjunga*, p124), where you should ask for a local guide.

Wind around the north side of the lake to a large campsite in a valley to the west (3954m, 40 minutes, Finaid: Kimathanka, sheet: 2787 02, ref: 328 774). The trail to the Tibetan border, Popti Bhanjyang (4200m, 3 hours) can be seen heading north out of the valley. A small trail climbs a ridge to the south of the campsite, before heading southeast, then east to a rocky ascent that climbs a minor pass (4201m, 1 hour, Finaid: Kimathanka, sheet: 2787 02, ref: 316 767). Be careful not to take a small trail that heads south just before the pass. Just after the pass is a great view of Tin Pokhari and the eastern edge of the Makalu-Barun National Park. An easy-to-follow trail descends a ridge to your left; there will probably be some yaks around the lake. At a small lake on your left is another trail junction (30 minutes), go right and continue descending next to a small stream to the valley bottom. Cross the Dhunge Khola (the plank bridge is often washed away) to a large kharka on the far bank and continue down the valley to a drier campsite, which normally has a bamboo structure over a kharka (3590m, 1 hour, Finaid: Kimathanka, sheet: 2787 02, ref: 290 772).

A small trail through dense forest continues to follow the west bank of the Dhunge Khola. After 1½ hours, and rounding a ridge that draws you away from the main river valley, the trail forks beneath cliffs in the middle of a small clearing. Either descend a steep stream bed to your left (which doesn't look like a trail at all), or continue on a small trail that bears right and into the tributary valley of the Kholakharka Khola. The stream bed trail will take you to a large log (45 minutes) over the Kholakharka Khola, about 80m upstream of the confluence with the Dhunge Khola – after heavy rain this is a very difficult river crossing. The right-hand trail goes to a point where the river crossing over the Kholakharka Khola is safer but will add up to 1½ hours to your day. Either route will mean you remain on the west bank of the Dhunge Khola and can follow a small and overgrown trail to the Saldim Khola (2 hours, Finaid: Kimathanka, sheet: 2787 02, ref: 267 736). The trail passes a large hollow tree used by locals as shelter before descending a couple of metres to the watercourse. A large tree has been felled creating a bridge across the river, but you will require a couple of safety lines as the log can be slippery. A hard-to-find trail in dense rhododendron forest then climbs briefly, heading parallel to the Saldim Khola. The trail gets lost in the gouged-out river bed (almost certainly caused by a GLOF, Glacial Lake Outburst Flood) and you will need to find your own way through, across a boulder-strewn and shifting route (for about 1 hour) until you can see a large, slightly overhanging rock face on your left. Scout around and you should find a small trail that leads to the base of the rock face, which makes an acceptable campsite (3115m, Finaid: Kimathanka, sheet: 2787 02, ref: 259 738). Apparently there is an alternative trail up the real Saldim Khola to another possible camping spot, but we didn't see the trail junction.

Climb the watercourse a little further before exiting it on the left on a small trail that ascends just to the left of a much steeper watercourse, which looks more like a cascade. Ascend steeply (for 350m) between two streams on a small trail (1½ hours) before the gradient begins to ease; you can then cross the stream to your left and head up a shrub-covered slope. Pass a small lake and continue

ROUTE GUIDE

to climb to a waterless kharka and on to the ridge top (3855m, 1 hour), which you will follow before descending slightly to an east-facing kharka and possible campsite. You then climb a craggy trail around a ridge to a minor pass (4207m, 1 hour, Finaid: Kimathanka, sheet: 2787 02, ref: 252 711), before dipping through a shallow valley and climbing another ridge (4253m, 1 hour) to arrive at a black water lake (4192m, 30 minutes), where there is enough room to camp. Climb the next ridge to a pass (4624m, 1½ hours) before a steep, rocky descent, which is treacherous if snow-covered. From the valley bottom the trail climbs another ridge to a minor pass (4457m, 1½ hours), where you can see a large valley and campsite below you, it will take another 1½ hours to descend through dense rhododendron shrubs and walk a little way up the valley to a kharka (4097m, Finaid: Bala, sheet: 2787 05, ref: 206 696). The slight downhill to the lip of the valley gives you a moment to identify the blue-roofed Mumbuk teahouses on the far side of the valley before you enter a beautiful forest of fir, pine and large rhododendron, and the trail steepens. Before you reach the Barun Khola the trail descends northwest, past another rock overhang cave (3366m, 1½ hours), and then after crossing several pleasant streams, finally into the open valley bottom. You now follow the Barun Khola along an easy trail broken by occasional landslides to Yangla Kharka (3557m, 2½ hours).

You are now on the main Makalu Base Camp trail, which you should follow and then cross the Sherpani Col, West Col and Amphu Labsta before arriving in Chukhung in the Everest region. Good luck!

❏ Sherpa people

The famous Sherpa people live in the Solu-Khumbu (Everest) region, and are similar to the Bhotia of Helambu (north of Kathmandu) and other ethnic groups dotted through the eastern districts of Nepal. Their mountain settlements are always higher than anyone else's, no matter where they are living. During the cold winter only the elderly stay in the village to look after livestock, and the younger ones come down to the plains and valleys to look for manual work. Many Sherpas own or work for trekking and mountaineering companies, while others run lodges and shops in Kathmandu or along popular trails. Most families make a part of their income from tourism. Sherpa people keep yaks, dzum and dzo (a cross between cattle and yak) to work the fields, carry loads and provide meat, milk and wool.

The traditional Sherpa house has two storeys made of stone with a sloping shingle roof. On the ground floor potatoes and firewood are stored, and this is where their livestock will be sheltered during bad weather. The family lives upstairs, normally in one large room, which functions as bedroom, sitting room and kitchen. Sherpas follow Tibetan Buddhism and generally pick their own marriage partner. They grow millet, maize and barley, and make their own alcohol, called chang, which is a fermented beer.

Solu-Khumbu (Everest region)

Mt Everest, known as Sagarmatha to most Nepalese and Chomolungma to the local Sherpas, has become Nepal's premier trekking destination. The proliferation of comfortable teahouses (many with en-suite rooms) and well-maintained trails means tens of thousands of tourists visit each season. The region is popular for good reason; some of the most spectacular and beautiful mountain scenery in the world combines with the famous friendliness and hospitality of the Sherpa people to make a visit a must for any walker.

The Everest Region, known locally as the Solu-Khumbu, fans out into a series of impressive glacier-filled valleys above the main trading centre of Namche. The main trail route to Everest Base Camp and the viewpoint of Kala

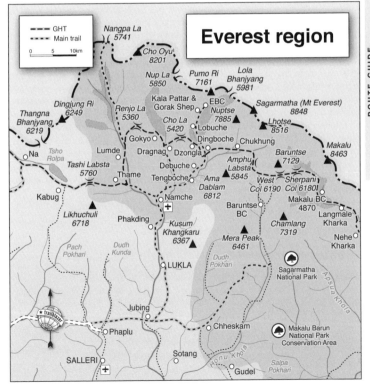

ROUTE GUIDE

> ### ❏ The Himalayan Trust
> Schools and programs operated by The Himalayan Trust, started by Sir Edmund
> Hillary, are famous for kick-starting the economy of the Solu-Khumbu region.
>   The key to the success of its projects is the involvement of locals. Sir Edmund
> believed locals could help themselves if given sufficient opportunity and resources.
> The Trust mostly provides funds and the villagers provide land, materials and labour.
> This approach means that the villagers 'adopt' the projects and take pride in maintain-
> ing and further developing schools, hospitals and bridges all over the Solu-Khumbu.

Pattar form the eastern side of the fan, along with the Chukhung valley that
leads to the Amphu Labsta (see *Sherpani Col, West Col and Amphu Labsta*,
p130) and the popular trekking peak of Imja Tse (Island Peak). The centre of the
fan is the Gokyo valley, which contains a series of turquoise glacial lakes
beneath the impressive bulk of Cho Oyu (8201m). To the west is the less frequently visited Bhote Koshi valley system that leads first to Thame and then
west to Tashi Labsta (see *The Rolwaling & the Tashi Labsta*, p144) or north to
the Nangpa La, a pass used by Tibetan traders and refugees.

   The vast majority of visitors to the Solu-Khumbu now fly into and out of
Lukla rather than doing the four- to five-day trek from Jiri. Beyond Lukla,
Namche offers a convenient and comfy acclimatisation stop and the opportu-
nity to get to know the local Sherpa people a little better. Khumjung and
Khunde are above Namche, and this is where Sir Edmund Hillary began his
pioneering work with local development projects. The famous Tibetan Buddhist
gompa at Tengboche is only a day further, and then the highest settlements of
Pheriche and Lobuche lead you to Gorak Shep, a staging-post for both Everest
Base Camp (where there isn't a view of Mt Everest's summit) and the viewpoint
of Kala Pattar (where there is). A popular side trip is to Chukhung, or over the
Cho La to Gokyo, which for many is a worthy destination in itself. The Renjo
La offers perhaps the best viewpoint of the entire region and leads to the Thame
valley, which can feel eerily remote compared to the main trails.

   Sagarmatha National Park was declared a World Heritage Site in 1979 and
has a comprehensive management structure. Use of firewood is prohibited, and
locals rigorously monitor environmental protocols.

EVEREST BASE CAMP, THE CHO LA AND THE RENJO LA

Many trekking groups who only visit Gorak Shep do the return trip to Lukla in
about 14 days, but if there is any chance of staying longer the effort will pay
dividends. Crossing the Cho La and adding the viewpoints of the Ngozumba
Glacier and Gokyo Ri increases your trek duration by a mere four days. Another
great add-on is Renjo La and a trip to Thame, which take just one more day than
returning down the main Gokyo valley. In short, this is the most convenient
place to experience the immensity of the Himalaya in Nepal.

There is almost no bad time of year to visit the Solu-Khumbu as there is always something going on. A major re-forestation program in the 1980s and 1990s has once again given a bloom of colour to the lower slopes in the pre-monsoon. The most popular season is October to December, when the air is clear and offers the best shots of the highest mountain in the world. The popular passes of the Cho La and Renjo La are open for most of the year except for a brief period from mid-February to March. All of the main routes in the valleys are open year-round.

The region used to have a reputation for tough trekking but a significant increase in teahouses and trail repair has made it an option for novices and experienced trekkers alike. Access is very easy with multiple daily flights to Lukla year-round, just remember to reconfirm the day before you fly as waiting lists can be long in peak season. For comprehensive trail, accommodation and local information see Jamie McGuinness's, *Trekking in the Everest Region*, also from Trailblazer.

> ## EVEREST BASE CAMP, THE CHO LA AND THE RENJO LA TREK
>
> Everyone should see Mt Everest at least once in their life. Trek to the famed Kala Pattar viewpoint, cross the Cho La and Renjo La, enjoy the natural openhearted friendliness of the Sherpa people – if you only visit Nepal once, this is the trek to do.
>
> **Duration**: 20 days
>
> **Highest Point**: 5550m
>
> **Best Season**: Mar-May/Oct-Jan
>
> **Accommodation**: teahouses or camping

ROUTE GUIDE

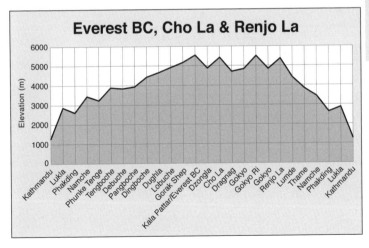

DAY 1: KATHMANDU – LUKLA – PHAKDING   4HRS

The flight to Lukla (2840m) has great views of about 200km of the eastern Himalaya; sit on the left hand side of the plane for the best views. Many guides like to meet your crew and purchase supplies in Lukla, so do not be surprised if you are delayed before heading out of town.

From the airport head north along the main paved trail crowded with shops to a *kani*, where you then head downhill. After 45 minutes you should reach Chheplung (2660m), the first of many collections of teahouses and the carved *mani* stones, prayer wheels and chortens built by all Buddhist communities throughout the Himalaya.

The trail now undulates through Nurning and Ghat, punctuated by short sections of scrubby pine forest and painted mani stones, until you reach Phakding (2610m, 2 hours). Many trekking groups stay in this extensive village so you might want to continue for another 20 minutes to Zam Fute (2730m), or 1 hour to Benkar (2630m).

DAY 2: PHAKDING – NAMCHE 5HRS

From Phakding the trail crosses a long suspension bridge before again following an undulating route, which many Nepalese would call 'flat'. A pretty waterfall attracts photographs just before Benkar (2630m, 1½ hours), after which you re-cross the Dudh Koshi and climb a little to the village of Monjo (2835m, 40 minutes). Ahead, you can see the trail climbing to a cleft between by a huge finger of rock and the hillside, which is the site for the Sagarmatha National Park entry post where you register.

Stone steps descend to another suspension bridge, which crosses to Jorsale (2740m, 45 minutes). Continue on a broad trail to another bridge and an easy riverside track and then a slight climb to the Larja bridge (40 minutes) festooned with prayer flags. From now until you finally sit down and rest in Namche (3440m, 2½ hours), you will be walking uphill.

Early on the first section of switchbacks the trail turns a sharp left on the edge of the ridge and you can catch your first glimpse of Mt Everest. The trail climbs switchbacks, which gradually ease as the trail follows a route that winds northwest through pine forest. There is a police check post 15 minutes before entering Namche where you must register.

DAY 3: NAMCHE   ALL DAY

As you have now passed the 3000m mark, it is a good idea to take an acclimatisation day and rest from the previous day's climb. Namche is an extensive market town, where there is always something to see and places to explore.

If you are here on a market day (Saturday) make sure you get up early to see Tibetan and Sherpa traders bargaining before the tourists arrive.

If you have the time it is worth completing a looped day walk to the Sagarmatha National Park Museum (on the ridge above the town), and the combined villages of Khunde (3840m) and Khumjung (3780m), which is the site of the first Himalayan Trust school, as well as many chorten and mani walls.

DAY 4: NAMCHE – DEBUCHE 5½HRS

It is a good idea to get an early start today, as the trail up to Tengboche can be hot and dusty in the afternoon. First climb to the ridge above Namche and the Sagarmatha National Park Museum and then continue along a slightly rising trail to Khyangjuma (3550m, 45 minutes), where a couple of teahouses enjoy a wonderful view of Ama Dablam on the far side of the valley.

A stone paved trail descends to Phunke Tenga (3250m, 1½ hours), before climbing switchbacks through pine forest and traversing across Tengboche hill to a final switchback only 5 minutes from the gompa, campsite and some teahouses (3860m, 2¼ hours).

Accommodation has been problematic in Tengboche for many years as the local teahouse owners sometimes take an aggressively commercial approach to trekking groups. A way to avoid this is to visit the monastery and then continue to Debuche (3820m, 20 minutes) or Milingga (3750m, 40 minutes) through a delightful pine, rhododendron and birch forest.

DAY 5: DEBUCHE – DINGBOCHE
3½HRS

Wake up early and head back up to Tengboche for the morning *puja* (prayers), which you should try to get to by 7 to 7:30am. Please enter the gompa as quietly as possible and remember to make a donation before you leave. Bring a khadag (silk blessing scarf) to offer as thanks if you want to receive a blessing from the abbot or senior monk.

This Nyingmapa sect gompa is a World Heritage site, originally built in 1916 but destroyed by an earthquake in 1934. The rebuilt gompa was again destroyed in 1989 by fire, but the grand new buildings are true to the original designs and form an idyllic setting for the thirty or so young monks who live here.

Once you have finished exploring the gompa it is worth the effort to climb the ridge that rises from Tengboche. Views of the surrounding peaks including Mt Everest and Ama Dablam improve with height once you reach a chorten after climbing for 30 minutes.

Leaving Debuche you first descend an easy trail before crossing a bridge and climbing to Pangboche (3930m, 1 hour), which boasts the oldest gompa in the region.

Note: Many people stay at lower Pangboche as part of a slower acclimatisation program.

The trail from Pangboche follows the Imja Khola and leads to a major trail junction (4175m, 1½ hours) and the site of a teashop. The left fork leads to Pheriche (site of the Trekker's Aid Post), but take the right trail and descend to a bridge. The trail continues up above the Imja Khola on a broad trail to Dingboche (4410m, 1 hour).

DAY 6: DINGBOCHE   ALL DAY

The ascent to Dingboche (or Pheriche) frequently produces mild altitude sickness symptoms so an acclimatisation day is an excellent idea. There are three options for a day walk from Dingboche of varying difficulty. Perhaps the most impressive, and exerting, is a trail that crosses the Imja Khola by a small wooden bridge at the southern end of the village. From there, climb about 400m (2 hours) to a valley with a series of small

lakes at the base of the north face of Ama Dablam. Continue up a slight ridge on your left, where you can see the pyramid summit of Makalu in the distance.

For a walk of similar duration but on easier trails it is a good idea to follow the main trail to Chukhung (4730m, 3 hours) but stop short and return. As you climb through the Chukhung valley the popular Island Peak becomes increasingly dominant ahead and the massive Lhotse wall dwarfs everything. There are good views of Tabuche, Cholatse and Ama Dablam.

The easiest day walk climbs the ridge to the north of Dingboche to a series of chortens and good views of all the surrounding peaks.

DAY 7: DINGBOCHE – LOBUCHE
3½HRS

Take any one of a number of trails that lead to a white chorten on top of the ridge behind Dingboche. The ridge is the edge of an ancient lateral moraine and the trail takes an obvious route along the top, providing views of Ama Dablam (behind), Pheriche (below) and Lobuche Peak (ahead) among others on either side.

The trail will eventually descend to cross a small river that emits from the end of the Khumbu Glacier, across from the small settlement of Dughla (4620m, 1½ hours). Climb the lateral moraine on the north side of the glacier snout on a well-defined trail to a series of stone memorials for climbers killed on the surrounding peaks.

Cross a bridge over a stream flowing from Lobuche Peak and continue to the often crowded teahouses of Lobuche (4910m, 1½ hours).

DAY 8: LOBUCHE   ALL DAY

Some trekkers decide to take an acclimatisation day at Lobuche despite the cramped conditions. However, you may choose to continue to Gorak Shep if you are not suffering from the gain in altitude, and explore around Lobuche on your return trip.

Directly behind the teahouses is a ridge that climbs to form the east flank of Lobuche East Peak. There is a small trail that climbs to about 5400m (2½ hours) and

ROUTE GUIDE

really good views of the surrounding peaks including Everest.

Alternatively, cross the Khumbu Glacier on a good trail and climb a scrambly, rocky track to the Kongma La (5528m, 3½ hours), where it is possible to continue on to the summit of Pokalde (5806m, another 1½ hours), but remember it is a long descent to Lobuche (or the Chukhung/Dingboche valley) so exercise caution if you decide to continue.

DAY 9: LOBUCHE – KALA PATTAR – GORAK SHEP   5HRS

The trail continues on the same side of the glacier past the trail junction to the Italian Research Centre pyramid and over the Changri Shar glacier snout. Kala Pattar (meaning black rock) is clearly seen ahead and Gorak Shep is the cluster of teahouses beside the small lake.

Your crew will want to go to straight to Gorak Shep (5140m, 3 hours) to deposit their loads, and you should take a rest to check everyone for symptoms of altitude sickness before attempting to climb Kala Pattar. It is important to take your time and monitor your group for symptoms of altitude sickness throughout the climb and when resting on the summit.

From the teahouse, climb north by northeast to a prayer-flag-covered rocky summit (5550m, 1½ hours) for one of the best views of the highest point on earth, Mt Everest, and the surrounding peaks of Nuptse, Lhotse, and Pumori.

Your descent will take 45 minutes, or longer if you wait until sundown (when it gets very cold very quickly).

DAY 10: GORAK SHEP – EBC – LOBUCHE   4HRS

From Gorak Shep the trail curls around the base of Kala Pattar, continuing along the side of the Khumbu glacier. After 1 hour you will move on to the glacier itself and care needs to be taken not to walk off the track. As you approach Everest Base Camp (5350m, 30 minutes) views of the notorious Khumbu Icefall appear on your right, it looks far more intimidating from here than from other viewpoints.

Most expeditions do not appreciate you walking around their camps for security reasons, so respect their wishes and avoid intruding. The return trip to Gorak Shep along the same trail takes about 45 minutes.

DAY 11: LOBUCHE – DZONGLA 5HRS

Descend from Lobuche for about 20 minutes towards Dughla and turn right before crossing a stream (4835m); after crossing a flat area, follow an obvious trail that climbs up and around a grassy hillside, with views all the way to Pheriche and beyond.

The trail continues to climb an easy gradient up natural contours in the hillside, the turquoise Chola Tsho (lake) lies below the rugged summits of Cholatse and Arakam Tse. The teahouses of Dzongla (4830m) are across another stream and up a small rise, and should be reached in 2 hours from the Lobuche-Dughla turnoff.

If you are camping continue for another 40 minutes to a large meadow surrounded by a horseshoe of impressive peaks.

DAY 12: DZONGLA – CHO LA – DRAGNAG (THANGNAK)   5HRS

An obvious trail loops over a grassy hill behind Dzongla then gradually climbs a large meadow to a rocky bluff near the end of the valley. The trail switchbacks up to a rock face and then climbs to the right, up a worn boulder-strewn trail to an area of smooth rock slabs covered in cairns, next to a glacier.

Stick to the south side, rather than climbing onto the glacier immediately, on a track that is frequently covered in snow, before crossing the glacier just before the Cho La (5420m, 2½ hours). There aren't any views of the highest peaks but there are many lesser peaks that fill the western horizon.

Beneath is a steep rocky trail that will be covered in parts with snow and ice. Take care on the descent but keep moving as the lower section is prone to rock fall from a craggy peak to your left. In less than 1 hour you should reach an easier gradient; cross a minor boulder-covered ridge, which leads to a good campsite in a trough.

Climb the grassy hill on the far side of the campsite to a large obvious boulder and then a long steep descent brings you to the teahouses and campsites at Dragnag (Thangnak, 4700m, 1½ hours).

DAY 13: DRAGNAG (THANGNAK) – GOKYO RI – GOKYO 5½HRS

Of all the glaciers in the Everest region the most impressive is the Ngozumba, which you must cross on a trail to the west of Dragnag. Ask locals which route is currently recommended and take your time while crossing the glacier to catch mountain reflections in the turquoise lakes.

Once on the far side of the glacier turn right and join the main Gokyo trail just before a large lake (1 hour from Dragnag).

The trail to Gokyo (4790m), located on the east bank of another large lake, takes a further hour. After depositing unnecessary gear in your teahouse or camp, head out of the village on a trail that crosses a broad shallow watercourse crossed by stepping stones and rock platform.

The track up Gokyo Ri is badly eroded in the lower section but it soon becomes a substantial ridge trail all the way to the summit (5483m, 2½ hours). This rocky, prayer-flag-covered peak offers one of the best views of Mt Everest and surrounding peaks in the entire region. It will take an hour to descend back to Gokyo.

DAY 14: GOKYO ALL DAY

A great day out is to explore more lakes and Cho Oyu Base Camp; without crossing the watercourse, head north on a good trail from Gokyo in the ablation valley caused by the Ngozumba Glacier.

You will soon come to the fourth of Gokyo's lakes (1 hour) surrounded by craggy peaks. Continue on the same trail to the picturesque fifth lake (4990m, 1½ hours).

Here you have three options: climb one of the higher lumps of glacial moraine for views of Mt Everest reflecting in glacial lakes; or climb a ridge that comes down to the north-eastern corner of the lake to an excellent view point at roughly 5500m (at least 1½ hours); or continue on a smaller trail which turns left to the foot of Cho Oyu which reflects in the sixth lake (1½ hours).

For groups with camping equipment it is worth spending a night in the sixth lake

area and enjoying all of these options as well as potential sunset views of Mt Everest.

DAY 15: GOKYO – RENJO LA – LUMDE 6½HRS

From Gokyo head to the base of the Gokyo Ri climb, but instead of heading up the hill take the left-hand trail that heads around the lake. There are two trails, do not take the one by the lakeshore; instead, take the other which climbs slightly.

In 1 hour you should reach the bottom of a steep switchback trail where the ground is loose and climbs an unrelenting gradient for another 1 hour. At the top of the climb the gradient eases a little and heads across a rocky section, which can be icy from December to March.

You now enter a broad valley, which can make an ideal high camp for those with tents. The trail heads due west across the valley and then climbs again around a rocky spur before heading up to the pass (5360m, 1½ hours) via a stone staircase. The trail is much easier to follow now that the people from Thame have completed a major reconstruction project. This is especially true on the western side of the pass, which is now a stone staircase in good repair.

The view from the pass is one of the best in the entire Solu-Khumbu, and a terrific lunch spot. The trail down the western side of the pass rapidly brings you to the edge of a glacial lake, where the stone steps finish.

Beyond is another lake, Relama Tsho (4905m, 2 hours), which is a popular camping spot for those approaching the pass from the Thame side. A broad trail now winds around the eastern side of a hill above the lake before descending to a large sandy kharka.

At the very end of the kharka the trail descends rapidly into the Bhote Koshi valley and in 1 hour you should reach the few teahouses at Lumde (4368m).

DAY 16: LUMDE – THAME 3HRS

An easy trail descends from Lumde to a bridge at the village of Marulung (4210m, 1 hour), where there are some more teahouses.

You now descend the western bank of the Bhote Koshi along a broad and easy-to-follow trail to Thame (3820m, 1½ hours), where there are many teahouses beyond a large moraine with some stupas on top.

If you have time, it is worth climbing this moraine and following a trail through juniper and fir forest to Thame's major gompa (at the entrance to small valley heading west from the main village), which is the site of a Mani Rimdu festival in May.

DAY 17: THAME – NAMCHE 3½HRS

The trail from Thame descends to the Bhote Koshi and crosses a steel-box bridge at the end of a canyon section carved by the river. The locals believe this is an auspicious place and have painted the rock face above the bridge with Buddhas and prayers.

The trail now climbs a little before settling into an easy downhill gradient to Thamo (3480m, 1 hour). Cross the Thesbu Khola and continue on a broad trail through pine forest all the way to Namche (3440m, 1½ hours), where you will arrive next to the new helipad and many painted mani stones on the hill above the western side of the town.

DAYS 18 – 20: NAMCHE – LUKLA – KATHMANDU

Return to Lukla via Phakding, then fly to Kathmandu on the following day.

OTHER MAJOR TRAILS IN THE SOLU-KHUMBU

Before commercial flights to Lukla became the most popular method of accessing the Solu-Khumbu, trekkers would start from the road head town of Jiri. The number of trekkers taking this route is now so small that those who do often find it a major highlight of their trek. Rather than the crowds and rush of the higher trails, the Sherpa, Gurung and Rai communities of the lower trails have time to exhibit their natural hospitality and friendliness. There are a number of route options, including the viewpoint of Pikey Peak, which can take from seven to ten days to Namche.

The road now continues past Jiri and a jeep trail reaches as far as Bhandar; perhaps buses will reach there soon too.

In 2007, the Nepali government removed trekking restrictions for the Nangpa La (5716m) at the head of the Thame valley. Camping equipment is necessary as well as experience in glacier travel. This is a rough and wild route, and absolutely do not cross into Tibet at all from here.

Perhaps the most popular trekking peak in Nepal is Island Peak above Chukhung. However, even if you are not going to climb to the summit a visit to the base camp area is an impressive day walk of about 5½ hours return.

GHT – SOLU-KHUMBU

After crossing the Amphu Labsta from the Honku Basin follow a good trail to Chukhung (4730m, 2½ hours). The Great Himalaya Trail now follows main trails down through Dingboche, and then over the Cho La (via Dzongla) to Gokyo and then over the Renjo La to Thame. A long day brings you to the base of the Tashi Labsta, which crosses to the Rolwaling – see *The Rolwaling & the Tashi Labsta*, p150 for more details.

The Rolwaling

Often overlooked by tour companies, there is a culturally diverse and challenging trekking region just a day's drive to the northeast of Kathmandu, known as The Rolwaling. Whether you want passes, mountains and glaciers, or charming villages amid old-growth forests, this region will both surprise and delight the intrepid trekker.

Although the name, Rolwaling, specifically applies to a river that is fed from the glaciers around the Tsho Rolpa lake, it now includes all the valleys, hills and ridges as far west as the Arniko Highway (the road to Lhasa from Kathmandu). To the east of the region is the Solu-Khumbu (see *Solu-Khumbu/the Everest Region*, p135), to which it is linked by the formidable Tashi Labsta pass. The

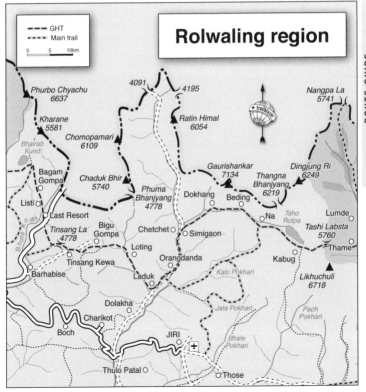

Great Himalayan Range comes to an abrupt stop at the Gaurishankar Himal as the Tama Koshi cuts through the mountains. Beyond, to the west, are Tamang, Gurung and Sherpa communities, as well as some rarely explored rhododendron forests that are home to red panda and black bear.

A road is being built up the Tama Koshi valley to Tibet, which is now increasing access to the Rolwaling as a whole. At the time of writing, another road from Barhabise to Bigu Gompa was not open due to landslides, but probably will be open soon. A good place to start exploring the eastern Rolwaling is the Last Resort on the Arniko Highway, where you can follow a series of ridges up to the Tinsang La. From here you traverse around the Chilingkha Danda through Sherpa, Tamang and Gurung villages to Laduk. It is possible to travel by bus from Kathmandu to Singati Bazaar, and reach Laduk in one day. Then it is a six-day trek to Na either via Simigaon or a mountaineering route via the Yalung La before climbing the Trakarding and Drolambu glaciers to the Tashi Labsta. The GHT can follow any of these trails, but the most northerly combination provides the simplest route through the region.

The Rolwaling is not protected by any conservation plan or environmental code of practice. As you cross the Tashi Labsta you enter the Sagarmatha National Park where your permits will be checked at Monjo.

THE ROLWALING & THE TASHI LABSTA

If you have limited time then you could begin your trek from Singati Bazaar and head over the Yalung La to Na and then cross the Tashi Labsta (a 16-day trek). Alternatively, when the road is finished, bus to Chetchet and reduce this itinerary to 14 days. Some groups like to combine this trek with a trekking peak like Ramdung (5930m), Yalung Peak (5630m) or Pachermo (6273m). Remember to include an additional acclimatisation day in the Thame valley if you are going to attempt the Tashi Labsta from the Solu-Khumbu.

The best times of year to visit the Rolwaling are the two main trekking seasons of March to May, and October to December. However, for those wanting to cross the Tashi Labsta, October offers much better conditions than in the spring months when there is less compacted snow. The approach and crossing of the Tashi Labsta can cause problems as even light snow can make the route finding very difficult and the trail treacherous on both the ascent and descent. The glaciers on the eastern side of the pass are hazardous and crevassed. You should also ensure

---

THE ROLWALING & THE TASHI LABSTA TREK

Diverse cultures, picturesque villages and one of the most challenging passes in the Himalaya. A trek through the Rolwaling will delight, surprise and provide a genuine physical test for even the most experienced trekker.

Duration: 23 days

Highest Point: 5760m

Best Season: Apr-May/Oct-Nov

Accommodation: camping and some teahouses.

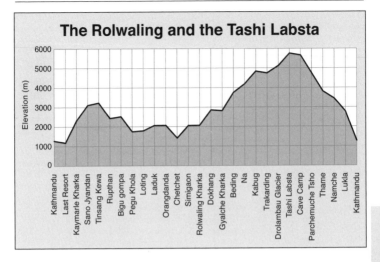

The Rowaling and the Tashi Labsta

Elevation (m): 0, 1000, 2000, 3000, 4000, 5000, 6000

Kathmandu, Last Resort, Kaymarle Kharka, Sano Jyandan, Tinsang Kewa, Rupthan, Bigu gompa, Pegu Khola, Loting, Laduk, Orangdanda, Chetchet, Simigaon, Rowaling Kharka, Dokhang, Gyalche Kharka, Beding, Na, Kabug, Trakarding, Drolambau Glacier, Tashi Labsta, Cave Camp, Parchemuche Tsho, Thame, Namche, Lukla, Kathmandu

that you have rock and ice climbing equipment with you, to help negotiate steep snow and/or blue ice.

Despite being a fertile area, food is often scarce in the Rowaling so ensure that you are as fully supplied as possible before leaving Kathmandu. Crossing the Tashi Labsta requires that you have sufficient food and fuel for at least eight days prior to arriving at Na. An Austrian development project, Eco-Himal, have built a series of teahouse-style lodges and campsites from near Barhabise on the Arniko Highway to Orangdanda, which provide an ideal route for a cultural trek via Bigu Gompa. It is worth employing a local guide to show you how to avoid the new road up and over the Tinsang La from Barhabise.

DAY 1: KATHMANDU – THE LAST RESORT   4HRS

The drive from Kathmandu up the Arniko Highway is best done early in the morning before the traffic becomes too heavy. If you reach Barhabise within 3 hours you have had a fast trip: the public bus can take much longer.

If you are going to stay in the Eco-Himal lodges then you will need to alight at Barhabise and trek to Karthali where Mr Sunil Rokka runs a teahouse and can organise a local guide for you. However, if you are planning to follow the route described below, then continue to the Last Resort (1170m, famous for the highest bungee jump in Asia), about 1 hour from Barhabise.

DAY 2: THE LAST RESORT – KAYMARLE KHARKA   5½HRS

There are many confusing forest trails from the Marmin Danda to the Tinsang La, so you must organise a local guide at The Last Resort. From The Last Resort cross the bridge and climb stone steps to Tyanthali village (1390m, 30 minutes).

At an old service road, turn right and continue past the village school. About 400m beyond the school take a trail that turns up hill (left) and slowly climbs as it traverses to Sakhuwa village (1480m, 40 minutes).

After passing through some scrubby forest the trail swings around a corner to some broad terraced fields belonging to Cati village (1520m, 20 minutes). Stay close to the base of the steep hillside above, which will involve stepping up from terrace to terrace. Do not enter the village.

Continue on a trail that heads across a small stream on the northern side of the village and then climbs into scrubby forest that covers the hillside above. You will now climb a well-worn switchback trail to Mandre (2180m, 2½ hours).

From above Mandre village, take a major trail that turns southeast (right) where you will find the gradient eases as it traverses the south-facing slope of a prominent hill.

In another 1½ hours you will reach a natural saddle between the Khagdal Khola and Gulche valleys. Camp on the terraces or saddle (2285m, Finaid: Barhabise, sheet: 2785 04, ref: 925 811). There is a permanent water source on the north side (Gulche village side) where there are a couple of houses.

DAY 3: KAYMARLE KHARKA – SANO JYANDAN   5½HRS

Today you leave the villages behind and head up to a large forested ridge, which ultimately leads to the Tinsang La. Take your time and enjoy the views, and if you begin early each day there is a good chance of seeing red panda.

Follow a trail to your east that heads up from the kharka along an obvious ridge. As you climb, the forest becomes thicker and after about 400m of ascent (1¾ hours) the trail veers away from the ridge and onto the northern slopes of the Nambarjun Danda.

After 40 minutes you reach a dry watercourse which you should climb to another saddle and potential campsite at Sindurche Kharka (2780m, 1 hour). The trail from the kharka continues east, back up onto the forested ridge. The trail sometimes edges against the precipitous edge of the ridge, with views down to the Khagdal Khola 700m below.

As you continue along the ridge the trail rises and falls for short sections and there are small seasonal shelters used by locals when they take their cattle to the high pastures during the monsoon months. Do not take any cross trails, stick to the obvious track, as close to the top of the ridge as possible.

After about 2 hours you will arrive at a kharka with two stone shelters in a large saddle, Sano Jyandan (3127m), where there is permanent water in the rhododendron-forested gully to the north of the campsite.

DAY 4: SANO JYANDAN – TINSANG KEWA   4HRS

Head due east on a trail that traverses beneath a forested hill to a very large kharka with many stone shelters called Palati Jyandan (3210m, 30 minutes).

Note: camping is not advisable here as water is scarce during the trekking seasons.

Continue to the far side of the kharka and re-enter the forest. You soon come to the head of a dry watercourse (25 minutes) which you should follow as it winds down between two hills and away from the ridge.

A further 30 minutes from the kharka, the trail swings east (right) and away from the watercourse and into an old-growth rhododendron forest. Continue on a good trail, which in 20 minutes from the watercourse brings you to Marmin Jyandan (3250m), where there are a few stone shelters but not permanent water.

From this kharka the trail heads out across a steep rocky hillside, you should check the weather before beginning, as rain will make sections difficult. Climb back onto the ridge for 30 minutes before the trail slowly climbs and traverses a steep rock and grass covered hillside.

In 45 minutes you will connect with a long north-south ridge, which leads to the Tinsang La. You should be able to see the motor road leading up to the pass about 2km away.

Once you join the main ridge you are back in rhododendron forest, but do not descend all the way to the pass. Instead follow a large trail that swings east, away from the ridge, and in 20 minutes you drop down to a series of plateaus that lead to a campsite at Tinsang Kewa (3266m, 15 minutes).

DAY 5: TINSANG KEWA – BIGU GOMPA   4½HRS

You will frequently cross the road as you descend via multiple short cuts through the forest. In 2¾ hours you will reach the hamlet of Rupthan (2400m) where you cross a small bridge.

From here the trail begins to climb back into the forest on an easy gradient. A local guide is useful to pick the right combination of short-cut trails up to the broad plateau of Bigu Gompa (2516m, 1¾ hours), and the Eco-Himal teahouse and campsite.

Bigu Gompa is a nunnery dedicated to the thousand-armed Buddha, Avalokiteshwara (Compassion of all Buddhas), who is the all-seeing, all-knowing remover of obstacles. The nuns are happy for visitors to attend morning prayers and a donation is appropriate for even brief visits.

DAY 6: BIGU GOMPA – LOTING
4HRS

From the Sherpa village of Bigu, there are two routes to Loting. The main trail descends to the Pegu (Amatol) Khola (1700m, 2½ hours), crosses it and then climbs a little before descending to a bridge over the Sangu Khola and then climbing to Loting (1768m, 1 hour and 20 minutes).

Alternatively, head east and gradually descend to the village of Alampu, which covers the southeast-facing hillside above the Kotheli Khola. A steep trail descends through the village to a bridge (1732m, 2 hours), which you should cross to a small hamlet.

Follow the river downstream for about 30 minutes to just before the confluence with the Sangu Khola and veer left to climb about 200m through scrubby forest. In 1 hour you round the hillside and enter the Gurung village of Loting where there is an Eco-Himal teahouse and campsite.

DAY 7: LOTING – LADUK   6HRS

A trail leads around the edge of some terraced fields before descending slightly to the Dorun Khola to the southeast of Loting. Climb the far bank past a large chautara and continue ascending a gradual gradient around a hillside, which is steeper on its southern flanks.

There are many trails around the hill and you should try to stick to the highest obvious track. Descend to and then cross a seasonal watercourse before climbing easy

trails to Chilingkha (1839m, 2 hours), where there is an Eco-Himal campsite but no teahouse facility.

Climb through the village to another scrub-covered hillside, which was affected by a bushfire at the beginning of 2009. The trail traverses around the hillside to the small village of Chyasarpa (2020m, 1 hour and 20 minutes), where you descend to another watercourse. From here the trail becomes broader as it passes through a small forest and then climbs an easy gradient all the way to the Eco-Himal teahouse and campsite at Laduk (2050m, 2½ hours).

Note: from Laduk it is possible to descend to the road at Singati and return to Kathmandu within 7 to 8 hours.

DAY 8: LADUK – ORANGDANDA
4HRS

A broad trail climbs an easy gradient from Laduk through pine forest that covers most of the hillside above. In 1 hour and 20 minutes you will reach a ridge above Bulung where you might be lucky and catch your first views of the Gaurishankar Himal. Descend to the village (1890m, 15 minutes), where there is a community-owned campsite.

A trail winds around the top of the village to a chautara with two chorten where you join another trail from the valley below. Take the left fork, which heads north and descends to a stream before climbing an easy gradient across a grassy hillside to the small village of Yarsa (2020m, 45 minutes).

The trail descends to a small dry watercourse on the northern side of the village, which you have to climb for about 40 metres to a track that swings right and climbs to terraced fields. In about 50 minutes you enter the ridge-top village of Orangdanda (2029m) where there is another Eco-Himal teahouse and campsite.

There are great morning views of the Gaurishakar Himal from this teahouse, which is the last one along the Rolwaling trail. From here you can descend to the road in the valley below (about 700m down, 3 hours) where you can return to Kathmandu.

To continue towards the Rolwaling Khola from this point requires camping equipment.

DAY 9: ORANGDANDA – RIVER CAMP 4¾HRS

Looking north from the Eco-Himal teahouse you will notice that the homes have changed from the previous days as you are now entering Tamang communities. From the entrance to the lodge, the trail contours around a broad, terraced hillside to a large landslide. There is a good trail across the very top of the landslide, do not cross lower down.

Once on the far side, descend terraces to a stream, and then climb a little to the village of Deulang (1900m, 1¼ hours). You soon reach the top of large village of Thare where you should follow the main trail that descends through the centre of the village.

As you reach a cluster of homes towards the bottom of the village (1820m, 45 minutes) the trail swings north and descends an easier gradient to a small Sherpa village above Gongar (1430m, 1¾ hours), which is in the valley below.

Stone steps lead down to the road, which you will need to follow for about 1 hour to a bridge at Chetchet (1377m). Cross the Tama Koshi to a campsite on the far bank.

If you are feeling strong and have enough time, you could combine today with tomorrow's trek.

DAY 10: RIVER CAMP – SIMIGAON 3½HRS

From the campsite a stone staircase climbs up and around a rocky spur that juts into the river valley. Climb steps which switchback for about 400m to the lower homes of Simigaon village (2 hours).

Once you reach the first terraces the gradient eases as the trail winds between homes. It will take another 1½ hours to reach the few teahouses and campsite (2036m) on the ridge above the village, where a new gompa is being built.

DAY 11: SIMIGAON – DOKHANG 6HRS

From the gompa you can see the trail winding around the hillside to the northeast to a minor ridge (30 minutes) where the trail descends through forest to a small kharka about 30m above the Rolwaling Khola (2060m, 40 minutes).

Note: if you are doing this route in reverse there is a trail junction about 10 minutes into the forest from the kharka – you must take the left fork and climb from here, do not descend to the river.

From the kharka the trail begins a long and sometimes steep climb through forest. After 2 hours you should reach a large waterfall, which has a cool pool of water to soak your feet if it's a hot day.

Continue to climb for another 2 hours to Gyalche Kharka (2832m) where there is a small shop and campsite. It is now an easy descent through forest and then beside a small stream to the spacious campsite at Dokhang (2791m, 40 minutes).

DAY 12: DOKHANG – BEDING 5¼HRS

After the steep climbs of yesterday, the trail gradient is now much easier as it winds a course along the south bank of the Rolwaling Khola. Rhododendron, pine and juniper shade wildflowers in mossy glades, and the river cascades beside the trail. There are a few small landslides to cross, which make ideal places to spot birds catching insects above the river.

In 2 hours you should reach a bridge to the north bank of the river, and in another 15 minutes you will reach a bridge over the Themlung Khola, which is surrounded by cairns. If you stand in the middle of the bridge and look up the steep ravine to the north you will see Gaurishankar looming overhead. From the bridge the trail climbs a few hundred metres away from the V-shaped river valley and towards the U-shaped glacial valleys above.

As you reach the top of the climb you will notice that juniper and fir trees become more common, and the snow and ice covered bulk of Tsoboje peak fills the end of the valley ahead.

The gradient eases once again and you should reach the village of Nyamare (3550m) in another 2 hours. Beding (3740m), where there are teahouses and a campsite, is now less than 1 hour away.

DAY 13: BEDING – NA 4¾HRS

Today is a relatively short and easy trekking

day, so take a little time to visit the gompa in the village. It is said that a Buddhist monk came and lived in a cave behind the gompa before the village was established. To mark the site, a chorten was built and to offer a khadag to the chorten is considered to bestow good luck on the giver for as long as the scarf remains attached. Please offer a donation to the gompa if you want to admire the wood-panel frescoes inside.

The trail climbs an easy gradient away from Beding through miniature fir trees along a sometimes rocky trail. After 2½ hours you should notice that the valley is becoming broader and flatter and some large boulders dot the landscape. One of the boulders has been carved with the Buddhist prayer, *Om Mani Padmi Hum*, and must be the largest single mani stone anywhere.

Just beyond is another boulder with a large painting of Padmasambhava (aka Guru Rinpoche, the Lotus Born, who first took Buddhism to Tibet in the 8th century) and a small shrine.

Na (4180m, 2¼ hours) is a scattered village on a broad alluvial fan where there are many camping options and a teahouse.

DAY 14: NA   ALL DAY
It is a good idea to take a day to acclimatise in Na, and there are a couple of good day trip options. The most popular day-trip is to head up valley to a small kharka and then turn right on a small trail to Yalung Peak base camp (5 hours return trip).

Alternatively, climb to the end of Tsho Rolpa lake for views of Kang Nachago above Na (4 hours return trip).

DAY 15: NA – KABUG   5HRS
The trail above Na climbs a slight gradient to a bridge over the Tsho Rolpa outflow. From here you have two options: the main trail ascends an ablation valley to the south; alternatively, climb the terminal moraine wall that acts as a dam for the lake.

Once at the lake, the trail winds around and descends slightly to the ablation valley to the south. About half way along the side of the lake, at Chhukyima, are a couple of small teashops run by locals from Na and a good campsite (4580m, 3 hours).

Continue to the end of the valley and climb a steep hillside for 250m (1½ hours) to a viewpoint of the lake and surrounding peaks. It is now a short descent to the broad sandy plateau of Kabug campsite (4820m, 30 minutes).

DAY 16: KABUG – GLACIER SNOUT
6½HRS
Cross the plateau to the furthest corner above the glacier and then descend a loose earth trail to the southern edge of the Trakarding Glacier (4735m, 40 minutes).

From here there are a number of routes that cross the glacier. If you have started early in the morning, the most obvious trail crosses almost immediately to a trail that then ascends the northern side of the glacier. However, this route is extremely prone to rock fall from mid-morning onwards.

Alternative routes begin in about 30 minutes and again in 1 hour up the south side of the glacier. As with all glacier crossings care should be taken at all times, and your party should remain together throughout the crossing.

Once on the north side of the glacier, follow a trail that leads to the snout of the Drolambu Glacier. There is a large campsite at place called Noisy Knob Camp (4880m, 3½ hours).

If you have time, continue to the far side of the glacier snout to where a rock scramble (use a hand line for porter safety) brings you to another campsite beneath ice cliffs (5085m, 2 hours and 20 minutes).

Note: many maps show a rocky route up the western side of the Drolambu Glacier snout, this route is no longer used owing to rock fall danger.

DAY 17: GLACIER SNOUT – TASHI
LABSTA CAMP   6½HRS
On the east (right) side of the glacier a stream has carved a rocky trail, climb this to access the top of the glacier (5350m, 1 hour). Stay in the valley bottom all the way to the base of the glacier flowing down from Pachermo (5435m, 2½ hours).

The snout of this glacier has receded and you might need to put in a hand line for porter safety. Once onto the glacier, climb a

ROUTE GUIDE

natural ramp that leads all the way to the summit of the Tashi Labsta (5760m, 3 hrs).

The pass is a rocky ridge, which is normally reached by climbing an icy slope on the lower flanks of Pachermo. From the top of the pass the high camp is beneath an overhanging rock face about 100m down from the summit.

Note: close to the base of the overhang is safe from rock fall, whereas camping on the glacier below is dangerous.

If there is already a group camped here, head a little higher on the northern flank of Pachermo to a snowy plateau that is often used as a base camp for groups climbing Pachermo.

The strong social and economic links between the Rolwaling and Thame valleys mean that you could even meet a wedding party camped up here during the summer.

DAY 18: TASHI LABSTA CAMP – LAKE CAMP / THYANGBO KHARKA   5 – 6½HRS
From the high camp a trail traverses due east along the base of south-facing rock face of Agole Peak. In less than an hour you should reach a broad notch in the cliff face below, you will probably need to set a safety line for porters.

The descent is about 70m to an obvious trail down rocky slopes to the campsite at Ngole (5130m, 2 hours and 20 minutes).

A steep trail leads down moraine from the camp to a shallow basin where there is a trail junction. The fastest route down to Thyangbo Kharka climbs the smaller moraine wall on the far side of the basin and descends around a black cliff face before winding down the northern side of the valley to Thyangbo Kharka (4320m, 3 hours).

Alternatively, turn right in the basin and head down to a series of three lakes where you can camp beside the largest, Parchemuche Tsho (4780m, 1½ hours).

DAY 19: LAKE CAMP / THYANGBO KHARKA – THAME   2 – 4HRS
The trail down to Thyangbo Kharka (4320m, 2 hours) is along the northern side of the valley and provides good views of a series of pinnacle-like peaks to the south.

From the Kharka, where there is a teahouse and good campsite, it's an easy 2 hours, passing the famous gompa, down to Thame.

DAY 20: THAME – NAMCHE 2½HRS
The trail from Thame descends to the Bhote Koshi and crosses a bridge at the end of a canyon section carved by the river. The locals believe this is an auspicious place and have painted the rock face above the bridge with Buddhas and prayers.

The trail now climbs a little before settling into an easy downhill gradient to Thamo (3480m, 1 hour). Cross the Thesbu Khola and continue on a broad trail through pine forest all the way to Namche (3440m, 1½ hours) where you will arrive next to the new helipad and many painted mani stones on the hill above the western side of the town.

DAY 21: NAMCHE – PHAKDING   4HRS
The trail from Namche leaves the southern entry to the town and descends almost 800m to the Bhote Koshi below (2 hours). The trail then winds down the river valley first to Monjo (2840m, 1 hour, the Sagarmatha National Park entry post), then Benkar (45 minutes) and then to Phakding (2610m, 1 hour), where there are numerous teahouses.

DAYS 22 – 23 PHAKDING – LUKLA – KATHMANDU   4HRS
An easy undulating trail leads to Ghat (2590m, 1 hour) where there are some fine painted mani boulders. It is then an easy climb to Lukla (2840m, 3 hours) where there are many teahouses and the famous airstrip with regular flights to Kathmandu.

❏ **The Bhotia**
Rather than being a distinct ethnic group, Bhotia people are immigrants from the Tibetan Plateau who have settled in mountain valleys along the length of the Himalaya. They can therefore be considered the 'ethnic cousins' of other Mongoloid groups like the Sherpa and Tamang, who have also migrated from the north.

Bhotia homes can be either single or double storey, and are usually made of stone for the ground floor and wood for the upper levels. Communities tend to be compact, with only small fields for growing crops and keeping livestock and a few dozen homes. Bhotia always follow Tibetan Buddhism and the particular sect they belong to is often a clue as to where they originally came from. Marriages are normally within their own community, or another Bhotia village.

The term Bhotia is considered insulting by some ethnic groups, so don't use it unless you are sure you won't cause offence; calling them 'Lama' or 'Sherpa' is likely to be safer, even if less accurate.

OTHER MAJOR TRAILS IN THE ROLWALING

There are many ridge and valley treks in the Rolwaling waiting to be explored. Trekking groups can be organised from the Last Resort to explore the Kalinchok Bhagawati Danda (the ridge that flows south from the Tinsang La) and the Jimyal Danda (the ridge to the north of the Tinsang La).

For those who want to challenge themselves with more adventurous trekking, the restricted area to the north of Lamabagar is now accessible with the purchase of a US$90 trekking permit from Kathmandu. Alternatively, create a spectacular technical alpine trek by starting from Lukla, cross the Tashi Labsta to Na, then over the Yalung La to join with the passes to the south of Yalung and Ramdung Peaks that link the upper Rolwaling with trails to Jiri, Bhandar, Junbesi and routes that approach Lukla from the south.

GHT – THE ROLWALING

The trek described in this chapter follows the entire Great Himalaya Trail route through the Rolwaling. By combining it with the Renjo La trek in the *Solu-Khumbu (the Everest Region)*, see p137, and then the Bhairav Kund route to one of the Tilman Passes (see *GHT – Langtang*, p163) via The Last Resort, this becomes perhaps one of the most accessible areas of the GHT throughout Nepal as there are multiple road access points in the eastern Rolwaling valleys.

Helambu and Langtang

Just a day to the north of Kathmandu is the third most popular trekking region in Nepal, Langtang National Park, where there are mountains, glaciers, wildlife and rhododendron forests galore. The intermingling of Bhotia, Tamang, Brahmin, Newari and Chhetri people throughout the region is a wonderful example of Nepal's harmonious ethnic diversity. Add some folklore and some sublime

Helambu & Langtang region

- GHT
- Main trail

0   5   10km

Langtang Ri
7205

Langtang
Lirung
7225

Dagpache
6575

Dorje Pahad
6979

Nagthali

Briddim

Langshisa Kharka

Tatopani

Gatlang

Kyangjin Gompa

Dorje Lapka
6986

Rimche

Ghoratabela

Kanja La
5122

Tilman Pass
5308

Phurbo
Chyachu
6637

Syabru Besi

Thulo Syabru

DUNCHE

Sing Gompa

Langtang
National Park

Saraswati
Kund

Gosainkund

Kharane
5581

Phedi

Panch
Pokhari

Tembathan

Bhairab
Kund

Ghopte

Helambu

Mangengoth

Chogormogor
Kharka

Bagam
Gompa

Ta di Khola

Kutumsang

Listi

Last
Resort

Chisopani

Tinsang La
4778

Shivapuri Watershed
& Wild Life Reserve

Sundarijal

CHAUTARA

Lamosangu

Barhabise

Tinsang
Kewa

KATHMANDU

Nagarkot

Indrawati

Kirtipur

BHAKTAPUR

PATAN

Boch

sacred lakes, and it's fair to say that Helambu and Langtang have it all.

Three glaciers converge at Langshisa Kharka and form the headwaters of the Langtang Khola, which flows east to west between two chains of snow-covered peaks: the Langtang and Kangja Himals. The ridges and river valleys that shape the south-facing flanks of the Kangja Himal are broadly called Helambu. An extensive trail network runs throughout the region providing treks from just a few days up to a month. However, most trekkers stick to the tea-house routes from Dunche to Kyangjin Gompa and Sundarijal to Gosainkund, which begins on the rim of the Kathmandu valley.

Of the two main trails in the region the Dunche or Syabru Besi to Kyangjin Gompa through Bhotia villages is by far the more popular. If you have camping equipment, continue up the valley into an unspoilt mountain wilderness, which is home to snow leopard and three challenging passes: the Ganja La, Tilman Pass and Tilman East Pass.

Note: if you are exploring the region on your own it is wise never to leave your camp unattended while on day trips.

There are dozens of trails through Helambu that link the sacred lakes of Gosainkund, Panch Pokhari and Bhairav Kund to villages nestled in rhododendron forests that are a blaze of colour in April. A major feature of this region is the ease of access; regular bus services from Kathmandu run to Dunche and Syabru Besi in the west, and Melamchi, Chautara and Jalbire in the east. All of these route options mean you can design your own unique GHT experience in this region and it's all just a stone's throw from Kathmandu.

Established in 1976, the Langtang National Park has a reputation for being well managed, where locals actively help to maintain Park biodiversity and ecology. Human impact is limited but not absent as grazing is allowed in high pastures and permanent communities are permitted to exist in the heart of the Park.

ROUTE GUIDE

HELAMBU TO GOSAINKUND TREK

To the north of Kathmandu is pure Himalayan magic – traditional cultures, great views, well maintained trails, plenty of wildlife, sacred lakes, rarely another trekker in sight and one of the best wildflower displays in Nepal during the spring season.

Duration: from 9 days

Highest Point: 4462m

Best Season: Mar-May/Sep-Nov

Accommodation: camping and tea-house route options

HELAMBU TO GOSAINKUND

The trail out of the Kathmandu valley is a step back in time, to an age when all expeditions started from the valley rim. The feeling of walking away from Nepal's capital is unique and it allows you to 'grow' into the trek. Once over the rim, you head for a mountain range that fills the horizon. To the main north-south route a series of interconnecting trails from the east and west offer an opportunity to trek to your heart's content.

The trek to Gosainkund tends to have a long trekking season from early October through to mid-February, and then re-opening in March

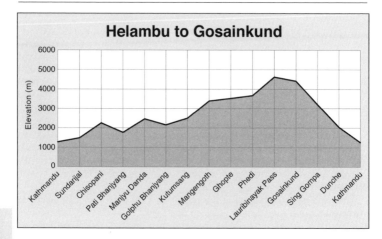

until the monsoon begins in June. However, snowfalls are very common on the Lauribinayak Pass throughout the year and trekkers should be careful not to become isolated on the higher trails. A major highlight is the magnificent rhododendron forests that bloom throughout April across the southern boundary of the National Park. If you want to connect with the holy lakes of Bhairav Kund and Panch Pokhari in the east of Helambu, you should be aware of sudden storms that can occur throughout the year, but they never deter the thousands of pilgrims who visit them during the monsoon months. If you have the time, consider a one-day side trip to the summit of Shivapuri and spend a night watching the twinkling of Kathmandu's city lights beneath a heaven full of stars.

Multiple daily bus services run to and from Sundarijal, Melamchi, Gaon, Dunche and Syanbru Besi.

DAY 1: KATHMANDU – SUNDARIJAL – CHISOPANI 6HRS

From the centre of Kathmandu, a bus trip of less than an hour in the early morning brings you to the road head of Sundarijal (1460m).

A large trail, mainly paved, leads north from the town centre up a small climb beside a large water pipe to the entrance of the Shivapuri National Park (1600m, 45 minutes) where you will need to register.

The trail ascends through forest to a scattered Tamang community called Mul Kharka (1900m, 1¼ hours). From here the trail continues to a ridgeline that encircles the Kathmandu valley and a small pass, Borlang Bhanjyang (2420m, 2½ hours). An easy downhill gradient with views of Shivapuri (behind) and Himalayan peaks (ahead) passes through an oak forest to the teahouses and campsites of Chisopani (2215m, 1½ hours).

DAY 2: CHISOPANI – KUTUMSANG 6HRS

The trail continues down a pronounced ridge to a saddle at Pati Bhanjyang (1770m 30 minutes) and then climbs to a fork where you should take the left hand trail to another saddle of a similar height, called Thankune Bhanjyang.

The trail then ascends an easy gradient before steepening to switchbacks and arriving at the village of Chipling (2170m, 2 hours). A final climb to the top of the Manjyu Danda ridge (2455m, 1 hour) brings you to a large chorten, teashop and a good viewpoint of the mountains to the north.

Descend for 45 minutes to the saddle village of Golphu Bhanjyang (2130m), where there are some teahouses and a camping ground next to the school if you cannot face the next climb.

The trail continues to climb a ridge to the north, take the larger track at each junction, until you reach another saddle and the Sherpa community of Kutumsang (2470m, 1½ hours).

There is a Langtang National Park office here and you will need to show your park receipt and may need to register your details.

DAY 3: KUTUMSANG – MANGENGOTH   4HRS
Water can be hard to find in dry months on the next trail section so carry a good supply.

Continue up the eastern side of a ridge from Kutumsang, first through oak forest and then through an impressive forest of red, white and pink-flowered rhododendron.

The gradient eases and from grassy meadows there are good views of the broad lower valleys and Shivapuri behind you.

The trail steepens again as you climb a gully before arriving at Kyuola Bhanjyang (3220m, 3½ hours) where there are some teahouses. The trail descends a little before climbing an easy gradient to Mangengoth (3390m, 30 minutes), which has a few teahouses and a large campsite surrounded by rhododendron forest.

DAY 4: MANGENGOTH – GHOPTE   4½HRS
The trail follows the undulating ridgeline north through dense rhododendron forest until it climbs to the hamlet of Therapati (3510m, 2 hours) and a major trail junction where you must go left (right descends to Melamchi village).

There is frequently snow covering the trail from here to the pass during the spring season, which could slow your group considerably. It is also important to note that

you are now at a height where many people feel the effects of altitude so you may want to stop and rest for the night.

If you look ahead it is possible to see the trail slowly ascending as it traverses through forest and then rocky hillside to the few teahouses and small campsite at Ghopte (3530m), which is 2½ hours away.

DAY 5: GHOPTE – PHEDI   3HRS
Most trekkers now stop at the teahouse and campsite at Phedi (3630m, 3 hrs) as it makes acclimatisation easier and you have the chance of reaching the pass while the weather is still relatively clear.

Attempting the pass from Ghopte is a long and strenuous day and means making the crossing in the afternoon when clouds often obscure the view.

The climb to Phedi is along a well-established trail but the rocky terrain can be hazardous in snowy conditions. There are also a couple of waterfalls that need to be crossed and these are normally frozen in the mornings.

DAY 6: PHEDI – GOSAINKUND 5HRS
The trail from Phedi climbs a rough trail past a chorten and up into a valley dominated by Surya Peak to the north.

Cross a wet or icy section of trail before ascending a series of easy climbs as you approach the Lauribinayak Pass (4610m, 4 hours). The pass is a broad saddle between the lower slopes of Surya Peak (to the north) and Chhyarkung Chuli (to the south) and connects with a complex series of shallow valleys to the north and northeast.

Each valley has at least one small lake and as many of them are sacred they each have a name.

From the pass descend into a valley past a couple of small lakes, and then over a slight rise where you can see the holiest of the lakes, Gosainkund (4380m, 1 hour). There is a Shiva shrine beside the lake adorned with bells to deter demons, as well as some spacious teahouses.

If you have time climb the slopes of a rocky hillside to the north for good views of Surya Peak and the lakes.

ROUTE GUIDE

❏ **The legend of Gosainkund**
Thousands of pilgrims gain merit by circumambulation of and/or bathing in the lake on the full moon in July and August. There are many legends concerning Gosainkund – perhaps the most famous involves Shiva, the Hindu god of creation. It is said that the gods were once churning the ocean, hoping to obtain *amrit*, the water of immortality. However, they extracted a burning poison that Shiva, in an effort to save the gods and the world, drank. This made his neck blue and the burning sensation forced him into the mountains to find something soothing to drink. He struck his trident into the ground and three streams poured forth, creating Gosainkund. Shiva drank from the lake and quenched his thirst. There is rock in the centre of the lake that resembles a Shiva *linga*, the sacred symbol of Hindu creation, and pilgrims often say they can see Shiva reclining on a bed of serpents in the lake's water.

DAY 7: GOSAINKUND – SING GOMPA   4HRS

An exposed trail from Gosainkund first traverses beneath and then climbs a ridge that runs westwards. Cresting the ridge brings you to a minor pass (4165m, 1 hour) and a series of chorten.

You can see the ridge descending to a collection of teahouses at Laurebina (3900m, 1 hour). There are good views of the Langtang range to the northeast and the Ganesh Himal to the northwest.

From Laurebina continue on the southern side of the ridge on a large trail, which enters rhododendron and then pine and fir forest. The trail switches to the north side of the ridge and continues through a forest that locals believe is haunted.

After 1½ hours the trail switches back to the southern side of the ridge and then descends to the village of Sing Gompa (3150m, 30 minutes) where there are teahouses and campsites.

DAYS 8-9: SING GOMPA – DUNCHE – KATHMANDU   3½HRS

The trail descends rapidly through an impressive forest all the way to the Trisuli river (2000m, 2½ hours), where there is a great spot to soak your feet in the river.

Cross the bridge to the south bank of the river and continue on a slightly undulating trail that meets the road out of Dunche (2030m, 1 hour), which is just a short walk away.

❏ **The life of a teahouse owner**
Running a teahouse is a tiring and often difficult occupation, but few can have had more challenges than Pasang Bhotie Sherpa, Namaste Lodge, Gokyo (see p141).

The eldest of four sisters, Pasang was sent to tend her family's yak herd in the Gokyo valley at the age of 12. While her sisters went to school, Pasang sold firewood and tea to trekkers from her cold and lonely stone huts, which she inhabited up and down the valley depending on the weather. After 6 years she had learnt basic English and was sending significant funds home to the family. She decided to run a small teashop at Gokyo's third lake and started saving every rupee. At 25 she met and fell in love with a Nepali trek leader with whom she has run a slowly expanding teahouse business for the last 19 years. She hopes that one day one of her sons, both of whom have a good college education, will return and continue her legacy.

Langtang valley

When you are sitting in the congested and noisy tumult of Kathmandu, it is amazing to think that in a day's bus drive you could be on the edge of pristine wilderness. Viewpoints above and beyond Kyangjin Gompa offer some stunning mountain vistas, and the opportunity to really immerse yourself in the Himalaya. Three high passes link to trails through Helambu and can be used to provide a range of loop itineraries.

The Langtang valley is trekkable year-round, and although the mountains are covered in cloud during monsoon, carpets of wildflowers compensate handsomely. The most popular seasons are early October through to mid-February, when the weather is clear and stable, and then from March to the end of April when rhododendron forests are in full bloom. Care should be taken when attempting any of the high passes; the Ganja La, Tilman Pass and Tilman East Pass are susceptible to sudden, fierce storms and snowfall at any time of year.

LANGTANG VALLEY TREK

Stunning views of glaciers and mountains, amazingly photogenic sunsets, sacred lakes, Buddhist monasteries, Tibetan culture, and the possibility of seeing rare wildlife – Langtang is a culturally rich and beautifully diverse national park.

Duration: 10 days

Highest Point: 4984m

Best Season: Sep-May

Accommodation: teahouse/camping

ROUTE GUIDE

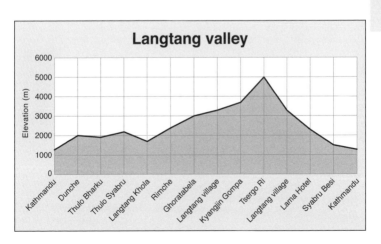

Comfy teahouses are in every village from Dunche and Syabru Besi to Kyangjin Gompa after which you will need full a camping kit. Supplies are expensive in Kyangjin so try to carry in as much as possible. If you want to attempt the high passes then you will need ropes and rock, ice and snow climbing equipment.

DAY 1: KATHMANDU – DUNCHE
8HRS
The drive from Kathmandu offers good views of Manaslu, Ganesh Himal, and Langtang and brief glimpses of village life in the Himalaya.

The first section is sealed road to Trishuli before a precipitous dirt road (which is due to be upgraded from 2010) to the National Park and police check posts on the edge of the bustling trading town of Dunche (2030m, 8 hours).

There are many teahouses and some campsites at the far end of the main street.

DAY 2: DUNCHE – THULO SYABRU
4½HRS
It might be possible to catch a lift with a vehicle heading towards Syabru Besi and jump off at Thulo Bharkhu (1860m, 1 hour), if not, it can be a dusty walk, so make sure you have a scarf to cover your face.

Thulo Bharkhu is a small place and a large sign towards the end of the village indicates the start of the main trail, which quickly climbs up through oak and pine forest to Barbal (2190m, 1½ hours).

If you can, take a rest break here and visit the gompa (and make a donation). It is now an easy undulating trail through temperate forest with occasional glimpses of the Ganesh Himal and Langtang valley.

You'll reach the ridgetop Tamang village of Thulo Syabru (2210m) in 2 hours, where you may have to register again at the check post.

DAY 3: THULO SYABRU – RIMCHE
5HRS
The trail cuts back into a gully to a bridge before rounding the hillside and dropping about 300m to the Langtang Khola below (1660m, 1½ hours). Once at the main valley trail turn east (right) and follow the Langtang Khola up stream.

In 20 minutes you will drop to the riverside and there may be a bamboo and log bridge to a hot springs on the far bank. The springs are not always accessible as landslides affect the area regularly.

Just beyond the springs is a teashop and for the next 1 hour and 20 minutes the trail passes through some small riverside glades and small up and downs as you approach Bamboo (1970m).

From behind the topmost of three teahouses with flower gardens the trail begins to climb more steadily. Head up into forest to avoid some landslides, although you will return to the riverside a few times before finally crossing a suspension bridge (2150m, 50 minutes).

Cross a couple of small landslides and then begin a switchback climb to Rimche (2399m, 1 hour), where there are a couple of pleasant teahouses, a small campsite and views down the valley.

DAY 4: RIMCHE – GHORATABELA
4HRS
From Rimche the trail climbs a little before dropping to the village of Lama Hotel (2487m, 40 minutes).

Note: if you are camping you will probably have to stay here rather than at Rimche.

Lama Hotel doesn't have any cultivation and relies exclusively on tourists for income. You should check and confirm all fees before committing to a teahouse; some even charge you just for sitting in the dining room.

From Lama Hotel you enter some beautiful oak, birch, hemlock and mountain-bamboo forests. Spanish moss hangs from trees giving the whole place a mysterious feeling.

Try to make an early start from Rimche to give yourself the best chance of spotting monkeys and the many birds that feed near the river. At first the trail undulates through the trees before coming to a lone teahouse at Gumnachok (2670m, 1 hour) in the forest. From here the trail climbs steadily for more than 200m to Ghoratabela (3030m, 2 hours and 10 minutes), where there are a couple of teahouses and a campsite.

If you have time, consider visiting the small monastery, which the local headman will open for a donation.

DAY 5: GHORATABELA – KYANGJIN GOMPA   4¾HRS
Beyond Ghoratabela is an army camp where your permits will be checked.

The valley now broadens and the gradient eases; Thyangsyapu (3120m, 1 hour) marks the end of the dense forest and the beginning of alpine country. The small settlement of Chyamki (3110m, 15 minutes) soon appears, before you then reach the gompa at Kangtangsa (3220m) in a further 45 minutes.

If you are feeling the effects of altitude it's a good idea to rest here for the night.

A short climb up to views of the classic glaciated U-shaped valley and the village of Langtang (3330m) in a further 30 minutes, the administrative centre for the valley. There are many teahouses and camping grounds to choose from, and remember to register at the check post.

From Langtang it is an easy climb through two Bhotia hamlets, Mundu and Sindum (3410m, 45 minutes). Ahead are views of Ganchenpo (Fluted Peak) and Langshisa Ri, and Langtang Lirung climbing above you to the north.

The trail then climbs the terminal moraine of the Lirung Glacier and descends to the gompa and many teahouses of Kyangjin Gompa (3830m, 1½ hours).

If you arrive early enough, sample the nearby cheese factory, visit the gompa, and consider trekking up trails that run on either side of the Lirung Glacier to see ice falls and spot musk deer or blue sheep.

DAY 6: KYANGJIN GOMPA ALL DAY
The easiest viewpoint is from a hill to the north of Kyangjin Gompa, many prayer flags, which can be seen from the village, indicate the summit (4360m, 2 hours).

For the more adventurous there are many good views on the climb of Tsergo Ri (4984m, 3½ hours climb). There is an excellent look-out with magnificent views of Langtang Lirung and its surrounding peaks – it can be reached by climbing the slopes immediately behind Kyangjin Gompa.

Further to the east of Tsergo Ri, is Yala Peak (5500m, 6 hour climb), which is more spectacular, and requires mountaineering skills and equipment.

Alternatively, a trek further up the valley towards Langshisa Kharka (4160m, 7 hour return trek) provides great views of the ranges bordering Tibet and a chance for some animal spotting in the early morning.

DAYS 7-10: KYANGJIN GOMPA – SYABRU BESI – KATHMANDU
Retrace your steps on the main trail. You might want to stay in different places on your descent or return to see friends.

Either way a clearly marked trail follows the river to Syabru Besi (1503m) where there are many teahouses and a regular bus service to Kathmandu (10 hours).

ROUTE GUIDE

OTHER MAJOR TRAILS IN HELAMBU & LANGTANG

Shivapuri
The highest point on the northern Kathmandu valley rim offers a stunning viewpoint (2732m, 6 hours) of the city below, especially on a clear night when the lights imitate the stars above. There are many trails, which often causes confusion, so take a guide who knows the way.

Panch Pokhari
A pilgrimage site and location of a Mahadev Temple, these five sacred lakes (4010m) can be reached in five days from the road head town of Chautara. The

lakes are in the southern section of the Langtang National Park and can be combined with treks to/from Helambu, Gosainkund and over the Ganja La or the Tilman Passes (see *GHT – Langtang*, p163) to the Langtang valley. Chautara, where you then begin a long ridge climb, is a few hours drive from the centre of Kathmandu.

The trail ascends the Kamikharka Danda above the Indrawati Khola before linking with the Hutprang Danda and on to the lakes. During the first few days you pass through Hindu, Tamang and Bhotia villages. You then walk through extensive rhododendron, pine and fir forests, which surround the Langtang National Park. The sacred lakes of Panch Pokhari ('Five Lakes') lie above the tree line and offer great views of the Kangja Himal.

Most return routes cross the Indrawati watershed to Tarkeghyang and involve camping for 12 to 15 days. Alternatively, you could go on to cross either Tilman Pass or Tilman East Pass, or if you want to further explore local cultures consider combining it with Gosainkund or Bhairav Kund for a doubly auspicious trek.

Ganja La

This pass should only be attempted by experienced trekking groups with appropriate climbing and camping equipment. The Ganja La offers a great circular trek back through Helambu, some fantastic views of the Langtang range and an approach to the popular trekking peak, Naya Kanga.

From Kyangjin Gompa, retrace the trail towards Langtang village and after about 20 minutes take the left fork, which drops down to the river and a small wooden bridge. A small but obvious trail climbs through birch and rhododendron forest to simple teahouses and a good campsite, Ngegang Kharka (4430m, 2 hours). Continue climbing, staying on the west bank of a watercourse, across steep ground until you reach the base of moraine deposited by the glacier above, and a potential campsite (4640m, 2 hours).

The pass is a further two-hour climb up a steep rock scramble, which is often made treacherous by snow. Mountaineering skills and a fixed rope may be necessary to reach the pass (5130m) and to descend. There is a steep descent on loose moraine for 3 hours, do not head towards the glacier rather, stay on the east-facing (right) slope of the valley.

Continue descending past some kharka and staying high on, but not on top of, a ridge that runs almost due south above the Yangri Khola. There is a good campsite (4420m) after another 2 hours with water from a tributary of the Yangri Khola. Continue to traverse the ridge without losing height; the next campsite is Dhukpu (4030m, 6 hours). Follow the ridge until the trail swings up to some prayer flags (1 hour) and then descends steeply to Tarkeghyang and the main Helambu trails.

The main route continues to Melamchi Bazaar (870m, two days via Sermathang) or via Tharepati and Chisapani (see reverse of *Helambu to Gosainkund*, days 1-4, pp154).

For notes on Bhairav Kund, **Tilman Pass, and Tilman East Pass** see following pages.

GHT – LANGTANG

This section of the GHT requires excellent navigation skills and/or local guides, and technical climbing experience for either the Tilman Pass or Tilman East Pass. Only fully equipped camping groups will be able to attempt the route, there are no teahouses or major resupply opportunities between the Bhote Koshi and Kyangjin Gompa.

The route described here is from the Last Resort on the Arniko Highway to Syabru Besi via Tilman Pass, however, GHT options also include linking Panch Pokhari, the Ganja La and Gosainkund.

Leave the Last Resort on the Arniko Highway from the main gate and pass through Panlan village immediately to the south. From here the trail climbs a steep hillside with little shade. The trail ascends rapidly to Baldun (1890m, 1¼ hours), which the locals might refer to as Listi. However, Listi (2260m, Finaid: Barhabise sheet: 2785 04, ref: 893 866) is a plateau further up the hill from this Tamang village and is reached in another 1 hour and 10 minutes. As you approach the ridge above you will clearly see a Hindu Temple, beneath which is a community health post where you can camp.

Continue on the temple ridge to a series of chorten overlooking Listi and then swing northeast keeping to the ridge. Do not traverse around the ridge (to your left, or more north). After 1½ hours you reach the top of the ridge above Listi and a broad grassy place (2650m) where cremations occur, so treat the area with respect. From here you can see the trail traversing a hillside to your north to a minor pass where a Sherpa village called Bagam (2705m, 45 minutes) is home to some of the three hundred nuns from Bagam Gompa, situated below the ridge. There is also a school here, which would make a good campsite. To the north can be seen a steep forest-covered ridge and the trail leads from Bagam straight up to 3286m (1¾ hours) to a temporary dharamsala which is just below the main ridge.

At the top of the ridge there is a trail crossroads, turn left and continue on the ridge proper. At first the trail looks like a watercourse and you are tempted to bear right, but don't stray from the ridge and the trail soon becomes a pleasant flat walk through pine forest. Shotang Kharka (3379m, Finaid: Barhabise, sheet: 2785 04, ref: 887 920) is reached in 20 minutes; you will need to ask any herders to show you where the water source is located.

From Shotang the trail continues north, climbing a ridge with good views of mountains to the northeast in Tibet and northwest in Langtang. Pilgrims who come for the August festival have made the trail broad and easy to follow to Chogomogor Kharka (3924m, 2 hours, Finaid: Barhabise, sheet: 2785 04, ref: 887 949), which is a major trail junction both north-south and east-west. If you do not wish to continue to Bhairav Kund you should camp here. To reach the sacred lake climb a little to a chorten and then head northeast across the east-facing flanks of a rising series of craggy peaks, there is a dharamsala and campsite at the lake.

The following morning retrace your steps to Chogormogor Kharka and take a trail that heads east-north-east to a kharka on the Paulan Dada (3812m, 2 hours, Finaid: Barhabise, sheet: 2785 04, ref: 873 956). Be careful to stay on the west-ridge trail from this kharka as many tracks lead into the forest. Descend a trail, which gradually becomes very steep as you enter dense forest.

In 2 hours you reach a temporary dharamsala and series of chorten directly above Kyansin village (2520m) to which you descend in 30 minutes. A trail then traverses a hillside to the northeast and once around the ridge descends steeply to the Nyasem Khola (1861m, 2 hours), where there is a camping place on the far side of a suspension bridge. Do not camp close to the bridge as there are quite a few ticks and lice in the area; instead pick an area about 20 or 30 metres upstream.

Climb a trail on the far side of the river for 300m to Nimatol village (2158m, 1 hour) where there is a new trail that traverses the sometimes steep hillside to Tembathan (2160m, 45 minutes). You will need to employ a local guide from this village, as the trails ahead are frequently overgrown and rarely used. There are two options from Tembathan, firstly a long route to Hille Bhanjyang to Panch Pokhari (three days); alternatively, head upstream and then climb a steep hill to Panch Pokhari (two days). The first option is a more substantial and easy to follow track, but a local guide is required for the climb via Hille Bhanjyang, where there is a main trail along the ridge top.

For the second route, follow a flat trail north from the village to a wooden suspension bridge over a tributary. Do not cross the bridge. Instead take a small trail that crosses the river about 10 metres downstream and then winds onto flat ground where there are some well-used kharkas. From the northern end of the kharka descend to the river side.

Note: the enormous landslide area on the far bank destroyed Mahathan village and most of Thipu village but, incredibly, with no loss of life.

The trail now climbs the eastern side of the rivers course to the hamlet of Tegu where you again follow a trail along the bank. In 1½ hours from Tembathan you will reach the remains of Thipu village. There is a good campsite by the river before the village area.

Do not cross the river at the village, instead continue on the east bank for 1 hour to a small bamboo and log bridge. Cross carefully and then continue north on a sometimes scrubby trail through forest to Chedupa Kharka (2513m, 1 hour, Finaid: Dorle Pahad, sheet: 2885 16, ref: 774 062). From this large kharka a small trail heads north for about 50 metres before heading up the steep hillside to your left. There are ticks and leeches along this track so be vigilant. Climb for about 800m to Salingling Kharka (3323m, 3¾ hours, Finaid: Lantan, sheet: 2885 15, ref: 765 057), where you might be able to find water in a gully to the south. If not, then continue for another 45 minutes to Nemagchukpa Kharka (3578m), where there is permanent water.

Continue along the ridge through rhododendron forest to an intersecting ridge, which leads to Panch Pokhari. There is another, small kharka campsite at 4048m (2¼ hours) on the ridge. From here it is only 1½ hours to the lakes of Panch Pokhari (4074m), which you reach by crossing the main north-south ridge at 4229m (Finaid: Lantan, sheet: 2885 15, ref: 747 034).

Directly to the east of the temple at Panch Pokhari is a short climb back to the ridgeline (4245m, 40 minutes), which you should cross and descend to a broad kharka (4070m, 20 minutes). Follow the obvious trail north as it rises to cross a hill spur into another shallow basin. For the next 1½ hours continue north crossing similar spurs and basins between 4000m and 4200m. In the fourth basin you will see a trail junction where the left trail climbs towards a rocky outcrop and the right trail swings away to the northeast. You can take either trail, but if the north facing slopes are covered in snow and/or ice you might find the longer, but lower, northeast trail safer. The higher route climbs to a small lake (Lingsing Kharka, 4450m, 1 hour) whereas the northeast trail contours lower slopes at 4000m +/- 30m for 2 hours before climbing and rejoining the higher trail at a small basin with a well-built stone kharka (4273m, Finaid: Lantan, sheet: 2885 15, ref: 749 092). From this kharka continue north, climbing for about 100m before the trail levels and you then drop through a small valley to ascend a final ridge above Tin Pokhari (4255m, 1½ hours, Finaid: Lantan, sheet: 2885 15, ref: 754 110), although the three lakes have dried up.

From the ridge above Tin Pokhari you have a clear view of both glacier approaches to Tilman Pass and Tilman East Pass. In clear weather it is even possible to see the rocky ridge of Tilman East Pass at the base of the west ridge of Dorje Lakpa peak. Your choice of which pass to attempt will depend on time available, weather conditions and skill level. The easier route is Tilman Pass (the western of the two glaciers, described in full below), however Tilman East Pass is a spectacular option for experienced groups and is worth considering if you have time available.

Tilman Pass

From Tin Pokhari follow a trail that drops into an ablation valley to the northwest, trek through some kharka and climb for 2¼ hours until you reach a campsite (4646m, Finaid: Lantan, sheet: 2885 15, ref: 731 134) at the valley's end, marked by a steep moraine wall. There are a few large boulders on top of the moraine wall, climb to the most northerly of them and descend beside a small glacial lake. From the lake cross to the middle of the glacier and follow an indistinct trail marked by occasional cairns. In 2 hours you will reach a campsite (4867m, Finaid: Lantan, sheet: 2885 15, ref: 732 150) on the glacier just as the valley narrows, and in a further 20 minutes you will reach the base of the pass (4848m).

There appear to be two routes up the lower rocky section of the pass, but the right hand rock-climbing option is exposed and prone to rock fall so you might prefer ascending the loose scree to the right of the icefall (and to the left of the rock-climbing route). Once above the rock band, traverse around to your left and climb mixed ice and rock to the right of the icefall and beneath a steep rock face. Once at the rock face traverse left to the glacier and then climb directly onto the pass snowfield. Tilman Pass (5308m, 2¾ hours, Finaid: Lantan, sheet: 2885 15, ref: 727 166) is through a narrow notch to the northwest of the snowfield. Beware of rock fall on both sides of your approach.

ROUTE GUIDE

Once on the pass descend a steep snowy slope to the northwest. Beware of crevasses on your descent, it is wise to rope everyone because the descent becomes steeper as you approach a broad plateau covered in avalanche debris at 5130m (45 minutes), where you could camp. Follow a snowmelt stream on the western side of the plateau to a steep drop to a glacial lake in a valley below. This section can be treacherous and care should be taken on the rock and ice filled gullies; a handline may be needed in places. In less than 2 hours you should reach the lake, where you can camp on the northern shore (4756m, Finaid: Lantan, sheet: 2885 15, ref: 727 185). Alternatively, continue to the left (northwest) of a moraine wall to an indistinct campsite at 4720m (30 minutes).

Continue to descend northwest to a small, level, sandy place (20 minutes) about 200m above the Langshisa Glacier. Do not descend to the glacier, the moraine here is very unstable, steep and prone to rock fall. Instead climb a rough hillside beneath black cliffs to your east (20 minutes). You soon come to a small gully, which you should cross as high as possible near a rocky outcrop. Contour to a second gully and cross it beneath the continued rock outcrop (10 minutes). Then descend heading northwest to a small ablation valley, which leads to the end of the Langshisa Glacier valley (4285m, 1½ hours, Finaid: Lantan, sheet: 2885 15, ref: 703 214).

There are no good trails that descend to the river so use cairns to roughly direct your approach. Wade the river at the shallowest point (normally near a large boulder on the northern bank) and move directly away from the river to find the main trail to Kyangjin Gompa (3900m, 3 hours to your west). From Kyangjin Gompa follow the main Langtang valley trail to Syabru Besi (1503m, 9 hours).

Tilman East Pass

This is a relatively new route and has only been completed a few times by groups with Sherpa staff and experienced porters. The descent from the northern side of the pass has many crevasses. Both sides of the pass are prone to rock fall. Care should be taken, as well as rock, snow and ice climbing equipment.

From Tin Pokhari follow a trail that drops towards an ablation valley to some small kharka to the northwest, the first of which has a trail that turns north (4210m, 15 minutes, Finaid: Lantan, Sheet: 2885 15, ref: 745 118). Drop to the river that flows from the Tilman Pass glacier and ascend moraine above a glacier that flows down from the northeast. The trail climbs steeply at first but as it nears an intersecting glacier from the northwest it becomes flatter. There isn't a good campsite beside the glacier so continue north and camp far enough away from hanging ice at 4675m (4¼ hours, Finaid: Lantan, sheet: 2885 15, ref: 763 152). Head out into the centre of the glacier (eastwards) and then bear north, staying clear of any rock fall from crags to your left. Ascend a slight step to a snowy basin and then climb again to Tilman East Pass (5368m, 3 hours, Finaid: Dorle Pahad, sheet: 2885 16, ref: 777 178), which is a rocky ridge about 30m high. It is then a steep descent across crevassed snowfield to the north-north-west, to the upper reaches of the Langshisa Glacier. Continue down the southern edge of the glacier to Langshisa Kharka (4550m, 12 hours from the pass).

Ganesh and Manaslu Himals

In the centre of Nepal are two trekking gems, the Ganesh and Manaslu Himals, and both are the country's best-kept secrets. Many would argue that the Manaslu Circuit trail is the best general trek in the country, with colourful cultures and

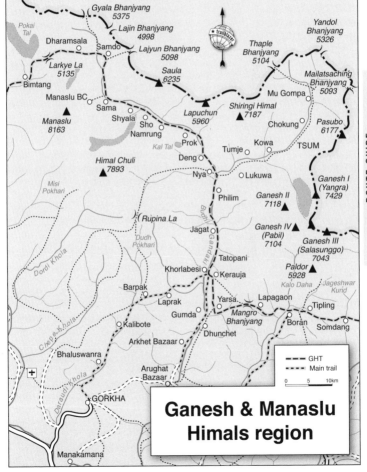

ROUTE GUIDE

Ganesh & Manaslu Himals region

Legend:
- – – GHT
- ···· Main trail

0   5   10km

dramatic valleys against a backdrop of classic Himalayan peaks. The Ganesh Himal is one of the least visited regions in Nepal, and offers the adventurous trekker some wonderful opportunities for genuine exploration.

Lying to the west of the Langtang valley, the Ganesh Himal is a collection of seven major peaks (one in Tibet, six in Nepal or on the border) that form a natural barrier with Tibet. Named after the Hindu elephant god, Ganesha (Ganesh IV is said to look like the head of an elephant), the range is bordered by the Budhi Gandaki river to the west and extensive forests across the southern flanks that flow to Dhading District. Beyond the Budhi Gandaki, to the west, rises a collection of peaks dominated by the 8163m summit of Manaslu. Throughout both himals Gurung, Tamang, Magar, Ru-Pa, Larke and Siar people blend to create perhaps the most ethnically interesting series of valleys throughout the Himalaya.

Itinerary options abound and provide some of the most fantastic range of GHT routes in the whole of the Nepal Himalaya. The Tamang Heritage Trail can be combined with more strenuous routes into and around the Ganesh Himal. Tsum, a remote Larke valley to the north of the Ganesh Himal, is accessible from the Manaslu Circuit. If you want to do the full Circuit trek and cross the impressive Larkye La, a large saddle to the north of Manaslu, you can explore the massive natural amphitheatre of mountains at Bimtang before descending to the Annapurna Circuit.

The Tamang Heritage Trail region was opened to tourists only in 2002 when the Chinese and Nepali governments resolved all border claims; in contrast the Manaslu region was opened in 1992, yet has been largely ignored. Neither region is protected by National Park status, so logging and poaching remain unchecked. Hopefully, the Nepali Government will one day safeguard these regions as part of a broader trans-boundary animal migration corridor with China.

TAMANG HERITAGE TRAIL TREK

An excellent trek along an easy-going route combined with authentic villages that offer a homestay program in traditional homes, and great views of mountains in Tibet, Langtang and Ganesh Himals, set against rhododendron forests, and just a day from Kathmandu.

Duration: 10 days

Highest Point: 3600m

Best Season: Oct-May

Accommodation: teahouse/camping

TAMANG HERITAGE TRAIL

The Tamang Heritage Trail is one of the newest trekking routes in Nepal and was created by some Nepali NGOs who worked hard with villagers to improve local trails; the result is an easy-going route through pristine mountain scenery. The main trail can be extended in a number of directions, including to Dudh Kund ('Milk Lake') on the northern slopes of Langtang Lirung, Sangjung Kharka and Kalo Pokhari near Paldor Peak, Jaisuli Kund above Somdang and connecting trails to valleys to the southwest of the Ganesh Himal.

The Tamang heritage Trail has

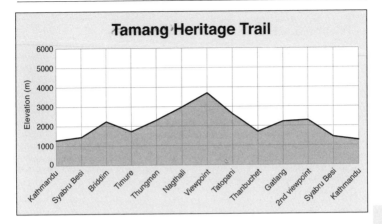

Tamang Heritage Trail

Elevation (m): 6000, 5000, 4000, 3000, 2000, 1000, 0

Kathmandu, Syabru Besi, Briddim, Timure, Thungmen, Nagthali, Viewpoint, Tatopani, Thanbuchet, Gatlang, 2nd viewpoint, Syabru Besi, Kathmandu

been designed to showcase the local Tamang culture and is best when combined with one of the many festivals throughout the year, making the route a genuine year-round trekking option. The highest point of this trek, at 3600m, also makes it ideal for those who are susceptible to altitude sickness but who still want to experience the high Himalaya. The best time for views is December to January when the air is free from haze and the mountains in Tibet can be seen clearly. The main trekking seasons (both pre- and post-monsoon) see a few small trekking groups visiting, but the region is most popular with independent trekkers who are in search of something different. The openhearted hospitality of the Tamang people makes any welcome something special, especially if you visit during the monsoon festivals.

One of the highlights of the trek is the opportunity for a 'home-stay' in the village of Briddim. This involves staying in a traditional Bhotia house for up to three nights.

DAY1: KATHMANDU – SYABRU BESI 8 HRS

The drive from Kathmandu offers good views of Manaslu, Ganesh and Langtang Himals as well as brief glimpses of village life in the Himalaya.

The first section is sealed road to Trishuli before the precipitous dirt road to Dunche, where there is a National Park and police check post. Continue to Syabru Besi (1503m), where there are many teahouses and a campsite.

As most of the day's drive is on dirt roads, a light scarf to protect your face against dust may be useful.

DAY 2: SYABRU – BRIDDIM (HOME STAY) 4 HRS

Make your way north through Syabru Besi to the check post located above the steps that lead to a suspension bridge across the Bhote Koshi. After leaving your details, cross the bridge and then turn left on a trail that climbs briefly before following an easier gradient to the village of Wangel (1633m, 1 hour).

There is a water pipe in the centre of the village, take the trail, opposite the pipe, that climbs between houses. You will enter mixed pine and rhododendron forest after roughly 30 minutes. Stay on this main trail for the rest of the day, and at any trail junc-

❏ **A Briddim folktale**
Long ago the field near the gompa was a *tal* (a small lake), which the villagers sometimes used for washing. One day, a great and famous high lama came to the village. He stayed in the gompa and the villagers looked after him. When he was here the villagers asked him if he could do something about the tal; they already had a good river for washing and water so the tal wasn't very useful (Tibetans refuse to kill animals and therefore place little value on fish). So the lama recited some powerful *mantras* (Tibetan Buddhist prayers) and all of the water and laundry that was around and in the lake spiralled up into the clouds and disappeared.

The fish that had lived in the water all jumped out of the tal and into a large rock beside the field. So the tal became a field, which the lama said the villagers must protect, as it was now sacred. The villagers may only sow three crops per year there, at most, and sometimes when they plough the field they find *dzee* stones (sacred stones believed by some to be fossilised caterpillars). Ask the locals to show you the fish in the rock.

tions always take the noticeably larger track. It's mostly an easy gradient as you traverse hillside, but there are two steeper sections in the forest.

A deserted house is reached after 1½ hours; monkeys can often be spotted here. For another hour the trail winds around another ridge before arriving on the edge of a basin above Briddim (2229m).

You can descend and walk up through the village or traverse around to a trail above the village and then walk down. The school offers a small campsite and there is a basic teahouse, however it is far more enjoyable and convenient to stay in one of the home-stays.

Many people elect to stay for two or three nights in the home-stay to really get the feel for what life is like in a Himalayan village. There are local trails to explore up the Briddim Khola that runs beside the village and along the ridge to the south of the village. Alternatively, see how a typical household works, spin wool, and learn about traditional culture.

DAY 3: BRIDDIM – TIMURE   3½ HRS

Take your time with farewells and buying any souvenirs you may want, as it is a short trek to Timure (1762m) where there are simple teahouses. There are two trails to choose from:

Descend through Briddim to Lingling (1737m, 1 hour) and then continue to the

Bhote Koshi (20 minutes). Follow the new road route beside the river for 2 hours to Timure. Alternatively, take the trail that leaves the village past the gompa and traverse through forest above Lingling and then descend a steep trail to the Bhote Koshi (2 hours). Then follow the road route for 1½ hours to Timure.

After the monsoon rains have receded the locals dig out some shallow pools at a hot spring just after the bridge to Thungmen. To find them, walk north along the riverbank from the bridge for about 400m, then rock hop beside the river to beneath a small cliff of loose earth. You should approach with caution as locals may be bathing and it is polite to give them a chance to cover up.

Alternatively, you can walk up to Rasuwa, the border with Tibet and the site of a ruined fort that was built in the early nineteenth century. Or, if you have made an early start from Briddim, you could continue straight to Thungmen and miss out Timure.

DAY 4: TIMURE – THUNGMEN/ THUMAN   4 HRS

Retrace yesterday's route to the bridge near the hot-springs (1650m), just over 1 hour from Timure. You may have spotted the bridge the day before as before you descended to the river trail. Cross the bridge and climb narrow switchbacks for 1½ hours to the terraces, and the village of Dalphedi (2317m). The trail climbs more gradually

❏ A local legend
One of the villagers from Briddim joined our camp one evening and told an intriguing tale: 'A long time in the past, the Chinese and Nepalese had a brief war, which resulted in the Chinese army marching through Rasuwa and occupying the hills to the south of Dunche. The defending Nepalese were caught off guard and with few troops were not going to be able to halt the Chinese. As the invaders established their camps overlooking the valleys around the Trisuli river, the Nepali general devised a cunning plan. Each night he lit small braziers and mounted them on cattle, which the Chinese were led to believe were the countless camps of the growing defending forces. The Chinese general believed the ruse and withdrew, which saved Nepal from an embarrassing loss.'

from Dalphedi to a ridge to the south of the village. A pronounced rock outcrop marks a minor pass (visible from Dalphedi) decorated with prayer flags. The trail descends some rough stone steps and then traverses a rock face before turning west and providing the first views of Thungmen (2338m, 1½ hours). An easy trail traverses around to the Palpachhe Khola before climbing slightly to the village.

There isn't a good campsite in Thungmen, but there are some simple teahouses and a decaying wooden Nyingmapa sect gompa that is said to be 450 years old,

and is definitely worth a visit. The locals don't seem to care about the state of the gompa, so please leave a donation with the key-holder who tries his best to maintain the building. If you are camping, continue up through the village to a school (15 minutes) and a series of grassy fields, which can all be used as campsites.

DAY 5: THUNGMEN – NAGTHALI
4 HRS

The trail is sometimes steep and there is no reliable water source so make sure you pack enough supplies. Climb a well-established

ROUTE GUIDE

❏ The Tamang
Tamangs mainly live in the hills that circle Kathmandu, where you may see them on the streets, carrying their *dhoko* by a *namlo*, and always with their *khukuri* knife tucked into their cloth belt. No self respecting Tamang fellow would leave the house without his knife. *Tamang* means horse-trader in Tibetan, and they believe that they originated from Tibet and moved to Nepal countless centuries ago, where they continue to practise Buddhism. Theirs is the major Tibeto-Burman speaking community in Nepal.

They generally prefer to live in congested paved villages with stone houses and wooden shingle or slate roofs. Most houses have two floors, the ground floor is where grain is stored and livestock shelters overnight, and the family live upstairs. The first floor has three wooden windows surrounded by intricate carvings and sometimes overhangs the ground floor, forming a veranda where the inhabitants will take tea, chat and work during the day. They grow their own crops of wheat, maize and millet and keep a few animals such as chickens, goats and buffalo.

Tamangs are skilled craftsmen and tuneful singers. So their festivals are often lively affairs, which continue into the early hours for days on end. They are strong, easygoing and hardworking – many are employed as porters for trekking groups as well as local delivery work. They are the most highly sought after domestic staff because of their honesty, kindness and work ethic.

trail that leads up to a series of terraces and pastures before reaching the forest (roughly 2750m, 1½ hours) above Thungmen.

You are now in a fine rhododendron, juniper, pine and oak forest that attracts birds. The trail switchbacks up to a small, derelict chorten (2870m, 1 hour), where the trail forks: take the left trail into a small valley. Remain on the south (left) bank of a small stream, as the trail continues to climb. Locals have cut young trees to leave stumps about 1m high as trail markers.

As you near the end of the small valley the track crosses the stream before climbing a short section to a large kharka (3010m, 1 hour). There are two trails to the top of the hill, the left hand track loops around a large thicket of dense rhododendron bushes and climbs some steps. The second heads from the herder's shelter through a narrow track that climbs a sometimes-slippery slope directly to the hilltop.

There are few trees on the top of Nagthali (3165m, 30 minutes) and you should easily spot the small gompa and new simple teahouses as you approach. There are plenty of places to camp or share a room for a small fee.

DAY 6: NAGTHALI VIEWPOINT
5 HRS

To the north of the gompa, nestled against the forest, is a small stone meditation hut for Buddhist hermits who visit from Tibet. You will see a track leading off to the right, which then winds around the hill through one of the most beautiful old-growth rhododendron forests in Nepal.

The trail swings to the north again (3310m, 1 hour) and stays on top of a narrow ridge offering views of the Ganesh Himal and Chilime valley below.

During the winter months and just after dawn, red panda can be spotted in the forest along this ridge. The track then climbs again before turning right (3400m, 45 minutes) and away from the forest and on to an open hillside of dwarf azalea bushes.

This track can be hard to follow when it gets overgrown, especially when it swings north (left) towards a copse of rhododendron festooned with Spanish moss.

After another 45 minutes you should reach a rarely used kharka with a small stream. This eerie forest section again gives way to dwarf azalea as you continue to ascend an easy gradient to a magnificent viewpoint (3720m, 1 hour) of countless peaks in Tibet, the Ganesh and Langtang Himals. Take the same route back to Nagthali (1½ hours).

DAY 7: NAGTHALI – TATOPANI
3½ HRS

From Nagthali the trail heads southwest over the edge of the plateau – ask the locals in the teahouse if you are unsure. The trail drops to a small copse before turning back on itself and descending steeply, heading north-northwest.

As you descend you will notice the small village of Brimdang (2848m, 1¼ hours), where there is a large chautara above a stone stairway. If you look at the houses while facing north you should see a small track that heads into the dense forest behind the buildings.

If you ask the locals they might guide you along this shortcut to Tatopani ('Hot Water'). However, the main trail continues down the steps and becomes a larger track that heads north past terraces and small, forested sections.

The hot springs of Tatopani (2607m, 2 hours) are ahead, marked by many prayer flags in some places. These hot springs are probably the largest in Nepal, and perhaps the most popular. Most evenings, locals and visitors congregate in the three pools and sing songs to each other.

DAY 8: TATOPANI – GATLANG
5¾ HRS

Your crew will probably be in the hot springs soon after dawn – feel free to join them for a dip before breakfast. From the centre of Tatopani follow a rough stone-paved trail, which descends to a single farm building before flattening out to an easy gradient.

The trail steepens again before entering Gonggang (2227m, 1 hour). A lone teashop marks the end of Gonggang and a steep descent to the Chilime Khola and a suspension bridge. On the far bank take the left hand trail that climbs to Chilime village (1762m, 45 minutes), where there is an old wooden gompa. The locals here are friendly but the village is frequently dirty.

Take the trail that leaves Chilime passing a small school and a series of chorten and mani walls. A long, derelict mani wall marks the entry to the Gatlang valley, and the trail again forks.

If you want to return to Syabru Besi from here, turn left and cross the suspension bridge to Thanbuchet and head straight down the valley on a trail on the north bank. At the end of the valley you will meet the Bhote Koshi, where you cross the Chilime Khola and head south to Syabru Besi (2½ hours).

To visit Gatlang, turn right and cross another bridge about 200m upstream from the mani wall. The trail now climbs through oak and rhododendron forest before meeting the terraces of Gatlang (2238m, 4 hours). Along the trail are large chorten decorated with beautiful mani stones. There is a community teahouse at the bottom of the village, and a private teahouse at the very top. If you are camping, you will probably be directed to the school above the village.

This is a friendly village, although a little dirty, and the local Mother's Group is always willing to provide a show of traditional songs and dancing for a donation.

DAYS 9-10: GATLANG – SYABRU – KATHMANDU

From Gatlang head up to the dirt road above the village and follow it east (turn left once on the road) for 3½ hours to a small pass, Rongga Bhanjyang (2187m) above Syabru Besi. If you have time, climb to the viewpoint to the north of the pass (2320m, 15 minutes).

The trail continues north from the viewpoint (or directly down from the pass), descending into forest before turning back on itself and descending rapidly to Syabru Besi (1503m, 2 hours).

OTHER MAJOR TRAILS IN THE GANESH HIMAL

Directly you leave the main Tamang Heritage Trail the paths, primarily used by herders and people gathering firewood, become small.

From Timure there is a small trail to Dudh Kund on the northern slopes of Langtang Lirung. WH Tilman was the first European to trek in Nepal in 1949, and this was the first place he tried to reach, but he couldn't find it as the trails were bad, and they're not much better today.

From Tatopani in the Chilime valley you can ascend the Chilime Khola to the border with Tibet and then climb a steep rocky hillside to your west (left) to the Sangjung Kharka (two days from Tatopani), a pretty valley that lies beneath Paldor and the Ganesh Himal. To the west of Paldor is Kalo Pokhari ('Black Lake'), the starting point for a mountaineering circuit around the trekking peak (four days).

Gatlang is a good place from which to head up to Jaisuli Kund (two days), to the south of Paldor and another potential route to Sangjung Kharka (further two days). It is also on the main GHT route to Somdang (see *GHT – Langtang*, p161). Once in the valleys to the southwest of the Ganesh Himal there is a number of 'shikari' or hunter trails that you could explore to the southern slopes of Pabil, or Ganesh IV (7104m) and Salasungo, or Ganesh III (7043m).

MANASLU CIRCUIT

There are a number of ways to begin your Manaslu adventure:
- Drive to the market town of Arughat Bazaar, where the road is being extended northwards along the Budhi Gandaki river to Arkhet Bazaar. Beginning from either of these towns offers the shortest overall itinerary of 15 to 16 days, and they are the most popular starting points.
- Drive to the ancient Nepali capital of Gorkha and then walk to Arughat Bazaar via Khanchok. This adds two days to option one.
- Drive to Gorkha and then head north up the Daraudi Khola, then climb to Barpak and cross the Gupsi Danda to Laprak, and join option one at Khorlabesi. This route adds four days to option one and is described in full below.
- The Rupina La is rarely crossed and should only be attempted by experienced and acclimatised trekking groups. Drive to Gorkha and then head north up the Daraudi Khola but instead of turning to Barpak continue up the valley and cross the Rupina La to Jarang. This route adds at least five days to option one, joining at Nya (before Deng).

MANASLU CIRCUIT TREK

A true gem of the Himalaya, the Manaslu Circuit has it all: stunning mountain vistas, enchanting cultures, some of the most beautiful sections of trail in Nepal, and all around the 8th highest mountain in the world.

Duration: 19 days

Highest Point: 5135m

Best Season: Mar-May/Sep-Nov

Accommodation: camping

The Manaslu Himal has a long trekking season from early October through to mid-February. It then re-opens after a brief winter in mid-March, and can be trekked until the monsoon begins in June. However, snow can block the Larkye La at any time of year and it can be icy, requiring a rope. Delays occur in all seasons, except monsoon, so you should make sure you can adjust your itinerary if necessary.

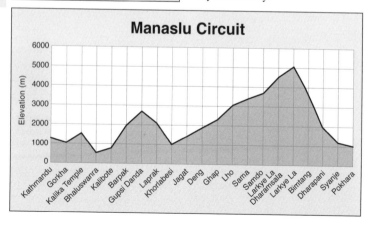

Manaslu Circuit

Elevation (m) plotted against route: Kathmandu, Gorkha, Kalika Temple, Bhaluswanra, Kalibote, Barpak, Gupsi Danda, Laprak, Khorlabesi, Jagat, Deng, Ghap, Lho, Sama, Samdo, Larkye La, Dharamsala, Larkye La, Bimtang, Dharapani, Syanie, Pokhara

DAY 1: KATHMANDU – GORKHA – KALIKA TEMPLE   ALL DAY

It is a good idea to leave Kathmandu early to avoid the traffic gridlock, and (all being well) arrive at Gorkha (1060m) by lunchtime (it's roughly a 6 hour bus trip).

Towards the top of the town is Tallo Durbar, or lower palace, of Prithvi Narayan Shah who unified Nepal in 1769. This palace is being turned into a museum and is not always open to tourists.

Opposite the palace entrance is a series of stone steps that climb up between traditional Gurung homes to the ridge above. At the top is the World Heritage Listed original palace, Gorkha Durbar (1490m, 1 hour) and Gorkha Kalika (temple to the Goddess Kali). Remove all leather garments (including shoes) before entering the temple.

The Goddess Kali traditionally represents death and destruction and is supplicated through animal sacrifice. These days she represents time and change, but she is still revered with sacrifices.

There is a good campsite about 10 minutes beyond the temple.

DAY 2: KALIKA TEMPLE – BHALUSWANRA   4¼ HRS

The aim is to reach, and then follow the Daraudi Khola, which lies in the valley that stretches away to the north.

From the campsite, follow any of the trails that traverse, and slightly descend, to the village of Bhogteni (1330m, 30 minutes). The trail now descends steeply, initially on rough stone steps, but then on smooth mud through a forested section. This trail can be very slippery after rain, so take care.

The trail forks after descending about 300m: take the right-hand trail. If you miss the fork you will descend to a bridge across the Daraudi Khola to Sangu, where you can then follow a trail to Bhaluswanra.

Having taken the right-hand trail, continue to descend to Shikar (500m, 2½ hours) and then cross a broad shallow river, the Mese Khola.

An easy trail follows the eastern bank of the Daraudi Khola to Sopange and a suspension bridge over the Jarang Khola (45 minutes). After crossing the bridge, the track climbs a small hill for 10 minutes before once again turning north and following the Daraudi Khola.

The village of Bhaluswanra (550m, 20 minutes) is on both banks of the river and linked by a long suspension bridge. There is rarely a cleared campsite in the village, so continue up stream for about 10 minutes and look for a large grassy clearing beside the river below the trail.

DAY 3: BHALUSWANRA – (AFTER) KALIBOTE   5 HRS

A broad, flat and easy-to-follow trail heads north from the village before becoming rougher as you enter some riverside jungle sections. Mule trains ply this route and they tend to make a mess of the trail on ascents and descents.

You will pass through a few hamlets that do not appear on most maps. Just beyond Pokhartar (700m, 3 hours) is a bridge to Kalibote (20 minutes) and a potential campsite (750m).

If you have time, continue along the west bank of the Daraudi Khola until the next bridge across the river. There is a campsite before the bridge and a village school, where larger groups can camp (1½ hours).

DAY 4: (AFTER) KALIBOTE – BARPAK   5 HRS

After crossing the bridge, follow an easy trail northwards along the eastern bank of the Daraudi River.

In 1½ hours you will come to a small teashop (970m) just before a wooden suspension bridge. Take care crossing the bridge if it is wet or there are leaves covering the planks, it can be extremely slippery. From the bridge it is all up-hill to Barpak.

The trail first ascends through a broadleaf forest on steep switchback trails. After an hour you should notice some tall metal structures that look like small electricity pylons. They are the stanchions of a ropeway (a wooden box hauled up and down to Barpak), which broke, killing four locals.

The village of Lyawai (1450m, 1 hour) sits on a narrow ridge with good views up to Himal Chuli. Follow a large trail through the village to terraced fields above, which alternate with low scrubby bushes all the way to Barpak (1950m, 2½ hours) so make sure you have adequate sun protection.

Barpak is one of the largest Gurung villages, where many of the families have at least one male relative in the Royal Gurkha Rifles. There are good campsites close to the tree line above the village with views of the village, Manaslu, Peak 29, and Himal Chuli.

DAY 5: BARPAK – LAPRAK 4½ HRS

A large trail climbs up to and then through extensive rhododendron forest above Barpak. The gradient is unrelenting for 2 hours and then eases as you begin to near the top of the Gupsi Danda and a minor pass (2670m, 3 hours from Barpak).

There are good views of the entire Manaslu range from here. A broad grazing pasture, or kharka, provides an easy and enjoyable initial descent from the pass.

After 20 minutes the trail steepens and you can see another large Gurung village, Laprak (2100m, 1½ hours), where there is a large school ground to make camp.

DAY 6: LAPRAK – KHORLABESI
5 HRS

This section involves some tricky navigation, so it might be a good idea to employ a local guide from Laprak or Singla.

Follow the main trail through the village, which then descends directly, for about 300m, to a bridge across the Machha Khola. Over the bridge, the trail climbs roughly 200m before swinging eastwards and traversing the hillside.

There is a large tree with a chautara beside the trail, which marks where the main trail turns towards the northeast. It is important that you continue traversing at this height and do not descend towards the river.

There are no teahouses at the village of Singla (2020m, 2 hours), but you can camp in the schoolyard.

Continue through the village and be careful not to take some of the smaller tracks that descend towards the Machha Khola. After roughly 1 hour you will come to a fork where it looks like the right-hand trail begins to descend across unused terraces – do not descend. Instead, take the left trail that climbs for less than 100m.

If you or your crew accidentally descend you will find the trail ends in old terraces and you will have to climb back up.

In another 20 minutes there are good views of the Budhi Gandaki river and the main Manaslu Circuit trail, that you will reach in another 1½ hours at Khorlabesi (970m).

There is a good campsite at the junction of the Namrung Khola and Budhi Gandaki.

DAY 7: KHORLABESI – JAGAT
5½ HRS

The trail from Khorlabesi to Jagat is through a dramatic gorge with lots of waterfalls and some landslides.

Follow the broad track on the west bank of the river to Tatopani (990m, 1 hour) where the waterspouts make a good washing stop. At the end of the village, cross a suspension bridge to the east bank and continue through sometimes dense forest to Dobhan (1070m, 1 hour and 20 minutes), where there is a fine campsite in the centre of the village.

Continue on a broad trail on the east bank of the river to Yaruphant (1170m, 1 hour), where there are a few teashops on a broad grassy slope.

From here, the trail climbs about 200m up what was once an enormous landslide that blocked the Budhi Gandaki.

The trail descends a little from the top of the climb to the broad riverbed. In trekking season there are some temporary teashops (1 hour and 20 minutes from Yaruphant) at the confluence of the Yara Khola.

Vertical cliffs rise on both sides of the valley as the trail continues on the eastern bank for 15 minutes to a bridge where the Budhi Gandaki has cut a narrow gorge. After a short climb and descent of 20 minutes you reach a flat area where there is a teashop and two grassy campsites signposted 'Jagat'.

The village is actually ten minutes further up the trail, behind a rocky spur. As you enter Jagat (1340m) on a good stone-paved trail, there is a community owned campsite on your left and a couple of basic teahouses before the Manaslu Conservation Area Project (MCAP) and police checkpost. *Jagat* is a common village name in the high mountains as it means 'customs post' and is the traditional tax collection point for trade to and from Tibet.

DAY 8: JAGAT – DENG   6 HRS
Beyond the village is the Pangaur Khola, which is crossed using stepping stones and log bridges.

The trail now climbs an easy gradient to a chautara (1 hour), where there are good views of Shringi Himal to the north. Descend to Sirdibas (1420m, 40 minutes) and turn a sharp left turn at the end of the village to ascend a stream for about 50m before turning sharp right for the main trail.

Continue to a suspension bridge over the Budhi Gandaki (there is a police checkpost at the bridge) and climb 200m to the village of Philim (1570m, 40 minutes) and another MCAP check post.

This next section of trail is spectacular and well worth the effort of a long day's walk. Ekla Bhatti (1650m) is about 45 minutes from Philim, but take your time and admire the waterfalls on the west side of the valley.

After the monsoon, there is a large waterfall beyond Ekla Bhatti, after which you enter scrubby forest that gives way to large pine trees. Forty minutes from Ekla Bhatti you reach a trail junction, where you turn left (the right hand trail goes to *Tsum*, see p178). Descend (5 minutes) to a bridge, where the trail begins a gradual climb as the valley turns westwards.

After the initial climb away from the bridge there is a small trail junction where you turn right (the left trail climbs steeply to Nya). Another bridge across the Budhi Gandaki is reached in 45 minutes, which you cross to the north bank to avoid a steep cliff.

In another 15 minutes you cross back to the south bank using a dilapidated wooden suspension bridge, which, hopefully, will be replaced soon.

In 20 minutes you will reach Pewa and the junction with the high trail from Nya (this is where you join the Circuit trail from the Rupina La). It's a good campsite at Deng (1860m), which is now 50 minutes away along a pleasant trail with good views of the narrow gorge cut by the Budhi Gandaki.

DAY 9: DENG – NAMRUNG   5 HRS
As the Manaslu Circuit trail turns westwards, the shape of the homes changes to squat, dry-stone structures to reflect the changing demands of climate, and the architectural influences of Tibet.

Mani walls, chorten and kani are common along the trail. Rice and wheat are replaced by buckwheat, barley and maize in the fields.

The trail descends to a suspension bridge to the north bank of the Budhi Gandaki and then climbs roughly 100m to Rana (1910m, 35 minutes). The trail now climbs an easy gradient beneath the village of Umbaie (above which is Shringi Gompa) before winding through the Shringi Khola gorge to Bhi (1990m, 45 minutes).

Follow an undulating trail through sparse pine trees and hamlets to a large kani (1½ hours) that marks the entry to the Prok and Ghap communities. The paintings and mani stones on this kani are in good condition. The fierce blue and red characters on the kani ceiling and walls are protectors who are meant to stop evil spirits from entering the villages beyond.

There is a campsite at Prok, only 10 minutes further.

The trail now gradually swings back to the river, which you cross via a suspension bridge before a slight climb to Ghap, where there are a couple of teashops. The valley now narrows and you pass through fine broad-leaf forest to a spectacular canyon carved by the river (45 minutes), which you re-cross in another 15 minutes on a larger bridge.

Note: the Himal Chuli Base Camp trail veers left here and climbs the Sherang Khola valley.

From the second bridge, the trail climbs more steeply for almost 1 hour to Namrung (2630m), where there is a campsite and basic teahouse.

DAY 10: NAMRUNG – SAMA   5½ HRS
Leave Namrung by crossing Therang Khola along an easy trail that passes a waterfall on your left before entering the scattered village of Barchham (20 minutes). The trail now climbs a bit less than 300m on an easy

ROUTE GUIDE

gradient to Lihi (2920m, 50 minutes), where there is a campsite and teashop at the far end of the village.

Descend and cross the Hinan Khola on the far side of the village and ascend an easy trail to Sho (2880m, 45 minutes). It is now a gentle up-hill gradient to Lho (3180m, 1 hour), where there is a campsite and teashop, but take your time and enjoy the evolving mountain panorama around you.

Manaslu dominates the skyline at Lho and if you have time, explore the village's mani walls, kani and Ribang Gompa, which sits on a hill above the village.

The trail descends to the Thusang Khola and then climbs a steady gradient for 300m to Shyala (1 hour and 20 minutes), a community of mainly log cabins where there is another campsite and teashops.

Next the trail dips through the Numla Khola before descending slightly and then becoming flat all the way to Sama (3520m, 1 hour and 10 minutes), where there are a number of teahouses and campsites to choose from at the far end of the village.

DAY 11: SAMA   ALL DAY
It is a good idea to spend a day in Sama exploring the village and/or some of the surrounding viewpoints as part of an acclimatisation program.

One of the most popular places to visit is the Pung Gyen Gompa beneath the east face of Manaslu. To get there, back track on the

Shyala trail to a junction before the Numla Khola, where you turn right and begin a long and sometimes steep climb for 2¼ hours.

Once you've crested the ridge above the river the gradient eases and ahead you'll see the small gompa. You'll be expected to provide a donation to the gompa if you visit it.

Higher still is a cave gompa and hot springs, but relaxing in the grassy kharka near the gompa and enjoying the view of Manaslu is a popular pastime before returning to Sama in 1½ hours.

Alternatively, explore the village and gompas of Sama, or take a local guide to Birendra Kund for reflections of Manaslu and its northern icefall.

DAY 12: SAMA – SAMDO   2¼ HRS
An easy day to Samdo can be combined with a side trip to Birendra Kund. Leave Sama on a broad trail that runs north from the village across grassy kharkas. Remain on the western side of the valley, following a trail that runs parallel to the Budhi Gandaki.

After 45 minutes cross the outflow from Birendra Kund to the summer herding area of Kermo Kharka where there is an excellent view of Manaslu from the impressive mani wall.

The trail continues to climb an easy gradient for 1 hour before dropping to a bridge over the river. Climb to an impressive kani, which marks the entry to Samdo (3875m, 30 minutes). This is a Tibetan refu-

---

❏ The people of Larke and Siar
The high valleys around the back of the Manaslu range, and bordered by the Ganesh Himal to the east and Tibet to the north, are called the Larke region. There are two groups of people who live here, the Mongoloid Buddhist people in the Ro (Sama) and Tsum valleys, and the Siar people of mixed Gurung ancestry who occupy the hills above Gorkha and Dhading.

The people of the high valleys of Larke originally came from Tibet and are therefore enthusiastic followers of Buddhism. The Siar people share many of the habits and traditions of the Gurungs to the south, while still being ardent Tibetan Buddhism practitioners. Their economies are based on agriculture and trade, as their villages lie along two important trade routes to Tibet, which were possibly established by the Sherpas of the Solu-Khumbu. Tibetans exchanged salt and wool for food grains and Nepali merchandise. They are relatively poor, but kind hearted and fun loving, and always ready to share a glass or two of rakshi [fire water] or a pot of boiled potatoes.

> ❏ **The Ru-Pa people of Samdo**
> Former residents of Ru, an old Tibetan trading village and home to the famous Taiga Gompa, fled to Samdo after the Chinese occupied their village in Tibet. They had grazed their herds in the fields of the Nubri Valley for centuries, but they left everything, crossed the passes and began a new life.
>
> The first group arrived above Sama in spring 1962. They claimed Nepali citizenship, based on a set of copper plates granting them land rights over 600 years before. Villagers petitioned the King of Nepal and received the rights they so desperately needed to remain in Nepal.
>
> Since then, there has been an almost constant disagreement with the people of lower villages, such as Sama, over who has the right to these lands. They still maintain many of the Tibetan Buddhist and animist customs their forefathers followed, and live a mostly subsistence life, trading and carrying their goods across high passes on *dzo* (a yak and cattle cross breed).

gee settlement of about 40 homes, created after the Chinese occupation of Tibet.

The border runs along the top of the hills above Samdo and makes an ideal side-trip.

DAY 13: SAMDO ALL DAY
It is wise to add a day to your itinerary at this point for acclimatisation: consider climbing the Lajyung Pass that goes to Tibet (northeast of Samdo) or up the slopes to the north of Samdo for some great view of the entire Manaslu range.

DAY 14: SAMDO – LARKYE LA
DHARAMSALA 3 HRS
From Samdo the trail descends to a bridge across the Gyala Khola. Climb the trail on the far side to a large pile of mani stones (40 minutes), where you can look down upon Larkye Bazaar, a trading ground (there are no buildings as such) where Tibetans sell large herds of goats before the Nepali festival of Dashain in October/November.

The trail now climbs an easy gradient with views of Larkye Peak and the north face of Manaslu for 2 hours and 20 minutes to Larkye La dharamsala (4460m), where there is a large emergency shelter. Camp here and check that you are well prepared to cross the pass tomorrow.

DAY 15: LARKYE LA DHARAMSALA –
LARKYE LA – BIMTANG 7 HRS
The longest and toughest section of the Manaslu Circuit now awaits you, but also

the most magnificent views – Himalayan majesty and grandeur all around.

It is wise to start early, before sunrise, and climb an ablation valley to views of Cho Danda. Although there are some prayer flags at the top of the ablation valley (4690m, 1 hour and 20 minutes) you are not at the top of the pass.

The trail now crosses rough undulating moraines for 30 minutes to another dharamsala (4905m). From here the trail begins to climb more steeply to the top of the Larkye La (5135m, 1¾ hours), where you will be greeted by magnificent views of the upper Bimtang valley and a roofless dharamsala.

Views of Himlung and Cheo Himals, Gyagi Kang, Menjung, Kang Guru and Annapurna II fill the horizon.

Descend from the pass down a steep slope, which is often snow covered and icy (and may require a handline), for 1½ hours. Beneath you are three glaciers spotted with numerous turquoise lakes; head for the ablation valley to the left of all the glaciers.

An easy gradient then leads down to the campsite at Bimtang (3590m, 2 hours), which is serviced by four competing teashops.

DAY 16: BIMTANG – DHARAPANI
6¾ HRS
Continue to follow the ablation valley south from Bimtang, which soon gives way to lateral moraine after 10 minutes. There are good views of the west face of Manaslu

from here. Cross a branch of the glacial melt and then turn left, cross some more moraine before crossing the main stream of glacial melt and then climbing a ridge of lateral moraine topped by some prayer flags (20 minutes).

The trail descends a little steeply through pine and rhododendron forest for 15 minutes before levelling to a gentle downhill gradient. As you descend towards the Dudh Khola through forest the trail passes through a few kharka.

There is a lone teashop at Yak Kharka (aka Sangure Kharka, 3020m, 1 hour and 20 minutes) after a copse of mountain pepper trees. From here the trail can be a little difficult to follow across some large landslides and through scrubby forest to the scattered settlement of Kharche (1 hour).

The trail now climbs an imposing ridge that juts into the centre of the valley before a long descent to the many fields of Goa (2515m, 1½ hours), where there are two teahouses. It is now a gentle downhill to the large Gurung village of Tilije (2300m, 50

minutes), where you cross a bridge and pass a new school.

After 20 minutes you come to a trail junction; turn right and descend to Thonje (1965m, 50 minutes), which you reach after crossing a long suspension bridge.

Once at the village follow a stone-paved trail to a T-junction in front of a tea-house. Turn left onto a dirt track and pass the school; after a short descent, cross a suspension bridge over the Marsyangdi river to Dharapani (10 minutes), where there is a police checkpost and many teahouses.

Welcome to the Annapurna Circuit!

DAYS 17-19: DHARAPANI – SYANJE – KHUDI – POKHARA   7 HRS

Follow the Annapurna trail (see *Naar, Phu & the Thorong La*, days 1-3, p186), but in reverse.

A road is being built up from Besishahar so you will only need to walk to Syanje (1150m, 7 hours), before catching a jeep or small bus to Besishahar and transferring to a tourist bus to Pokhara.

OTHER MAJOR TRAILS IN THE MANASLU REGION

Gorkha to Arughat Bazaar

Instead of ascending the Daraudi Khola from the Kalika Temple above Gorkha, follow the dirt road to Khanchok (6 hours). Then descend to Arughat Bazaar (4½ hours) and continue to Arkhet Bazaar (2 hours). From there, trek to Machha Khola (5 hours), which is 30 minutes before Khorlabesi and then begin the *Manaslu Circuit* from day seven, see p174.

Tsum

The Tsum valley was opened to tourists in 2002 and is becoming a popular side trip to the Manaslu Circuit. The Larke communities here have three gompas all run by nuns.

Warning! Only experienced trekkers should attempt the Thak Khola exit route, as it is exposed and extremely dangerous; porters should not be taken.

Before descending to the Chumjet bridge over the Budhi Gandaki there is a right-hand fork (1½ hours from Philim), which climbs through pine forest. After 1 hour you will reach Lukuwa, where there are fine views up the Siyar and Budhi Gandaki valleys.

Descend through bamboo jungle to a wooden bridge that crosses the Gumrung Chu (30 minutes) – this is a good lunch spot. The valley now swings north and the trail climbs a rough trail through jungle and then on to grassy hillside with stone slabs. Once across the slabs, the trail descends again to a suspension bridge that crosses to the north bank of the Siyar Khola (1½ hours).

The main trail crosses the bridge (rather than going to Ripchet – see *Landan Kharka*, below) over the Siyar Khola. You then climb through terraces and scattered stone houses to Tumje (3230m, 1¼ hours), where you can camp in the school grounds. Do not leave anything unattended in this campsite, not even your toilet tent! Locals have a reputation for theft during the night and in all weathers. A pretty grass-covered trail descends to the Siyar Khola and passes a small gompa run by three nuns who will be glad to offer a cup of Tibetan tea for a donation.

Not far beyond the gompa is a bridge over the Sarpu Khola to Kowa (2630m, 1 hour). Here the trail forks, the right-hand track leads to Domje (2460m, 20 minutes), see *Landan Kharka*, below. Take the left-hand trail that leads through the village and past a row of chortens before climbing at a constant gradient through scrub rhododendron for 450m. A chorten and mani wall at 2970m mark the edge of a broad flat valley and the outskirts of Chokung (3031m, 3 hours) where there is another small gompa and campsite. Continue up the valley on an easy trail to Rachen Gompa, which houses sixty-three nuns and was established in 1927. Beyond is Mu Gompa, where the valley branches in two; each branch has a trail that leads to Tibet.

It is possible to return to Tumje in 5 hours from Chokung, where you then have to choose your exit route: either retrace your steps to Lukuwa and then join the Manaslu Circuit trail at the bridge to Chumjet, or take the high and difficult route via Thak Khola to Lana.

This route is for experienced trekking groups only, and no one with vertigo should attempt the route; it is exposed and very dangerous; porters should not be taken. Do not stop at Tumje, instead continue for 2 hours to Chumje (3020m), which is a small collection of homes before the Urgin Chu. The following day, follow a trail that crosses the Urgin Chu and then climbs out and up to a grassy ridge with three chortens (3150m, 2 hours). The trail now drops steeply before crossing a tricky section of steep ground covered in scrub. Climb another ridge and descend again through bamboo forest.

The trail can be hard to find and you must be careful on the slippery log ladders. Beyond the forest, the route again climbs a ridge on a trail that follows a stream. Once on top of the ridge you enter a small village, Durjung Kharka (2570m, 5 hours), where you can camp in the terraces beyond the village. From here, it is only 3 hours down to the main trail at Lana.

Landan Kharka (north face of Ganesh I)

From the trail junction before crossing the Siyar Khola bridge, take the right hand track to Ripchet (2420m, 1 hour) and then on to Domje (2460m, 2hours). You should check in Domje if the trail to Landan Kharka is accessible, and if there have been landslides it might be wise to employ a guide here. From Domje, climb a steepening forest trail on the north bank of the Landan Khola. After 3 hours you will reach a kharka with good views of Ganesh I (aka Yangra, 7429m).

ROUTE GUIDE

The trail continues through forest for another 2 hours before leaving the tree line and reaching an ablation valley on the north side of a nameless glacier. In another hour you reach the final kharka and campsite beneath a natural amphitheatre below the Ganesh Himal.

Exit via Begnas Tal

Those with a little extra time and who want a more complete Nepali experience, could take a trail from below Syanje over to the famous picnic spot of Begnas Tal (a short bus ride from Pokhara).

Descend the Annapurna Circuit as far as Khudi, where you cross the Khudi Khola on a suspension bridge. Next, take a right hand trail that leads to Sera (870m, 30 minutes). From here there is a long series of stone steps that rise above the Boran Khola to Baglungpani (1595m, 3 hours) where there are some great views of Manaslu, Lamjung Himal and the Annapurnas, with the distinctive Macchapuchhare (Fish Tail Peak) standing sentinel. A long ridge descent via Nalma (1240m, 2 hours) brings you to the Midim Khola, a broad valley that leads down to Karputar (490m, 2½ hours). From here it is 1½ hours to Begnas Tal, which is one of Nepal's favourite picnic spots. Catch a bus to Pokhara from here (less than 1 hour).

GHT – MANASLU

This section of the Great Himalaya Trail requires some navigation skill and/or a local guide, especially in the forested ridges that separate the Ganesh Himal from the Budhi Gandaki valley. As at July 2009, the Arughat Bazaar map from Finaid was out of print so the GPS coordinates are given instead.

There are two trails to Gatlang (2300m) from Syabru Besi: the first option follows the new valley road to the Chilime Khola valley into which you turn west (left) and follow a good trail to Thambuchet and then to Gatlang (see *Tamang Heritage Trail*, day eight, p170).

The second, faster, option from Syabru Besi is to climb a trail that begins beside the Buddha Guest House. This is a direct route to the Rongga Bhanjyang (2187m, 2 hours) above Syabru, and is also the route of an old road to Somdang. From the pass it is an easy 2 hours and 20 minutes along the road to Gatlang.

From Gatlang the road is not used by motor traffic as landslides and fallen trees often block it. Follow a large track from Gatlang school up to Parvati Kund (45 minutes) where the trail then intermittently cuts across the old road that winds through pine and rhododendron forest. At 3100m (1¾ hours) you come to a large kharka where you can camp. Not far above you re-join the road and follow it as it traverses a steep rocky hillside to another, smaller, kharka where the road does a U-turn. Here you take a small trail that climbs up and right, away from the road, into a gully filled with rhododendron to the Khurpu Dada Pass (3710m, 2 hours, Finaid: Somdan, sheet: 2885 13, ref: 194 171), which is where a line of old powerlines (now only poles) crosses the Khurpu Dada and is a trail junction.

To the north, along the ridge, is a small trail, which leads to Jaisuli Kund (Jageshwar Kund on the map, 3 hours), from where you could head to Paldor Peak Base Camp. Instead, head west and descend quickly, cutting across the road a few times, before following it as it gradually descends along to Somdang (3258m, 1½ hours), where there are some campsites and teashops.

From Somdang, the trail climbs up through forest and occasionally crosses an old road that was never finished. In 2¾ hours you should reach a small pass at 3780m, where the trail begins traversing steep, rocky hillside. If there has been recent snowfall care should be taken to avoid small avalanches along this section of track. The trail traverses above a large kharka before arriving at the Pansan Pass (3830m, 1 hour, Finaid: Somdan, sheet: 2885 13, ref: 153 165) where locals appear to be building a small gompa.

Descend through rhododendron forest for 1¾ hours, passing through a couple of kharkas, which are potential campsites. However, it is best to continue to the terraced fields of Lawadun or Tipling village (1890m, 1¼ hours), and camp in the school. Nearly all of the locals in this region of the Ganesh Himal are friendly Gurung Christians, who have decided to ban all alcohol from their communities.

Follow a main trail to Sertun (1920m, 1 hour and 40 minutes) and on to Boran (1560m, 2½ hours). As you reach Boran there is a stone house on the right hand side of the trail. Next to this house is a stone staircase that cuts down through the northern edge of the village to the Akhu Khola below. Either camp in the school grounds at the centre of the village, or descend to the river, cross a suspension bridge and camp in a small grassy field beside the Lapa Khola (1285m, 30 minutes, Finaid: Somdan, sheet: 2885 13, ref: 030 168). If you choose to camp by the river you will need to post a night guard on your camp as local thieves are likely to slash your tent in the early hours.

Note: it is possible to descend to the Dhading Besi road-head in three days from Boran by following the main trail to the south.

From the riverside campsite cross another suspension bridge and begin the long climb to Lapagaon (1850m, 2 hours), a large Tamang village, where the school grounds would make a good campsite. Unless someone in your group knows the trail ahead it is wise to employ a local guide from this village.

A new, steep trail climbs a hillside to the west of the village to a chautara with views back down the valley (2200m, 50 minutes). You now enter a section of mixed forest with many trails. After 1 hour and 10 minutes you reach a kharka with a dharamsala (GPS: 2441m, N 28° 10.246' E 084° 59.077'). The trail heads northwest up a gully with a rocky spur to the north. The gully steepens as it nears a ridge and the barely distinct Mangro Pass (2936m, 1¼ hours, GPS: 2782m, N 28° 10.102' E 084° 58.726'), which leads to the first of a series of shallow basins that make the next few hours tricky to navigate.

Descend into and then climb out of the first basin to another minor forested ridge in 45 minutes (GPS: 2728m, N 28° 09.908' E 084° 58.354'). The trail now heads northwest, first through forest and then across an exposed hillside to the large Myangal Kharka (50 minutes, GPS: 2936m, N 28° 09.468' E 084° 57.656'), where there is a dharamsala. However, rather than camp here, ascend an easy trail to a final forested ridge marked with a chorten (2975m, 10 minutes, GPS: 2975m, N 28° 09.475' E 084° 57.506'), which the locals call Myangal Bhanjyang. Descend a good trail through forest for 25 minutes to Nauban Kharka (GPS: 2750m, N 28° 09.732' E 084° 56.900'), which makes a better campsite.

The trail continues to descend, sometimes steeply, through dense forest for 2 hours and 20 minutes to a bridge over the Richel Khola (GPS: 1555m, N 28° 10.729' E 084° 55.522') from which it is less than 1 hour to Yarsa village (GPS: 1877m, N 28° 10.857' E 084° 54.773'). As you leave the village, the trail swings northwest into the large Budhi Gandaki valley and in 40 minutes you reach Kashigaon, where the school makes an ideal campsite.

You now follow a trail, which contours from 1950 to 2100m, for the next 3½ hours to the extensive village of Kerauja (GPS: 2074m, N 28° 14.198' E 084° 54.254'), where you camp at either the school or health post above the village.

Note: if you are following the GHT in reverse, it is possible to get a local guide from this village and reach Lapagaon in three to four days via a different trail to the one described here. Locals rarely use this route so it is important that you check the credentials of any guide.

Contour around the hillside to the north of Kerauja to a trail junction in 40 minutes. The left, descending trail crosses the Budhi Gandaki river just to the north of Khorlabesi (see *Manaslu Circuit*, day seven, p174). If you continue to Rumchet, you will need to descend to a bridge beyond the village and then contour through some small terraces to a tiny stone house and chorten, which mark a point where the hillside steepens. The trail now heads across scrubby hillside interrupted by unstable landslides and rocky scrambles for 3 hours until you finally reach the bridge beyond Tatopani where you join day seven of the *Manaslu Circuit* trek. Then follow the route described to Dharapani on the Annapurna Circuit (see *GHT – Annapurna*, p196).

Annapurna, Naar & Phu

For many years the Annapurna region was Nepal's premier trekking destination, only recently overshadowed by the Solu-Khumbu. The reason is the construction of two roads, one to Manang from Besishahar (due to be finished in 2011) and the other to Muktinath and Lo Monthang from Beni (completed in 2008), which have made much of the traditional route of the Annapurna Circuit less interesting for trekkers. However, a trail that avoids the new road is being developed from Muktinath south down the valley and should be completed by the time you read this. The Annapurna region is re-inventing itself, hoping to attract even more adventure tourists and pilgrims than ever before.

Nepal's second largest city, Pokhara (see pp96-112), is the ideal starting place for exploring the Annapurna region. For many, the early morning viewpoint of Sarankot provides the first rush of a Himalayan panorama, and whets the appetite for more. The Annapurna Himal, to the north of Pokhara, has over 20 major peaks, including Annapurna I (8091m) and the stunning Machhapuchhare, also known as Fish Tail Peak (6997m). To the north of the massive bulk of the Annapurnas is a valley system that leads to Tibet through the villages of Naar and Phu as well as the Mustang region. The airport and road hub of Jomsom is also a major trail junction for routes to the Dhaulagiri and Dolpo regions, so you can design treks of almost any length and difficulty, unlike anywhere else in the Himalaya.

The opening of new areas and increase in the range of facilities throughout the Annapurnas means there is a wide range of trekking-style options. From the comfort and convenience of the teahouses on the main Circuit trail, through camping treks with limited teahouse support, to remote wilderness experiences, there are some truly amazing treks on offer for every type of trekker. For those wanting to indulge in authentic cultures there are Tibetan villages in Naar and Phu, and the famous Manangba, Thakali and Gurung communities of the main trail. Or, for some serious mountain close-ups, consider visiting Tilicho Tal, or Dhaulagiri and Hidden Valley. For those with limited time, the Annapurna Sanctuary offers a wonderful mountain 'fix', and for the novice trekker, the famous sunrise panorama site of Poon Hill is still a must-see.

The Annapurna Conservation Area Project (ACAP) is the largest protected biodiversity area in Nepal. Local community groups are pushing hard for improved services and support from Kathmandu, and have invested heavily in tourism facilities. The more tourists attracted to the area, the more value local communities will feel their natural environment has to offer, and therefore, the more likely they will help to preserve their region. So use local facilities and services where you can and try to encourage sustainable practices at all times. For comprehensive trail, accommodation and local information see Bryn Thomas' *Trekking in the Annapurna Region*, Trailblazer.

ROUTE GUIDE

ROUTE GUIDE

Annapurna, Naar & Phu region

Larkye La 5135
Manaslu 8163
Ratna Chuli 7035
Himlung 7126
Pokai Tal
Bimtang
Goa
Bagarchhap
Dharapani
Tal
Svanje
Bahra Pokhari
Misi Pokhari
Dolal Khola
Marsyangdi
Khudi
BESISHAHAR
Kyang
Junam Goth
Singenge
Koto
Timang
CHAME
Jomsom Himal 6364
Phu
Naar
Pisang Peak 6092
Annapurna II 7973
Pisang
Humde
Tangting
Teri La 5529
Kang La 5322
Ngawal
Hunde
Siklis
Yakwa Kang 6482
Thorong La 5416
Thorong Phedi
Manang
Annapurna III 7555
Machhapuchhare BC
Machhapuchhare 6997
POKHARA
Muktinath
Thorong Peak 6201
Khatung Kang 6484
Annapurna BC
Machhapuchhare BC
Phewa Tal
Kagbeni
Tilicho Tal
Annapurna I 8091
Annapurna South 7219
Chhomrung
Ghandruk
Landruk
Pothana
Phalla
Tilicho Peak 7134
Tadapani
Ghorepani
Birethanti
JOMSOM
Ghorethanti
Marpha
Poon Hill
Dhampus Peak 6035
Dhaulagiri I 8167
Taglung
Kali Gandaki
Ghasa
Dana
Tatopani
BENI
Jirbang
Mukut Himal 6639
Dhaulagiri II 7751
Runma
Myagdi Khola

Legend

GHT
Main trail

0   5   10km

NAAR, PHU & THE THORONG LA

Opened to tourism in 2003, this trek can be combined with trails to or from Mustang, or via Tilicho Tal to produce some exceptional and challenging itineraries. To assist acclimatisation most people walk in from Syanje and then fly out of Humde or Jomsom. A new trail from Muktinath through the Kali Gandaki valley should be finished in 2011, which will provide a trekking route all the way back to Pokhara.

The Annapurna Circuit is rarely closed to trekking – only a period from mid-February to early March will see the Thorong La closed. However, large amounts of snow can fall in intense storms throughout the trekking season, so you should always be cautious of impending weather changes.

Lying in the rain-shadow of the Annapurna Circuit, beyond a steep-sided canyon to the north of Koto, the villages of Naar and Phu receive little rain throughout the year. Phu, where there is one teahouse, lies just a few kilometres from the Tibetan border, and is a medieval stonewalled village that sits precariously on a rock spur overlooked by Tashi Gompa, famous for the head Lama who is an expert in traditional medicine. Naar is to the south of Phu and behind Pisang Peak (6092m), a popular trekking peak, and has a couple of basic teahouses and shops where you can purchase staples.

> ### NAAR, PHU & THE THORONG LA TREK
>
> The trek to Naar and Phu represents the future of trekking in the Annapurna region; ancient Tibetan communities combine with the extraordinary alpine views from the Kang La; combined with the Thorong La this is a magnificent trek.
>
> **Duration**: 17 days
>
> **Highest Point**: 5416m
>
> **Best Season**: Mar-May/Oct-Dec
>
> **Accommodation**: camping/teahouse

ROUTE GUIDE

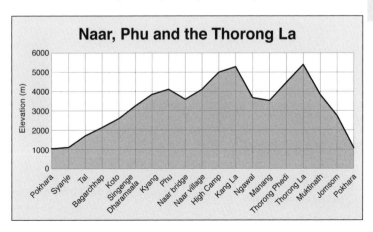

DAY 1: POKHARA – BESISHAHAR – SYANJE 10 HRS

A new road is slowly being built to Manang, and should be finished by 2011. The village of Syanje (1100m) is the current road head and takes about 10 hours by bus and/or jeep from Kathmandu.

The drive follows the Marsyangdi river, which you will follow in the days to come. Almost all of the villages in this region are Gurung communities, which are noted for their friendliness, jovial spirit and excellent work ethic.

DAY 2: SYANJE – TAL 4 HRS

From Syanje the Marsyangdi river has cut a gorge, which becomes steeper and steeper as the day goes on. Follow a trail out of the village on the west bank, heading north; like every riverside trail, it has lots of up and downs.

It takes 1½ hours to reach the inviting village of Jagat (1300m), which was once a customs post for the salt trade with Tibet. The trail continues to undulate beside the river, which causes frequent landslides during the monsoon. Beyond the village, cliffs form the far bank and the valley becomes noticeably narrower.

It will take an hour to reach Chamje (1430m), where you cross a suspension bridge to the east bank of the gorge. Climb about 200m to Sattale (1680m), which marks the narrowest section of the valley.

A landslide-prone trail then climbs a little to a broad flat-bottomed valley and the village of Tal (1700m, 1½ hours), which marks the official entry to Manang District.

DAY 3: TAL – BAGARCHHAP 3¼ HRS

Beyond Tal is a short landslide affected section, which drops down to a suspension bridge to the east bank of the Marsyangdi river (1½ hours); cross it to Khotro (aka Karte, 1850m).

The trail through this section has been blasted from rock to try to reduce the chances of landslide-blockage. Do not re-cross the river for the remainder of the day.

In 45 minutes you will reach the beginning of the Gurung village, Dharapani (1860m), which stretches beside the conflu-

---

❏ The Gurung

Gurungs usually live along the southern slopes of the Annapurnas, from Gorkha in the west to Lamjung in the eastern Gandaki zone. They first became famous in Nepal when they formed the bulk of the Shah armies of Gorkha, which conquered the Kathmandu valley in 1768 and united Nepal. This fighting tradition continues to this day, with many young Gurung men in the Gurkha regiments of the British and Indian armies, as well as the Nepal Army and police. Gurungs who are not in the armed forces survive on agriculture and livestock breeding. As many of the older men of a village receive service pensions they tend to hold only small amounts of land, and it is always a treat to see an elderly ex-Gurkha decked out in his neatly pressed uniform in a village in the middle of nowhere.

In April, Gurungs take their sheep or goats to high pastures, where they remain until about September. After the harvest they take their flock to lower altitudes to sell for the important Dasain festival, when every family will have at least one animal for dinner. Gurungs also cross the border to Tibet or India to trade.

The Gurung people are hardworking and fun loving, and the women especially are flirtatious, even with foreigners. Their round faces, bright eyes and broad cheeky smiles are hard to resist. Gurungs traditionally speak a Tibeto-Burman language, though many now speak Nepali. Gurungs uniquely have a system called *rodi* where young boys and girls have sleepovers in a house under supervision, as a method of courting. Couples, once married, do not live together, but remain with their respective parents until a child is born. The girl then finally leaves her parents and lives with the boy and his family.

ence of the Dudh Khola, flowing down from Manaslu.

Next, follow the route of the new road to the outskirts of Bagarchhap (2160m, 1 hour), which you cut through to rejoin the road on the far side of the village. There was a devastating landslide here in 1995; a memorial in the centre of the village only mentions the tourists who died.

At the far end of the village there are good views of the Annapurnas, and sections of the Lamjung Himal.

DAY 4: BAGARCHHAP – KOTO
4 HRS

From Bagarchhap, continue along the route of the new road to Danakyu (2300m, 35 minutes). Beyond the sprawling village, the trail climbs steeply for about 400m through thick pine and fir forest before arriving at Timang (2750m, 1 hour and 25 minutes).

There are a few teahouses in Timang, any of which make an ideal rest stop with great views of the Lamjung Himal. Continue along a flat-ish trail to Latamro (2695m, 45 minutes), where you descend to and climb away from a gushing tributary before arriving at Thanchok (2670m, 20 minutes).

This is a large and often dirty village, but there is a nice teahouse beyond the main settlement, just before rejoining the road for a long and easy descent to Koto (2600m, 50 minutes), where there are teahouses and campsites.

DAY 5: KOTO – SINGENGE DHARAMSALA
6¼ HRS

At the end of Koto village there is a traditional stone doorway and a police checkpost. After registering, descend and cross a suspension bridge and follow a trail that has been blasted out of a sheer rock face. The gorge quickly narrows and the surrounding pine and fir forest obscure any views.

After 2½ hours, cross a bridge to the east bank of the Naar-Phu Khola and pass a broad grassy campsite. In less than 30 minutes you will cross a suspension bridge over the Seti Khola tributary. Huge boulders almost obscure the river, which you follow for another 1¼ hours to the second major river obstruction.

The trail now becomes steeper and the gorge closes in to form a canyon. The river roars as it crashes against a third and then a fourth series of boulders deposited by ancient landslides. After the last series of boulders cross a wooden bridge (3180m, 30 minutes) to the west bank and follow a trail gouged from a cliff face.

After another 30 minutes re-cross the river and climb through a forested section of trail, then around a cut-away formed by a waterfall over the path before a short final climb to the stone huts of Singenge dharamsala (3230m, 1 hour), where there is a small campsite.

DAY 6: SINGENGE DHARAMSALA – KYANG
5½ HRS

The trail remains in the valley bottom for about 30 minutes then crosses a small bridge and climbs for about 250m to the seasonal settlement of Meta (3560m, 1 hour).

As you reach the top of the climb there are good views back down the Naar-Phu Khola to Annapurna II and Lamjung Himal. You can also see a large chorten in the valley bottom near some bridges, which eventually lead to Naar village over a deep gorge. The trail now makes an easy traverse of azalea-covered hillside to a broad clearing at Junam Goth (3690m, 2¼ hours).

The trail dips down to the Junam Khola and then climbs to the twin villages of Chyako (3720m, 30 minutes), which are seasonal settlements shared by both the Naar and Phu villagers.

From Upper Chyako, the trail climbs a little before crossing the Mruju Khola, which is the outflow of the Lyapche Glacier above. The trail now climbs and crosses an eroded section of moraine which offers excellent views back down the valley to Pisang Peak and to the north of Kyang (3850m, 1¼ hours), where there is a good campsite.

DAY 7: KYANG – PHU
4¾ HRS

The trail enters a narrow gorge that runs due north from Kyang; follow a trail cut away from a large cliff face before descending to the river.

Do not cross a small wooden bridge over the river, instead continue heading north on the same side of the river, which swings northeast after 2 hours. The valley now opens up and you pass some derelict chorten, the valley ahead looks completely uninhabitable. Look out for blue sheep on the cliff faces on the far bank.

The trail stays beside the river until you can see a large pinnacle of rock standing across the entrance of a gorge. With a little imagination you can see faces in the rock surface, which are said to be evil spirits that have been trapped by the valley guardian. A narrow and steep trail climbs to the left of the rock pinnacle to a doorway and mani wall (4020m, 2 hours), which offers views of the valley ahead.

The trail winds around the eastern hillside above a deep gorge before descending slightly to a series of deserted buildings and large chorten. Cross the bridge to the chorten or continue on the eastern bank to a suspension bridge just before the village of Phu (4100m, 45 minutes).

DAY 8: PHU   ALL DAY

The locals say that the dry-stone walled village of Phu has been here for 800 years, which is easy to believe when you start exploring. Take your time and if you are lucky you might be invited in to a home for some salt-butter tea.

On the far side of the river above Phu is a peninsula of loose rock carved by two rivers. Climb to the top to visit Tashi Gompa and the inspiring *amchi*, traditional Tibetan medicine doctor, Lama Karma. The Lama has many stories to tell and may invite you for a puja ceremony.

A couple of trekking/mountaineering groups have crossed from Upper Mustang to Phu via a series of snow plateaus and passes; it takes 8 to 10 days and is extremely challenging, involving mountaineering skills, difficult navigation and very high altitudes over 6000m.

DAY 9: PHU – JUNAM GOTH 4½ HRS

As today is an easy trek, you might try to organise a morning puja ceremony with Lama Karma. Retrace your steps down the Phu Khola, through Kyang and Chyako to the campsite at Junam Goth.

DAY 10: JUNAM – NAAR   5 HRS

Continue down the same trail to a point where you can see the bridges to Naar. A loose and sometimes steep trail descends towards the bridges, marked by an ancient and derelict tower (3570m, 1¾ hours).

You may prefer to cross the 80 metre deep gorge on the new suspension bridge rather than the original wooden and dry-stone version. From the bridge climb a broad trail, where there are good views of Pisang Peak and Kang Guru.

After 2¼ hours you will reach a large chorten and long mani wall where the gradient eases. Continue for less than an hour to Naar village (4110m), built in a natural bowl with many terraced fields beneath. There is an excellent camping area above the village.

Note: The valley behind (to the north) Naar is a route to Tangge in Upper Mustang, via the Teri La, see *Other Major Trails in Mustang*, p207. This route doesn't offer many water sources, especially in the pre-monsoon months of April and May.

You also need a special trekking permit from the Department of Immigration in Kathmandu to complete this route to Ghemi (five to six days).

DAY 11: NAAR – HIGH CAMP
2½-5¾ HRS

Leave the village on the trail that passes the small hydro plant and then climbs a little to a broad U-shaped valley to the west of Naar.

An easy gradient climbs past yak herding pastures and kharka for 2 hours to Kang La Phedi (4530m), where there is a good campsite. This is the largest campsite before the pass and you should consider staying here if you are in a group of more than 8 trekkers.

The trail climbs away from the pastures below and then steepens on a rocky trail, which is often icy.

After 2½ hours you will reach a small flat area of loose scree (5020m), where the trail again steepens before arriving at a small glacial lake (5245m, 1¼ hours), where there is a small campsite on scree.

DAY 12: NAAR – NGAWAL /HUMDE
4¼-7¾ HRS

If you camped at the kharka it will take less than 4 hours to reach the top of the pass. For those who camped at the glacial lake it will take less than 30 minutes to reach the summit of the Kang La (5306m). The pass is about 3 metres wide and decorated with many prayer flags. There are good views from the summit but they improve when you descend a little and can see past the rock wall to your right.

Peeking over the ridge joining Annapurna III and IV is the summit of Machhapuchhare (Fish Tail Peak). To the west you can spot Tilicho Peak and the entire Manang valley. The Annapurna Circuit trail lies about 2000m down in the valley below.

From the pass, descend steep scree slopes while being careful not to cause rock fall, to roughly 4500m (1½ hours) where the trail becomes firmer underfoot. The trail is easy to follow all the way to azalea and rhododendron bushes, where it then descends a ridge to the village of Ngawal (3660m, 2¼ hours).

If you are flying out from Humde (3280m, 1 hour), continue down through the village and cross a suspension bridge to the west of the airstrip and the village.

DAY 13: NGAWAL – MANANG 3 HRS

Follow any of a number of trails from Ngawal that descend to some large flat fields along the north bank of the Marsyangdi

river. These trails converge as you enter a pretty forest section that leads to Mugji (3330m, 1¾ hours).

You are now back on the main Annapurna Circuit road route which leads to the 500 year old village of Braga (3360m, 30 minutes) and then to Manang (3540m, 20 minutes), where there are many teahouses and campsites, as well as a maze-like village that dates back hundreds of years.

For trekkers on the Annapurna Circuit, Manang is an acclimatisation stop so there are many more services, restaurants and teahouses than you will have come across so far.

DAY 14: MANANG – THORONG PHEDI 5½ HRS

Just beyond Manang is the village of Tangki (3530m, 20 minutes), which overlooks the entire community. The trail now swings north and climbs gently to a stone wall with a gate that stops livestock from leaving the high pastures.

Do not allow any animals to pass through the gate, and if it is locked, use the stone steps to your right.

Not much further is Ghusang (3950m, 1 hour from Tangki), where you can enjoy some great views of the Chulu Himal, Annapurna III, Gangapurna, Tare Kang (Glacier Dome), Khangsar Kang (Roc Noir) and Tilicho Peak.

An easy gradient leads to a suspension bridge over the Ghyanchang Khola, where

---

❏ **The Manangpa**

The inhabitants of the Manang valley are more properly known as Nyeshang. They claim to be Gurung, although the Gurungs don't agree, and their language is different from any Tibetan dialect. They farm, cultivate and run successful businesses, both in the mountains and in urban areas.

Their houses are usually mud with flat stone roofs, with stables below and living areas above. They are built almost on top of each other up steep slopes, each roof forming the front and base of the next house up. Upper floors are reached using notched wooden ladders.

Houses in Manang itself, where there is more flat land, are the traditional mountain homes of stone or wood with storage below and living areas on the upper floor. They follow Tibetan Buddhism, although many gompas have fallen into disrepair over the years.

there are a couple of small teashops (40 minutes). In another hour you will reach Yak Kharka (4050m), where there are a few teahouses beneath a slight rise to another lone teahouse.

The trail now climbs fairly constantly at an easy gradient to Ledar (4200m, 40 minutes), where there are some simple teahouses, and continues across a hillside covered with many trails.

At the first major trail junction take the right, straight route rather than descending to the river. At the next trail junction, take the left hand straight route, rather than climbing.

After 50 minutes from Ledar the trail descends to a wooden bridge over the Kone Khola before climbing to a teashop that is expensive (20 minutes). It's now an easy 35 minutes to Thorong Phedi (4450m) where there are extensive teahouses and services.

DAY 15: THORONG PHEDI – MUKTINATH 9 HRS

It is a good idea to get a pre-dawn start from Thorong Phedi to avoid the strong winds that often affect the pass after 11am.

There are four large 'steps' up to the Thorong La (5416m); the first is a steep climb up scree to Thorong 'Base Camp', a decrepit and expensive teahouse and dirty campsite (4830m, 1 hour).

The trail now winds through a watercourse before climbing through another, larger gully formed by the melt from a glacier on the eastern side of Thorong Peak. One hour from 'Base Camp' you reach a well-built dharamsala at 5100m, which also offers a campsite for those wanting a genuine high camp (ensure you are well acclimatised).

From here it's 1½ hours across undulating moraine to the top of the Thorong La, where there is a teashop in peak trekking season, but expect to pay handsomely for a drink!

On a clear day you should be able to see some of the Annapurna range to the south and Mukut Himal bordering Dolpo to the west. From the pass the trail descends steeply over scree, which gives way to grassy meadows before reaching Muktinath (3760m, 3 hours).

This large village is a very important pilgrimage site for Hindus and Buddhists, who live in a sacred compound around an eternal flame-from-water. Take some time to visit the famous Hindu temple with 108 carved spouts from which holy water flows, making a cold shower for the brave.

❏ The price of progress

In 2005, the Nepali government embarked on an extensive road construction program in the Annapurna region. The plan was for two roads, one from Besishahar to Manang, and the other to link Beni (near Pokhara) to Lo Monthang (Mustang) and Muktinath. The Chinese had already built a dirt road to Lo Monthang from Tibet and, it was hoped, these new roads would increase development within the region.

The road to Manang is still far from complete. However, the road to Muktinath is finished and jeep traffic and small buses complete the journey from Beni to Jomsom in about seven hours. The impact on the tourism industry has been immediate and dramatic. Villages in the Kali Gandaki valley are suffering from a sudden and almost complete drop in tourism. Businesses that have flourished for more than twenty years have closed and locals are leaving the region in growing numbers.

Those who are staying are pinning their hopes on a government-backed plan to build a new trekking route from Muktinath to Poon Hill on the eastern side of the Kali Gandaki valley, but this isn't expected to be completed until 2011, and perhaps it will take another year or two before teahouses can be built and necessary services put in place. The owner of Mountain View Teahouse in Jomsom is expecting to have to rely on family savings for the next five years and the hope that one day trekkers may return.

Note: Muktinath is also a major trail junction to Dhi in Upper Mustang, see *Southeast of Lo Monthang*, p206.

DAY 16-17: MUKTINATH – JOMSOM – POKHARA   4¼ HRS

The valley around and beneath Muktinath has five Buddhist gompas and many Hindu shrines. The trail is broad and busy with four-wheel-drive cars and motorcycles ferrying Hindu pilgrims from Jomsom.

If you have time it is worth making a small side trip to Kagbeni (2810m, 2¾ hours), the official entry point to the Upper Mustang region to the north.

From Kagbeni or Ekla Bhatti (2740m, 3 hours), the trail descends along the windswept and dusty valley floor of the Kali Gandaki, said to be the deepest river gorge in the world because of the peaks of Annapurna and Dhaulagiri above.

The airstrip and comfy teahouses at Jomsom (2720m) are now only 1½ hours away. There are regular morning flights from Jomsom to Pokhara; the later flights have more potential to be delayed.

Note: If you are delayed because of bad weather in Jomsom, there is an excellent easy day trip down to Marpha village and back to Jomsom (4 hour round trip).

Marpha is the centre of the Thakali community and site of a good quality Apple Brandy distillery. The locals also make cider and apple pie, which are both very popular with trekkers.

❏ The Thakali

Thakali people come from the high valleys of the Kali Gandaki, about five days walk northwest of Pokhara. Their homeland is called Thak Khola, and extends south from Jomsom towards Tatopani. The hospitable Thakali people run most *bhatti*, or trailside teahouses, in the Annapurna region. Their homeland marks the transition between the mainly Hindu lowlands and Buddhist higher areas, although they look more similar to their northern neighbours with regular Mongoloid features of round faces, high cheekbones, flat noses and yellowish skin colour.

Thakalis have spread south and east through Nepal, since they were awarded a monopoly over the salt trade with Tibet in the nineteenth century. Along with the Manangba, these people have evolved into one of the most successful long distance trading groups of Nepal.

Thakali houses generally stand against each other in a line, much like western terrace houses, are built of stone and have flat roofs for drying grain. The insides of their houses are usually spacious, and many have an enclosed courtyard for shelter from the wind and keeping livestock, which then leads onto the main living room, with the kitchen off to one side. There are separate sleeping and storage rooms, as well as a family chapel.

Thakalis have a financial co-operative system called *dhigur*, where members pay a set amount each year into the 'community chest'. Every year one member is awarded the money, either because of a specific need, or by lottery, which he can use as he pleases. He must repay the principal sum, but keeps any profit and carries any loss he may incur. Dhigur has helped families to build large teahouses, and even businesses in Kathmandu and beyond.

Thakali religion is a complex mixture of Jhankrism (a shamanistic religion), Hinduism, Buddhism and Bon. They usually marry by capture where the boyfriend 'abducts' his girlfriend until the families agree to marriage. If no agreement can be made the boy's family must pay a fine, although the couple may elope instead.

ANNAPURNA SANCTUARY & POON HILL

The Annapurna Sanctuary has remained relatively unchanged since the first trekking boom in the mid-1990s, probably because local investment concentrated on the Circuit route and there are limited high trail combination options. From Poon Hill there are a number of trails that link to Khopra Ridge and Tadapani, and to the east of Landruk you could connect to the Mardi Himal trails and even go cross country as far as Siklis and the old (and high) monsoon route over the Namun Bhanjyang to Timang.

Lying to the south of the Great Himalaya Range, this region has a typical monsoonal climate: a long rainy season from June/July through to the end of September and then a period of stable weather through to mid-January. Later winter storms frequently fill the Sanctuary with large amounts of snow, often burying the teahouses completely. The spring thaw is in March and the trails soon re-open and remain so even through monsoon.

Excellent teahouse services line the main trail, but exploring further afield requires full camping kit.

> ### ANNAPURNA SANCTUARY & POON HILL TREK
>
> The Annapurna Sanctuary is a fabulous mountain amphitheatre with magnificent views of the surrounding peaks; en route there are relaxing hot springs, lush forests, fun loving Gurung communities, and it all begins with an incredible panorama from Poon Hill.
>
> **Duration**: 10 days
>
> **Highest Point**: 4234m
>
> **Best Season**: Sep-May
>
> **Accommodation**: camping/teahouse

DAY 1: POKHARA – BIRETHANTI – ULLERI   5 HRS

A short taxi or bus ride from Pokhara brings you to Nayapul (1070m) and the beginning of the trek.

From the bus stop, head north while descending a trail that runs beside the Modhi Khola. In less than 30 minutes you will reach a suspension bridge, which leads directly to Birethanti (1050m) on the far bank and a registration checkpost.

The trail that heads north from Birethanti, up the Modhi Khola, is a direct route to Annapurna Base Camp via Ghandruk. But it is worth first heading west and climbing Poon Hill so that you can combine the up-close mountain views of the Sanctuary with an impressive panoramic vista.

A well-made, broad trail heads west following the Bhurungdi Khola. Remain on the north bank of this river all the way to Ghorepani where you'll arrive the next day.

An easy gradient climbs to Lamdawali (1160m), Sudame (1340m), Hile (1430m), and on to Tikhedhungga (1540m, 2½ hours). The trail now steepens to well-made stone steps; apparently there are 3767 of them!

You should reach the Magar village of Ulleri (1960m) in 2 hours, where there are comfy teahouses and views of Annapurna South and Hiun Chuli.

DAY 2: ULLERI – GHOREPANI / DEURALI   4½ HRS

The trail continues to climb from Ulleri, leaving behind the cultivated section of the Bhurungdi Khola and head into oak and rhododendron forest.

In 1 hour you should reach Ban Thanti (2210m) and in another 1½ hours, Nangge Thanti (2430m), both of which now have good teahouses and make ideal rest stops. Continue climbing for another 90 minutes along the same track to reach Ghorepani

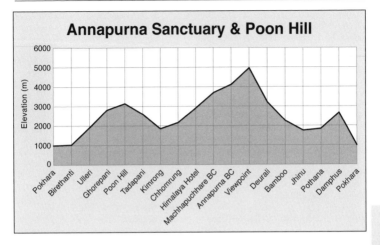

Annapurna Sanctuary & Poon Hill

(2860m) a large village with a checkpost.

Many trekkers prefer to continue for another 20 to 30 minutes and stay at Deurali (2920m), which has great views and is a good starting point for the easy climb to Poon Hill's viewpoint.

DAY 3: GHOREPANI / DEURALI – POON HILL – TADAPANI   5 HRS
The panorama of Machhapuchhare and the Annapurna and Dhaulagiri ranges from Poon Hill is one of the classic Himalayan views.

It takes about 1 hour to reach the top of Poon Hill (3210m) from Deurali, and many

trekkers get up early to enjoy the sunrise. There is a wooden viewing tower on the summit but you will need to be early to beat the crowds and get a good vantage point; remember to take water and a snack.

The crowds will begin to thin out about an hour after sunrise as people head down to their teahouse for breakfast and to prepare for the day's trek.

From Deurali, head back towards the centre of Ghorepani and then take a left fork that heads due east before the end of the village. The trail remains high on a forested ridge, which offers excellent views of

---

❑ The Magar
Magars have Mongoloid features and are more yellow skin-toned than other Nepali people. They speak at least three mutually unintelligible Tibeto-Burman languages, but most speak Nepali as a second language. Magars live in western Nepal, from the high Himalaya to the terai, around the Gorkha District, and in small pockets to the east, past Kathmandu. Many Magars become soldiers, and they are skilled craftsmen and hunters, so they spread across Nepal looking for work. Magars form the largest number of Gurkha soldiers outside Nepal. Their traditional home is a two-storey stone house, covered in whitewash, with thatch or slate roof. In the west, many smaller houses are round or oval and washed in red mud or ochre.

Most Magar villages will have a number of men away on army duties, and many older fellows who have retired from the service. Their marriages are similar to the other hill folk, with most young people choosing their partner to a certain extent. The majority of Magars are Hindu, and the most influential call themselves Thakuris.

Machhapuchhare, Annapurna and Hiun Chuli, especially when you crest a small pass with teashops, which is called Ban Thanti on many maps, after 1½ hours.

From here the trail drops steeply through rhododendron forest covered in Spanish moss to a stream, before climbing to a deserted quarry now occupied by teahouses. The trail now traverses to the hamlet of Liui Kharka before heading out on to a broad hillside above the Kimrong Khola and the teahouses of the pretty village, Tadapani (2630m, 2½ hours).

Note: from Tadapani you can descend to Ghandruk and on to Pokhara via Birethanti or Dhampus for a four to five day Poon Hill itinerary.

DAY 4: TADAPANI – CHHOMRUNG
3 HRS

At the end of the village the trail forks, turn left here to Chhomrung (turning right leads to Ghandruk). The trail descends slowly at first, but soon steepens before the cultivated fields above Chuile. Continue down through this hamlet on a stone track to a bridge over the Kimrong Khola (1820m, 1 hour).

The trail now climbs through the cultivated fields of Kimrong (1850m), before heading east to Taulung (2180m, 1½ hours). Some of the teahouses here offer excellent views of the countless terraced fields to the south that rise from the Modhi Khola below.

The trail heads north from Taulung along an easy downhill gradient to the Gurung village of Chhomrung (2170m, 30 minutes), and some more good views of Annapurna South and Hiun Chuli.

DAY 5: CHHOMRUNG – HIMALAYA
4¾ HRS

Descend a stone stairway and cross a bridge over the Chhomrung Khola and climb through some small terraces to Tilche (2010m, 40 minutes). Beyond the village, enter a bamboo forest and traverse above Bhanuwa and enter the Modhi Khola valley, which forms a striking V shape ahead.

The trail climbs to the last permanent settlement of Sinuwa (2360m, 35 minutes) and continues through oak and rhododendron forest interspersed with large stands of

bamboo. After another 45 minutes you should reach Kuldhigar (2540m), where there are a few teahouses and an ACAP post.

From here onwards, sections of the valley are affected by avalanche debris falling from the flanks of Hiun Chuli; you should check with ACAP staff if the trail is clear and safe. A short climb is followed by a steep descent on a well-prepared paved track to Bamboo (2310m, 30 minutes), where the trail now deteriorates with many tree roots and slippery sections forcing your pace to slow.

Three small bridges cross tributaries en-route to Dobhan (2600m, 1¼ hours), where there are a few teahouses. From Dobhan the forest becomes more impressive with large rhododendrons covered in Spanish moss and pockets of orchids.

The locals believe that the god Baraha protects the Sanctuary. Accidents are frequently explained as the unfortunate outcome of upsetting him by taking animal meat or eggs beyond a small shrine you'll find opposite a pretty 'weeping waterfall'.

In 1 hour you reach the village of Himalaya (2920m), so named because there was a single teahouse here, called Himalaya, and the village sprang up around the lone teahouse once the trek became popular.

DAY 6: HIMALAYA –
MACHHAPUCHHARE BASE CAMP
(MBC)   3¼ HRS

Continue to climb through dense forest to a large rock overhang (Hinku Cave, 3170m, less than 1 hour), once the site of a teahouse. Deurali (3230m, 45 minutes) can be seen ahead, beyond another avalanche-prone area.

The valley now broadens and a fine birch forest fills the far bank before you pass a small snow cave that has been slowly melting for years. Two obvious rock pillars mark the 'gateway' to the Sanctuary, which suddenly opens out to broad grassy slopes and a series of teahouses at MBC (3700m, 1½ hours). The last expedition to climb this sacred mountain was in 1957, and out of respect, it stopped short of the summit.

Many trekkers begin to feel the effects of altitude at MBC, so it is a good idea to initially rest and enjoy the views of Machhapuchhare, Gangapurna and Annapurna South on arrival.

❏ **Side trip from ABC**
For those who are acclimatised and have the time, there is an excellent viewpoint on the far side of the Annapurna South Glacier and above the Tent Peak Base Camp. From ABC descend to the glacier and look for a trail marked by cairns, which crosses the glacier to a large gully (**beware of rock fall**) cut by a stream through the moraine on the far side of the valley. Climb to the left of the gully to a grassy moraine and head west as a small trail winds around the base of some buttresses.

Before the rim of another deep gully (4350m, 1½ hours), climb straight up the face of a buttress which soon begins to level to a point where you can cross a small stream to the west bank and ascend a broad grassy slope that leads up to a viewpoint (4890m, 2 hours) of the entire western basin of the Sanctuary.

To the east is Tent Peak (Tharpu Chuli), to the northeast is Singu Chuli, to the north is Khangsar Kang (Roc Noir) and to the west is the massive face of Annapurna I (8091m). The southern horizon is filled with Annapurna South and Hiun Chuli.

Your return to ABC will take 2¼ hours.

If you are still feeling symptoms of altitude sickness later that evening or the following morning, you should rest for the day or consider descending to Himalaya.

DAY 7: MBC – ANNAPURNA BASE CAMP (ABC)   2 HRS
The trail climbs ancient moraine, now covered in grass, west of MBC. There are many trails that wind slowly up to ABC (4130m, 2 hours). Those on the edge of the moraine have views of the Annapurna South Glacier; those towards the lower slopes of Hiun Chuli give a better perspective of the Sanctuary.

There are four teahouses at ABC, which was the site for the 1970 British Annapurna Expedition, and a day spent wandering further up the valley or along the edge of the nearby moraine is a great way to absorb the majesty of the Himalaya.

DAY 8: ABC – BAMBOO   5½ HRS
Backtrack along the same route to Bamboo (2310m, 4½ hours), or if trail conditions allow continue on to Sinuwa (2360m, 1 hour from Bamboo).

DAY 9: BAMBOO – LANDRUK
5¼ HRS
Reach Sinuwa (2360m) in one hour from Bamboo and continue to Taulung (2180m, 1½ hours from Sinuwa). At the end of the village the trail forks: the right leads back to Kimrong, but take the left trail, which

descends steeply to Jhinu (1780m, 45 minutes). Before the track swings sharply west (into the Kimrong Khola valley) there is a small sign for a hot spring about 40 minutes to the north in the Modhi Khola valley.

If you don't want a hot bath, continue along the trail as it descends to a bridge over the river and climb the trail the far bank to Samrung (1750m, 30 minutes) before again descending to the Modhi Khola on a trail heading towards New Bridge (1340m, 20 minutes).

Just before the final descent to the bridge is a sign to another hot springs down a scrambly track to the north of the bridge. Cross the bridge and pass through some small villages before a short climb to the large Gurung village of Landruk (1565m, 1¼ hours).

DAY 10: LANDRUK – POTHANA – POKHARA   4¼ HRS
The trail now climbs an easy gradient sometimes on soft ground and sometimes on stone paving to Pothana (1890m, 2½ hours), which straddles the Manjh Danda ridge. There are fine views of Machhapuchhare and the Annapurnas to the north from along the next section of trail, making this one of the best final days on a trek in Nepal. Descend from Pothana along a large ridge trail to Damphus (1650m, 1 hour), before a final steep descent through forest to the taxi stand and car park at Phedi (1130m, 45 minutes), which is only a short drive from Pokhara.

ROUTE GUIDE

GHT – ANNAPURNA

The Great Himalaya Trail follows the main Annapurna Circuit trail (now partially road) from Dharapani to Kagbeni via the Thorong La. From Dharapani (1860m), follow the same route as described in days three and four of *Naar, Phu & the Thorong La* (p186) to Koto, where you should stop for the night.

The district centre of Manang is Chame (2675m), 20 minutes up the road-trail from Koto, where there are many teahouses and tourist services. Walk through the village on stone paving and cross a suspension bridge to a final couple of teahouses near a hot springs. Continue to follow the road route to Talekhu (40 minutes), where the valley narrows to steep cliffs on either side. In the middle of the next gorge section is Bhratang (1 hour), where there are a couple of simple teahouses. After the village, the trail descends to a bridge over the river (20 minutes) before climbing about 200m through fine pine forest to Dhikur (3060m, 1 hour), where there are some extensive teahouses. You have now walked through a massive bend in the Marsyangdi river and an enormous concave rock wall rises to your right.

The road route now levels and it is a very pleasant trek through sparse pine forest to Lower Pisang (3200m, 50 minutes), where there are many teahouses. Look for a large stuffed yak with lightbulb eyes in an ornately decorated teahouse on your left as you enter the village. The trail remains flat for 15 minutes or so beyond Lower Pisang, before climbing an easy gradient on the dirt road to a minor pass called Deurali Danda (3470m, 50 minutes). The trail descends to another long flat section to Humde (3280m, 40 minutes) where there is an airstrip, police checkpost and teahouses. A lack of shade through this section of trail can make it very hot going to Mugji (50 minutes), where there are a couple of basic teahouses. It is now only 30 minutes to the 500-year-old village of Braga (3360m) and then another 20 minutes to Manang (3540m), where there are many teahouses and campsites, as well as a maze-like village that dates back hundreds of years.

For details of crossing the Thorong La from Manang and then descending to Muktinath see days 14 and 15 of *Naar, Phu & the Thorong La*, pp189-90.

From Muktinath, take a trail that descends towards and then through Jharkot (3550m, 30 minutes). From here you can avoid the motor road (a 1 hour jeep trip to Jomsom, or 40 minutes to Kagbeni) by following a small irrigation stream to Khingar (3280m, 20 minutes) but from here you will have to take the road route. Make sure you have a scarf or similar to cover your face against dust kicked up by jeeps, or the fierce afternoon wind. Once you reach a broad, flat plateau as you enter the main Kali Gandaki valley there is a shortcut track to Kagbeni (2810m, 1 hour and 10 minutes), which avoids the road. Kagbeni is a delightful village that used to be on the Nepal/Tibet border, see *Mustang Circuit*, day two, p200. The gompa in the middle of the old village is in good condition, and look for the male and female protectors at either end of old boundary wall. There is a checkpost here, where you will need to show your permits to be able to continue to Dolpo. The airstrip at Jomsom is 1½ hours (or a 20 minute drive by jeep) to the south, where there are many teahouses and services.

Mustang

'Mustang is one of the few places in the Himalayan region that has been able to retain its traditional Tibetan culture unmolested...authentic Tibetan culture now survives only in exile and a few places like Mustang, which have had long historical and cultural ties with Tibet.'
The Dalai Lama

Closed to foreigners until 1992, the 'Forbidden' Kingdom of Mustang is where today collides with medieval Asia; where a vibrant culture dating back over a thousand years is coming to terms with a 21st century road. Fortunately, the communities and their traditions are resilient, as are their mud-walled towns and monasteries covered in original frescos, for now. A recently built road from Tibet runs through the heart of Mustang to Jomsom and on to Pokhara; it offers unprecedented change to this unique and ageless place. Jeeps and motorcycles have replaced decorated horses, and art experts are assessing the potential dangers of traffic vibrations to fragile artworks. Mustang may not last forever, see it while you can.

Lying to the northwest of the Annapurnas and extending onto the Tibetan Plateau, Upper Mustang is a large mountain-fringed basin home to the headwaters of the Kali Gandaki. The main trail runs north-south from Lo Monthang to Jomsom with some side trips en route, but none that conveniently connect to other trekking routes. So, until some serious trail work is completed there isn't a reliable route option through Upper Mustang for the GHT. Trails from Naar and Phu to Upper Mustang have sporadic water sources, are rugged and some require technical alpine skills. However, there is a good trail from Ghemi to Chharka Bhot in Upper Dolpo, but it can be used only in October or November. The locals in Ghemi restrict access to this route, as they believe that the mountain spirits will be offended and prevent rain from falling on their fields if anyone disturbs the pass from December to September. They have been known to defend this belief violently.

Mustang is part of the Annapurna Conservation Area Project (ACAP), which is the largest protected biodiversity area in Nepal. Referred to as a Trans-Himalayan Ecosystem (the lower, lush valleys of the mid-hills are linked with the arid Tibetan plateau), this is a culturally and environmentally sensitive and fragile region, which demands the utmost respect and care. Please take all precautions to tread softly and follow the *Great Himalaya Trail Code*, see p8.

In October 2008, King Jigme Palbar Bista's (b. 1930) reign over Mustang ended by Nepali Government order, which effectively terminated the monarchic tradition established in AD1350.

MUSTANG CIRCUIT

The standard return route from Jomsom to Lo Monthang takes 12 days, which works well with the 10-day Upper Mustang permit. There are some loop itiner-

Mustang region

- – – · – GHT
- – – – Main trail

0 __ 5 __ 10km

Kora La 4660
Phungphung La 5177
Chhatang Bhanjyang 5666
Chanchumi Bhanjyang
Parcheka Bhanjyang 5447
Ratna Chuli 7035
Himlung 7126
Lugu La
Gaugiri 6110
Bhrikuti Sail 6364
Jomsom Himal 6364
Phu
Damodar Kund
Siyawa La 4817
Gharphu
LO MONTHANG
Dhi
Yara
Luri
Tengge
Teri La 5529
Yakwa Kang 6482
Thorong La 5416
Thorong Phedi
Mansail 6235
Namgyal
Lo Gekar
Tsarang
Ghemi
Geling
Rangchyung
Chhusang
Muktinath
Arniko Chuli 6034
Sang La 5584
Chhunggar
Samar
Kagbeni
Thorung Peak 6201
Pindu Bhanjyang 6583
Ghami La 5694
Ghok
Santa
Phalla
JOMSOM
Marpha
Jungben La 5550
Nulungsumda Kharka
Niwas La 5124
Dhampus Peak 6035
Chharka Bhot
Mukut Himal 6639
Barbun Khola
Tinjegaon
Dhaulagiri II 7751

aries to the north of Lo Monthang and those with mountaineering experience could try the eastern link via Luri Cave Gompa and the Damodar Glacier to Phu (7-10 days). The western link, which ascends the Ghemi Khola valley and crosses the Khyaklum Himal to Chharka Bhot is only open from October to November.

Most routes in Mustang open in late March or early April when the sun is strong enough to melt large volumes of snow dumped by winter storms. From June, the effect of the monsoon is significantly reduced due to the 'rain-shadow' effects caused by the Annapurna and Dhaulagiri massifs. This means that trekking routes are pleasant even in the middle

MUSTANG CIRCUIT TREK

Like nowhere else on earth does modern day collide so obviously with the Middle Ages, where life is both booming and threatened by progress. Try to coincide your visit with the Teeji festival to immerse yourself in a timeless culture set amid dramatic mountain scenery on the 'Plain of Aspirations'.

Duration: 12 days

Highest Point: 4070m

Best Season: Mar-Nov

Accommodation: camping and basic teahouses

of the monsoon, as rainstorms have less intensity than in the rest of the country. After the monsoon has finished, a long period of cold but stable weather interspersed by occasional intense storms continues to early December, when snow accumulates on the passes and the trekking becomes challenging.

Mustang has remained an exclusive trekking destination because of the large trekking permit fee, which was reduced in 2009 to US$350 per person for 10 days (Kagbeni to Kagbeni). To visit the northernmost settlements and valleys

ROUTE GUIDE

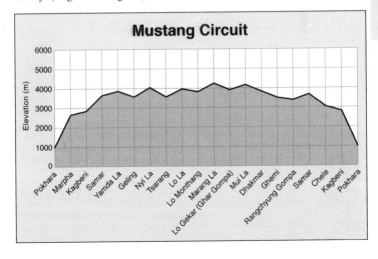

above Lo Monthang you must have an extended permit before you arrive in Lo Monthang, without a fully paid extension and a specified route you will not be permitted to trek beyond Lo Monthang.

DAY 1: POKHARA – JOMSOM – MARPHA   ALL DAY

The ascent of the Kali Gandaki valley can cause altitude sickness so it is wise to include acclimatisation periods. One of the most popular first stops is to stay at Marpha (2670m), whether you fly to Jomsom and then walk for 2 hours (20 minutes by vehicle), or drive up from Beni. Marpha is a picturesque stone-flagged village surrounded by apple orchards, from which the locals produce cider and brandy.

The Kali Gandaki valley is one of the oldest and most important trade routes between Nepal and Tibet. Dating back to the 1400s, the local Thakali people were renowned traders in all goods, especially salt and wool (from Tibet), and grains (from Nepal). This valley is said to be the deepest natural river gorge in the world, as it runs between two 8000m peaks, Annapurna I (8091m) and Dhaulagiri (8167m).

DAY 2: MARPHA – KAGBENI 4½ HRS

The trail to Jomsom (2720m, 2 hours) is normally busy with local traffic and can be reached in 20 minutes by vehicle. The town is spread along the road and crosses the Kali Gandaki beyond the Nepal Army barracks. A broad dirt road now follows the east bank of the river to Ekla Bhatti (2740m, 2 hours) where there is a fork: the right track climbs to Muktinath (see day 15 of *Naar, Phu & the Thorong La*, p190), but you continue along the valley bottom to Kagbeni (2810m, 30 minutes), which can be seen ahead.

Your Mustang permit is from Kagbeni onwards so it is important that you arrive here the day before it becomes valid.

The official entry to Upper Mustang is at Kagbeni, an oasis-like settlement of narrow flagstone-paved paths, flat-roofed homes, and dominated by an old but still functioning Tibetan Buddhist gompa of the Sakyapa sect. The remains of an old fort lie on the northern edge of the village and would have looked formidable before the local king fell on hard times and his

dethroned descendants moved on. A male spirit-protector guards the northern gateway of the village (there is a smaller female protector at the southern entrance) and beyond is a mani wall, next to which is the ACAP registration office and information centre.

Beyond the village there are excellent views of the gompa with Nilgiri, Tilicho, Annapurna and Dhaulagiri rising above.

DAY 3: KAGBENI – SAMAR   6 HRS

From Kagbeni the trail continues on the east bank of the Kali Gandaki, often traversing slopes of loose rock where you might be lucky and find ammonites.

The valley narrows and a large cliff face on your right is dotted with ancient cave dwellings before opening out again at the village of Tangbe (3060m, 2½ hours). The valley undulates across what looks like moonscape to Chhusang (2980m, 45 minutes), where there is a small teahouse. If you have time, ask one of the locals to guide you to a small but impressive cave gompa dedicated to White Tara (Buddha of Success and Achievement) about 20 minutes from the village.

There are also impressive rock formations and some meditation caves in the cliffs on the west bank of the Kali Gandaki. Chhusang is bordered to the north by a broad river, which can be tricky to ford after heavy rain.

The valley ends abruptly at a narrow canyon with more meditation cliffs above and a metal bridge that leads to Chele (3050m, 45 minutes). There are a few teahouses here and good views back down the Kali Gandaki valley, with the peaks of Nilgiri and Tilicho in the distance.

The trail climbs through the centre of Chele and up a loose rocky slope where the gradient eases. From here you can see the trail enter an eroded valley, on the far side of which is the rarely visited village of Ghyakar. Continue on a track blasted and chiselled from an enormous cliff face, which eventually leads to a small grassy

❑ Baragaunle people

These people live south of Lo Monthang and north of the Thakalis, and usually prefer to be thought of as Gurungs. They are more widely travelled then the Lopa (from Mustang) and the region in which they live is slightly more advanced. Their major villages are Muktinath and Kagbeni, both of which form the border to Mustang, and are often visited by trekkers crossing the Thorong La.

Their houses are similar to the houses in Lo, built of mud and poorly ventilated. They are, however, quite warm and manage to keep out most of the wind that howls up the valley every day from about 11am. Their clothing, like the Lopa, is Tibetan in style and often brightly coloured. The Baraguan villages used to supply large numbers of bonded servants to rich Thakalis. They follow Tibetan Buddhism with some Bon influences.

basin and the Dajori La (3735m, 1½ hours) pass with views down to the Samarkyung Khola. Samar (3660m, 30 minutes) is a small, picturesque village surrounded by poplar trees, *chatta* on tall poles, and terraces used for cultivating millet.

DAY 4: SAMAR – GELING   6¼ HRS

The trail runs through the centre of the village to an old kani where the track rapidly descends into a heavily eroded watercourse and then climbs a steep trail on the far bank.

Cross a short section of flat grassy ground, past an old stupa before reaching another eroded watercourse, which you cross by another switchback trail. Once you reach the top of the far bank the trail forks: the right fork climbs a ridgeline and ultimately leads to Rangchyung Cave Gompa, but this is best saved for your return trek, so turn left and continue up towards the Bhena La (3838m, 2 hours).

The trail dips and then climbs again to the Yamda La (3860m, 1 hour) and your first expansive views of Upper Mustang. Ahead is range after range of copper, chocolate, grey, ochre and coffee-coloured hills, scarred by deep canyons forming a maze of windswept depths. The trail descends rapidly into a small valley, which you descend on an easy gradient before contouring to the left and around a steep hillside.

The trail steepens again as you near Syanboche village (3800m, 45 minutes), which is where the Rangchyung Cave Gompa trail rejoins the main trail. There are a few

teahouses here should you want to rest. On the far side of the village the trail climbs to another pass before descending an easy gradient to a fork marked by a painted cairn.

The left trail traverses the upper slopes of the valley, past an enormous stupa at Chhunggar, but the next teahouse is at Ghemi on this route. So turn right at the cairn and descend to a broad flat-bottomed valley and the village of Geling (3570m, 2½ hours). There are not many rooms available in Geling so you may want to send someone ahead to reserve accommodation.

There are two Ngor-pa sect (an offshoot of the Sakyapa) gompas in the village, which date to the sect founder Ngorchen Kunga Zangpo in the 15th century. The main gompa is dedicated to Maitreya (the Future Buddha) and contains frescos of the Thousand Buddhas of the Bhadrakalpa (a time when all thousand Buddhas shall appear).

The second, smaller gompa is high on the rocks above the village, and is called the Gonkhang. This is where the village spirit-protectors are stored, and is a very holy and powerful shrine. The resident lama may not be willing to uncover the fierce-looking deities for fear of angering them.

DAY 5: GELING – TSARANG
6¼-7 HRS

There are two trail options from Geling; the fastest route climbs a steep hillside above the two gompas before heading due north along a shallow valley to a pass (4025m, 2 hours) with excellent views back towards the

Annapurnas. Then descend to the main road route and on to Ghemi (3520m, 1¾ hours).

The second, slower trail takes an easier gradient climb up the main Geling valley to the road route over the Nyi La (4010m, 2½ hours), which also offers some great views. A long but easy descent brings you to Ghemi (3520m, 1 hour), where there are a couple of teahouses. From the centre of Ghemi descend a rough and sometimes-slippery trail next to a stream out-flow from the village.

Cross the suspension bridge in the valley bottom, and ascend the far bank to a valley with the longest mani wall in Mustang. Follow the trail beside the mani wall and then swing right into a small valley where the trail climbs another pass, the Tsarang La (3870m, 2 hours).

Another long, easy descent brings you the old capital of Mustang, Tsarang (3560m, 1½ hours), which is dominated by a huge crumbling fort that used to be the royal residence. The extensive gompa and library here has similar but larger frescos and statues to those in Geling's gompa.

DAY 6: TSARANG – LO MONTHANG
4½ HRS

The trail from Tsarang drops into a river course to the north of the town; you will need to duck under a metal water pipe as you descend to the Charang Khola. Climb the far bank and ascend to the mouth of the Thulung Khola and the dirt road, which you follow for 2½ hours, past a large stupa, to a broad plateau where there is a lone teashop.

In the cliff face above the teashop you can see more cave dwellings. Continue to follow the road to the Lo La (3950m, 1¼ hours), where there are fine views of Lo Monthang (3809m) and northern Mustang. From the pass it is an easy downhill for 45 minutes to the ancient walled capital, which sits upon the Plain of Aspiration.

Only the (ex-) King of Mustang is allowed to ride through the main gateway, all others must walk into the 600-year-old mud-walled city. It is worth spending at least two days exploring Lo Monthang, which is crammed with about 150 homes linked by narrow, twisting alleyways. The flat roofs of each home are used for drying crops during the daytime, and at night young lovers are able to climb easily from roof to roof for liaisons.

Established as the capital of Lo by Raja Amapal in the 1380s, the people of Lo Monthang avoid building homes outside the city walls, believing that bad spirits will cause havoc in their households if they do.

❏ The Lopa
The Lopa people of Mustang live in mud-brick homes that are whitewashed on the outside and decorated on the inside, much like Tibetan homes. Lo Monthang also boasts the Raja's Palace and many beautiful monasteries, which are currently being restored by art historians from Italy and other European countries. The land around Lo Monthang is arid and windswept, and not at all conducive to agriculture. The altitude is between 3000m and 3500m. Where there are small streams, however, willows grow and wheat, potatoes and barley are cultivated.

The Lopa traditionally traded with Tibet but in the mid-eighteenth century the Thakalis to the south were granted a monopoly on the salt trade, so the Lopa lost a great deal of income. Local wealth deteriorated further when Tibetans began crossing the border in 1959 and encroached on the small pastures the Lopa used to feed their sheep, yaks, donkeys and mules, causing great hardship.

They practise Tibetan Buddhism, and have marriages by parental agreement, capture and elopement. Like many people who live in harsh landscapes, they are kind and generous but also shrewd businessmen.

The most famous festival in Lo Monthang is Teeji, which is generally in April/May, when for three days the lamas and monks perform costumed dances in the village square.

The Lamas, who circumambulate the city during festivals blessing the walls as they go, perpetuate many such superstitions.

The former Raja, 'Lo Gyelbu', named Jigme Palbar Bista, fulfils a mainly ceremonial role when in residence although he is loved and respected throughout his Kingdom. It is said that he keeps some of the best horses, Lhasa Apsos, and the most ferocious Tibetan mastiffs in Mustang. The Raja's palace is an imposing four-storey building in the centre of the city. Rani is from an aristocratic family in Lhasa.

DAY 7: LO MONTHANG   ALL DAY

Apart from the intriguing town itself, there are three major gompas to explore, Jhampa, Thupchen, and Chhoede, all of which have undergone expert restoration over the last 20 years.

The oldest gompa is Jhampa Lhakang (meaning 'god house'), begun in 1387 during the reign of king Amapal, and later designed by Ngorchen Kunga Zangpo (who also established Geling and Tsarang gompas). Jhampa is said to contain 1000 hand-painted Yogatantric mandalas of amazing intricacy, as well as a large gilded clay statue of Maitreya (Future Buddha), which is two storeys tall. The ground floor is undergoing long overdue restoration, but the second floor is accessible. So too is a third floor sanctum leading to a flat roof, which offers excellent views of the city and surrounding countryside.

Nearby is the great gompa of Thupchen, founded in 1412, which you enter through an entrance hall protected by baroque statues of the four Lokapala, who keep evil spirits at bay. Commissioned by King Chang Chen Tashi Gon, the grandson of Amapal, this is perhaps the most impressive of the three gompas. The main prayer hall has two rows of ornate statues. The larger row against the western wall includes Shakyamuni, Avalokiteshwara (Compassion of all Buddhas), Manjushri, and Padmasambhava (Guru Rinpoche). The lower one with displays Vajradhara (Primordial Buddha), White Tara, Amitaya, and Hayagriva (the wrathful manifestation of Avalokiteshwara).

❏ The Teeji festival

The Teeji (comes from the words 'ten che', meaning 'the hope of Buddha Dharma') festival is a three-day ritual known as 'The Chasing of the Demons', which centres on a local myth that tells of a deity named Dorje Jono, who must battle against his demon father (Dorje Sonnu) to save the Kingdom of Mustang from destruction. The demon father wreaked havoc on the Kingdom by creating a shortage of water (a precious resource in this very dry land), which caused all sorts of disasters including famine and animal loss. Dorje Jono eventually beats the demon and banishes him from the land, and the community is saved from a plague of misfortunes. Of course, the local population celebrates their salvation, as water will be plentiful again, and the balance and harmony of day-to-day life is restored.

Over three days, the lamas from Chhoede Gompa enact battles and folklore scenes through intricate mask-dances, which culminate in a fireworks and musket-firing melee outside the main gate of the city. Each of the three evenings, there is a cultural program in the centre of the city, where young and old come to enjoy dance and singing performances.

Teeji is a lively, vivid and amusing celebration and reaffirmation of a myth said to have been bought to Mustang by Padmasambhava in the 8th century. Apart from the symbolic ritual of cleansing the Kingdom, Teeji coincides with the end of the dry winter/spring season and ushers in the wetter monsoon season (the growing season in Mustang). So for everyone in Mustang, it is a 'must-see' event, where locals dress up in their finery and have a good time.

The walls are adorned with large frescos of Buddhist deity triads, which are flanked by hundreds of minor deities. An antechamber on the northern side of the gompa is still under renovation and was probably dedicated to the protector Mahakali.

The final gompa to visit is Chhoede, the main religious hub of Lo Monthang, and normally guarded by some fierce Tibetan mastiffs, so you are advised to secure the services of a monk to accompany you. Established in 1757, there are three notable places to visit. The main gompa prayer hall has many bronze, brass and copper statues and the sacred *thanka* of Mahakala and Dorje Sonnu (the evil demon ritually killed during the Teeji festival).

Note: the monks prohibit photography of these statues in an apparent bid to limit interest in them among collectors of stolen art.

In a small building next to the gompa is a large prayer wheel, which almost fills the room. It is said that circumambulation three times while spinning the wheel will drive away any bad dreams.

The final spot worth visiting is the monastic school beside the entry to the Chhoede compound, where the students and teachers welcome visitors and are keen to show off their language skills. A large new prayer hall opposite the school is where the monks prepare for their dances at each festival.

DAY 8: LO MONTHANG – LO GEKAR – GHEMI   6 HRS

Instead of retracing your steps back towards Tsarang, follow a smaller trail that slowly climbs to the southwest of Lo Monthang to Samduling Kharka (4080m, 1½ hours), where the trail forks. Take the smaller, right hand trail that climbs further up the valley before striking up towards the hills to the south.

Once on top of the gently curved hill the trail descends a rough but shallow valley formed by a stream running south. The valley gradually steepens, before reaching a relatively flat area with boulders washed down from the mountains to your right. A bridge crosses the upper Chharang Khola (3820m, 1¾ hours), which has carved a deep gully. Ghar Gompa (3950m, 20 minutes) sits in a grove of poplar trees on the hillside above Lo Gekar ('Pure Virtue of Lo').

Note: if you accidentally take the left-hand trail at Samduling Kharka you will cross the Marang La and then have to walk up the Tsarang valley, past Lo Gekar to Ghar Gompa.

From Lo Gekar, climb a section that is a bit steep before descending and crossing a tributary of the Chharang Khola. The trail now climbs to another pass, the Mui La (4170m, 1 hour), which leads to a broad flat valley. Some prayer flags mark a notch in the hillside on the far side of the valley where the path descends rapidly on loose

❏ Ghar Gompa

A local legend says that the Buddhist saint Padmasambhava founded Ghar Gompa in the 8th century, when he came to Mustang to do battle with evil powers out to destroy Buddhism. It is said that he came to Lo Gekar while he was on a journey through Mustang to Samye, where he established the first gompa in Tibet (built AD775–787), thus making Ghar Gompa one of the oldest Tibetan Buddhist gompas in the Himalaya.

The main statue in the inner prayer room is said to be a self-emanating image of the saint, flanked by his two principle consorts, Mandarava and Yeshe Tsogyal. Smaller statues of other deities are displayed around the room, which is decorated with some fine frescos. The anteroom is uniquely decorated with hundreds of wooden tablets each with a Buddhist deity painted in vivid colours. A large cavity in the north wall holds a very rare collection of wooden and clay statues, including one of Padmasambhava on a horse prepared for battle against the demons.

ground to the red and pink cliffs of Dhakmar (3820m, 1½ hours).

From the centre of Dhakmar follow a trail that first descends the left hand (northern side) of the valley before crossing a small river to the southern bank, then rises slightly to three decorated chorten before rounding the hillside and descending rapidly to Ghemi (3520m, 1 hour).

DAY 9: GHEMI – RANGCHYUNG CAVE GOMPA – SAMAR   7¼ HRS

Retrace your steps up to the Nyi La (4010m, 1¾ hours) and descend to a trail junction marked by a painted cairn. Take the right-hand trail, which contours across easy ground to the large painted chorten at Chhunggar (3750m, 45 minutes). Continue on a broad easy gradient up to Syangboche La (3850m, 1¼ hours).

From the top of the pass you should be able to spot a small trail that heads down the right side of the valley beneath the village, to Rangchyung Cave Gompa (3420m, 1 hour). The trail to the cave is sometimes steep and on loose ground, but for the most part it is easy.

As you descend into a canyon formed by a tributary of the Kali Gandaki, you begin to realise how mysterious this place must feel to the locals, who are used to the expansive, windswept plateau above.

The cave is in a cliff wall, about 100m above the junction of two small rivers.

Rangchyung chorten means 'the chorten that built itself', or appeared by a miracle. The cave has a large natural pillar, which appears to be supporting the roof of the cave temple. Locals also worship this pillar as a chorten.

From the entrance, go to the left of the pillar and climb a few steps into a dark passageway that runs behind the pillar. There are many carvings in the rock face worn smooth by devotees touching them.

It is said that the images are predominantly of Padmasambhava (8th century) and Atisa (11th century), the two great teaching lamas who founded what became competing Tibetan Buddhist sects (red hat and yellow hat respectively). However, scholars believe that the cave was of religious importance long before Buddhism arrived in Mustang and was probably a ritual site for an animist belief system.

The trail from the cave crosses a small bridge and then climbs relentlessly to a ridge to the north of Samar (3660m), which you will reach after 2½ hours.

DAYS 10-12: SAMAR – KAGBENI – POKHARA   5½ HRS

It will take about an hour to descend to Chele, and a further 4½ hours to Kagbeni (2810m), where you must register at the ACAP office. It is possible to drive to Jomsom and onwards to Pokhara, or take the short flight.

SIDE TRIPS FROM LO MONTHANG

If you have purchased an extended permit for more than 10 days, you are allowed to visit the villages to the north and east of Lo Monthang. However, camping equipment is recommended to explore these areas, as there are very few teahouses. In 2007, a team of archaeologists discovered a series of caves in a remote valley in Upper Mustang that had lain untouched for centuries. The team who made the discovery believe that there are more caves waiting to be discovered.

North of Lo Monthang

The heart of Mustang is two broad, fertile valleys that lie to the north of Lo Monthang, and makes an enjoyable two-day trek, or a one-day horse ride. An ancient trade route linking India with Tibet passes through these valleys, which were once much wealthier judging by the many decaying buildings that dot the landscape. If you want to stay in the teahouse in Gharphu then you should begin your circuit in the eastern, Chhosar valley. If you are riding, then it is probably best to head to Namgyal first to try to see some of the morning puja ceremony.

● **Chhosar valley, including Gharphu, Nyphu and Jhong Cave Gompas** – follow the dirt road from Lo Monthang along the main trade route to Tibet along the west bank of the Mustang Khola. Nyphu Gompa (3750m, 2 hours) is across the valley, its red walls stand out against the rugged cliff face above the east bank of the river. After another 45 minutes you reach Gharphu (3900m), also on the east bank of the river. Jhong Cave Gompa (3950m, 30 minutes) is further north on the east bank of the Mustang Khola and is reached by some wooden ladders and tunnels, ask at Gharphu if the gompa is open.

● **Thinggar valley, including Namgyal Gompa, Kimaling and Nyamdo** – from the northwest corner of Lo Monthang follow an obvious trail to Namgyal Gompa (The Monastery of Victory, at 3910m, 1 hour), set on a ridge with excellent views of walled city in the valley below. The Namgyal Thupten Dhargyeling Gompa was founded in AD1310, and continues to be the busiest and most important gompa outside of Lo Monthang. The abbot, or *khenpo*, Ven. Khenpo Tsewan Rigzin, is working hard to maintain both a school and the ancient gompa building, so donations are welcome.

On the far side of the ridge, a trail leads through the village of Namgyal to Thinggar (4025m, 30 minutes) where the Raja had his Summer Palace. Phuwa Gompa can be seen on the far side of the valley, about 30 minutes away. Kimaling (4030m) is 45 minutes from Thinggar, and the largest village in the valley. The locals here happily try to sell arts and crafts as well as handmade rugs. To reach Gharphu, continue up the valley and follow a trail that turns east at the Nyamdo Khola.

Southeast of Lo Monthang
● **Dhi, Tashi Kabum Cave Gompa and Luri Cave Gompa** – from Lo Monthang a small trail descends into the Kali Gandaki valley canyon, which you follow to Surkhang and Dhi (3390m, 6 hours). **Note: this route is only open during the winter months when the river is frozen.**

An alternative and easier route involves following the main trail to Tsarang. Just before you leave the Thulung Khola valley, descend to a bridge across the river and climb an easy gradient to a minor pass, which offers good views south. The trail then descends an eroded gully to a bridge over the Kali Gandaki; cross to the campsite at Surkhang (5 hours from Lo Monthang).

Note: you do not actually need to stay at Dhi, which is on the far bank a little upstream. However, when asking for directions, ask for Dhi as it is older and better known than Surkhang.

From Surkhang, ascend the Puyung Khola valley to the campsite at Yara village (3650m, 2 hours), which makes an ideal base to visit Tashi Kabum Cave Gompa (1 hour from Yara) and Lori Cave Gompa (2 hours from Yara). Both caves pre-date the main gompas in Lo Monthang by about 100 years and are good examples of Buddhist art before the Tibetan style was fully developed. Employ a local guide from Yara to find both gompas.

Other major trails in Mustang

From Dhi, you can ascend the Puyung Khola and then climb to the sacred lakes at Damodar Kund (4890m), which is the source of the Kali Gandaki. From the lakes you can exit Mustang via a high route to Muktinath, which is still used by pilgrims (seven to eight days). There is an alpine route to Phu village (via the Damodar glacier, seven days) for those with mountaineering skills and equipment.

To the south of Dhi is another village called Tangge (3240m, 6 hours), where there is a popular high route to Muktinath via the Baha La (4400m) and Gyu La (4077m), which takes three days from Tangge.

Note: water is not always available on this route.

Also from Tangge is a route to the southeast over the Teri La (5529m) to Naar, which takes seven days and has few water sources.

From Ghemi, there is a trail up the Dhuva Khola heading due west, which eventually leads over a pass to Upper Dolpo. The locals in Ghemi believe that powerful spirits live in the mountains along this route and will not allow anyone to approach the pass between March and September (it's closed during the winter months from December to February) out of fear of losing essential rainfall in the pre-monsoon season.

ROUTE GUIDE

❏ The 8000ers – the world's highest peaks

Rank	Mountain	Height (m)	Height (ft)	First ascent
1	Mount Everest/Sagarmatha/ Chomolungma	8848	29,028	1953
2	K2/Qogir/Godwin Austen	8611	28,251	1954
3	Kangchenjunga	8586	28,169	1955
4	Lhotse	8516	27,940	1956
5	Makalu	8485	27,838	1955
6	Cho Oyu	8188	26,864	1954
7	Dhaulagiri I	8167	26,795	1960
8	Manaslu	8163	26,781	1956
9	Nanga Parbat	8126	26,660	1953
10	Annapurna I	8091	26,545	1950
11	Gasherbrum I	8080	26,509	1958
12	Broad Peak	8051	26,414	1957
13	Gasherbrum II	8034	26,362	1956
14	Shishapangma	8027	26,335	1964

Dolpo

Dolpo is remote, wild and considered by many to be one of the most magical and mysterious of places in the Himalaya. Linked for hundreds of years to Tibet, this region lies among the high peaks, on top of the roof of the world. Trekking here is very different from much of Nepal; oasis-like villages dot barren landscapes, scarred by deep canyons, and all beneath velvet blue skies.

Boasting a diverse terrain and extraordinary biodiversity, Dolpo connects the Tibetan plateau with the pahar of Nepal, and has some of the highest continuously inhabited settlements on earth along the Thakchu Khola, at 4100m. To the south is a large east-west valley system called Lower Dolpo, and to the west is Mugu, which lies beyond the sacred Crystal Mountain and the Kanjiroba massif. To complete Dolpo's isolation, the Khyaklum and Dhaulagiri Himals create a natural border to Mustang and Annapurna to the east. A combination of ancient animist beliefs, Tibetan Buddhism, and Bon religions predominate throughout the region.

There are a number of trekking options that run through Dolpo; they are all magnificent and provide some good GHT options. Most trekkers enter and exit Dolpo via the dirt airstrip at Juphal in Lower Dolpo. Alternatively, experienced groups could consider the much more committing access routes from Mustang (east) or Mugu (west), where trail finding and acclimatisation pose additional challenges. Perhaps the most beautiful place in Nepal is Phoksundo Lake, in the centre of Dolpo, which can be combined with trails to Shey (Crystal Mountain) to access Bhijer, Saldang and the northern villages, or Dho Tarap and the valleys to the east. There are also route options that follow the Bharbun Khola, through Chharka Bhot and even to Hidden Valley to the north of Dhaulagiri.

Most of Dolpo and eastern Mugu are protected by the Shey Phoksundo National Park and Buffer Zone which covers a massive 3555 km² and is the largest such park in Nepal. Referred to as a Trans-Himalayan Ecosystem (the lower, lush valleys of the mid-hills are linked with the arid Tibetan plateau), this is a culturally and environmentally sensitive and fragile region, which demands the utmost respect and care. Please take all precautions to tread softly and follow the Great Himalaya Trail Code.

UPPER DOLPO CIRCUIT

There are many trails to and from Upper Dolpo, including the traditional salt-trade route through Dhorpatan to the south of Dunai and Tarakot, from Pokhara and/or Tansen. A less-used route is via Chharka Bhot in eastern Dolpo from Kagbeni in the Annapurna region. For the really adventurous there are two wild linking trails to Mugu from Pho, in northwest Dolpo, that climb through the Mugu Karnali Nadi valley system to Jumla. Within the region there are a number of loops

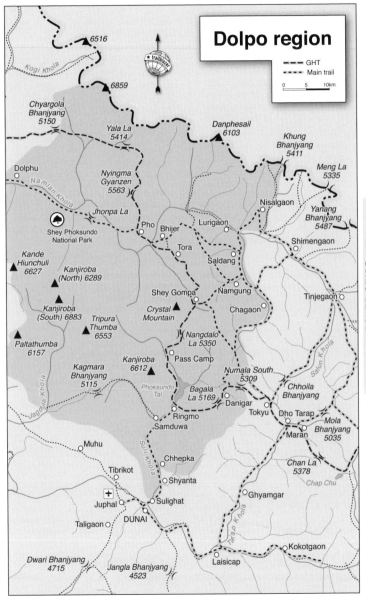

Dolpo region

— — GHT
····· Main trail

0   5   10km

6516

6859

Kogi Khola

Chyargola
Bhanjyang
5150

Yala La
5414

Danphesail
6103

Khung
Bhanjyang
5411

Meng La
5335

Dolphu

Namlan Khola

Nyingma
Gyanzen
5563

Nisalgaon

Yanang
Bhanjyang
5487

Jhonpa La

Shimengaon

Shey Phoksundo
National Park

Pho

Bhijer

Lurigaon

Kande
Hiunchuli
6627

Tora

Saldang

Kanjiroba
(North) 6289

Shey Gompa

Namgung

Tinjegaon

Kanjiroba
(South) 6883

Tripura
Thumba
6553

Crystal
Mountain

Chagaon

Salun Khola

Paltathumba
6157

Nangdalo
La 5350

Kagmara
Bhanjyang
5115

Kanjiroba
6612

Pass Camp

Numala South
5309

Chhoila
Bhanjyang

Jagdula Khola

Phoksundo
Tal

Bagala
La 5169

Danigar

Tokyu

Dho Tarap

Mola
Bhanjyang
5035

Ringmo

Maran

Samduwa

Suli Khola

Chan La
5378

Chap Chu

Muhu

Chhepka

Tibrikot

Shyanta

Ghyamgar

Juphal

Sulighat

Tara P Khola

Kokotgaon

Taligaon

DUNAI

Dwari Bhanjyang
4715

Jangla Bhanjyang
4523

Laisicap

ROUTE GUIDE

UPPER DOLPO CIRCUIT TREK

Mysterious and spectacular, Dolpo is one of the last genuine examples of traditional Tibetan culture. Add the stunning beauty of Phoksundo Lake and amazing ecological diversity, and this trek reveals the very best of the Himalaya.

Duration: 20 days

Highest Point: 5220m

Best Season: Apr-Oct

Accommodation: camping

that link Upper and Lower Dolpo, but any itinerary should include the stunningly beautiful Phoksundo Lake.

Dolpo has a similar weather pattern to Mustang as it lies in the 'rain-shadow' region behind the Annapurna and Dhaulagiri massifs, meaning the main trekking season is from May to October. Although the high passes are only closed in winter, you will need to brave extreme cold out of season. Large storms that dump huge amounts of snow can hit at any time before or after the monsoon so have some flexibility in your itinerary.

Upper Dolpo was opened for trekking in 1992, but a substantial permit fee of US$500 per person for 10 days has deterred many trekkers from exploring this magnificent corner of Nepal. Those who have braved the expense wholeheartedly say it was worthwhile.

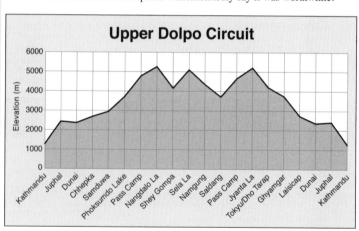

Upper Dolpo Circuit — elevation profile (m) from Kathmandu, Juphal, Dunai, Chhepka, Samduwa, Phoksumdo Lake, Pass Camp, Nangdalo La, Shey Gompa, Sela La, Namgung, Saldang, Pass Camp, Jyanta La, Tokyu/Dho Tarap, Ghyamgar, Laisicap, Dunai, Juphal, Kathmandu.

ROUTE GUIDE

DAY 1: KATHMANDU – NEPALGUNJ
ALL DAY

As the flight from Nepalgunj (150m) to Juphal (2475m) leaves before any flights from Kathmandu arrive, you have to overnight in Nepalgunj. There are some hotels in town and a few, more basic places to stay near the airport. Whichever option you

choose, it is essential to book in advance, as they are frequently full. There isn't much to see or do in Nepalgunj so perhaps book a mid-afternoon flight.

DAY 2: NEPALGUNJ – JUPHAL –
DUNAI   3 HRS

Make an early start to the airport for a 40

minute flight to the dirt airstrip at Juphal (2475m). Once back on the ground there isn't much to see, so make a start down hill on a broad trail, which descends between terraced fields.

The trail turns into a shallow gully before once again heading out to terraced fields and descending a bit more steeply. You will clearly see the trail angling down to a small group of buildings beside the Thulo Bheri Khola (2080m), which you should reach in 45 minutes.

At the river, follow the broad dirt track that was built as a service road between the airstrip and the sprawling district headquarters at Dunai (2140m, 2¼ hours), where there are some simple teahouses.

DAY 3: DUNAI – CHHEPKA   5¾ HRS

Dunai is the administrative centre for all of Dolpo, as well as the main trading centre.

From the centre of the town descend to a suspension bridge across the Thulo Bheri Khola and then turn left on a trail that heads upstream along a denuded hillside to the confluence of the Suli Khola.

There are two options, a higher, quicker trail that climbs over the lower Palihalna Danda, or the slightly longer riverside route, both of which converge at Sulighat (2282m, 1¾ hours), where you need to register at the National Park office.

The trail up the Suli Khola has little shade and seems to endlessly go up and down, but is faster and more convenient than taking the old higher route via Rahagaon, which is some 600m above.

From Sulighat continue on the east bank of the river for 1¼ hours to Raktang (2421m), where there is a teashop and the trail crosses to the west bank on a suspension bridge. In another hour you will need to re-cross the river at Shyanta, a winter settlement for Ringmo village.

Cross a large tributary, the Ankhe Khola, in 15 minutes, when the trail begins to climb for 1 hour to Chhepka (2720m), where there are two simple teahouses and a campsite.

If you have time, continue to an excellent campsite in a pretty walnut grove 20 minutes beyond Chhepka.

DAY 4: CHHEPKA – JHARINA HOTEL 6 HRS

Less than 10 minutes beyond the walnut grove the trail crosses the Suli Khola to the west bank but soon returns to the east bank (1 hour and 10 minutes) after avoiding a steep, landslide affected area. The trail continues through dense forest for another hour before crossing a tributary from your right and then climbing a switchback trail for roughly 380m to a broad grassy plateau (1 hour and 20 minutes).

An enjoyable flat trail does not last long, and in 45 minutes you descend to the river. There is a campsite on the far bank at Rechi (2940m, 30 minutes) but most trekkers continue from here to Samduwa (2960m, 1½ hours).

To reach Samduwa, continue on the east bank beyond Rechi for one hour to a bridge near the Tapriza Secondary School and gompa, which was established by a Swiss ethnology student, Marietta Kind, who spent a year and a half in Ringmo. The teachers and children are always happy to receive guests and please consider giving a generous donation as the school receives very little support from the government. See ⌨ www.tapriza.org for further information.

From the school, cross to the west bank of the Phoksundo Khola (previously called the Suli Khola). In 20 minutes you will reach the Jharina Hotel and campsite.

DAY 5: JHARINA HOTEL – RINGMO 4 HRS

The trail climbs slightly along the west bank of the Phoksundo Khola for 30 minutes to a campsite on the hillside above a wooden bridge that leads to Rike and the trail to Dho Tarap.

Do not descend to the bridge. Instead, continue climbing through cedar and pine forest on a trail that swings northwards. There is now a long climb past another small winter settlement, called Polam (3400m, 1 hour), where there is another checkpost.

Continue climbing switchbacks to a ridgeline with excellent views of the turquoise and cobalt blue Phoksundo Lake, and an enormous waterfall formed by the headwaters of the Phoksundo Khola (3800m, 1 hour and 20 minutes). The trail now descends through birch forest to the clear-running headwaters before climbing an easy gradient towards Ringmo village (3640m, 1 hour), where there is a simple teahouse.

On the far side of the village, cross a bridge to the National Park office and campsite (10 minutes), or you can also camp on the western side of the lake out-flow (but it is a little dirty).

Ringmo is undergoing transformation into a homestay village so check for details when you arrange your trip.

DAY 6: RINGMO   ALL DAY

Phoksundo Lake is a RAMSAR-registered wetland (The Convention on Wetlands of International Importance, especially to Waterfowl Habitat), and is Nepal's deepest, and second largest, lake.

Perched on the southern shoreline is Ringmo, a traditional Tibetan village, where the locals make a range of handicrafts.

About 1.5km away, on the south-eastern edge of the lake, is the Bon tradition Pal Sentan Thason Chholing Gompa. There is much conjecture about the Bon religion, but one well-respected expert David Snellgrove (in *Himalayan Pilgrimage*, Shambala Publications, pp41-54) asserts that it is contemporary with, and extremely similar to, Tibetan Buddhism.

The most important distinction is that all movements are opposite to Tibetan Buddhist practice, so for example, you should pass a mani wall or chorten on your left side, and when walking around or within a gompa, you should walk anti-clockwise.

DAY 7: RINGMO – PHOKSUNDO
KHOLA CAMP   5½ HRS

This day begins with one of the most spectacular sections of trail in Nepal: from the western side of the lake outflow, head towards the cliffs to your west (left), which you traverse along a precipitous trail.

For the first 40 minutes the trail doesn't climb very much but does feel exposed in places, and there are excellent views of the lake and village. After crossing a small stream, the track steeply climbs about 400m before contouring around a rock face at roughly 4140m (1¼ hours). It is amazing to think that yaks frequently use this trail.

After 1¼ hours the trail descends to the flood plain of the Phoksundo Khola at the northern end of the lake (3630m), where there is an excellent grassy lunch place or campsite. This valley is overgrown in the lower reaches with black caragana bushes, which have needle-like thorns.

After 35 minutes cross the river and enter patchy pine forest which is soon replaced by silver birch (the bark of which is often used by Tibetans for writing prayers to leave on passes and important chorten) as the valley narrows.

Cross the river via stepping-stones several times as you ascend the valley. After another 1¼ hours the valley begins to narrow to a cliff-lined gorge and the trail remains on the northern bank. You will pass

---

❏ The Evil Lake of Reng

For many locals throughout Dolpo, Phoksundo Lake is referred to as 'the evil lake of Reng' and the gompa is sited here to keep any bad demons at bay. It is believed that long ago there used to be a village where the lake now is. The valley was flooded by a spiteful demoness who was fleeing from the wrath of the Buddhist sage and magician, Padmasambhava, who was on his way to Tibet to convert the people there to Buddhism.

In an effort to confuse the sage, the demoness gave the people in the village a turquoise, making them promise not to tell her pursuer that she had passed that way. But Padmasambhava turned the turquoise into a lump of dung. Thinking the demoness had tricked them the people told the sage where she had gone. In a rage of revenge, she flooded the valley killing everyone.

❏ The Legend of Shey

Shey means crystal, a name derived from Crystal Mountain due west of the gompa, which is streaked with quartz veins. An annual festival in June/July is based at the gompa and involves circumambulating Crystal Mountain in honour of Drutob Senge Yeshe who defeated a demon and converted Dolpo to Buddhism a thousand years ago.

Joel Ziskin, in his *National Geographic* article (see Vol. 151, No 4, April 1977), was the first to relate the legend, '*Many years ago, the Buddhist ascetic Drutob Senge Yeshe came to Dolpo and found here a wild people whose supreme god was a fierce mountain spirit. The lama went directly to this mountain and meditated. There he attained enlightenment...A flying snow lion* [a legendary companion of the Snow Leopard] *had served the yogi* [male practitioner of various forms of religious practice] *as a mount.*

When the mountain god resisted with an army of snake-beings, this loyal lion reproduced itself 108 times and overcame them. Drutob Senge Yeshe then transformed the earth spirit into 'a thundering mountain of purest crystal.' A white conch shell fell from the sky, and the yogi rose on his lion and pierced a hole in Shey's summit. Rainbows arced across the heavens.'

through a few copses of silver birch, which could make a campsite, but continue for 30 minutes to a large copse at the mouth of a tributary gorge of the Tuk Kyaksar Khola (3750m) with a red-pink western (left) cliff line and a dark grey eastern (right) cliff.

There are also some cairns beside the small river that flows from this gorge, which mark a rough trail. There is a trail that continues up the main valley at this point so you will need to be vigilant not to miss the gorge and campsite.

DAY 8: PHOKSUNDO KHOLA CAMP – PASS CAMP   5½ HRS

From here there are two routes to Shey Gompa: the first, which initially continues up the Phoksundo Khola, is used by pack animals and takes a little longer. The second route is more direct but rougher and not suitable for pack animals.

From the campsite it is only a few minutes to the mouth of the gorge, which is more safely ascended in the morning when the river is lower. The trail winds up the gorge, crossing the river many times. There are many animal tracks in the gorge so take care when route finding.

The sound of the river reverberating from the cliffs makes conversation difficult, so make sure to keep your group together.

The gradient eases after 1½ hours as the gorge widens. In another hour there is a small campsite (4435m) of about eight flat plots scraped out of rocky ground on the western side of the valley. However, there is a far better camp at the head of the valley where a small waterfall has carved a gully (4717m, 30 minutes).

From here you have two choices. If the flow of water through the waterfall is low you should probably camp at this spot, as there will be little or no water higher up. If the flow is strong, such that it fills the bottom of the gully (you might need to climb for about 100m to check), then continue to the higher camp above.

Climb the switchback trail to the east (right) of the waterfall and after about 100m the gradient eases. You now ascend the upper reaches of the river valley, which gradually broadens, to a large basin. A large scree slope rises on the west (left) side of the basin and the pass (Nangdalo La, 5350m) is on the above ridgeline, which is called the Churan Lekh.

Do not be tempted towards either of the easier looking saddles to the north and north-east. There are plenty of flat areas in the basin (4810m, 2½ hours from the previous camp), the most popular is at the base of the long curving trail that leads up to the pass.

**DAY 9: PASS CAMP – SHEY GOMPA
5 HRS**

The trail to the pass is over loose slate-scree up an unrelenting gradient for 2½ hours. From the top of the Nangdalo La (5350m) you can see a broad valley descending to the north carved by a substantial stream, which you should reach in 1 hour from the pass.

The trail now follows an easy gradient down the valley, crossing the stream a few times depending on your chosen route. This valley is popular with yak and sheep herders so try to buy some fresh yoghurt, butter, or milk as you descend.

In 1½ hours, you will reach the red-painted walls of Shey Gompa (4343m), ringed with mani walls and chorten, set amid a large pasture.

DAY 10: SHEY GOMPA   ALL DAY

It is worth spending a day at Shey to explore both the Kagyupa sect gompa as well as the hermitage at Tsakang.

There are many legends surrounding the founder of Shey Gompa and Tsakang, Tsan-zin Ra Pa, who lived in the early seventeenth century, making this one of the most sacred valleys in Dolpo.

Locals insist that the killing of any animal is prohibited in or around Shey Gompa, and this perhaps explains why it is relatively common to spot blue sheep and snow leopard in the valley.

Perched on the cliffs of Crystal Mountain, about an hour north from Shey, is the hermitage of Tsakang. Traditionally the Lama of Shey lived here, although the current incarnate is at school in Kathmandu. However, if you can find the key-holder to let you in, the frescoes here are worth the climb. See *Shey to Shyamling & Dho Tarap*, p217 for details of other trails from Shey.

**DAY 11: SHEY GOMPA – NAMGUNG
6-6¾ HRS**

From the gompa, head east into the arid Sephu Khola valley, following a trail along the north bank. After 1¼ hours, the trail forks where a tributary flows down from the north.

Turn left into this tributary valley and climb on loose ground for 2½ hours to the Sela La (5095m). From the pass, descend into a shallow valley, where a number of trails seem to converge from different directions, to an obvious fork in 1 hour.

The right-hand trail descends beside a watercourse to a campsite upstream from the small village of Namgung (4360m, 1 hour).

Alternatively, take the left-hand fork, which climbs a ridge and then descends a parallel watercourse to the old Kagyupa

---

❏ **The Dolpopa**

West of the upper Kali Gandaki, at around 4000 metres, lies the remote area of Dolpo. Surrounded by mountains over 6000m, this landscape can only be successfully inhabited by tough, hardy people. There are 25 or 30 villages spread over an area of about 1300 square kilometres. The Dolpopa (-pa means people) are very hospitable and kind, and grow most of the crops they need, as well as keeping yaks, sheep and goats for meat, wool and milk products, or to be sold or traded. Their houses are built of rough stone and all huddled together, as though trying to gain warmth and comfort from each other. This often makes the villages look like forts.

Their traditional 'fancy' dress for women includes a striking headdress made of two rectangular brass plates with edges that turn up over the top and back of the head. These headdresses are adorned with coral and turquoise and often represent the wealth of the family.

They marry by choice or arrangement, and follow Buddhism and Bon. The 1998 movie *Caravan* (also called *Himalaya*) was shot here and told the tale of the now defunct salt caravans. You can still find locals in villages such as Saldang who appeared in the film.

sect Namgung gompa set high on a cliff face (1¼ hours), from where you can walk downstream along the Namga Khola to the campsite (less than 30 minutes).

DAY 12: NAMGUNG – SALDANG
2¾ HRS

From Namgung there are a number of trails that climb over the ridge on the far side of the valley and then descend to Saldang; do not follow any trails that head down the Namga Khola valley.

Once over the ridge that forms the northern bank of the Namga Khola, descend to the Nagon Khola in 1¾ hours. The trail continues north, to the commercial and administrative centre of Upper Dolpo, Saldang (3770m, 1 hour), where there is a school established by some German trekkers who first came in 1995.

A horse racing festival in July to honour the Black Goat King, who once ruled central Dolpo, begins from the newly decorated gompa in the village.

Trails from all over Dolpo converge at Saldang; to the north are interesting gompas in the Karang valley (2½ hours), Luri (Sunger Gompa) and Nisalgaon (Yangze Gompa, a further 2 hours from Karang). Circling around via Nisalgaon, or crossing the Khoma La to the east of Saldang, is the village of Shimengaon, which leads to a route via Chharka Bhot, Niwas La, and Kagbeni to Jomsom (10 days). Heading east, over the Neng La, is the route to Bhijer, Pho and onto Mugu (see *GHT – Far West* p235). To the south, is the main trading route to Dho Tarap.

DAY 13: SALDANG – CHAGAON
3 HRS

The Nagon Khola valley has gently sloping hills on its south-eastern (left) bank across which runs an easy undulating trail.

Settlements merge into one another and provide glimpses into the day-to-day lives of this seemingly inhospitable region. An easy 3 hours from Saldang is Chagaon (3840m), where you can see a gompa beside the river. There is another hermitage gompa, popular with local and Tibetan lamas, high on the ridge above.

Camp in or near Chagaon, there are many spots to choose from.

DAY 14: CHAGAON – PASS CAMP
6½ HRS

As you continue south the valley walls become steeper and the terrain more desolate. A crumbling fort stands as an impotent guard above the river beyond the last village, Chasip (less than 30 minutes). Continue along the main trail as it slowly climbs beside the river.

After 1½ hours cross the river to the west bank, and a couple of stone houses at Rakyo Kharka. From here you may need to wade through the river a few times if floods have damaged the trail, but try to remain on the west (right) bank.

In a further 2 hours a large tributary, the Dachung Khola, flows into the valley from the south as the main valley swings westwards. Cross the Nagon Khola to the east (left) bank and turn into the Dachung Khola valley, do not cross the river.

A further 1¾ hours brings you to another major river junction with rivers from the southeast and southwest. Turn right, crossing the Dachung Khola, into a steep-walled valley (the southwest option to your right) and reach a flat grassy campsite at 4700m, in 45 minutes.

DAY 15: PASS CAMP – TOKYU
5 HRS

A steady gradient climbs about 500m from the campsite to the top of the Jyanta La (5220m, 2 hours). Take care when route finding as there are many trails in the area, it might be easier to try and stay in the middle of the valley to avoid moving off course.

Descend into a huge shallow alpine valley, which is boggy (and normally frozen) at the bottom, beside the Jyanta Khola. The gradient remains gentle on the west (left) bank of the river until you reach a loose wall of terminal moraine after 1½ hours. Once down the moraine the gradient eases again and you cross the river to the eastern bank.

You will pass a series of mani walls and chorten on either side of the valley as it widens. A final descent brings you to the upper reaches of the Dho Tarap valley, and a campsite near to the village of Tokyu (4209m, 1½ hours).

DAY 16: TOKYU – GHYAMGAR
6 HRS
The large, fertile Thakchu Khola valley is home to ten Magar and Bhotia villages, which almost merge together. This is one of the highest permanent settlements on the planet at an average of 4100m, and a popular place for Tibetan nomads to graze their yak herds.

There are both Buddhist and Bon gompas in the valley, although they are not as old as those in Upper Dolpo. The trail down through the valley is an easy and enjoyable walk past villagers busy with daily life.

Some French donors have built the Crystal Mountain school towards the end of the valley (where you can camp), just before the trail turns south past some large kani and mani walls, and enters Dho Tarap (3950m, 1½ hours), the last village in the valley.

If you have time, visit the nunnery of Ribum Gompa and Regu Chorten on the hillside above the village, which has a large and well-preserved statue of Tsong Kharpa. A tributary branches west (left) from Dho Tarap and leads to Chharka Bhot, see *GHT – Dolpo* p218.

From Dho Tarap, continue to descend the now narrowing Tarap Khola valley. The trail through this valley can be affected by landslides, which slow your progress. There are a few campsites so consider which to use to suit your group's speed.

At first, the valley doesn't descend too rapidly as it follows the east bank of the river. After 2½ hours there is a campsite, called Kama or Langa Kharka (4010m) at the confluence of a tributary, Klang Khola, flowing from the east (left).

Cross the Tarap Khola to the west bank beyond the campsite and descend a rough rocky trail through scrubby patches of forest, it might be a surprise to see and smell trees again after the denuded slopes of Upper Dolpo.

The trail descends rapidly to the Sisal Khola, where woodcutters have made a rough camp. The trail swings back into the Tarap Khola and descends rapidly to a bridge in a narrow gorge. You might be able to spot Blue Sheep on the rock face on the far bank.

Beyond the bridge is a climb of about 200m over a small peninsula in the valley called Ghyamgar (3755m, 2 hours), where there is a small campsite.

DAY 17: GHYAMGAR – LAISICAP
7 HRS
The valley now becomes a sheer sided canyon with the river in a white rage beneath a bridge to the west bank. The gradient eases to a more gradual descent on an undulating trail for the next 2½ hours to another major tributary junction with the Nawapani Khola where there is another campsite.

The trail soon crosses back to the east bank for a short section before returning to the west bank at Chhyugar (3440m, 1 hour), where locals sometimes camp beneath a large rock overhang.

The trail has been blasted and gouged from rock as it now descends more rapidly to a steep switchback section that drops to a pretty lace-waterfall at Laina Odar (3370m, 2½ hours). The trail soon descends rapidly again and suddenly the Tarap Khola valley merges with the Thulo Bheri Khola valley.

Either camp at an excellent site in a fine pine forest near a deserted police post before crossing the river, or continue to a smaller campsite before entering Laisicap village (2775m, 1½ hours).

DAY 18 : LAISICAP – DUNAI
After days of descending treacherous trails it is a relief to be walking on a broad thoroughfare beside the Thulo Bheri Khola. However, a lack of shade can make this a hot walk on a sunny day, so have plenty of water and sun cream.

About 1 hour beyond Laisicap is a fine kani at the entrance to Tarakot (2540m), a popular winter settlement for people from Dho Tarap. Beyond Tarakot the trail crosses to the north, exposed bank of the Thulo Bheri Khola and resumes a typical up and down profile all the way to Dunai (2140m, 4 hours).

**DAYS 19-20: DUNAI – JUPHAL –
NEPALGUNJ – KATHMANDU**
Retrace your steps from the first day of trek-
king to the airstrip at Juphal (2475m, 3½

hours), where you can fly back to Nepalgunj
and then catch a late morning or afternoon
flight to Kathmandu.

OTHER MAJOR TRAILS IN DOLPO

● **Lower Dolpo Circuit** – from Ringmo (see *Upper Dolpo Circuit*, day six, p212) descend to the Maduwa Khola valley and head eastwards to the Bagala La (5210m, two days). Cross the pass and camp again at or near Danigar (4631m, one day), which is a popular herding pasture. From Danigar, it is a long day up and over the Numala La South (5238m, see *GHT – Dolpo, Chharka Bhot to Pho via Dho Tarap, Phoksundo and Shey*) to the upper reaches of the Dho Tarap valley, where you will rejoin the *Upper Dolpo Circuit* on day 16, see p216.

The Lower Dolpo Circuit is typically a trek of 10 to 12 days in total and does not require the $500 trekking permit, only the standard $10 per week permit.

● **Shey to Shyamling & Dho Tarap** – From Shey (see *Upper Dolpo Circuit*, day 10, p214) there are a number of route options. To the north is a high ridge-top trail to another important gompa complex at Shyamling (aka Samling, two days via Tra).

This route can be linked with a long and difficult trek from Pho, the remot-est village in Upper Dolpo, to the Namlan Khola system in Mugu and then on to Jumla (12 to 16 days from Shey). This is a hazardous and challenging route, only for experienced groups and you should employ local guides (you need at least two for safety reasons), see *GHT – Far West*, p236, for further detail.

The Sephu Khola behind Shey gompa leads to a major trail junction, the right-hand fork leads over two high passes (Lanmuse La and Numala La North) to the Dho Tarap valley (three days).

GHT – DOLPO

Trail options abound throughout Dolpo and the first decision is where to start, from Kagbeni or Ghemi in Mustang? You then need to cross a major dividing ridge system running north from Dhaulagiri to Tibet. This is a very remote area, and it is a pleasant surprise to bump into a wandering nomad. However, the locals in Ghemi are very superstitious and will only allow trekking groups to cross the Ghami La in October and November. They believe that the mountain spirits will be offended and prevent rain from falling on their fields if anyone disturbs the pass from December to September. They have been known to defend this belief violently.

The main trail is from Kagbeni via Santa and Ghok and is open throughout the main trekking seasons. You could also approach Chharka Bhot from Marpha, Dhampus Pass and Hidden Valley and then connect to the main trail near Ghok. This route is easily closed by small amounts of snow so be sure to check weather forecasts.

Trails from the Kali Gandaki valley converge at Chharka Bhot and then separate off again to the north and west. Running parallel with the Tibetan border is a remote route to Shimengaon and the Saldang valley, before heading northwest to the remotest village in Dolpo, Pho. Heading west and then north from Chharka Bhot are trails to Dho Tarap, Phoksundo Lake and Shey gompa, which also lead to Pho. It is also possible to head south from Chharka Bhot and wind around the Thulo Bheri Khola through Lower Dolpo to eventually arrive at Jumla (although this last route doesn't run through the Great Himalaya Range). Of the first two options, the route via Dho Tarap and Ringmo is longer than the Saldang route but it visits some 'unmissable' highlights of Dolpo. For the trails from Pho to Mugu and the Namlan Khola, see *GHT – Far West*, p236.

There are many good tourist maps of the entire Dolpo region, so rather than quoting Finaid map references, GPS coordinates are used for places that could be hard to locate.

Kagbeni to Chharka Bhot

Wind through the southern end of Kagbeni (2810m) village to a suspension bridge behind the school. From the far bank there are two trail options, a steep switchback climb or the longer, easier route up the Kali Gandaki valley to Tirigaon (1 hour). If you take the steep route take the right fork after about 250m, which leads to a grassy plateau (40 minutes). The trail from Tirigaon forks just before the village, take the left trail and climb an easier gradient to a small gully where there is a slight scramble up to the grassy plateau (1 hour). Once on the plateau there is a main trail that leads to a kharka (3478m, 1 hour), where there is a water source in a deep gully to your left.

From the kharka ascend to a saddle to the north (3810m, 50 minutes), where the trail then climbs the hillside to the west; do not descend. The gradient increases as you enter a gully and pass some caves frequently used by locals as a bivouac. The trail follows the watercourse in the gully for about 50m before switchbacking again. At 4050m you meet the larger main trail from Phalyak and turn west (right) and continue to climb on a much easier gradient to a ridgetop pass (4306m, 1½ hours). From here the trail continues west and contours through two basins before climbing a little more to the Bhima Lojun La (4460m, 1 hour). Now make an undulating traverse for the next 1½ hours to a small spur. Head down into a large ravine where some camping groups have cleared tent platforms. From here the trail contours across a loose scree-covered hillside to a flat point on a ridge marked by chorten. Take the left, slightly higher trail at the first chorten and then descend steeply to the compact village of Santa (3777m, 1¼ hours) where there are some stone walled fields to camp in that belong to an old man called Wangyel.

From the western end of the village follow a trail that heads through two gullies before reaching a switchback climb to Jhansye (4195m, 2 hours). The trail now stays relatively flat as it crosses steep hillside for 1 hour before a steep and loose descent to the Kyalunpa Khola (25 minutes). There used to be a river trail to the west but it has been cut by landslides and the locals no longer use it. Instead, cross a simple wooden bridge and climb the trail to Ghok, but when you reach a grassy plateau before the village turn west (left) and continue to climb towards a narrow gully. Do not go to Ghok. The trail climbs up though the steep gully made by the Ghalden Ghuldun Khola before reaching a campsite among juniper trees and scrub (1 hour and 50 minutes, GPS: 4247m, N 28° 54.813' E 083° 37.259'). There is another potential campsite in 20 minutes (4380m) but it has less shade and shelter from the afternoon winds. From here it is a continual climb to the Gharchak Chuksa Danda and the Jungbenley La (5122m, 2¾ hours), which is finally reached via a rocky gully. Descend into a shallow valley on the far side of the pass before climbing very slightly to a potential campsite at 5140m beside the Lhanimar Khola (45 minutes). The Jungben La (5550m, 1½ hours) is on the ridge to your west and once at the top you'll have excellent views of Hidden Valley (south) beyond which the very top of Dhaulagiri can be seen. The Annapurnas are on the horizon to the southeast, and to your west is the Kanjiroba range. Descend on an easy trail from the pass to the large plateaus of the Niwas La (5120m), where a cairn marks the high-point, in 1 hour and 20 minutes. From here it is an easy descent for 30 minutes to the Nulungsumda Kharka (4987m) campsite at the confluence of the Malun and Thasan Kholas.

Note: if you are trekking this route in the opposite direction, it is essential you do not descend into the valley on the eastern side of the Niwas La plateaus. Instead follow the obvious trail that climbs a ridge extending northeast from the plateaus.

From the Nulungsumda Kharka, follow the Thasan Khola along the northern (right) bank to another good camping spot, where a river joins from the north (right), in 40 minutes. There is another campsite, where the Yalku Khola joins from the south (left), in another 1 hour and 20 minutes. The trail does not cross the river at this point. Instead it climbs for 40 minutes to avoid a landslide area before a long descent to the end of the valley where it joins the Chharka Tulsi Khola (4380m, 2 hours and 20 minutes). Walk along the top of the long peninsula that divides the two rivers. Continue to the very end and then descend to your left to a suspension bridge (15 minutes). Do not descend to the right on an old trail that crosses the Chharka Tulsi Khola.

Note: the Chharka Tulsi Khola is the route to the Ghami La and on to Ghemi in Upper Mustang (four days).

Climb an easy gradient for about 15 minutes before following an easy trail for 1 hour to a rigid metal bridge to the north bank of the Chharka Tulsi Khola. The large village of Chharka Bhot (4302m) is now only 20 minutes away. Many groups take a rest day here and explore the ancient village and Bon gompas. It is also a good place to restock with food staples like rice and flour.

Chharka Bhot to Pho via Dho Tarap, Phoksundo and Shey

The main trail to Dho Tarap takes a southerly route around the craggy peaks that dominate the western end of the valley from Chharka Bhot. However the route requires many river wades and would be difficult in, or soon after, rain. There is a northerly route that crosses two passes but you will need a local guide as trail finding is very difficult before the second pass, and you should not take pack animals as the descent from the second pass is challenging.

● **Northern route** – take the main trail west out of Chharka Bhot to an old chorten, which marks a trail junction (40 minutes), turn right and then climb a steady gradient for 2 hours to the Mola La (5030m). On the far side is a large plateau and the Myantikti Khola which you should follow to the confluence with the Pandi Ladum Khola (2 hours) where many nomads camp. Ascend this river valley to the Jhyarkoi Bhanjyang (5360m, 3 hours), where the trail descends on a steep cliff-face trail, which is usually not suitable for pack animals. Descend the Maran Khola to Maran (4350m, 2 hours), where you meet the southern route.

● **Southern route** – take the main trail west out of Chharka Bhot to an old chorten, which marks a trail junction (40 minutes), turn left and descend an easy gradient to a small confluence with the Chuchen Khola (roughly 4300m, 20 minutes). Descend the Chharka Tulsi Khola for 10 minutes on the west bank before wading to the east bank which you follow for 15 minutes before wading back to the west bank. In another 35 minutes cross again to the east bank for 10 minutes before crossing back for the final time to the west bank. Then climb for a short section before descending to a minor tributary from the west (left), which is crossed by stepping-stones.

The trail then climbs for 45 minutes to a small lake, the Chap Chu (4320m), where there is a campsite. Continue up the valley on a trail that frequently crosses back and forth for 2¼ hours to a gully that leads to a basin and an easy gradient to the Chan La (5378m, 45 minutes). The trail descends switchbacks to a small valley before ascending about 100m to follow a ridge above the Sheru Khola, which is to your south (left), and the Tarpi Khola to your north (right). At a chorten (50 minutes) on the ridge, head down into the Tarpi Khola valley, and continue to Maran (4350m, 1 hour and 50 minutes), where you meet the northern route.

From Maran it is an easy 1 hour to Dho Tarap (3944m), which is a large trading village and a good re-stocking point.

Note: you can descend the Tarap Khola to Laisicap (two days) and then carry on to Juphal (two days).

Above the village of Dho Tarap is the nunnery of Ribum Gompa and Regu Chorten, which is well worth a visit. The Tarap valley makes for an enjoyable and easy walk as you slowly climb past small villages to Tokyu (4209m, 1 hour), where there is a major trail junction. To the north (right) is the main trail to Saldang, see *Other Routes to Pho*, p222, whereas this GHT route heads west (left) to Ringmo and Phoksundo Lake.

Continue up the Tarap valley for another 1 hour to a point where a valley enters from your south (left) and there is a monastery perched on the hillside to your north (right). Do not cross the small stream flowing out of the valley, instead climb into the valley's mouth to a campsite marked by a small, roofless dharamsala (4440m, 25 minutes), which can be used as a kitchen. Follow a trail on the southeast (left) bank of the river to a point where the valley bends and climbs sharply to the south (left). Instead of following the river, cross it and climb a small stream from the west (right). The trail soon emerges onto grassy slopes and the gradient eases as it rounds into a basin dominated by snow-covered craggy peaks to the south (left). From the melt-water stream in the centre of the basin, ascend the north-western (right) side of a gully between two obvious peaks for about 300m to what the locals confusingly call the Numala La South (3¼ hours, GPS: 5309m, N 29° 10.542' E 083° 05.965'). There are three points to cross the Numala ridge, including the southern pass, the other two are: a pass to the north which is an alternative route to Saldang, and a central pass that is marked on many tourist maps as the southerly route but is very rarely used. Descend steeply from the pass for roughly 800m to the Gyampo Khola, which you follow to a trail junction (1¾ hours), where you should take the left fork.

Note: the right fork is a long route to both the central and northern Numala passes.

The trail now climbs 200m as it rounds a craggy ridge and then descends to the picturesque campsite at Danigar (4512m, 1 hour), which is dominated by Norbung Kang (6085m) at the head of the valley. From the campsite, cross the Panklanga Khola and climb a switchback trail for 1¼ hours before the gradient eases to a long traversing ascent to the Bagala La (5169m, 1 hour). On the far side of the pass is a steep rocky descent to a flat-bottomed valley (4686m, 1 hour), which is the high camp for groups coming the other way. Another steep descent brings you to Temche (3995m, 50 minutes), a large grassy kharka that trekking companies refer to as the Bagala La Base Camp.

In another 40 minutes is the even larger Yak Kharka (3860m). As many animals are kept here it is frequently dirty. The trail now traverses steep and craggy hillside for 1 hour and 10 minutes before a couple of short climbs high above the confluence with the Phoksundo Khola. The views down the valley from here are very pretty. The trail now swings north into pine forest, where you should look for views of a spectacular cascade on the far hillside, and in 40 minutes reach the village of Ringmo (3641m), where there is a simple teahouse and campsites. One of the most beautiful places in Nepal, Phoksundo Lake, is a few minutes beyond the village. There is a National Park office on the foreshore where you should register.

See *Upper Dolpo Circuit*, days 7-10, pp212-4, for route and additional information to Shey Gompa.

From Shey Gompa, take a trail that climbs up from the campsite for about 400m (1 hour and 10 minutes) before swinging into a small valley. The trail descends slightly to the stream, which you cross, before climbing the far hillside for another 100m or so (35 minutes) to a ridge (4860m) with views of the Tartan Khola and Tsankang Gompa opposite. Traverse the broad hillside before dropping into the Den Khola valley, where there is a kharka of the same name (4553m, 1 hour). The trail then heads back up to a minor ridge (1 hour) before traversing past some monsoon kharkas to another ridge (4810m, 30 minutes). A final undulating traverse brings you to the last minor pass of the day (4840m, 25 minutes), which is decorated with prayer flags and chorten.

An easy descent leads to the large kharka of Tora (1 hour) where there are three trails. The most northerly (right) trail climbs rapidly to the ridge above, the middle takes an easier gradient to a point further along the ridge and the

> **❏ A Bhijer folktale**
> Long ago, a lama came from Tibet on the Saldang trail and when he was on the pass
> he saw a large Blue Sheep, which he followed to a big valley. The lama became
> thirsty so he dug into the ground and a river came forth. Deeper in the valley, he saw
> a giant rat which attacked him. In defence, he killed it with an arrow through the
> heart. The arrow struck the ground and he left it there. Sometime later an apricot tree
> grew where the arrow lay and when donations are made at the gompa the tree bears
> fruit. The locals have never cut the tree, which stands in the gompa forecourt.

more westerly (left) descends to the village of Tata and on to Shyamling (aka
Samling). Do not take the path on your right. If you have time, visit Shyamling
Gompa (2 hours) and then take the round-about trail to Bhijer (1½ hours). The
direct route to Bhijer (3850m, 1¾ hours) is the middle trail that makes an easy
ascent of the ridge before a sometimes steep descent to the village where there is
a campsite. The lama at the gompa in Bhijer is also an *amchi* (a Tibetan medicine
doctor) and he tells an intriguing tale of the first settlement of the village.

Wind through the village to a trail that climbs to some chorten to the north.
Switchbacks ascend a ridge, where there is a cairn and some prayer flags
(4605m, 2¼ hours). You now enter a basin beneath the rocky Yambur Peak.
Traverse the rocky trail for 40 minutes to the base of the final steep climb to the
Yambur La (4813m, 30 minutes). Descend a steep trail on the far side of the
pass to a large kharka, which makes a good lunch spot (4030m, 1¼ hours).

The next section of trail has had some extensive maintenance but is still
steep and slippery in places. Descend into the Tora Khola canyon on a trail
carved from cliff faces to a large wooden cantilever bridge (roughly 3400m, 1
hour and 10 minutes). The crisp, clear water here makes it an excellent site for
a cool swim. The trail winds around some craggy cliffs before ascending a steep
gully via switchbacks to the terraces of Pho (4087m, 2¾ hours), where there are
a couple of campsites. If you haven't already employed a local guide you will
definitely need to get one here at Pho. The next section to Mugu is one of the
toughest parts of the GHT.

Other routes to Pho
● **Via Dho Tarap and Saldang** – from Tokyu take the northern trail via the
Jyanta Bhanjyang to the Saldang valley (three days). From Saldang there are
trails direct to Shey and Bhijer (both two days).
● **Via Shimengaon and Saldang** – from the large kharka after the Mola
Bhanjyang (from Chharka Bhot) head north along the Kehein Khola for two
days to Tinjegaon. It is then a long day to Shimengaon. There is a cross-country
trail to Saldang (two days) as well as a round-about route (three days) via
Nisalgaon. From Nisalgaon there is a high route to Pho over two rarely used
passes, which the locals believe to be the homes of dangerous spirits.

The Far West

The Far West districts of Nepal have remained isolated and untouched while the rest of the country has been developing. Poor infrastructure, scarce resources, and marginalised ethnic groups are among many issues that have held the region back in years past. However, since 2008 a massive effort has been underway to develop and promote this region, which is considered by many to be a future adventure tourism 'hotspot'. If you are looking for an authentic trekking experience in pristine mountain scenery interlaced with legend and folklore, then look no further – this region is for you.

Covering about 25% of Nepal's Great Himalaya Range, the Far West is massive compared to the other trekking regions, but despite its size there are few recognised trekking routes. Dividing the region in two is the Karnali Nadi, one of the great Himalayan rivers. To the east, are Kanjiroba Himal and the mountains of Dolpo, to the west are the Api and Saipal Himals and the border with India. The second largest district in Nepal, Humla, fills the entire northern boundary with Tibet, and the southern districts of Bajura and Bajhang lead to the pahar. Villages are largely subsistence based, so don't rely on purchasing any foodstuffs, and accommodation is frequently limited to finding a flat pasture. The entire experience is similar to that of the first trekkers to Nepal in the 1950s, when the country first opened up. And that is part of the wonder and joy of visiting the region; the logistical effort in reaching these districts is far outweighed by the welcome you will receive and the feeling of wonder that every day brings.

Trekking is in its infancy throughout all these districts, trails are rough and take an unrelenting approach to ascent and descent. There are two routes through Mugu from Pho in Dolpo and they are both rough and wild trails. Rara Lake National Park, near Jumla, receives the occasional trekker, as does the Yari valley (near Simikot, popular with groups trekking to Mt. Kailash) and Khaptad National Park. Mountaineering groups have explored both Api and Saipal Peaks, but trekkers here are extremely rare. No doubt things will change.

The two smallest National Parks in Nepal, Rara and Khaptad, are the only protected areas in the pahar of the Far West (other than Bardia National Parks, Sukla Phanta Wildlife Reserve and the Blackbuck Conservation Area on the terai). However, special trekking permits are required to visit many of the areas along the Tibetan border. Maps are hard to find, especially for the areas around the Api and Saipal Himals. This region will benefit enormously from tourism in the years to come, and as one of the first to trek here, it is important that you lead by example. Please follow the Great Himalaya Trail Code in every respect and help make a positive difference to a region that desperately needs all the help it can get.

ROUTE GUIDE

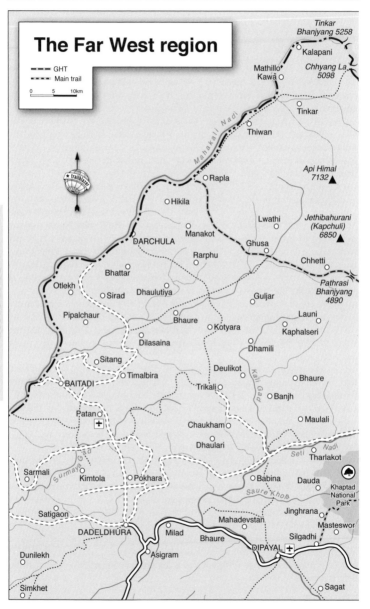

The Far West region

- - - GHT
- ·- Main trail

0   5   10km

Tinkar
Bhanjyang 5258

Kalapani

Mathillo
Kawā

Chhyang La
5098

Tinkar

Mahakali Nadi

Thiwan

Api Himal
7132

Rapla

Hikila

Jethibahurani
(Kapchuli)
6850

Lwathi

Manakot

Ghusa

DARCHULA

Chhetti

Rarphu

Bhattar

Pathrasi
Bhanjyang
4890

Otlekh

Sirad

Dhaulutiya

Guljar

Pipalchaur

Launi

Bhaure

Kotyara

Kaphalseri

Dilasaina

Dhamili

Sitang

Deulikot

Bhaure

BAITADI

Timalbira

Trikali

Banjh

Patan

Maulali

Chaukham

Dhaulari

Kali Gad

Seti Nadi

Sarmali

Kimtola

Pokhara

Babina

Tharlakot

Dauda

Khaptad
National
Park

Surmaya Gad

Saure Khola

Satigaon

Jinghrana

Mahadevstan

Masteswor

DADELDHURA

Milad

Bhaure

DIPAYAL

Silgadhi

Dunilekh

Asigram

Simkhet

Sagat

6422

Halji

Jang

Sarpe
Bhanjyang
5012

Timure

Cyau Khola

Chhunsa
Lake

Lasa
6189

Numuche
Tuppa 5250

Chhuimun

CONTINUED OVERLEAF

Jyachhun
6388

Chimala
Bhanjyang
5092

Yari

Tumkot

Kermi

Humla Karnali Nadi

Muchhu

Yokapahad
6644

Thado Dhunga
Tuppa 5638

Puiya Yangar

Saipalgaon

Urai Bhanjyang
5207

5627

Timure

SIMIKOT

Garaph

Seti Nadi

Siyanban Khola

Shankha Lagna
4709

Chhipra

Dahachaur

Saipal Himal
7031

Sain

Chaurapani

Chhuphu
Tal

Dhuli

Ghat Khola

Gompa

Baniya

Surma Tal

Buradhaula

Kangarkot

Bauri

Lauthi

Kawadi Khola

Bichharo

Loland

Jethibahurani

Seragaon

Kidannagaon

Damoligoth

Ghatal

Dugun

Bateli
Bhanjyang

Dogragoth

Rugin

CHAINPUR

Pokhara

Dadagiri
3309

Kolti

Boldhik

Yaz
Bazaar

Gorkhali

MARTADI

Thini

Khalet Khola

Khaptad
National
Park

Dugurbani

Kedar

Karnali Nadi

Khaptad
Daha

Budhiganga Khola

Bargaon

Ukhari

Bomarle

Lamabagar

Thirpu

Sanphebagar

Dopalta

Bindabasini

Sirkun

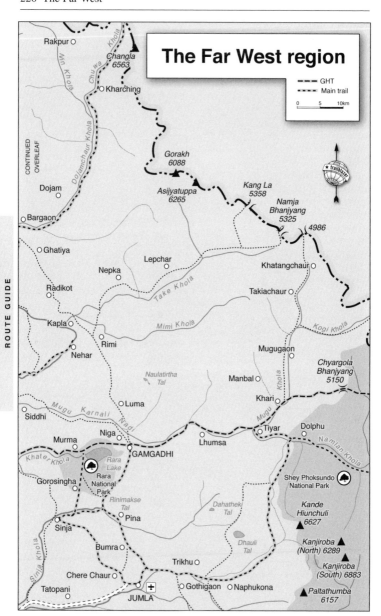

The Far West region

- — — GHT
- ∙∙∙∙ Main trail

0   5   10km

RARA LAKE CIRCUIT

This loop trek from Jumla can be done in either direction, but is slightly easier if you start via Sinja. Connecting trails to Simikot (north, five days), Mugu (northeast, three days), Dhorpatan and Lower Dolpo (southeast, 10-12 days) and Khaptad (west, six days) mean you can link to many other trekking routes, including to Mt Kailash, and Saipal and Api Himals. A new dirt road runs from Jumla to Surkhet to the south if you want to explore the wild mid-hills of west Nepal.

Nepal's largest lake is at its prettiest during spring when wild flowers cover the forest floor. The monsoon is very unpredictable with extremely heavy rains, causing serious flooding, mixed with week-long periods of relatively light rain. From October through to January, cold temperatures accompany clear skies for great photography. Migratory birds are common at the lake throughout the year, and there are some spotting-towers near the Park headquarters.

When the Park was established in 1976, the only two villages within the Park were resettled to Bardia on the terai, a decision that is still controversial to this day. The nearby town of Gamgadhi is the only place where you could purchase supplies in any quantity, but even here food is scarce. A series of failed rainy seasons and marginal farming land has created a food-crisis throughout much of the Far West, and the World Food Program is busy trying to establish

ROUTE GUIDE

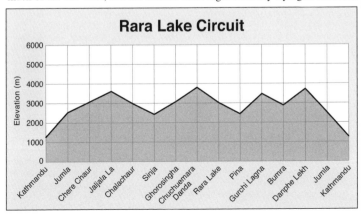

Rara Lake Circuit

Elevation (m): Kathmandu, Jumla, Chere Chaur, Jaljala La, Chalachaur, Sinja, Ghorosingha, Chuchuemara Danda, Rara Lake, Pina, Gurchi Lagna, Bumra, Danphe Lekh, Jumla, Kathmandu

a long-term solution. Your group must therefore be completely self-sufficient, which probably means bringing all supplies with you from Nepalgunj to either Jumla (daily flights) or Gamgadhi (weekly flights).

DAY 1: KATHMANDU – NEPALGUNJ
ALL DAY

As the flight from Nepalgunj (150m) to Jumla (2540m) leaves before any flights from Kathmandu arrive, you will have to overnight in Nepalgunj.

There are some hotels in town and a few, more basic places to stay near the airport. Whichever option you choose it is essential to book in advance, as they are frequently full. There isn't much to see or do in Nepalgunj so most airlines recommend that you book a mid-afternoon flight.

DAY 2: NEPALGUNJ – JUMLA

As if to make up for the inconvenience of having to overnight in Nepalgunj, the flight to Jumla (2540m) is terrific. First you cross the Nepali terai, covered in dense jungle, before climbing over the pahar of west Nepal.

Vast forests pass under the wings; this is one of the least densely populated areas of the Himalaya, aside from the very highest mountain regions. The approach to Jumla involves a diving 180° turn over a forested ridge to the grass airstrip; it's quite a thrill!

Once outside the heavily controlled airstrip, head west (turn right out of the gate) and follow a large, dusty trail to the main bazaar of Jumla, which is about 15 minutes away. The centre of town, called Khalanga Bazaar, is paved in large flagstones and is a busy trading post for the region.

Beyond the many shops are two interesting Hindu temples, Chandan Nath, which commemorates the yogi who introduced rice farming to the valley some 900 years ago and is dedicated to Vishnu, and Bhairavnath, a newer temple dedicated to Shiva.

These temples were built at the beginning of the Malla Empire, a Khas dynasty that dominated western Nepal, Tibet, Ladakh and Kashmir for centuries, see boxed text opposite. A strong wind blows through the valley in the afternoons, so if you arrive early enough it is a good idea to complete tomorrow's trek.

DAY 3: JUMLA – CHERE CHAUR
4½ HRS

Head due north from Khalanga Bazaar, following a large trail into a shallow valley and towards the Karnali Technical College. The trail is lined by buildings for the first hour and remains on the western (left) side of the valley.

When you reach a section of trail with fields on either side you will come to a bridge to the east bank. Cross the bridge and continue towards a large tank of water before the technical college (30 minutes). The trail winds around the college and then begins to climb an easy gradient on a trail with little shade for 3 hours to Chere Chaur (3055m).

This is a large, grassy plateau and makes an excellent campsite with views back down the valley to Jumla.

DAY 4: CHERE CHAUR –
CHALACHAUR   5 HRS

At the northern end of the plateau the trail forks; here you need to turn left and enter a pine forest.

Note: the right fork enters a short section of forest before climbing an exposed hillside to Danphe Lekh pass (3685m).

Having turned left, the trail climbs steadily as it contours around the top of a small river basin to a couple of buildings at Chor Khola (3170m, 45 minutes). From here the trail climbs steeply through forest to the upper pastures of the Dori Lekh and the Jaljala La (3585m, 2½ hours).

An easy descent on the north side of the pass soon brings you to a broad grassy pasture, Jaljala Chaur (3420m, 30 minutes). To reach the few buildings on the far side of the pasture continue along the northern tree line to a trail that crosses a small bridge over a stream. If you take any of the earlier, direct routes, you will have to wade a number of small streams and cross boggy ground. Camp on a patch of cleared ground in front of the buildings should you want to stay here.

From the buildings the trail descends rapidly through forest into the Jaljala Khola valley, where there is a good campsite at Chalachaur (2980m, 1¼ hours).

DAY 5: CHALACHAUR – SINJA
4½ HRS

You are now in a fine deciduous forest with the sparkling Jaljala Khola leading the way. Cross the river several times, over bridges with traditional carvings on the handrail supports. After 45 minutes a large tributary valley merges from the right and the first small plots of farmland appear.

The trail now remains on the southern side of the valley, and climbs a small spur before continuing to descend an easy gradient. As the valley broadens the terraces of smallholdings appear and you pass through the scattered settlement of Garhigoth (2740m, 2 hours).

The next settlement, Chauki (2500m, 1 hour), is a larger Thakuri village with its distinctive red and white painted homes. Walking through the village you are able to see the end of the valley ahead, and a rocky promontory with commanding views.

The trail winds around the southern base of the promontory and then drops to a bridge across the outflow of the Jaljala Khola to a peninsula with the Sinja Khola on the far side. Camp on the peninsula next to the health post (2405m, 45 minutes), the main part of the village is on the far side of the valley and can be reached by another bridge.

DAY 6: SINJA
ALL DAY

The promontory that you passed the previous day is one of the most important sites in medieval Nepali history.

The western hills of Nepal were once the centre of the largest kingdom ever seen in the Himalaya, prior to the unification of Nepal: the first Malla Empire, and the winter capital was here, at Sinja. The only remains are some ruins of the royal palace and the ancient Hindu Kankasundri Temple on top of the promontory, called Lamathada.

Two large stone lions at the entry of the temple are certainly from the right period,

ROUTE GUIDE

❏ The Khasas

Khas people are found in the remote valleys of the western hills of Nepal, mainly in Mugu District. Known as Khasas, they have traditionally been illiterate, backward people who originally followed Tibetan Buddhism, until Indian Brahmans, fleeing the Islamic invasion of India (9th to the 14th centuries), arrived here and converted them to Hinduism. Since then they have had very limited access to education or opportunities. Most modern Khas people will not refer to themselves as Khas (they consider it to be humiliating), instead calling themselves Chhetri, or Thakuris, after the caste that converted them.

The Khasas were a warlike tribe who built three capitals over time: Taklakot in Tibet, and Sinja and Dullu in Nepal. From the 11th century, their powerful kingdom, known as the Malla Empire (not related to the Malla Kingdoms of Kathmandu Valley), grew, covering most of west Nepal, Ladakh, Kashmir and western Tibet. As the Empire fell apart from the 14th century, many of the ruling families migrated throughout Nepal, so today many common Nepali surnames (Thapa, Basnet, Bista and Bhandari), as well as the national language, have their roots in the ancient and once proud Khas kingdom.

Most of the men can speak Nepali, however, women, who generally do not leave the village, can only speak the Khas language. Their houses are built of stone and mud with flat roofs of mud or thatch depending on their altitude. They are dark and poorly ventilated and not usually kept very clean. Ground floors are usually for livestock and a notched wooden ladder provides access to the first floor and wooden veranda. Most marriages are arranged when the child is still young. The Khas continue to worship their shamanic mountain deities, and rarely adhere to traditional Hindu rituals.

but identifying other artefacts within the temple is impossible.

Throughout the region are many stone pillars, or *stele*, that declare land owner-ship changes, or places of historical inter-est, but they nearly all date from the 17th century onwards.

From the top of Lamathada you look down into a deep ravine to the west, and some caves on the far bank, where the fifth Dalai Lama is said to have meditated.

The old border with Tibet is not far away, in the Mugu Karnali Nadi valley, and local legends tell of a time when Sinja was the most important place in the Himalaya ranges. To the southeast, about 5 hours walk away is a large cave, where locals believe the five Pandava brothers (from the Hindu epic, the *Mahabharata*) were exiled.

An annual horse race, in July, is held from Lamathada to the cave and back.

The local people call themselves Thakuri, a noble Chhetri caste, which means you will probably not be invited into homes.

DAY 7: SINJA – GHOROSINGHA
4 HRS

From the campsite, cross the suspension bridge to Sinja village but turn right (not left to the village) and follow a dirt trail that climbs a little as it heads through the gorge behind Lamathada.

From the gorge it is easy to see why Lamathada was such an obvious choice for a fort palace, any attacker from here would have no chance of success. Continue on the north bank of the Sinja Khola along a trail that continues to climb, do not take any smaller routes that descend to the riverside.

After 1½ hours you should reach the outlying homes of Bhota at the entrance of the Ghatta Khola valley (2600m). Unless you want to detour to the main part of the village stay on the west (left) bank of the river.

A detour to the village, which is on the east (right) bank of the river, will add 45 minutes to 1 hour to your day. At trail fork to Bhota take the left hand, smaller track, and begin ascending the Ghatta Khola. The valley soon narrows and climbs steeply up an exposed trail that passes many grinding wheels. At the top of the ancient moraine wall (3050m, 2½ hours) you are greeted by

a meandering stream flowing through a broad grassy valley, and perhaps one of the most inviting campsites you will ever come across, Ghorosingha.

DAY 8: GHOROSINGHA – RARA LAKE
6¼ HRS

The trail now winds through beech and pine forest as it continues to ascend the valley. After 40 minutes you will pass a derelict army and National Park entry post. Climbing further the valley forms a grassy basin and then the river turns sharply to the northwest (right) into a much narrower gorge. Continue along the north side of the boulder-filled valley to the bottom of a steep switchback trail that climbs to a saddle on the Chuchuemara Danda (3804m, 2¼ hours).

Traverse the northern slope to your right on a small but defined trail to a ridge (3756m, 30 minutes) overlooking Rara Lake, which makes an ideal lunch spot if the weather is clear.

The trail now descends, slowly at first, but more steeply once you enter rhododen-dron forest for 1½ hours to the main track along the Khatyar Khola (2965m). A wood-en bridge leads over the Khola to the north bank, where you turn right and ascend an easy gradient to the western end of Rara Lake (3010m, 30 minutes).

The main campsite (45 minutes) is beside the National Park office on the north-ern shore of the lake, you will have to reg-ister here as well.

DAY 9: RARA LAKE
ALL DAY

Rara Lake is an idyllic place; the astound-ingly clear water surrounded by protected forest is a nature-lover's dream. A walk around the rim of the lake (13km, 5½ hours) is really worth the effort – see if you can spot the stele marking the cardinal points, nobody knows how or why they are here.

On the north-eastern bank is Rara Mahadev Temple, decorated with wood-carvings of elephant, peacock and people. On the full moon in July/August locals gather here to honour the god Thakur, who, legend says, created the lake by firing an arrow at the western shore and then built the eastern bank by stamping down the earth. Swirling rock formations at the eastern end of the lake are said to be his footprints.

There are some old canoes near the army camp that you might be able to use, and a fishing permit for snow trout (the only fish found in the lake) can be purchased from the National Park staff.

The lake water is extremely clear for swimming, but cold, and Park rules stipulate that you must use buoyancy aids.

DAY 10: RARA LAKE – PINA 4¾ HRS

Take the lakeside trail back to the western end of the lake and the bridge over the outflowing Khatyar Khola.

Cross the bridge and continue around the lake to a trail junction in the south-western corner, the left hand trail continues around the lake, but this time take the southern (right) fork and climb an easy gradient through forest.

Crest the grass-covered ridge (3060m) to the south of the lake in 2½ hours from camp. Descend through a fine cedar forest to Jhari (2550m, 1¼ hours) to a trail junction. There is a newer trail that avoids Pina and takes an almost direct route south to the Gurchi Lagna, which is reached in 6 hours.

You need local knowledge to follow this route, which is committing as the first campsite is in the valley on the far side of the pass.

Alternatively, the older route descends to Pina where there is a good campsite. To take this route descend to the small river in the valley, which you should cross. Keep descending for another 20 minutes before a slight climb to a grinding mill, beyond which are the cultivated fields of Pina (2440m, 30 minutes).

Do not descend through the village, instead contour through the upper parts of the village to a campsite next to an old teahouse (10 minutes).

Note: if you want to take an extra day to reduce daily trekking hours, it is possible to break the return trek to: Rara Lake to Jhari (day 10), then to Chauta (day 11), then Padmara (day 12), Jumla (day 13) and fly to Kathmandu on day 14.

DAY 11: PINA – BUMRA   7¼ HRS

To the south of Pina a valley climbs up towards the Gurchi Lagna (3445m) to the south. The trail follows a stream through forest and some rocky spurs; it takes 3½ hours to reach the pass.

From the top of the pass there are good views of Kanjiroba Himal. Descend into a small valley that soon forks, take the larger south-westerly (right) route that continues to descend. The valley then curves westward and another tributary joins from your left, again continue right and descend.

Once you reach about 3100m the valley turns to the south and enters forest; pass the National Park office and enter Chauta (2745m, 1¾ hours from the pass). Descend through the village to a trail junction, turn south (left) and contour about 150m above the Sinja Khola.

It is now 2 hours to Bumra (2850m) where you can camp, but if you have time, continue for another 20 minutes or so to some better campsites beside the river.

DAY 12: BUMRA – JUMLA   7 HRS

If you camped in Bumra, descend to the Sinja Khola and head south along a broad trail to a bridge (2720m, 1 hour). The trail now climbs an unrelenting gradient through birch forest for 3½ hours to some pastures where there is a trail junction (3520m).

The left-hand fork, which continues across the meadows, leads to Padmara (3060m, 2½ hours) and will add an extra day to the return to Jumla.

A smaller trail branches right towards a tree line; you might have to scout around for this if the meadow is overgrown. Climb through the forest, which soon ends, and emerge onto another grassy pasture that leads up towards the Danphe Lekh pass (3685m, 30 minutes).

From the top you can see the broad meadow of Chere Chaur, where you camped the first night out of Jumla, descend to it (40 minutes) and continue on the same trail back to Jumla (1½ hours).

DAY 13: JUMLA – NEPALGUNJ – KATHMANDU

Reconfirm your flights as soon as you arrive in Jumla. Depending on schedules you should be able to fly to Nepalgunj in the morning and then catch one of many afternoon flights to Kathmandu the same day.

ROUTE GUIDE

KHAPTAD NATIONAL PARK

Lying on the junction of four districts Bajhang, Doti, Achham and Bajura, in the far west of Nepal, is the small and thoroughly picturesque Khaptad National Park. The Park covers a large plateau thrust up from amid the pahar, just to the south of the Great Himalaya Range. Trails criss-cross the region to the remote district of Darchula (12 days), the Saipal and Api Himals (eight days), Rara Lake (six days) and dozens of sites throughout the mid-hills.

> ### KHAPTAD NATIONAL PARK TREK
>
> This is an idyllic Nepal trekking experience interlaced with intriguing history, sacred pilgrimage sites, pristine forests filled with wildlife and an unbeatable 300km panorama of the Himalaya.
>
> **Duration**: 9 days
>
> **Highest Point**: 3276m
>
> **Best Season**: Mar-May / Oct-Dec
>
> **Accommodation**: camping

Since it was established in 1984, the Park has received roughly 250 registered visitors, an amazing contrast to the thousands of pilgrims who come on the full moon each August (during the monsoon) for a *mela* and to honour a famous yogi. However, the monsoon rains are unpredictable, with sudden heavy downpours closing roads and infrastructure for weeks at a time. Winter snow closes the Park from late December to the end of February before the spring sun brings life back to *patans* (grassy meadows) and forests. The post-monsoon period has clear skies for landscape photography, whereas spring is famous for perhaps the best wildflower and medicinal plant display in Nepal.

A six-hour drive from the Mahendra Highway is the road head town of Silgadhi, and the main trail to the Park headquarters. Alternatively, you could

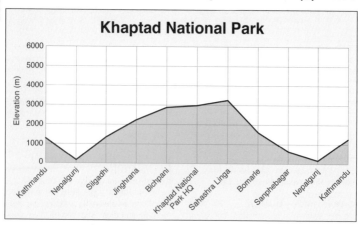

charter a flight to Chainpur (Bajura District), Dipayal (Doti District), Kolti (Bajura District) or Sanphebagar (Accham District) and take one of the many minor trails to the Park. This itinerary starts at Silgadhi and end at Sanphebagar, although the most popular route is to return to Silgadhi on the same trail.

DAY 1: KATHMANDU – NEPALGUNJ/ BARDIA   ALL DAY
Whether flying or driving to Khaptad National Park you will probably overnight in Nepalgunj.

If you driving the entire way from Kathmandu then you could combine your trip with a few days at the beautiful nature reserves at Bardia or Suklephanta National Park to break the journey.

DAY 2: NEPALGUNJ – SILGADHI   ALL DAY
A 9- to 10-hour drive from Nepalgunj (7-8 hours from Bardia) along a road with relatively low traffic volume brings you to Silgadhi (1340m), which is a sprawling town perched on a south-facing ridge.

The Saileshori Temple, in the centre of the town, is surrounded by a large stone-paved square, and is one of Nepal's most important pilgrimage sites. The Temple is dedicated to the combined manifestation of Shiva and Parvati, who, it is believed, honeymooned in the picturesque forests and grassy patans at the centre of the Park, as mentioned in the Hindu epic, the *Mahabharata*.

The local market cannot be relied upon for a comprehensive range of provisions so stock up in Kathmandu, Nepalgunj or along the Mahendra Highway.

DAY 3: SILGADHI – JINGHRANA   6 HRS
Climb through the village to the main ridge above the town, then turn north (right) and follow a large dirt trail, which climbs steadily. You can see an aerial mast next to an army camp (1570m, 1 hour) not far ahead, where you register before continuing.

The trail climbs an easy gradient past some small farms before steepening on an exposed dirt trail to a viewpoint at 1860m (1 hour and 20 minutes). The trail is now predominantly through rhododendron and beech forest as it continues to climb to a small teashop beside an apple orchard

(2100m, 1 hour), where you can camp. However, it is better to continue along a flat ridgetop trail heading due north before contouring around the head of a small valley to an intersecting ridge, cresting at 2500m in 1½ hours.

Pass a small Shiva temple and follow the ridge past a pond, which used to provide water to the temple. This area would make a good campsite if there was a reliable water supply as it has excellent views both east and west.

The trail climbs slightly as it traverses beneath another ridgeline before descending slightly to a saddle and the National Park entry at Jinghrana (2250m, 1 hour). There is a good campsite here, beyond the Park entry post and the army camp.

DAY 4: JINGHRANA – BICHPANI   4½ HRS
Just past the army camp, at the edge of the forest, is a trail junction. A sign proclaims that the left hand trail is only for humans, whereas livestock can be taken up the right trail. If you are a strong walker and enjoy steep, muddy climbs then take the left trail, everyone else should go right.

The 'only for humans' (left) track takes a direct route to a shallow valley (2760m, 3½ hours), where it climbs again for 120m to join the main trail that has wound around the eastern side of the same hill (4½ hours). You are now at Bichpani (2905m) where there is a teashop and campsite.

DAY 5: BICHPANI – NATIONAL PARK HQ   4¼ HRS
From the campsite the trail climbs about 100m before heading east along an undulating ridgeline that forms the southern edge of the Khaptad plateau.

Pass a small deserted building in 1½ hours near to a small stream and a popular place for herders to rest their flocks. The first patan you come to is Suketa (3070m, 1¼ hours), where a dharamsala was built in memory of some soldiers who died of exposure in a sudden storm.

From the end of the valley are views of Api Himal to the north. The dharamsala also marks a trail junction; to reach the National Park HQ, head right, and climb a little into forest. Do not take the smaller trail that descends at the end of the valley.

After a short climb through some beautiful woodland descend to a large patan, and follow the main trail which swings right and descends to a small temple, from here Tribeni (3010m, 1 hour) can be seen in the ahead.

Tribeni marks the confluence of three rivers and is the site of a Shiva temple. Some old statues and stele line the walls inside the temple, which is the focal point of the *dashara mela* held during Jestha Purnima (August full moon). The empty buildings near to Tribeni are shelters for the pilgrims who attend the mela.

From Tribeni, continue northeast along a main trail that follows a stream. In 5 to 10 minutes, pass a large boulder where offerings have been made. The valley curves to the east and the National Park office and army camp can be seen ahead; camp in a saddle between the two (3020m, 20 minutes).

DAY 6: NATIONAL PARK HQ
ALL DAY

Geologists believe that a massive geographic distortion has elevated the sandy plateau that forms much of Khaptad National Park.

The excellent drainage and fertile earth here mean that 400 of the 700 medicinal plants found in Nepal can be found in a single day's walk across the rolling hills of grassland fringed by rhododendron and birch forests. If you have some time, explore the patans that form a giant diamond shape and are home to wild cat, fox, bear and musk deer.

From the centre of the park there are a number of interesting things to do: a visit to the famous Khaptad Baba's Ashram (also referred to as Khaptad Swami locally, 1½ hours return trip) should be high on your list. Khaptad Daha (lake) offers some sublime reflections and is another pilgrimage site, as locals believe that Shiva bathed here.

The lake lies beside the trail to Kolti (Bajura District, three days). Sahashra Linga (3276m) is the highest point in the park and a favourite pilgrimage spot (5 hours return walk).

The views from a grassy hillock near to the National Park office are also excellent. In clear weather you can see from the Kumaon Himal in India to the west, the Saipal and Api Himals to the north, the ranges of Dolpa to the northeast, and finally, shimmering on the eastern horizon, the massive bulk of Dhaulagiri and the Annapurnas. That's a 300km panorama of the Himalaya that anyone can appreciate.

DAY 7: NATIONAL PARK HQ –
BOMARLE 7½ HRS

The other trails in and out of Khaptad are not as well defined as the one from Silgadhi. The route described here takes two days to Sanphebagar, where there is a dirt airstrip, and is perhaps the toughest of the alternative routes.

Note: you may need a local guide from the trail junction to the ridge.

ROUTE GUIDE

❏ Khaptad Baba

The yogi, Sachidanda Saraswati Khaptad Baba, spent fifty years meditating and administering herbal remedies from his cave hermitage using the incredible range of local medicinal plants. Legend says that the Baba was once a doctor in India, but his life before he started living in a cave, deep in the forest, is largely a mystery.

During the 1950s, locals built a simple shelter before the buildings were expanded to the current size by order of King Birendra, who became a follower of the Baba, who died in 1996. A statue of the yogi sits on the south-facing porch, where visitors can leave donations.

From the National Park HQ head towards the viewpoint, but before you get to the end of the patan take the small left-hand fork that leads to Sahashra Linga. Follow this trail for 1 hour to a trail junction; turn left (right goes to the Linga) and traverse through scrubby woodland to a ridge that emanates from the Linga viewpoint (3030m, 45 minutes).

Descend a sometimes-steep trail to a series of kharkas, each of which has many small trails, however, do not deviate more than a few metres from the ridgeline for the next hour. You then reach a junction where a small trail continues along the ridge and a larger track descends southwest through woodland (2815m, 1 hour).

Take the larger track, which descends steeply through oak and rhododendron forest to about 2600m at the top of a small watercourse (1 hour). Descend the watercourse but before reaching the valley floor swing left onto the hillside and traverse a recent landslide.

Once past the landslide the trail gradient eases and you traverse to a small, dirty village (2010m, 2½ hours), where you can camp in the school at the bottom of the village. If you have time, it is better to continue to the upper reaches of Bomarle village (1605m) in 1¼ hours. Camp in the school grounds at the top of the village.

DAYS 8-9: BOMARLE – SANPHEBAGAR – SILGADHI – KATHMANDU   5¼ HRS

Descend directly through Bomarle to the river, crossed by a small wooden log bridge (1220m, 45 minutes).

Note: if the river is high you have to cross by a suspension bridge a little upstream from the village.

Climb to a main trail on the far bank (1400m, 1 hour) through dense jungle. The gradient now eases as you follow a trail that links a series of villages, each with a pretty Shiva shrine, until you round the valley end and head west into the Budhiganga valley (1200m, 2½ hours).

There are trails from each subsequent village that descend to the dirt road in the valley bottom (1 hour), where you can get a lift on a tractor trailer to Sanphebagar (620m, 1½ hours by tractor).

At the centre of Sanphebagar is a bus park with regular services to Silgadhi (2½ hours) and Nepalgunj (10 hours).

There is a dirt airstrip outside Sanphebagar that will accept charter flights. Flights operate throughout the day from Nepalgunj to Kathmandu, but instead of heading straight back to Kathmandu, take a day or two and enjoy animal spotting in Bardia National Park, where there is an excellent chance of seeing tiger, rhino, elephant and many other animals.

ROUTE GUIDE

GHT – FAR WEST

There are two major route options in the far west for the GHT:

● **Through Mugu to Gamgadhi, then up to Simikot and the Yari valley to the Tibetan border**. This route is appealing as it follows the route of the Humla Karnali river across the Great Himalaya Range to the Tibetan plateau, but here it ends as you cannot cross the border, nor can you trek to the further Indian border. So as far as a continuous trail is concerned this route is a picturesque dead-end. There could be a potential pass from Simikot to the north side of Saipal and then you could trek to Chainpur and on to the Mahakali Nadi, but attempts to find and cross such a pass have failed so far.

● **Through Mugu to Gamgadhi, then cross country via Rara Lake to Kolti and thence to Chainpur and on to the Mahakali Nadi**. This route has the appeal of providing a continuous route to the Indian border, but runs across the southern flanks of both the Saipal and Api Himals and is therefore not through the centre of the Great Himalaya Range.

As at July 2009, there have been three recent attempts to find a pass that runs west from Simikot, or southwest from Muchhu and all have failed. So for the time being the GHT route described here will only be the one via Kolti and Chainpur. However, the high trail from Chainpur to the Mahakali Nadi has been cut by two major landslides and is not expected to be open before the pre-monsoon season of 2010. This effectively ends the GHT in Chainpur for the time being.

There are also two route options from Pho to Mugu, both of which are challenging. The lower southern route is only accessible when trekking from west to east as the only local guides who know it live in Dolphu (the last village on the Mugu Karnali Nadi). If you want to try this route all of your party should have rock climbing experience and equipment, as there are three difficult rock sections plus two wire-rope river crossings that require pulleys. The higher northern route can be trekked in either direction; employ a guide either in Pho or Mugugaon. Accordingly, the northern route is described here in detail and only a summary is given for the southern.

Pho to Mugu – the Higher Northern Route

From the top of the village climb to a painted chorten (10 minutes) where the northern and southern trails diverge. Take the right fork and climb switchbacks across scrubby slopes to the first ridgeline at 4645m (1½ hours, Finaid: Phophagau, sheet: 2982 04, ref: 889 675), from which there are good views back down to Pho. The trail then climbs at an easy gradient though a basin to a major ridge, the Gyallo Raud Lekh, that descends from the large rocky peak above you to the south (left). The ridge has a large cairn and prayer flags at which you should turn north (right) and follow a gradually ascending ridgeline. The trail rounds a rocky hill to then follow a sharp and craggy ridgeline, which steepens considerably to the Nyingma Gyanzen La (5563m, 2 hours and 50 minutes, Finaid: Phophagau, sheet: 2982 04, ref: 857 714). This pass sits in the very centre of the Great Himalaya Range, with the Kanjiroba Himal to your south and a line of slightly lower snowy peaks along the Tibet border to your north. It is like no other place on the Nepal GHT and makes you feel like you are walking along the spine of the planet.

Descend a steep trail that continues to follow the craggy ridgeline down to a notch marked by a large triangular rock and prayer flags (5450m, 20 minutes). Cross through the notch and continue to descend steep ground into the valley to the northeast of the pass. The trail winds down the centre of the valley, but stays in the central scrubby vegetation rather than on the left or right side. After about 900m of descent you will reach the end of the valley (1 hour and 40 minutes) but do not continue to the river confluence. Instead, follow a track that winds beneath a cliff line to your north (left).

Note: if you are trekking this route in reverse, it is critical that you do not head further downstream than 4440m, Finaid: Phophagau, sheet: 2982 04, ref: 876 737. Beyond this point the river valley becomes extremely dangerous.

The trail then slowly descends to the Swaksa Khola (4440m), where there are a few tent platforms scraped out by nomads. However, there is a far better site on the eastern (right) side of the valley on the grassy Pung Kharka (4650m, 55 minutes). In another hour, pass a river that flows down from the west (left) through a huge kharka area of grassy hillocks. There are some small caves on the east (right) bank opposite the river confluence, and just beyond them cross to the west bank. Continue to follow the Swaksa Khola up a valley that becomes flatter as you reach another large kharka and potential campsite (4820m, 50 minutes).

Locals have established a new pass, which is not marked on the Finaid map; they say too many people died from rock fall on the old pass. The new Yala La (5414m, 2¼ hours from the kharka, Finaid: Phophagau, sheet: 2982 04, ref: 866 817) is reached by climbing a steep grassy hillside, and then traverses beneath a rock band to a small basin of red and orange rocks. Climb through the basin towards the rocky ridge above, where a series of large cairns and chorten can easily be seen from below. There is a steep descent on the far side to a shallow basin before another steep descent into the large grass covered valley of the Chyandi Khola (4830m, 1¼ hours). Snowy mountains surround you, and as there are no settlements for miles round, the sense of wilderness is palpable. There are many potential campsites in the valley for the next 40 minutes.

The trail follows the northern bank of the river before moving right next to the water's edge. You may need a 20m hand line in places as the trail can be a bit tricky. Approaching some forest, the trail suddenly starts to climb and descend steeply to avoid a series of landslides. A final slippery descent brings you to a confluence with a small river entering from the north (3995m, 2 hours and 50 minutes, Finaid: Mugu, sheet: 2982 07, ref: 778 828). All of the river names on the Finaid maps differ from those used by guides, who also disagree with each other!

Cross the simple log bridge over the river and climb a steep switchback trail straight up a shallow gully to a ridgeline at 4365m (1¼ hours, Finaid: Mugu, sheet: 2982 07, ref: 775 832), which is marked by a chorten. The trail now traverses a broad hillside, with great views of the valleys to the south. A final rocky scramble brings you to a last ridge marked by four large cairns (4495m, 1 hour), before a steep descent through silver birch forest to the Takla Khola (3785m, 2 hours), where a few small logs to act as a bridge. There is a good campsite on the far bank in a grove of silver birch (Finaid: Mugu, sheet: 2982 07, ref: 737 836).

Leave camp by following a trail up the forested river valley to your west (rather than the larger river to your north). After 40 minutes pass a tributary that flows down from the north (called the Chhyugulden Khola on the Finaid map). Continue on an easy gradient ascending ancient moraine and landslide debris for about 1 hour to a small lake, after which the trail slowly crosses a boulder-filled watercourse to the beginning of the pass-climb (4410m, 15 minutes from the lake). Follow switchbacks that climb a grass and wildflower-covered slope to a scree-filled basin. The trail climbs the left hand side of the basin across rocky ground to the cairn-covered Chyargola Bhanjyang (5150m, 2½ hours). A good trail descends from the top of the pass, and at roughly 4600m (1¼ hours)

ROUTE GUIDE

there is a potential campsite. Follow the ancient moraine on the north (right) side of the valley down to an enormous flat-bottomed valley called Thajuchaur (4050m, 1¼ hours).

Note: if you are trekking this route in reverse then look for a black rock with a white cairn that marks the route up to the moraine.

The trail now descends into a V-shaped valley and frequently climbs away from and descends back to the Chham Khola. There are many trail junctions, at each one follow the largest or freshest route. After 30 minutes the trail crosses to the middle of the river and then back to the northern (right hand) bank to avoid a landslide. In another 1 hour you reach a large flat, pine-forested area that makes an excellent campsite (roughly 3500m, Finaid: Mugu, sheet: 2982 07, ref: 599 818). From here, cliffs rise on both sides but a good trail leads down to the end of the valley. There used to be a both a cantilever and log bridge to the south bank of the Chham Khola but ignore them all. Instead, scramble over some boulders to the very end of the valley along the northern bank. Once you have reached the Mugu Khola (1 hour), turn north (right) and follow an easy trail for 30 minutes to a bridge that crosses to the west bank of this much larger river. It is not necessary to go all the way to Mugu. Instead, turn south (left) and head downstream through the Shilenchaura Kharka (2945m, 20 minutes), opposite the Chham Khola confluence and a good campsite. In fact, for the next 3 hours there are a series of riverside glades that would all make good campsites. The river performs a massive S-bend and on the second curve a tributary joins from the north (right) and is crossed by a rigid metal bridge. After 3 hours from Shilenchaura the valley narrows and in 45 minutes you reach another major confluence, at Tiyar, with the Namlan Khola, which the locals also call the Karnali Nadi. Just before the confluence, cross a wooden bridge to the west bank of the Mugu Khola and climb a dusty trail to some large chortens. Just beyond the chorten is a gompa with a grassy forecourt that makes an excellent campsite (2418m). The Padma Dundul Choling Gompa was used as an 'education' camp by the Maoists but is now being restored by the resident lama.

Dolphu to Pho – the Lower Southern Route

The trail that connects Dolphu with Pho mainly follows the Namlan Khola, also called the Mugu Karnali Nadi by locals. This route is difficult and requires rock climbing skills and equipment, and two local guides from Dolphu. Locals in Pho neither have the equipment nor trail knowledge to guide this route. From Dolphu expect the route to take six to eight days, depending on group size, as the climbs and wire-ropes slow progress considerably.

Dolphu is one day from the Padma Dundul Choling Gompa, where there is a trail that follows the north bank of the Namlan Khola before coming to a large gully. Climb through the gully on a trail that scrambles up the far wall and then traverse through terraced fields to Dolphu. You can camp by the gompa and it will take at least a day to find, and then negotiate with, local guides. From Dolphu the trail descends to the Namlan Khola to a wire-way. If you have made an early start you should cross the wire, but normally locals camp in a scrubby campsite before crossing. You need pulleys (the local guides should have some home-made pulleys) and about 60m of rope, plus harnesses. Once on the far side the trail climbs to a cliff line, which you need to climb. On top, cross a flat grassy area before descending a very steep rock section, requiring a handline; on the far side is a good campsite. This was the base camp location for the first snow leopard survey in 1981.

For the next couple of days negotiate three more rock sections of varying difficulty before arriving at a large grassy area as the river swings north. Climb the hillside to the west of the campsite past ancient juniper trees to a deep gully. Ascend the gully to a point where the cliff line on the far side (north or left) runs out and you should see some log ladders. Camp here, in the gully, as there are no more sites on this side of the pass. Ascend the ladders and the sloping rock face above and continue up the ridgeline towards an obvious saddle on the ridge above. The approach to the pass is beneath the north (left) cliff line. From the top of the pass the gradient steepens, descending rapidly to a gully and then climb a short section, before again gradually descending back to the Namlan Khola (Mugu Karnali Nadi). You have just cut through a huge curve in the river.

Once again, cross a wire-way to a campsite on the far bank. The trail is now hard to find as it ascends the loose scree slope to the east of the campsite. Climb to a minor rock band and then traverse eastwards (right). The trail climbs a little to a small flat area on a ridge above a confluence with a small river that flows down from the north (left). Follow the cliff line around to the north (left) to a large rock overhang just before a final descent to the river. This is the best place to camp before the next passes.

Cross the river and climb up through forest to a minor ridge where the trail turns southeast and ascend another ridge line (4790m, Finaid: Bhijer, sheet: 2982 12, ref: 852 616). Swinging due north the trail now climbs around another ridgeline before crossing a spectacular saddle to a kharka, but there is no water here for much of the year. From the kharka, climb switchbacks to another ridge-line to your northeast (right). Once on the ridge turn east (right) again to climb towards a minor peak (shown as point 5096m on Finaid: Bhijer, sheet: 2982 12, ref: 874 643) before traversing northeast (left). There are amazing views of northern Dolpo and the Kanjiroba Himal. There is a tricky section of loose fine scree beneath a black cliff line before a long steep descent to the village of Pho.

Tiyar to Gamgadhi

Retrace your steps past the chorten and cross back to the north bank of the Mugu Karnali Nadi. Once on the far bank, turn west (left) and climb an easy gradient to the main trail, which you follow for 3¼ hours to a large blue suspension bridge.

Note: there's a small shop just before the bridge that sells rice and flour.

Cross the bridge and continue heading west (right) for 30 minutes to a major bend in the river where there might be a small water source near a large bank of river stones. In another hour is a campsite in a small copse beside the Mugu Karnali Nadi (Lhumsa, where there is a small shop is another hour). Continue on the south (left-hand) bank all the way to the end of the valley, marked by a small school with a large stele in the forecourt (2 hours). There are more of them behind the school and they either declare land rights, or mark the old border between Tibet and the Khas Kingdom. The trail swings south (left) and descends into a smaller valley. At a large trail junction, take the left, higher fork, then descend to and cross the Gam Gad river via a small wooden bridge (15 minutes). It is a 40 minute climb up a hillside where a few pine trees offer some shade to the large bazaar of Gamgadhi (2095m). There is a teahouse as you enter the village and no campsite.

Gamgadhi to Chainpur

Head up through the bazaar on a stone paved trail to the end of the town to a main trail junction. The right-hand trail continues to climb past the police post towards a minor ridge. Do not descend at any point through the bazaar or on the exit trail. The trail crosses a new road a couple of times, before following it as it traverses west (left) beneath a ridge. There are a few small carpenters' homes (1 hour and 20 minutes) just above the road to your right, after which the trail climbs on an easy gradient. In 15 minutes you come to a few homes in a shallow gully, which the locals call Bougarie, where the trail again branches. Take the right, higher trail, climbing up through the gully towards forest that can be seen ahead. At times the trail has been badly eroded by runoff and is sometimes quite steep. Pass the final few homes to a grassy area in front of the forest where the trail again forks. Take the larger, right hand trail to an old broken down check-post building (2850m, 1 hour), where power poles now mark the trail you follow. The trail winds up through pretty pine forest to the rim of the Rara Lake basin, where again the trail forks (3050m, 1 hour and 10 minutes). Take the right hand, larger trail, which undulates through forest. In 20 minutes pass 3 stele beside the trail and in a further 10 minutes a small temple on the left. Another 25 minutes brings you to the army post through which you must follow a rocky path to the campsite and National Park office, where you need to register. For more see *Rara Lake Circuit*, day nine, p230.

In the early morning, it's a delightful walk around the southern shoreline of Rara Lake to the outflow, which becomes the Khater Khola. Follow the north (right) bank of the river down to Murma (1 hour) and cross the river.

Note: the left hand trail is the route to Sinja and Jumla, see *Rara Lake Circuit* days one to eight, pp228-30.

Continue to follow the river on a trail, crossing the growing stream a few times before staying on the north (right) bank. In 2¼ hours you should reach the next village of Baunpani; beyond is a bizarre shrine, which some locals say is the Hindu God Mahakali and consort. The trail now descends past many villages as the valley broadens.

The people here call themselves Thapa (a Chhetri name), but they are more likely Khas. They wear a confusing mix of clothing items, some Gurung, some Chhetri, that is explained away as current fashions. Beyond the village of Jamiya follow the new road that is being built from Kolti. Locals hope this will eventually cut through the National Park to Gamgadhi, which would destroy the peace of Rara. After roughly 3 hours of descending the road there are a couple of potential campsites. Post night guards if you choose the second at Tak Bazaar (1854m, after Chimadungri). The valley narrows again and at Bagar (after 1½ hours) the trail crosses to the south (left) bank, which you follow for another 1 hour and 20 minutes to the end of the valley.

When you get the first views of the now large Karnali Nadi, you will see a suspension bridge crossing back to the north bank – do not cross this bridge. Instead follow a small trail beside an irrigation channel (1190m) winding around cliffs on the left. In 25 minutes you reach a large suspension bridge across the Karnali to Boldhik village (1170m). After crossing the bridge the trail forks, the southern track (left) takes a shortcut route around a rocky bluff. This trail is exposed and tricky. The right-hand fork goes through the village and follows the main trail up and over the bluff. Both trails then meet again on the far side of the bluff before descending to a teashop beside the Karnali; it is possible to camp on a small beach beside the river here (1180m, 50 minutes).

An easy trail continues on the west (right) bank of the Karnali as it winds south and after about 40 minutes the trail moves next to the river before climbing a little to a trail junction. Take the left-hand trail, traversing beneath Badu village to cross a tributary flowing down from the north (right). On the far side is a large flat area where you could camp (50 minutes). The trail now climbs a little as it winds around a hillside that forms the northern mouth of the Kunda Khola, which leads to Kolti. A large cairn near a chautara marks the entry to the valley (30 minutes). It is then an easy walk up the northern (right) side of the valley to the airstrip and bazaar of Kolti village (1513m, 2 hours). The original village is 15 minutes beyond the bazaar and at its centre is a large grassy area that makes an excellent campsite. You need a local guide to take you from here to Chainpur. The best person to ask is Pradeep Kumar Giri who has a large house near the campsite. He will probably find a guide from a nearby village, which will take a day or two.

Take a path to the left of Pradeep's house that climbs through the village and then through a small gully. The trail stays on the north (right) side of the Kunda Khola and passes through small villages to a point where the river forks. However, before you get to the confluence look for a shortcut log bridge to a large grassy area. The trail then winds around scrubby hillside, past the suspension bridge to the villages of Jagar and Ghodakot (2½ hours from Kolti). Turn left in the village to a trail that climbs steep hillside to Tari (2170m, 1 hour). Walk through the village and slowly descend about 100m to a small river (40 minutes) that flows down from the south (left).

On the far bank the trail climbs through scrubby forest but be careful, there are many tracks here and you should stay close to the ridge on your right. There are many trails all the way up this ridge and your local guide should be familiar with a small forest campsite about 5 minutes away from the main route (2750m, 2 hours and 20 minutes from the small river, Finaid: Kolti, sheet: 2981 07, ref: 554 650). After 30 minutes there is a kharka at the top of which there is another potential campsite. Continue to climb on an easier gradient on a trail, which has more and more traversing sections as you head towards the main ridge. In 45 minutes you reach the main ridge, which you follow north (right) for another 30 minutes to a small pass marked by a decorated cairn, Dadagiri (3309m, Finaid: Kolti, sheet: 2981 07, ref: 540 654). After a short traverse descend to the large Shingtua Kharka (3148m, 30 minutes).

ROUTE GUIDE

Ascend a trail to the northwest up a scrub and grass covered hillside to the small village of Bugaidaya (3460m, 45 minutes, Finaid: Kolti, sheet: 2981 07, ref: 524 658), where the trail climbs a little more to the final pass across the main ridge (3565m, 20 minutes). Descend along the top of a spur from the ridge before branching right, down a shikari (hunter's) trail, which is both difficult and dangerous, for 4 hours to a small river. There is a campsite (2170m, Finaid: Kolti, sheet: 2981 07, ref: 493 661) just after the confluence with the larger Madi Khola, about 5 minutes downstream.

From the camp, head downstream; you will have to cross a few times before finally meeting a trail that climbs the north (right) bank in 15 minutes. The trail climbs an easy gradient for 20 minutes to Madigaon village (2300m). Head through the village on a trail that continue to climb to a ridge line offering views of the surrounding valleys and the lower snow-covered peaks of the Api range. Follow the ridge to a stinging-nettle-choked village called Pokhara (2290m) where the trail then descends rapidly to a bridge over the Buriganga Khola at Sim (1636m, 2 hours and 50 minutes). The trail climbs the west (right) bank of the Buriganga Khola for about 200m before traversing to the village of Dahakot. Walk through the village on the main trail to a bridge beneath the school, which makes a good campsite (1662m, 1¼ hours). There are in fact two trails from here to Chainpur: a direct route on a small track leads up the valley from Dokot to cross the Binayak Dada via Dhalkada (estimated time 5 to 6 hours). This trail then descends a long, forested ridge to Chainpur (7 to 8 hours).

Alternatively, take the main trail, which is both easier to follow and a little faster. Ascend the switchbacks beyond the bridge to a saddle on the Mel Lekh (2233m, 1½ hours) before descending to Kaudakot (2197m, 30 minutes, Finaid: Martadi, sheet: 2981 10, ref: 398 624). The trail then traverses scrubby hillside for 45 minutes to Manakot and on to Kotgau (1 hour), where you can find local guides for the next section.

Climb through Kotgau and up to a small spur on a ridge that marks a tributary valley that flows down from the north (right). The trail swings into this valley and descends to the river, which you cross before climbing steeply for 2 hours and 15 minutes to a forested ridgeline. The ridge soon broadens and there is a small campsite among the trees at (2979m, 20 minutes, Finaid: Martadi, sheet: 2981 10, ref: 623 355) but the water source is about 15 minutes further up the trail, as it begins to traverse towards the main ridge. Just beyond the water source is another potential campsite among some trees just beneath the trail on your left.

In another 20 minutes you reach the Bateli Bhanjyang (3200m, Finaid: Talkot, sheet: 2981 06, ref: 323 640) with views of the Api Himal to the northwest and Saipal Himal to the north above the Seti Khola valley. It's a rapid but easy descent from the pass on a muddy but good trail through dense forest. Stay on the south (left) side of the valley throughout the next 2 hours as you descend about 1000m to a forest campsite beside the Karal Khola (Lachhi Gad on the Finaid map). The trail is now confusing as it has many junctions and log walks through dense scrubby sections but eventually you reach clearer forest and another couple

ROUTE GUIDE

of potential campsites (another 1½ hours). You come to a large kharka (at 2227m), which would make an ideal campsite, (Finaid: Talkot, sheet: 2981 06, ref: 297 668), before crossing to the north bank and climbing to Tutigaon (1 hour), where you could camp in the school grounds. Descend slowly back to the Karal Khola and cross it before climbing a spur that projects into the valley.

A long undulating traverse leads to the mouth of the river valley but you cross a saddle into the Dungri Gad / Musabhui Khola valley, where you turn west (right) to approach Chainpur (1270m, 3 hours and 10 minutes). The main trading bazaar for Bajhang District is on the far side of the Seti Khola and is a good place to restock. A motorable road to Chainpur should be open soon.

The Seti valley is a rarely visited trekking route to Nampa, Api and Saipal base camps, which are about five days to the north.

Chainpur – Darchula

As at July 2009, the first section of this route to Chhetti has been cut by two large landslides and is not in use. The locals expect to have the trail opened soon as they are currently concentrating on building a motorable road to Chainpur from Dhadeldura. The end of the GHT is at Rapla, two days north of the bazaar town of Darchula. It takes 10 to 12 days from Chainpur to reach Rapla.

Routes via Simikot and to Rapla will be researched in the 2010/11 seasons.

Appendix A: Bibliography

Adhikary, Surya Mani – *The Khasa Kingdom* Nirala Publications, 1988

Bista, Dor Bahadur – *People of Nepal* Ratna Pustak Bhandar, 2004; *Fatalism and Development* Orient Longman, 2001

Chorlton, Windsor – *Cloud-dwellers of the Himalaya* Time-Life Books, 1982

Doig, Desmond / Bhagat, Dubby – *Down History's Narrow Lanes: Sketches and Myths of the Kathmandu Valley* Braaten Books, 2009

Drs Duff, Jim & Gormly, Peter – *Pocket First Aid and Wilderness Medicine* Cicerone, 2007

Jest, Corneille – *Tales of The Turquoise. A Pilgrimage in Dolpo* Mandala Book Point, 1993

McGuinness, Jamie – *Trekking in the Everest Region* Trailblazer, 2009

Rogers, Clint – *Secrets of Manang* & *Where Rivers Meet* Mandala Publications, 2004 & 2008

Schaller, George B – *Stones of Silence. Journeys in the Himalaya* Bantam Books, 1982

Shaha, Rishikesh – *Ancient and Medieval Nepal* Manohar Publishers, 2001

Shakya, Sujeev – *Unleashing Nepal* Pengiun Books 2009

Snellgrove, David L – *Himalayan Pilgrimage* Shambala Publications 1989; *Four Lamas of Dolpo* Himalayan Book Seller, 1967

Stiller, Ludwig F – *Nepal Growth of a Nation* Human Resources Development Research Centre (HRD), 1999; *The Rise of the House of Gorkha* (HRD), 1995

Thomas, Bryn – *Trekking in the Annapurna Region* Trailblazer, 2006

Toffin, Gerard – *Man and his house in the Himalayas* Sterling Publishers, 1991

Tucci, Giuseppe – *Journey to Mustang* Bibliotheca Himalayica, 2003; *Nepal: The Discovery of the Malla* E. P. Dutton & Co, 1962

Wright, Daniel – *History of Nepal with an introductory sketch of the country and people of Nepal* Asian Eductional Services, 2003

Ziskin, Joel F – *Trek to Nepal's Sacred Crystal Mountain* National Geographic, April 1977

Appendix B: Glossary

Ablation valley – an often-shallow valley created by snow and/or ice melt from a glacier

Amchi – a traditional doctor in Tibetan medicine

Amrit – mystical water of immortality

Bato – Nepali word meaning path, track or trail

Bazaar / Bazar – trading place or town

Bergschrund – gap where a glacier meets rocky ground

Bhanjyang – pass, see also *Deurali* and *La*

Bhatti – trailside teashop or simple lodging, see also *Teahouse*

Cairn – pile of stones marking a route ('stone men')

Chang – fermented beer made from millet, barley or other grain

Chatta – vertical prayer flag normally mounted on a bamboo pole

Chautara – a resting place beside the trail, often shaded by two giant trees

Chu – Tibetan word meaning running water, often used for stream or small river, see also *Gandaki*, *Khola*, *Koshi* and *Nadi*

Chorten – Buddhist memorial or decorated cairn built on passes, ridges, or other significant spots

Crampons – spikes that strap on to boots that aid walking on ice

Crevasse – dangerous crack in a glacier

Deurali – minor pass, see also *La* and *Bhanjyang*

Dhal bhat – Nepal's national dish of rice, vegetable curry, lentil soup and some pickle

Dharamsala – emergency shelter usually without windows or doors

Dhigur – Thakali financial co-operative system

Dhoko – woven basket of various sizes used to carry goods throughout the Himalaya

Dorje – also known as the **vajra**, is a short metal weapon; like a diamond it can cut any substance but not be cut itself; symbolises the thunderbolt (irresistible force)

Dzee stone – precious stone found in the Himalaya often believed to be a fossilised caterpillar

Dzo – infertile male yak/cow crossbreed. See also *Dzum*

Dzum – fertile female yak/cow crossbreed. See also *Dzo*

Gandaki – a sacred tributary network of seven rivers that flow from Nepal to the Ganges. They include the Daraudi [Khola], Seti [Khola], Madi [Khola], Kali [Gandaki], Marsyangdi [river], Budhi [Gandaki] and Trisuli [river]. See also *Chu*, *Khola*, *Koshi* and *Nadi*

Gaon / Gau – Nepali word for village (the 'n' is barely pronounced)

Gompa – Buddhist temple (literally: 'meditation')

Gurkhas – one of a number of fierce army regiments in the British Army (Royal Gurkha Rifles) and Indian Army (6 regiments of Gorkha Rifles), which were first established by recruiting soldiers from the Gorkha Kingdom, most notably after the Gurkha War in 1815

Guru – Hindu or Buddhist sage or holy man, although the term is widely used for 'teacher'. See also *Khenpo*, *Lama*, *Sadhu* and *Yogi*

Guthi – (pronounced Goot-hee) Newar club or association that comes together for religious services, social events and public services

Himal – snowy mountain range

Himalaya – the 'eternal snows'

Jagat – a common village name in the high mountains that means 'customs post'; a traditional tax collection point for trade to and from Tibet

Kang – Tibetan origin word meaning 'mountain'

Kani – entrance gateway to Buddhist communities to cleanse evil spirits

Kharka – pasture used during part of the year to graze livestock

Khola – river or stream, see also *Chu, Gandaki, Koshi* and *Nadi*

Khadag / kata – Buddhist prayer scarf

Khenpo – Tibetan Buddhist Abbot or highly respected meditation practitioner. See also *Guru, Lama, Sadhu* and *Yogi*

Koshi – alternative name for river, see also *Chu, Gandaki, Khola,* and *Nadi*

Kund – lake, see also *Tal, Pokhari* and *Tsho*

La – a pass, see also *Bhanjyang* and *Deurali*

Lama – Buddhist priest, and a surname in some ethnic groups. See also *Guru, Khenpo, Sadhu, Yogi*

Lhakang – Lopa word from Mustang meaning 'god house'

Linga – a stone pillar representing the Hindu god Shiva's fertility

Lumdar – prayer flags strung together

Mani / Mati stones – carved prayer stones sometimes piled up in large numbers referred to as a mani wall

Mantra – Tibetan Buddhist prayer

Mela – Hindu religious festival

Mitai – any form of sweet treat

Nadi – very large river, see also *Khola, Koshi, Gandaki, Chu*

Namlo – often referred to as the 'Nepali passport', it is the sling used to carry loads, mainly *Dhokos*

Pahar – the mid-hills or Central Himalaya Ranges

Patans – rolling grass-covered valleys

Pokhari – lake or large pond, see also *Kund, Tal, Tsho*

Puja – Hindu or Buddhist prayer(s) ceremony

Rakshi – crudely distilled 'fire-water' from almost any grain or root vegetable

Rodi – traditional Gurung method of courting where young boys and girls have sleepovers in a house under supervision

Sadhu – Hindu holy man who has taken a vow of renunciation and is respected as a mystic, an ascetic, practitioner of yoga and/or wandering monk. See also *Guru, Khenpo, Lama* and *Yogi*

Shikari bato – Nepali phrase meaning 'hunter trail'

Sirdar – Nepali guide or the person in charge of trekking crew (literally 'trail finder')

Tal – small lake or pond, see also *Kund, Pokhari* and *Tsho*

Teahouse – what Nepali people call a mountain lodge or basic hotel, normally owned and operated by a family. Distinct from teashops, which are common throughout the hills, teahouses are normally only found on regular trade and tourist routes, see also *Bhatti*

Terai / tarai – the plains area, once covered in dense jungle, which forms the southern border to India

Thanka / thangka – traditional Tibetan Buddhist painting on paper or cloth, often displayed in *gompas*

Tongba – drink made from fermented millet, barley or other grain and drank from a bamboo flask, or plastic jug, which is refilled with hot water

Tsho – word of Tibetan origin meaning lake or pond. See also *Kund, Pokhari* and *Tal*

Yogi – male practitioner of various forms of religious practice, female is yogini. See also *Guru, Khenpo, Lama* and *Sadhu*

Appendix C: Nepal Trekking Agencies

There are now over 650 registered trekking agencies in Nepal, some are large highly experienced operations, whereas others are small owner-guide companies. This list is a selection of companies currently registered with the Trekking Agents Association of Nepal (TAAN) and is not an endorsement or recommendation of any service or advice that you may be given. For more information about these and other operators see TAAN website ▢ www.taan.org.np.

Trekking Agencies	Email	Contact Person	Telephone Number
Active Holidays Nepal treks & Expedition	ilte@wlink.com.np	Yogendra Tamang	+977 1446 1636
Adventure 6000 Company	norbu@adv6000.wlink.com.np	Ang Norbu Sherpa	+977 1448 0614
Adventure Dreams Unlimited	adut@wlink.com.np	Lal Tamang	+977 1442 2285
Asia Adventure Excursions	info@asiatravel.com.np	Rinku Das Thapa	+977 1442 8344
Adventure GEO Treks	info@adventuregeotreks.com	Niru Rai	+977 1437 7290
Adventure Mountain Club Treks & Expedition	info@mountain-club.com.np	BN Dhakal	+977 1441 0856
Adventure Specialist Trekking	ast@mos.com.np	Nawaraj Maraseni	+977 1442 8914
Adventure Thamserku Treks & Expedition	lukla@mos.com.np	Dawa Geljen Sherpa	+977 1472 0685
Adventure Zambuling	info@advzambuling.com	Bhai B Tamang	+977 1446 7712
All Nepal Trekking	alltreks@mos.com.np	Krishna Bahadur Sha	+977 1425 5690
Alpine Asian Treks & Expedition	nepaltrek@wlink.com.np	Shekha Bahadur Thapa	+977 1422 6896
Alpine Trekking & Expedition Service	atesnimi@wlink.com.np	Nimi Sherpa	+977 1422 6980
Amuse Treks & Expeditions	amusetreks@wlink.com	Dawa Gyalsen Sherpa	+977 1443 6243
Arun Treks & Expedition	aruntrek@wlink.com.np	P Chhwang Sherpa	+977 1437 4929
Asian Heritage Treks & Expeditions	asianheritage@wlink.com.np	Nihari Bastola (Nilam)	+977 1426 8638
Asian Trekking	asianadv@mos.com.np	Ang Tshering Sherpa	+977 1444 2424
Barunche Treks & Expeditions	barunche@ntc.net.np	Pemba Rinji Sherpa	+977 1442 3000
Bird's Eye View Adventure	bev_adventure@yahoo.com	Sharada Thapa Shrestha	+977 1553 7770
Bochi-Bochi Trek	info@bochi-bochitrek.com	Tikaram Gurung	+977 1622 3356
Cho Oyo Trekking	nim.kar@cho.wlink.com.np	Nima Nuru Sherpa	+977 1442 9097
Chomolhari Trekking	chomotrek@infoclub.com.np	D B Koirala	+977 1423 1039
Chomologma Pilgrimage Trekking	chomo@wlink.com.np	Chhering Sherpa	+977 1449 6315
Churen Himal Treks & Expedition	churen@mos.com.np	Mulal Gurung	+977 1444 1121
Climb High Himalaya	raj@climbhighhimalaya.com	Ranjen Thapa Magar	+977 1437 2874
Community Action Trekking	catreks@wlink.com.np	Mahesh Kumar Sewa	+977 1472 0677
Cosmo Trek	cosmo@mos.com.np	Kamal Dhoj Joshi	+977 1441 6226
Destination Nepal Trek & Expedition	info@destination.com.np	Pancha Bahadur Tamang	+977 1425 9538

Agency	Email	Contact	Phone
Discover Adventure	trektour@mail.com.np	Vinod Rana	+977 1444 5858
Discover Himalayan Sherpa	discover@wlink.com.np	Hari Bahadur Kadel	+977 1442 8248
Eagle Treks & Expedition	info@eagletreks.com	Ramesh Bhattarai	+977 1441 0588
Edelweiss Treks & Expedition (Nepal)	edelweiss@wlink.com.np	Gam Bahadur Rai	+977 1559 2682
Equator Nepal Treks & Expeditions	equator@mos.com.np	Manish Singh Thapa	+977 1470 0854
Explore Alpine Adventure	exploretrek@wlink.com.np	Bhim Pd Khanal	+977 1470 0714
Explore Himalaya Travel & Adventure	enquiry@explorehimalaya.com	Suman Pandey	+977 1441 8100
Family Alpine Trek & Expedition	sherpaft@enet.com.np	Lakpa Nurbu Sherpa	+977 1435 7478
Friends Adventure Team	lamateam@wlink.com.np	Kabindra Lama	+977 1436 4838
Glacier Safari Treks	glacier@gst.mos.com.np	Dhruba KC	+977 1441 2116
Global Adventure Trekking	gat@wlink.com.np	Suman Dahal	+977 1470 0355
Hard Rock Treks & Expedition	hrt@hardrock.wlink.com.np	Rana Bahadur Khadka	+977 1425 9067
High Country Trekking	hcountry@ecomail.com.np	Sumba Rinji Sherpa	+977 1443 1855
High Mountain Wave Trekking	info@highmountaintrek.com	Tej Bahadur Jarga	+977 1470 0870
Highland Excursions (Nepal)	highland@mos.com.np	Uma Khakurel	+977 1441 4783
Highlander Trekking & Expedition	highlnder@wlink.com.np	Hari Dharel	+977 1470 0563
Himaland Adventure Treks	trek@himaland.wlink.com.np	Tilak B Lama	+977 1443 9654
Himalaya Aventura Treks & Expedition	aventura@wlink.com.np	Samundra Man Bajracharya	+977 1424 0785
Himalaya Expeditions	himalaya@mos.com.np	Keshav Rayamajhi	+977 1554 5900
Himalaya Adventures	himad@mos.com.np	Tshering Lama	+977 1472 1657
Himalayan Cultural Treks & Expeditions	hicten@wlink.com.np	Ram (Ratna) Kumar Tamang	+977 1447 6118
Himalayan Garden Treks & Expedition	higatenepal@wlink.com.np	Min Dhan Rai	+977 1444 0583
Himalayan Glacier Trekking	hgtrek@ccsl.com.np	Sagar Pandey	+977 1442 1780
Himalayan Guides Nepal Treks & Expedition	himguidenp@hons.com.np	Ishwari Poudel	+977 1426 0205
Himalayan Holidays Trekking	namaste@himhols.wlink.com.np	Bibhuti (Bibu) Chand Takur	+977 1442 7705
Himalayan Journey	info@gohimalaya.com	Ashok Pokharel	+977 1422 6138
Himalayan Mountain Guides Expeditions	info@himalayanmountainguides.com	Gauri Thapa	+977 1437 1927
Himalayan Sherpa Adventure	sherpadv@mos.com.np	Phurba Gyaltsen Sherpa	+977 1448 0064
Himalayan Society	himso@wlink.com.np	Chanda Sherpa	+977 1441 3330
Himalayan Trails	mads@himalayan-trails.com	Mads Mathiasen	+977 1441 0661
Himalayan Treasure Trekking	himatreks@wlink.com.np	Lakpa Sherpa	+977 1444 5522
Himalayan Waves Trekking	htreks@hwt.wlink.com.np	S B (Deepak) Bhandari	+977 1441 6831
Himalayan Windhorse Adventure	info@himalayanwindhorse.com	Nawang Dorjee Sherpa	+977 1444 5679
Holiday Mountain Treks & Expedition	info@tripsnepal.com	Abir Malla	+977 1425 3776

Nepal Trekking Agencies (cont'd)	Contact Person	Email	Telephone Number
Iceland Trekking & Expedition	Tendy Sherpa	tendy@mos.com.np	+977 1423 2216
Independent Himalayan Adventure	Chandra Niraula	independent@mail.com.np	+977 1424 9214
International Adventure Treks & Expeditions	Harka Raj Pariyar	treks@iate.wlink.com.np	+977 1422 0664
International Trekkers (In-Trek)	Phintso Lama	nepal@intrek.wlink.com.np	+977 1437 0714
Kailash Himalaya Treks	Santa Subba	himtravel@wlink.com.np	+977 1224 1249
Khumbu-ila Mt & Trekking	Pemba D Sherpa	khumbila@mail.com.np	+977 1448 3660
Khumbu Shangri-La Nepal Trek & Expedition	Tashi Tshering Sherpa	tasjo2009@hotmail.com	+977 1443 3398
Kulung Ethnic Treks & Expeditions	Nirmal Kumar Rai	kulungtreks@wlink.com.np	+977 1441 0685
Lama Adventure Treks & Expedition	Santa Bir Lama	iate@mos.com.np	+977 1441 3950
Langtang Ri Trekking	Pamfa Dhamala	info@langtang.com	+977 1442 4268
Marvel Treks & Expedition	Dhruba Prasad Lamsal	marvel@wlink.com.np	+977 1442 2504
Mongolian Trekking & Expedition	Min Thapa	mongolian@treks.enet.com.np	+977 1421 6491
Monte Rosa Treks & Expedition	Ganesh Bahadur Neupane	monte@ccsl.com.np	+977 1470 0348
Monviso Treks & Expedition	Chhogba Lama Sherpa	monvisotreks@yahoo.com	+977 1621 4202
Mount Pumori Adventure Treks & Expedition	Surya Prasad Bastakoti	mpumori@mos.com.np	+977 1470 1247
Mountain Adventure Trekking	Deepak B Roka	mtnatrek@mos.com.np	+977 1425 4607
Mountain Madness	Kili Sherpa	mountmad@wlink.com.np	+977 1437 9845
Mountain Tribes Trekking	Babu Sherpa	mtribes@wlink.com.np	+977 1470 0382
Multi Adventure	Chenga Sherpa	multiadv@ccsi.com.np	+977 1425 7791
NE-KO Treks & Expeditions	Ang Dorjee Sherpa	nekotreks@ecomail.com.np	+977 1441 3471
Nepal Exploration (NEPA) Treks	Dinesh Kumar Magar	trek@dineshmgr.wlink.com.np	+977 1442 8585
Nepal Myths & Mountain Trails	Ngima Dorgi Sherpa	nmmt@mos.com.np	+977 1482 1901
Nepal Sanctuary Treks	Tulsi Gvawali	sanctuary@mail.com.np	+977 1441 4492
Nepal Trans Himalayan Explorer	Pasang Dawa Sherpa	sat@wlink.com.np	+977 1442 2656
Nepal Village Trekking	Prem Kumar Lama	nvt@wlink.com.np	+977 1470 0207
Nima & Neema Treks	Nima Thundu Sherpa	tenzings@mos.com.np	+977 1448 0327
Nireekha Treks	Kumar Rai	hotaka@nireekhatreks.com	+977 1443 4760
Nomad Nepal Trek & Mountaineering	Dawa Sherpa	nomadnepal@wlink.com.np	+977 1442 3572
Numbur Himal Treks	Pasang Nundu Sherpa	numbur@wlink.com.np	+977 1424 0446
Om Mane Trekking	Om Man Shre;stha	mane@mos.com.np	+977 1553 1427
Parikrama Treks & Expeditions	Bal Kumar Basnaryet	treks@parikrama.wlink.com.np	+977 1620 2341
Peak Promotion	Wongchu Sherpa	peak@mos.com.np	+977 1424 3296
Peaks of Nepal Treks & Expedition	Jangbu Sherpa	zangbu@wlink.com.np	+977 1442 8329
Pema Treks & Expedition	Pema Tshiri Sherpa	info@pematrek.com	+977 1442 7058

Agency	Email	Contact	Phone
Project Himalaya	info@project-himalaya.com	Jamie McGuinness	+977 98021 49789
Ramdung Go Treks & Expeditions	info@asianexpedition.com	Saila Tamang	+977 1442 3361
Rasuwa Treks & Expedition	rasuwatreks@mcmail.com.np	Balaram Neupane	+977 1208 2383
Regal Excursions	lakpa@regal.wlink.com.np	Lakpa Norbu Sherpa	+977 1442 9044
Rolwaling Trek & Expedition	seagull@mos.com.np	Nabin K C	+977 1444 2019
Royal Orchid Treks & Expedition	temba@rotreks.wlink.com.np	Pasang Temba Sherpa	+977 1448 9640
Sea to Summit Trekking	ttshering@wlink.com.np	Chhering Doma Sherpa	+977 1447 8109
Shambhala Trekking Agency	shambhala@enet.com.np	Kesh Ram Ghale	+977 1216 0220
Shangri La Reisen	visit@wlink.com.np	Kami Ringi Sherpa	+977 1446 4777
Sherpa & Swiss Adventures	sherpaadv@wlink.com.np	Lhakpa Gyalzen Sherpa	+977 1437 1218
Sherpa Alpine Trekking Service	sata@wlink.com.np	Tshiring Ongel Sherpa	+977 1441 0118
Sherpa Shangri La Treks & Expeditions	shangrilatreks@hins.com.np	Jiban Ghimire	+977 1449 0984
Sherpa Society	pasang@mos.com.np	Meena Sherpa	+977 1424 9233
Shiva Treks & Expeditions	shivatreks@shivaholidays.com	Mangal Man Maharjan	+977 1442 9848
Snow Leopard Trek	snowlprd@trek.wlink.com.au	Yankila Sherpa	+977 1443 4632
South Asian Treks	southtreks@infbclub.com.np	Rinchin Sherpa	+977 1448 9253
Su-Swagatam (Nepal) Trek	swagatam@ccsl.com.np	Mima T Sherpa	+977 1447 9216
Summit Nepal Trekking	trekking@wlink.com.np	Sangye Sherpa	+977 1552 5408
Summit Treks & Adventures	statreks@wlink.com.np	Hari Bahadur Thapa	+977 1426 0970
Taro Treks & Expedition	shilichung@wlink.com.np	Bishal Battharai	+977 1443 9085
Thamserku Trekking	info@thamserkutrekking.com	Lhakpa Sonam Sherpa	+977 1435 4044
Tip Top Trekking	tiptop@wlink.com.np	Lhakpa Sherpa	+977 1441 9973
Trans Himalayan Trekking	ththev@wlink.com.np	B S Ghimire	+977 1422 4854
Trekking Team Group	info@trekkingteamgroup.com	Shreehari Thapaliya	+977 1422 7506
Trinetra Adventure	trinetra@mos.com.np	Sunar Bahadur Gurung	+977 1425 2462
Tseringma Treks & Expedition	dawaguide@yahoo.com	Mingma Phuti Sherpa	+977 1482 1618
Wilderness Experience	wildexxp@ecomail.com.np	Deepak Lama	+977 1441 7932
Windhorse Trekking	winhorse@wlink.com.np	Ang Karma Sherpa	+977 1437 6641
World Adventure Trekking & Mountaineering	worldadv@mos.com.np	Nima Temba Sherpa	+977 1425 9796
World Records Expeditions & Treks	worldrecords@wlink.com.np	Fur Geljen Sherpa	+977 1441 3458
World Summit Explorer	worldsummitexp@live.com	Jangbu Sherpa	+977 1424 9118
Yala Adventure	info@yalaadventure.com	Yadu Lamichhane	+977 1441 4095
Yeti Mountaineering & Trekking	ymtrek@ccsl.com.np	Gana Sham Poudel	+977 1442 5896
Zambuling Treks & Expeditions	zambuling@info.com.np	Palden Tamang	+977 1442 1222

Appendix D: Wind chill chart

Temperature °C

	5	0	-5	-10	-15	-20	-25	-30	-35	-40	-45	-50
5	4	-2	-7	-13	-19	-24	-30	-30	-41	-47	-53	-58
10	3	-3	-9	-15	-21	-27	-33	-39	-45	-51	-57	-63
15	2	-4	-12	-17	-23	-29	-35	-41	-48	-54	-60	-66
20	1	-5	-12	-18	-24	-30	-37	-43	-49	-56	-62	-68
25	1	-6	-12	-19	-25	-32	-38	-44	-51	-57	-64	-70
30	0	-6	-13	-20	-26	-33	-39	-45	-52	-59	-65	-72
35	0	-7	-14	-20	-27	-33	-40	-47	-53	-60	-66	-73
40	-1	-7	-14	-21	-27	-34	-41	-48	-54	-61	-68	-74
45	-1	-8	-15	-21	-28	-35	-42	-48	-55	-62	-69	-75
50	-1	-8	-15	-22	-29	-35	-42	-48	-56	-63	-69	-76
55	-2	-8	-15	-22	-29	-36	-43	-50	-57	-63	-70	-77
60	-2	-9	-16	-23	-30	-36	-43	-50	-57	-64	-71	-78
65	-2	-9	-16	-23	-30	-37	-44	-51	-58	-65	-72	-79
70	-2	-9	-16	-23	-30	-37	-44	-51	-58	-65	-72	-80
75	-3	-10	-17	-24	-31	-38	-45	-52	-59	-66	-73	-80
80	-3	-10	-17	-24	-31	-38	-45	-52	-60	-67	-74	-81

Wind speed km/h

Risk of frostbite in prolonged exposure	-25 to -34	Frostbite possible in ten minutes if warm skin is suddenly exposed.	-35 to -59	Frostbite possible in two minutes if warm skin is suddenly exposed.	-60 and below

Appendix E: Heat index chart

Temperature versus Relative Humidity

	90%	80%	70%	60%	50%	40%	30%	20%	10%
18°C	19	18	18	17	17	16	16	15	15
21°C	22	22	21	20	20	19	19	18	18
24°C	27	25	24	24	23	23	22	22	21
27°C	31	30	29	28	28	27	26	25	25
29°C	39	36	34	32	31	30	29	28	26
32°C	49	44	41	38	36	34	32	30	29
35°C	61	55	50	45	42	38	36	33	32
38°C	76	68	61	54	49	44	40	37	35
41°C	93	83	73	65	57	51	45	41	38
43°C	113	100	87	76	67	58	51	45	41
46°C	135	119	103	90	77	67	58	50	44
49°C	160	140	121	104	89	76	65	55	48

Source: www.crh.noaa.gov/pub/heat.htm

Note: Exposure to direct sunlight can increase the HI by up to 9°C

27°C – 32°C	Fatigue possible with prolonged exposure and physical activity
32°C – 41°C	Sunstroke, heat cramps and heat exhaustion possible
41°C – 54°C	Sunstroke, heat cramps and heat exhaustion likely; heat stroke likely
54°C or more	Heat stroke highly likely with continued exposure

INDEX

Page references in **bold** type refer to maps

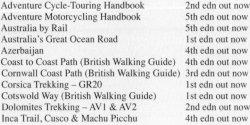

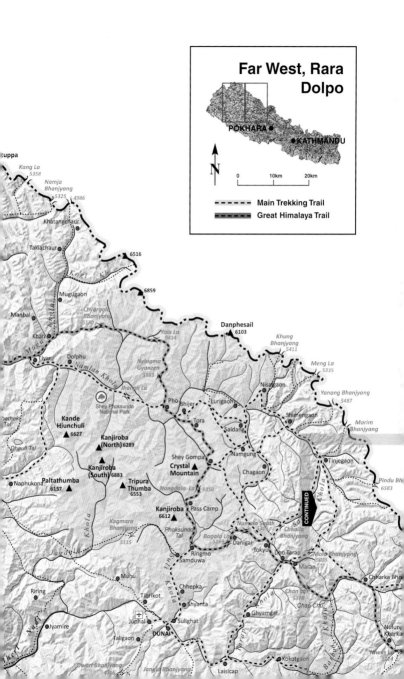

POKHARA
KATHMANDU

N

0   10km   20km

- - - Main Trekking Trail
━━━ Great Himalaya Trail

tuppa

Kang La
5358
Namja
Bhanjyang
5325   4986

Khatangchaur

Taklachaur

6516

Koin Kh

6859

Mugugaon

Manbal

Chyargon
Bhanjyang
5150

Yala La
5414

Danphesail
6103

Khung
Bhanjyang
5411

Meng La
5335

Khari

Dolphu

Tiyar

Namlan Khola

Nyingma
Gyanzen
5563

Jhongti La

Yanang Bhanjyang
5487

Nisaigaon

Marim
Bhanjyang

Pho

Bhijer

Lurigaon

Shimengaon

hathek
Tal

Kande
Hiunchuli
6627

Shey Phoksundo
National Park

Tora

Saldang

Kanjiroba
(North) 6289

Shey Gompa

Namgung

Tinjegaon

Dhauli Tal

Kanjiroba
(South)
6883

Crystal
Mountain

Chagaon

Pindu Bh
6583

Paltathumba
6157

Tripura
Thumba
6553

Nangdala La 5350

Naphukona

Kanjiroba
6612

Pass Camp

Numala South
5309

CONTINUED

Chhalla
Bhanjyang

Kagmara
Bhanjyang
5115

Phoksundo
Tal

Bagala La
5169

Danigar

Tokyu

Dho Tarap

Mola Bhanjyang
5035

Chepka

Ringmo
Samduwa

Maran

Chan Sa
3370

Chkarka Bho

Muhu

Tibrikot

Chhepka

Ghyamgar

Chap Cho

Riring

Shyanta

Jyamire

Juphal

Sulighat

DUNAI

Taligaon

Kokotgaon

Nulung
Kharka

Dwari Bhanjyang

Jangla Bhanjyang

Laisicap

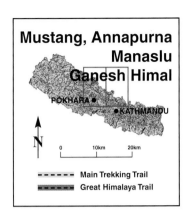

Mustang, Annapurna
Manaslu
Ganesh Himal

POKHARA
KATHMANDU

| 0 | 10km | 20km |

- - - - - Main Trekking Trail
- - - - - Great Himalaya Trail

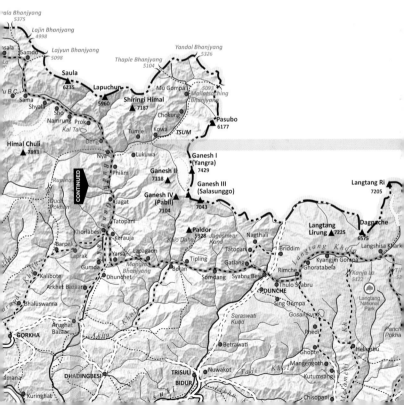

ala Bhanjyang
5375

Lajin Bhanjyang
4998

Lajyun Bhanjyang
5098

Yandol Bhanjyang
5326

Thaple Bhanjyang
5104

sala
Samdo

Saula
6235

Lapuchun
5960

Mu Gompa
5093
Mallatsothing
Bhanjyang

u B.C.
Sama
Shyala

Sho
Namrung Prok
Kal Tal

Shiringi Himal
7187

Chokung

Pasubo
6177

Himal Chuli
7893

Deng
Nya

Tumje Kowa *TSUM*

Lukuwa

Ganesh I
(Yangra)
7429

Langtang Ri
7205

Philim

Ganesh II
7118

Ganesh III
(Salasunggo)
7043

CONTINUED

Jagat

Ganesh IV
(Pabil)
7104

Langtang
Lirung 7225

Dagmache
6575

Langshisa Khark

Tatopani

Khorlabesi

Paldor
5928

Jageshwar
Kund

Nagthali

Kyangjin Gompa
Ghoratabela

Barpak

Kerauja

Lapagaon

Kulo Dahal

Tatopani

Briddim

Kanja La
5322

Til

Laprak

Yarsa

Manaro
Bhanjyang

Tipling

Gatlang

Rimche

Kalibote

Gumda

Botan

Somdang

Syabru Besi

Arkhet Bazaar

Dhunchet

Thulo Syabru
DUNCHE

Langtang
National
Park

Bhaluswanra

Sing Gompa

Gosainkund

GORKHA

Arughat
Bazaar

Saraswati
Kund

Phedi

Panch
Pokha

āmana

DHADINGBESI

Betrawati

Ghopte

Helambu

Kuringhat

TRISULI
BIDUR

Nuwakot

Ghopte

Mangengoth

Kutumsang

Chisopani

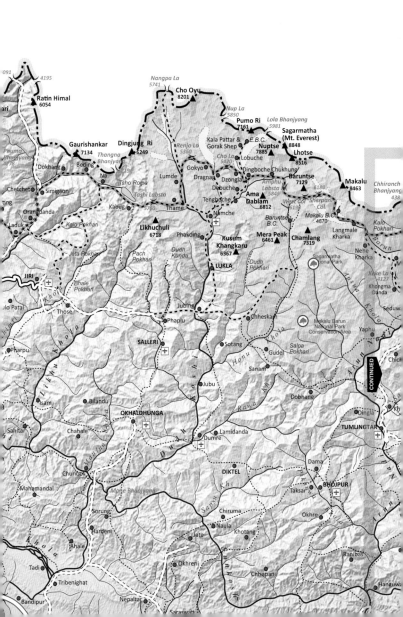

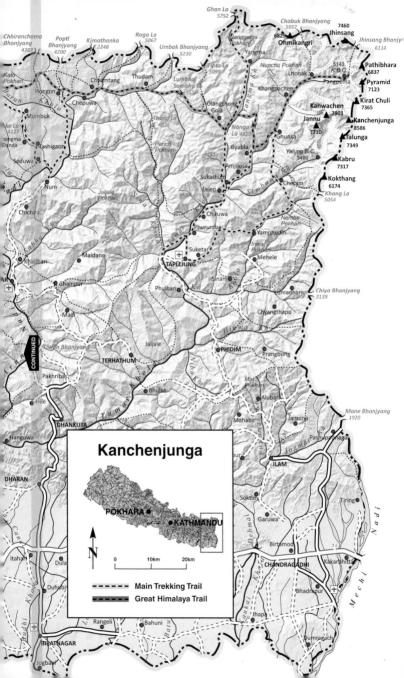